POLITICAL RESEARCH METHODS
Foundations and Techniques

POLITICAL RESEARCH METHODS
Foundations and Techniques

BARBARA LEIGH SMITH
University of Nebraska

KARL F. JOHNSON
University of Missouri , Kansas City

DAVID WARREN PAULSEN
University of Nebraska , Omaha

FRANCES SHOCKET

HOUGHTON MIFFLIN COMPANY
BOSTON
Atlanta
Dallas
Geneva, Illinois
Hopewell, New Jersey
Palo Alto
London

Cover photo by Cary Wolinsky, Stock, Boston

Printed in the U.S.A.
Library of Congress Catalog Card Number: 75-31030
ISBN: 0-395-20363-5

CONTENTS

PREFACE

Political science has changed substantially in the last thirty years. Many textbooks and most professional journals cannot be understood fully without some minimal acquaintance with the philosophy of science or social science and a wide range of empirical and statistical methods including computer science, various forms of statistical analysis, content analysis, survey research, and many others.

It has become increasingly apparent to us that there is a need for an elementary methods textbook which begins by discussing the evolution of the discipline terms of its scope, methods, and various objectives, and which systematically discusses the current research methods employed in the discipline and the problems they raise. This text, we hope, aims in this direction. To aid students in understanding the current place of these methods, we briefly trace the development of political science as a discipline. Attention is given to traditional questions and methods and various factors that led to certain fundamental changes in approach. Current methods then are discussed briefly with due recognition of their particular shortcomings and implications. To facilitate thorough knowledge of the contextual and procedural considerations entailed in current research methods, we have drawn broadly from a number of different areas such as the philosophy of science, questions of ethics, computer machine technology, and others.

The text is designed to be introductory, however, and it assumes that students have no previous acquaintance with basic research methodology, statistics, and other more specialized methodological coursework. A course employing this text would therefore logically precede, rather than follow or replace, more advanced work in research methodology. This text should not be taken as a substitute for more advanced work. We feel that students interested in the basic issues raised throughout this text would benefit from exposure to more advanced work in philosophy of social science, statistics, experimental design, and/or multivariate analysis, to name but a few.

We also feel that students too frequently have been "thrown" into courses in statistics or computer science, without understanding the purpose behind the techniques and the general context that makes such coursework relevant and important. All too often the result has been the divorce of substantive problems from the methods of approaching them, which sometimes leads to a presumptuous triumph of method over substance. Too many students trained in this manner have discarded advanced empirical and/or quantitative methods out of hand simply because their relevance to substantive problems was never made explicit. We enter the debate of hard versus soft methodology only to suggest that methodological techniques and concerns should neither triumph over substantive concerns nor be discarded out of hand. We view this debate as more than occasionally resting on spurious arguments and essentially feel that well-informed students of social science should be well grounded in both methodology and substance with the relationship between the two firmly recognized. The two should complement one another.

Barbara Leigh Smith initiated the project of writing this book and had overall editorial and supervisory responsibility. She is the sole author of Chapters 5, 7, 8 and 10 and primary author of Chapters 1 and 3. David W. Paulsen is sole author of Chapter 2 and made substantial contributions to Chapters 1, 3 and 4. Karl F. Johnson is sole author of Chapter 9 and primary author of Chapter 4. Frances Shocket is sole author of Chapter 6 and did editorial work on other sections of the book.

The general outline of the text is as follows: After tracing the evolution of the discipline in Chapter 1, we discuss the meaning of "science" in Chapter 2. The treatment of "science as an approach to knowledge" stresses the assumptions concomitant with adopting this particular approach and the benefits of scientific methods.

Chapter 3 extends the discussion of scientific method into an analysis of ethical considerations in social research and general questions of values. We hope this chapter will help students to think more seriously about their own valuational conclusions on the basic questions raised. To this end, the discussion is essentially open-ended and directed toward raising questions rather than providing definitive answers. This chapter uses several case studies to examine the problems of scientific reception and the problems of the relationship between science and government. It is our general feeling that ethical questions and general questions of value must be recognized and dealt with throughout the study of social science in its methodological as well as its more substantive concerns.

Chapter 4 discusses research design, measurement, and operationalism in social science research. Various problems are raised in this regard, including problems of definition, operationalization, and the question of the most appropriate level and type of measurement.

Chapter 5 discusses sampling in social science research.. Considerations of sample size and sampling methods are discussed in the context of an examination of the major types of probability and nonprobability sampling. The actual procedures for executing different sampling designs are outlined in detail.

The second part of the text, beginning with Chapter 6, provides a more detailed examination of specific data collection and analysis techniques widely used in social science. Pretested short- and long-form exercises are included with each chapter. Experience has shown that many methodological procedures and problems are most effectively learned by actual work with them in the field. We hope that students will find the exercises a significant part of the learning process.

The research tool most frequently used in political science and sociology is probably the survey research technique. There is a large empirical substantive literature based upon this technique as well as a large methodological literature on the subject. Chapter 6 discusses the development of the survey research approach, the mechanics of questionnaire construction, and the more general problems associated with this technique.

Chapter 7 deals with scaling in political research. The chapter begins with a general discussion of the purpose of scaling. A variety of scaling methods are then discussed, including Likert scaling, Thurstone scaling, Guttman scaling, and the semantic differential. In addition, one scaling method frequently applied to legislative voting, cluster bloc analysis, is discussed.

Chapter 8 discusses content analysis. The development of this research method is traced briefly through a historical examination of its use and purposes. The assumptions underlying content analysis then are delineated, and basic problems associated with the technique are pointed out. The latter part of Chapter 8 outlines specific procedures for executing content analysis, including the Q-sort method, evaluative assertion analysis, and the paired-comparison method.

Chapter 9 provides a general introduction to statistics. The purpose of statistics is briefly covered, and the requisite assumptions for each of the techniques are delineated. Descriptive statistics commonly found in the literature and common measures of association are included.

Data processing is the subject matter of Chapter 10. The development of computer services and its impact on political science is briefly discussed. The chapter then turns to specific procedures that students would use to analyze data with the aid of data processing equipment. The operation of the key punch and the counter-sorter is discussed, as are considerations in coding. Finally, various canned computer programs are outlined. This chapter logically follows the format of the text, but it can be read easily at an earlier point in the syllabus, and probably more profitably, if students are expected to execute projects using this tool.

Finally, the text includes a number of appendices. Appendix A is a lengthy discussion and listing of some major library resources available in political science. Appendix B provides basic guidelines on writing a research paper. The remaining appendices include basic statistical tables to be used in conjunction with the various chapters of the text.

In writing this text we necessarily have incurred many debts. Various students throughout the past three years patiently endured the constant revision and redefinition of our research methods courses. They more than adequately proved that undergraduates can handle this material with a high degree of proficiency.

Several students were particularly helpful in gathering bibliographic material and indexing, and we wish to thank Jeffrey Martin, David Capek, and Gerald Carlson for their assistance in these tasks. Friends and colleagues also have been helpful and supportive. We wish particularly to thank William Blizek, Mike Gillespie, Gary Blum, Peter Shocket, Susan Welch, Mary Leigh Smith, and John Peters for their comments on various chapters of this text. Michael R. Kagay (Princeton University), James D. Hardy (Queens College, CUNY), David B. Meltz (Georgia Institute of Technology), and G. Wayne Peak (Colorado State University) deserve special thanks for providing extensive criticisms and encouragements on the entire manuscript. Finally, we gratefully acknowledge the assistance of Carol Dunklau, who patiently typed and retyped the manuscript.

POLITICAL RESEARCH METHODS
Foundations and Techniques

There is no waste more criminal
than that of erudition running, as
it were, in neutral gear, nor any
pride more vainly misplaced than
that in a tool valued as an end
in itself.

Marc Bloch

1
THE DEVELOPMENT
OF POLITICAL SCIENCE

A 1909 catalog from a Midwest university lists coursework in political
science including a "Seminary on Bad Government," a course on
"Modern Social Betterment Movements," and a course on "Social
Reformers." Reformism was an important objective of political science
in this period. The 1889–1890 catalog, by contrast, emphasizes institutional analysis. The course, "Methods of Legislating," is typical. It
is described as "a comparative view of the rules and practices of
modern legislative assemblies, with special reference to the machinery
of congressional and legislative action in the U.S."

The title of this book and the subject matter it represents encom-
pass an area of academic study virtually unknown seventy-five years
ago. In this chapter we provide a general overview of the development
of political science with special concentration on the changes that have
occurred in the last three-quarter century. Our focus will be on differences and changes in scope, methods, and objectives introduced
during this development.

"Scope" generally relates to the basic definitions of the boundaries of a field and the central questions that it poses. "Methods," in
a broad sense, relates to the pattern of justification to the questions
that are posed, and, in a narrow sense, to the tools and procedures

used to provide answers to them. "Objectives" deals with the desirable answers and end products of inquiry. Simply stated, scope deals with *what* is appropriate for study, methods with *why* it is appropriate and *how* it can be studied, and objectives tell *for what* purpose it is studied.

Obviously, these components are interrelated; changes in what is considered the proper method of political inquiry are, for example, closely connected to the possible scope of that inquiry. Students of politics have continually reinterpreted what are appropriate subjects of inquiry and tools of investigation. The methodological emphasis of this text is a product of such historical changes and can be best understood initially in terms of the evolution of the field.

The development of the discipline: a brief chronology

A number of available studies suggest a general chronology and explanation for some of the more pronounced changes within political science. An outline of this development is recorded in the time line found in Figure 1-1. Political Science, like all the social sciences, developed out of moral philosophy during the nineteenth century. We can date the emergence of institutional analysis from political philosophy to the last half of the nineteenth century. Various intellectual movements conspired during the first quarter of the twentieth century to generate behavioralism in political science. Finally, the last decade has seen the appearance of a new orientation that has been dubbed "post-behavioralism." It must be noted at the outset that these phases in the development of political science do not represent discrete, successive stages in its evolution. Contemporary political theorists continue to investigate political and social philosophy, and many political scientists analyze political institutions. In recent years, contemporary proponents of these two older facets of the field have been grouped together and collectively referred to as "traditionalists," a group opposed to various tenets of behavioralism.

Building upon the work of Charles Merriam in charting the history of the discipline, we can distinguish several phases in the development of political science: the classical period, the institutional period, a period of transition, and the behaviorial period.[1]

> *Phase 1: The Classical Period, to 1850* Up to 1850, a philosophical emphasis prevailed with extensive reliance upon deductive methods of explanation.

[1] Charles Merriam, *New Aspects of Politics*, 3d ed. University of Chicago Press, Chicago, 1970.

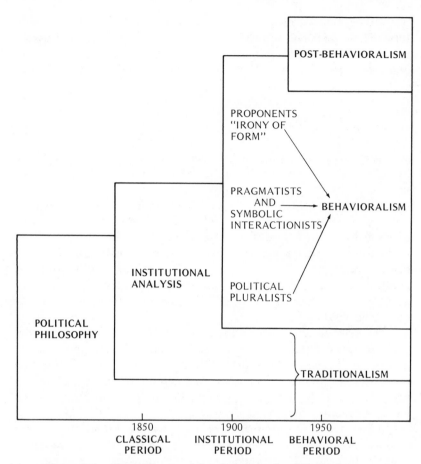

Figure 1-1   Chronology and development of political science

Phase 2: The Institutional Period, 1850–1900   In this period historical and comparative methods were predominant, and the focus was on formal government institutions.

Phase 3: Transitional Period, 1900–1923   The first quarter of the twentieth century emphasized observation, survey, and measurement. It was a period in which several intellectual movements strongly affected the field. Reformism was also a continuing concern during this period.

Phase 4: The Behavioral Period, 1923 to the present   This period is characterized by increased reliance upon psychological variables in the treatment of politics and by an emphasis on the individual and/or the group as the unit of analysis. Measurement techniques are increasingly more refined, and the quest for general empirical theory begins.

Succeeding sections of this chapter examine each of these periods in turn. Then we shall consider the debate that still exists between traditionalists and behavioralists. Finally, we shall mark recent developments in the field by a discussion of the postbehavioral revolution.

THE CLASSICAL PERIOD

The study of politics practiced during the classical period tended to be normative in concern and deductive in method. Typically the pattern of deductive reasoning employed argued from a general premise to more specific conclusions. The work of Thomas Hobbes and John Locke is characteristic of this emphasis. Both Locke and Hobbes were concerned with the nature of political obligation. Although Hobbes and Locke came to rather divergent conclusions on the nature of the social contract, the "proper" form of government, and the general nature of political obligation, each of their conclusions is more or less directly deducible from their initial general assumptions about the nature of human beings.

The classics are perhaps best remembered as normative studies that are concerned with the setting of standards and the "ought" dimension of politics. They deal with human nature, the justification of values, and the reconciliation of obligation and liberty. Plato, for example, discussed the question of justice in *The Republic* through his classic examination of the ideal state.

Machiavelli is sometimes regarded as the father of modern political inquiry, because he sought to explain the actual operation of existing forms of government and institutions. His treatment of politics was highly pragmatic and instrumental, and his analysis was based upon the empirical method of careful observation. Based upon this observation of political institutions and processes in Florence, Machiavelli offered advice to the Medici on how they could best maximize their power. Machiavelli's empirical approach was, however, the exception rather than the rule: by and large students of politics in this period turned their attention to utopian states, to the justification of institutionalized value preferences, and, rarely if ever, to the real-world operation of existing governmental institutions.

The early concern with the justification of values is not surprising in light of the intellectual dominance of the philosophic-religious tradition at that time. The first split in the generally holistic treatment of knowledge occurred with the breaking away of the natural sciences and the great breakthroughs by Galileo, Newton, and others. At this point, scholarly inquiry became divided into natural philosophy and moral philosophy. Eventually, further subdivision took place, as philosophy gradually lost hold of the social as well as the natural sciences.

THE INSTITUTIONAL PERIOD

The institutional period in the United States saw the establishment of political science as an area of graduate study at Columbia University under John Burgess in 1880. The boundaries of each of the social sciences progressively narrowed.

During this period there was a basic shift in the scope, methods, and objectives of the field. The research was mainly descriptive and generally concerned with describing existing political institutions and processes. The emphasis was on legally constituted governments with legal documents and constitutional strictures providing a major data base. Human nature was frequently taken as a constant during this period with an accompanying emphasis on institutional structures as important independent variables. Political institutions were regarded as important factors governing and influencing human behavior rather than vice versa.

THE TRANSITIONAL PERIOD

The transitional period saw a rather decisive reorientation of the discipline in terms of the data and methods it used. This shift in methods resulted from the inadequacies of past methods and from rising faith in the application of the methods of the natural sciences to the social sciences.

Although these tendencies toward greater methodological sophistication did not come into full fruition until the 1940s and later, the 1920s and 1930s were important years in the development of the field. Merriam and other notable scholars at the University of Chicago were working at the frontiers of the discipline, and the cry they raised was for a more scientifically based study of politics. As Somit and Tannenhaus point out, Merriam's "quest for scientific politics sprang from his concern with social policy." [2] He was not interested in a science of politics for the sake of knowledge itself. Merriam looked especially to psychology and statistics for relevant models for politics. He encouraged students to make the transition from library resources to field work to supplement and enrich traditional data bases.

Other notable early proponents of a scientific approach to politics included G. E. G. Catlin and William Bennett Munro. Catlin saw the model of classical economics as possessing special relevance. He also wrote one of the most fully developed early discussions of the presuppositions of a scientific study of politics, *Science and the Method*

[2] Albert Somit and Joseph Tannenhaus, *The Development of American Political Science: From Burgess to Behavioralism,* Allyn and Bacon, Inc., Boston, 1967, p. 111.

of Politics (1927). Munro, in may ways, was the most outspoken advocate of science. He maintained that it was both desirable and feasible to search for and discover fundamental laws of political behavior. Munro was particularly fond of citing the relevance of developments within the field of physics. Potential laws of possible significance to politics that he cited included geographic determinism, racial determinism, and above all, the law of the pendulum, which holds that extremes always generate their opposites.[3]

These early advocates did not go unchallenged. William Yandel Elliott, Edward S. Corwin, and Charles A. Beard were among the most sophisticated and outspoken critics. They argued that a scientific study of politics was impossible, and they questioned the quest for ethical neutrality in particular. The arguments they raised were prophetic of the coming traditionalist-behavioral debate that later would question the scope, methods, and objectives of political science.

How do we account for the succession of periods that have marked the development of political science? The historian and philosopher of science, Thomas Kuhn, has discussed the factors governing substantial change within a scientific discipline, a process of "scientific revolution." One important factor is the *anomaly*. An anomaly—or a departure from the expected rules, findings, or methods —is recognized as a major threat to previous theories and methodologies. This results in the recognition that the solutions to questions posed and the approaches are in need of revision. An anomaly typically comes to be considered as such, however, only after some viable alternative has been offered.[4]

On occasion the discovery of anomalous findings will be almost totally accidental to the main purposes of the inquiry.[5] To this extent, the introduction of new approaches is a somewhat fortuitous process. In some instances, events external to the scholarly community may exert influence by focusing on anomalous events that cannot be explained by existing approaches within the scholarly community. External events may also call attention to questions that the scientific community has not considered. The perception of anomalous findings undoubtedly played a role in bringing about change within political science. The recognition that these findings were true anomalies, and not just unsolved questions for older approaches, was possible because of three influences during the period of transition that paved the way for the development of behavioralism. The following sections of this

[3] Ibid., pp. 111–114.
[4] Thomas S. Kuhn, *The Structure of Scientific Revolutions*, University of Chicago Press, Chicago, 1964.
[5] See, for example, Bernard Barber and R. C. Fox, "The Case of the Floppy-eared Rabbits: An Instance of Serendipity Gained and Serendipity Lost," *American Journal of Sociology*, 64 (September 1958), 128–136.

chapter examine these three influences: (1) the irony of form, (2) pragmatism and the symbolic interactionists, and (3) the political pluralists.

The irony of form   As we have pointed out, traditional institutional approaches to the study of politics tended to take human nature as a constant—as a beginning assumption, rather than as a subject for empirical inquiry. Early in the twentieth century a number of sociologists began to question this assumption and the extent to which institutional form could adequately describe and explain political behavior and processes. Their efforts cast doubt on the explanatory power of the previous institutional emphasis. Moreover, they indicated that the social sciences *must* make a distinction between normative assumptions and empirical descriptions; their interest in the latter led to a basic reevaluation of the premises underlying the former, and their work contributed to a major redefinition of the methods appropriate for inquiry.

Roberto Michels[6] and Gaetano Mosca[7] are among the better-known early critics of traditional formulations about the relationship between leaders and citizens. They disputed, among other things, the prevailing assumption that ostensibly "democratic" institutions would in fact result in a "democratic" decision-making process. Indeed, they raised doubts about the very possibility of "democracy" (in the traditional sense of the term) in a complex, industrial society. They questioned the openness of the selection process by which leaders are recruited in various political systems as well as the criteria that citizens use in making basic electoral choices. Their work called assumptions of scholar and reformer alike into question. Michels' classic study of political parties, for example, attacked the naïveté of the prevailing conceptions surrounding these supposedly "democratic" organs of citizen participation. Michels suggested that:

> Our consistent knowledge of the political life of the principal civilized nations of the world authorizes us to assert that the tendency toward oligarchy constitutes one of the historical necessities . . . from which the most democratic modern societies, and, within those societies, the most advanced parties, have been unable to escape. By giving themselves leaders, the workers create with their own hands new masters, whose principal means of domination consists in their technical and intellectual superiority and in the inabilities of the masses to control the execution of their commands to the leaders. . . . Thus one can place one's

[6] Roberto Michels, *Political Parties*, The Macmillan Company, New York, 1962.
[7] Gaetano Mosca, *The Ruling Class*, McGraw-Hill Book Company, New York, 1939.

finger upon the flagrant contradiction which exists, in mature parties, between democratic declarations and intentions, on the one hand, and the concrete oligarchic reality, on the other.[8]

Another movement appeared almost simultaneously. It also was concerned with the inadequacies of prevailing institutions and existing normative formulations of the democratic process. This movement, however, was largely a reform-oriented response that began from the previous assumptions of institutional determinism.[9] The assumption underlying these reform efforts was that the current structuring of the institutions was at fault for the "improper workings of the political system." These neoinstitutionalists saw structural reform as the solution. "More democracy" became the antidote for political corruption, and reformers attempted to remove city government from the influence of corrupt partisan politics through the institution of professional city management and nonpartisan elections. They argued also for more direct citizen access through such devices as the direct election of officials and the initiative, referendum, and recall procedures.

The conclusions of this reform-oriented movement differed greatly from those reached by the leaders who empirically demonstrated the irony of form. Michels' work, for example, suggested that institutional reform of the type advocated by these reformists would be largely irrelevant. The dynamics of the situation lay elsewhere. Changing the institutional forms would not necessarily lead to a change in circumstances.[10]

The influence of pragmatism and the symbolic interactionists   The symbolic interactionists and the pragmatists also exerted influence in redirecting the discipline away from an institutional emphasis. The leaders of these movements included, among others, James, Park, Mead, Cooley, and Dewey.[11]

[8] Roberto Michels, "Some Reflections on the Sociological Character of Political Parties," *American Political Science Review*, XXI (November 1927), 760–776.

[9] The Populist and Progressive movements were major forces advocating institutional reform in the United States.

[10] See, for example, Robert Merton, *Social Theory and Social Structure*, The Free Press, New York, 1957, pp. 71-81, for a discussion of the functional aspects of the political machine. The implication of Merton's analysis is that a functional understanding of an institution is necessary to explain the institution and to guide reform.

[11] Some prominent work in this connection includes the following: John Dewey, *Democracy and Education*, The Macmillan Company, New York, 1961; and *The Public and Its Problems*, Henry Holt and Company, New York, 1927; and *Reconstruction in Philosophy*, New American Library, New York, 1952; William James, *A Pluralistic Universe*, Longmans, Green & Co., New York, 1920; and *Pragmatism: A New Name for Some Old Ways of Thinking*, Longmans, Green & Co., Ltd., New York, 1925; Sidney Hook, *Political Power and Personal Freedom*, The

Symbolic interactionism was both an experimental and an intellectual movement in psychology that was influential in the 1930s. Symbolic interactionists challenged existing notions about human nature and behavior, particularly the assumption that human nature could be taken as a constant. The underpinnings for the old notions came from instinctual psychology, which depicted human nature as largely fixed, the product of immutable, genetically determined characteristics. While Freudian analysis had posited a dichotomy and inherent conflict between the individual and society, the symbolic interactionists argued that people were social beings who were largely products of their interactions with others. The logical implication of this reasoning was a dissolution of the distinction between self and society, the social and the individual—a dichotomy that had plagued social scientists and particularly political philosophers for centuries. A further implication was that political behavior could only be understood from the perspective of the individual through the interaction of individual perceptions, images, and roles. The implied emphasis was on interaction-oriented paradigms and process models. Symbolic interactionists also argued that questions of human nature and human behavior must be empirical, experimental questions. Governmental forms and reforms could not be deduced from a priori assumptions about immutable human characteristics.

Pragmatism, a philosophical correlate of the psychological implications of the symbolic interactionist movement, largely reinforced these conclusions. Prominent in the 1920s and 1930s, pragmatism was a reaction against nineteenth-century metaphysical philosophers. Pragmatism is a philosophical position which maintains that ideas or actions can be judged only by their results, that they have only a posteriori value and achieve legitimacy only by their consequences. This position contrasts sharply with previous ones that actions and ideas are to be judged in terms of their logic, morality, or consistency with other ideas or actions. Pragmatic logic results in a stress on hypothesis and process. As Michael Weinstein points out:

> The pragmatic movement in American political philosophy can be viewed as an attempt to achieve three goals. First, the pragmatists desired to create a method of analysis that would separate the actual consequences of political patterns and practices from the ideological justifications given to them. Second, the pragmatists attempted to develop a standard for evaluating public

Macmillan Company, New York, 1965; William James, *Essays in Pragmatism*, Hafner Publishing Company, Inc., New York, 1948; M. P. Follett, *The New State*, Longmans, Green & Co., Ltd., New York, 1918; G. H. Mead, *Selected Writings*, The Bobbs-Merrill Company, Indianapolis, 1964; *Symbolic Interaction: A Reader in Social Psychology*, ed. Jerome G. Manis and Bernard N. Meltzer, Allyn and Bacon, Inc., Boston, 1967.

activities. And finally, they tried to devise a descriptive political science to trace the effects of political activities on social groups and structures.[12]

Pragmatists found the conceptual apparatus of traditional political philosophy and its mode of explanation a deterrent to effective and meaningful explanation. Dewey's complaint exemplified the dissatisfaction of pragmatists in this respect:

> They [the classical theorists] took "causal agency instead of consequences as the heart of the problem." Dewey is not concerned with accounting for the origin of the state. Whatever the origin of the state may have been, it can only be described and justified in terms of its consequences for life in the here and now.[13]

William James made essentially the same point when he discussed the difficulties associated with the traditional facile definitions of "government." He advised that:

> The person who would understand government most completely would be wise not to waste time casting about for a definition purporting to give its essence.[14]

Such efforts, James warned, would be essentially wasted, and any unified definition would be more misleading than useful. He severely criticized what he termed the "stock rationalist trick" of treating a definition of a phenomenon as its explanation.[15]

In their efforts to devise a descriptive political science, pragmatists have probably had most influence through their functional orientation and their emphasis on the consequences of human activity. This emphasis has been of continuing relevance to all the social sciences. It is visible, for example, in the work of sociologists Talcott Parsons[16] and Robert Merton,[17] who have both influenced political science.

The influence of the political pluralists and the attack on the concept of sovereignty   While the lack of empirical substantiation of basic underlying assumptions played an important role in discrediting the

---

[12] Michael Weinstein, *Philosophy, Theory and Method in Contemporary Political Thought*, Scott, Foresman and Company, Glenview, Ill., 1971, p. 46.
[13] Ibid., p. 35.
[14] Ibid., p. 32.
[15] Ibid., p. 33.
[16] See, for example, Talcott Parsons, *The Structure of Social Action*, McGraw-Hill, New York, 1937; and *Toward a General Theory of Action*, ed. Talcott Parsons and Edward Shils, Harvard University Press, Cambridge, 1951.
[17] Robert Merton, *Social Theory and Social Structure*, The Free Press, New York, 1957.

traditional manner of approaching the study of politics, many other critics also focused on the inadequacy of traditional concepts. The attack on the concept of sovereignty by the political pluralists in the 1920s highlights this aspect in the reorientation of the discipline.

The scope of political science was traditionally defined in terms of the concept of the state. The major factor differentiating the state from other social institutions was *sovereignty*, a position of supreme and independent authority. Unfortunately this particular concept was not very useful from the standpoint either of understanding the evolution of the state and contemporary political systems or of comprehending the contemporary distribution of political forces. The concept was particularly inadequate for explaining governmental transformation and change. If sovereignty was an indivisible and enduring characteristic of the state, how did one account for the changing political fortunes and access of various groups within a society? The concept helped little to explain the change in the distribution of influence in American society at the beginning of the twentieth century. A greater shortcoming of the concept, perhaps, was its tendency to substitute a definitional truth to characterize the "state" for an adequate explanation for the process by which this absolute power is instituted, maintained, and transformed.

Leading political pluralists, including Arthur Bentley, Mary Follett, Sidney Hook, John Dewey, and others, further argued that the traditional unitary concept was inadequate because political power is in fact pluralistic.[18] People have many loyalties, and the distribution, number, and kinds of influence vary over time. Power is shared legitimately. Political parties, interest groups, and various formal and informal groups and individuals share in the exercise of political power.

Political pluralists were persuasive at the time, and their contention was much more radical than it appears today. It provided a means of analyzing the rise of new formal and informal groupings with the process of industrialization in America—a phenomenon with which the traditional conceptual apparatus could not deal. The pluralists argued for a definition of the political process that emphasizes the power aspect in a pluralistic context. They suggested defining the state in terms of its legitimate political power. Using the concept of legitimacy facilitates a more dynamic approach. With the shift to the concepts of legitimacy and power, the emphasis changes from institutional to interactional analysis and relationships, and to the consequences of interactions rather than a priori reasoning on the basis of the assumed residing features of an institution. Power is thereby

---

[18] See the citations in footnote 11 and also Arthur Bentley, *The Process of Government*, The Belknap Press, Cambridge, 1967; and Bentley's *Relativity in Man and Society*, G. P. Putnam's Sons, New York, 1926.

given a functional definition according to what it does. This shift in concepts has been important in redefining the scope of the discipline.

Unfortunately, space allows us to suggest only briefly some influences on the evolution of political science. The essence of these criticisms was that the methods then employed, the concepts used, and the types of questions asked were generally unsatisfactory. The three influences we have examined tended to reinforce one another in the following conclusion:

> Scientific discourse was the only language in which meaningful communication was possible, and every symbol in this universe of discourse was meaningful precisely because each was unequivocally grounded in empirical fact. Hence if political science was to deserve its name, a thorough purge was necessary. . . . Traditional categories of explanation had to be reformulated or cast aside because they were based on non-observable constructs. "Ghosts" was Arthur Bentley's contemptuous summation of the concepts of political science in his day [1908].[19]

This conclusion—which basically argued for an application of scientific method to the social sciences—eventually crystalized in a behavioral position in political science.

The behavioral period

Today behavioralism has become mainstream political science. Some contend the movement has been so successful that it will now disappear as a protest movement simply because it has become so thoroughly integrated into the discipline. Over the past fifteen years the broad outlines of the behavioral position have emerged. In answer to the two questions, "Is it possible for political science to more closely approximate a science, and if so, is it desirable to attempt to do so?" behavioralists have responded with a definitive "yes." Behavioralists usually have supported their arguments on the lines of the tenets we shall discuss in this section.[20]

1 Political Science can eventually more closely approximate a science capable of prediction and explanation. The goal of political science is the construction of systematic, empirical theory.

Implicit in this assertion is the assumption that human behavior is not random or unpatterned; certain regularities can be found.

[19] Don E. Bowen, "The Origins of the Behavioral Movement," in *The Political Experience*, ed. Michael Weinstein, St. Martin's Press, New York, 1972, p. 135.
[20] For a summary listing of the behavioral position see David Easton, *A Framework for Political Analysis*, Prentice-Hall, Englewood Cliffs, N.J., 1965, pp. 6–7.

Behavioralists regard it as incumbent upon political scientists to search out these regularities and the variables associated with them. This position would indicate a high priority on broad theoretical studies in contrast to narrow descriptive accounts of relatively unique events. It emphasizes explanation rather than pure description.

2   Research should be theory oriented and directed. There should be a close interplay between theory and data in social science inquiry.

Narrow empiricism and unguided data collection will not, in the long run, work toward the goal of broad, systematic general theory. Eventually we will have to move beyond merely reporting empirical findings and place them in a larger explanatory context. Theory incapable of, and devoid of, empirical substantiation is undesirable; and empirical findings unrelated to a larger explanatory framework are apt to be trivial.

3   It is desirable that questions of fact be kept analytically separate from questions of value.

Although social scientists disagree over the extent to which this analytical distinction is possible, it generally is accepted that recognition of this distinction is necessary. The argument underlying this point is that there is no way of scientifically establishing the truth or falsity of statements of value, whereas there are methods of tentatively establishing the truth-value of statements of fact. Understanding cannot be advanced by confusing these different kinds of questions and the modes of explanation appropriate to each.

4   There is an essential unity among the various social sciences. They could profit by working more closely together in an interdisciplinary manner.

Behavioralists have emphasized the essential unity of the social sciences by referring to them generally as the "behavioral sciences." This call for greater interdisciplinary interaction and synthesis rests upon the recognition that the division of inquiry into disciplines is essentially analytical—a convenient division of labor—together with the feeling that the boundaries between the social sciences are not as clear cut and well defined as current curricula might imply. We are not *only* political beings or *only* economic or social beings. We are all these things simultaneously, or at least sequentially. It seems reasonable to suppose that our economic and social aspects may have some bearing on our political aspect and vice versa. While abstracting and emphasizing one aspect may be defensible for manageability, a thorough understanding necessitates a broader, more integrated examination. The validity and generality of findings can be enhanced by working from a more integrated perspective.

Interdisciplinary integration and synthesis are not, of course, without their attendant difficulties. As Richard Snyder points out, much of the limited success of such efforts seems to stem from the fact that "in the absence of a general framework of political analysis it is very difficult to select from the data and techniques of other disciplines those most appropriate and useful for our purposes." [21]

Nevertheless, interdisciplinary work does contribute enormously to political science. Many important problems are essentially inter-disciplinary in nature and implication. How, for example, can we discuss political socialization without understanding various aspects of psychology such as developmental psychology, perception, learning, and thinking? Many current social problems that concern political scientists cannot be divorced from their economic, social, and psychological context. The environmental crisis is a good example of a problem that transcends the boundaries of any one discipline in terms of the origins of its problems, their implications, and its resolution. The frequent lack of a common vocabulary and methodology make inter-disciplinary interchange and synthesis difficult, but no less imperative.

While interdisciplinary work may be necessary in certain applied problems, it also may have the desirable effect of increasing sophistication within each discipline. Methodologically, this has been the case; political science has freely borrowed research methods from other social sciences with positive effects. Outside perspectives may suggest alternative assumptions, methods, and general questions. (It is interesting to note, for example, the variety of human motivational assumptions that underlie the social sciences). Finally, outside perspectives may play important roles of criticizing and clarifying. Economics presently has a profound impact on some political scientists. It is substantially altering how they pose questions and, on occasion, offering new conclusions and alternative explanations. [22]

5   Political scientists should become more self-conscious, precise, and sophisticated in their methodology.

Political scientists could profitably emulate the natural sciences by becoming more familiar with and making better use of precise

---

[21] Richard C. Snyder, "A Decision-making Approach to the Study of Political Phenomena," in *Approaches to the Study of Politics*, ed. Roland Young, Northwestern University Press, Evanston, Ill., 1966, pp. 4–5.

[22] See, for example, Mancur Olson's challenge to traditional group theorists, *The Logic of Collective Action*, Shocken Books Inc., New York, 1968. See also *Economic Theories of International Politics*, ed. Bruce M. Russett, Markham, Chicago, 1968. William C. Mitchell provides an excellent discussion of the developing influence of economics on political science in "The Shape of Political Theory to Come: From Political Sociology to Political Economy," in *Politics and the Social Sciences*, ed. Seymour Martin Lipset, Oxford Book Company, New York, 1969, pp. 101–136.

research methods. To a large extent, methods influence conclusions. It is important therefore that political scientists make every effort to be aware of and to discount or outline their own value preferences and biases in planning, executing, and analyzing research. Sophisticated contemporary research methods help social scientists check their biases at various stages of research design. A thorough understanding of methodological problems will result in more reliable, valid, and generalizable results. The import of this point will be a central focus of discussion throughout this text.

6   Analysis should focus on individual and/or group behavior rather than merely on political institutions.

Reacting against earlier emphasis on institutions and the inadequacies of that approach, contemporary behavioralists argue that the reduction of individual or group behavior to institutional prescription results in unrealistic and inadequate explanations. Instead, they contend, politicial scientists should concentrate on observable human behavior. While institutional behavior is an important concern of social scientists, it cannot be understood independently of the words and actions of those who carry out institutional functions. Past institutional reductionism has been inadequate on several grounds. First, human behavior is more complex and varied than an institutional position implies. Human behavior is not a simple response to a given institutional stimulus. To a very large extent human behavior depends upon intermediate perceptions and images that are not solely and uniformly determined by institutional factors. Second, whether behavior follows from institutional prescription is, in any case, an empirical question. Behavioralists argue that it is important for social scientists to develop more appropriate concepts. The concept of "role" is one example of a manner of profitability approaching the nexus between institutional constraints and individual personality factors.

The behavioral revolution represents a basic redefinition of political science as a discipline in terms of objectives, scope, and methods.[23] As discussed above, debates over these issues have been recurrent. Contemporary behavioral response will not finally answer these fundamental questions. Nevertheless, an understanding of current answers is important, since these shape inquiry. Table 1-1 summarizes basic distinctions among varying responses to questions of scope, methods, and objectives.

[23] There is a large literature dealing with the evolution of political science as a discipline and with the behavioralist-traditionalist debate specifically. Some useful works include the following: David Easton, *The Political System: An Inquiry into the State of Political Science*, 2d ed., Alfred A. Knopf, New York, 1971; Harold D. Lasswell, *The Future of Political Science*, Atherton Press, New York, 1964; Albert Somit and Joseph Tannenhaus, *The Development of American Political Science: From Burgess to Behavioralism*, Allyn and Bacon, Boston, 1967;

	Classical political philosophy
Theory and data	Data are viewed from a moral perspective. Explanation is combined with prescription.
Generalization and the unique case	Stress on uniqueness and differences.
Facts and values	Facts and values can't be separated; the two are intertwined in political life, which deals with moral choices.
Method and data	No self-conscious concern for methodology. Techniques must not become more important than substantive problems. Reliance on documents, limited field work, reporting qualitative observations.
Pure and applied research	Politics is a practical science. Knowledge is an end, but the knowledge should be put into action. Philosophers offer general advice to rulers.
Political science and other academic fields	Influence of philosophy and history. Stress on autonomy of political science.

Table 1-1   Major approaches to the study of political science

Adapted from *Political Life and Social Change: An Introduction to Political Science*, by Charles F. Andrain. © 1970 by Wadsworth Publishing Company, Inc., Belmont, California 94002. Reprinted by kind permission of the publisher, Duxbury Press.

Heinz Eulau, *The Behavioral Persuasion in Politics*, Random House, New York, 1963; Stephen L. Wasby, *Political Science: The Discipline and Its Dimensions*, Charles Scribner's Sons, New York, 1970; *Approaches to the Study of Political Science*, ed. Michael Haas and Henry S. Kariel, Chandler Publishing Company, San Francisco, 1970; *Essays on the Behavioral Study of Politics*, ed. Austin Ranney, University of Illinois Press, Urbana, 1962; *Changing Perspectives in Contemporary Political Analysis*, ed. Howard Ball and Thomas P. Lauth, Jr., Prentice-Hall, Englewood Cliffs, N.J., 1971; *Perspectives in the Study of Politics*, ed. Malcolm B. Parsons, Rand McNally & Company, Chicago, 1968; *The Political Experience*, ed. Michael A. Weinstein, St. Martin's Press, New York, 1972.

Institutional analysis	Behavioral science
Stress on accumulation of facts, which are self-explanatory. Rejection of abstract theorizing.	More inductive theory. Data are used for testing hypotheses. Theory and data are interdependent.
Human nature is constant; structures operate differently in each society.	Regularities of behavior can be found and expressed in generalizations (probability statements).
Facts and values cannot be kept wholly separate. Political science involves reformist impulses.	Facts and values should be kept analytically distinct. Scientists must control for personal biases of observer.
Qualitative methods. Reliance on documents (rules, laws, constitutions) and uncontrolled observation.	Methods are self-conscious, explicit, and quantitative. Use of statistical techniques.
Concern for practical reforms, that is, ways to check power. Stress on realizing democracy, constitutional government, representative government.	Knowledge of behavior is the main goal. Generalizations are partial, incomplete, and tentative. There are dangers of partial understanding.
Influence of law and history. Stress on autonomy of political science.	Influence of psychology, biology, statistics, and econometrics.

Although the behavioral debate has waned somewhat, a traditional rebuttal has been heard. The final sections of this chapter shall discuss the traditionalists' rebuttal and, finally, the most current debate in the discipline, which results in some instances in a merging of behavioral methodology with the classical moral concerns of traditionalists.

The traditionalists' rebuttal

Traditionalism in political science is represented by political scientists of several professional inclinations. Although it is more closely associated with practitioners of moral or social philosophy, it embraces institutional analysts as well. While behavioralists argue that social sciences can more closely approximate the methods and goals of natural sciences, traditionalists argue, to the contrary, that political science can never become a science in any real sense of the word, and that even if it were possible for political science to become a science, it would be undesirable to attempt it.[24]

To support their basic position, traditionalists raise a number of points about behavioralists' methods. In regard to the claim that political science can never really become a science, traditionalists have argued that units of analysis in political science are not comparable to those of natural science. Human beings, they claim, are not like the stable units found in natural science. It would, therefore, be inaccurate and presumptuous to aim at general predictive laws. Human beings are unique by virtue of their self-consciousness and capacity for altering and planning behavior on the basis of past, present, and future expectations and experiences. A related argument has been that political behavior is not amenable to experimental inquiry because it is, in a historical sense, unique and not recurring. According to this argument, the search for regularities is vain.

Traditionalists also have maintained that political science will never become a science because human behavior is too complex. Too many contingencies and variables are involved to use scientific methods. Because human behavior is complex, scientific methods can never deal adequately with the nearly infinite number of contingencies; and because science can never deal with all complexities and contingencies, it can never thoroughly and adequately deal with human behavior.

Traditionalists further hold that quantification and rigorous analysis does not suit political science. The discipline, it is said, lacks both precise concepts and required metrics. Significant questions usually cannot be quantified, and problems that can be quantified easily are usually trivial. A somewhat related problem involves traditionalists' concern over the extent to which significant human behavior can actually be apprehended and observed in a systematic manner.

---

[24] There is also a large literature representing the traditionalist position: Bernard Crick, *The American Science of Politics: Its Origins and Conditions,* University of California Press, Berkeley, 1959; *The Limits of Behavioralism in Political Science,* ed. James C. Charlesworth, American Academy of Political and Social Sciences, Philadelphia, 1962; *Essays on the Scientific Study of Politics,* ed. Herbert Storing, Holt, Rinehart and Winston, New York, 1962; Leo Strauss, *Natural Right and History,* University of Chicago, Chicago, 1953; Vernon Van Dyke, *Political Science: A Philosophical Analysis,* Stanford University Press, Stanford, 1960; Eric Voegelin, *The New Science of Politics: An Introductory Essay,* University of Chicago, Chicago, 1952; Peter Winch, *The Idea of a Social Science,* Routledge & Kegan Paul, London, 1958.

Traditionalists argue further that additional subject-matter differences between social and natural sciences confound efforts to emulate the methods of natural science. Social scientists, they argue, cannot treat their subject matter dispassionately; they can never achieve the objectivity required by the scientific method. In fact, the scientific method blinds social scientists to the realities of their own biases. They cannot, traditionalists argue, keep values and emotions separate from facts.

Because traditionalists and behavioralists hold different conceptions of appropriate methods, it is understandable that they also differ over appropriate scope and objectives. The appropriate objectives of scholars, in the traditionalist conception, are action oriented in the roles of humanitarian, advocate, critic, and reformer.

The traditionalist position implies a special characterization of scientific method. Unfortunately the debate is muddied because this conception is seldom fully articulated. On one level, rejecting scientific method entails claiming that the pattern of justification differs in natural and social sciences. On another level, the traditionalist position also involves the claim that scientific techniques of discovery differ in natural and social sciences. The former claim is more radical in import. Much of the debate fails to articulate this important distinction. Today a middle solution appears to have emerged that avoids the strawman positions of the various advocates:

> It is possible to define science and scientific inquiry so narrowly that only a few special areas in the physical sciences could qualify. On the other hand, it is possible to establish such broad meanings that almost any systematic accumulating of information could be so designated. When it is not clear what claims are being made for or against science there is an artificiality about debate. In recent years philosophers of science have persuasively stated the case for a view of science and scientific methods that falls between the above extremes.[25]

Chapter 2 takes up the philosophy of science in greater detail, and we articulate details and implications of the moderate characterization of science and scientific method.

The postbehavioral revolution

Harold Lasswell has frequently been at the frontier of the discipline. He was one of the first to urge political scientists to adopt scientific

[25] Malcolm B. Parsons, "Perspectives on the Study of Politics: An Introduction," in *Perspectives on the Study of Politics*, ed. Malcolm B. Parsons, Rand McNally & Company, Chicago, 1968, pp. 17–18.

methods, and he was a pioneer in political psychology. Though his early arguments concerning the future of political science were premature in the sense of failing to find a wide audience for some twenty years, they indicated the directions in which the field did eventually move. In a volume edited by Lerner and Lasswell entitled *The Policy Sciences* (1951), Lasswell finally was able to proclaim that "the battle for method is won." [26] Other political scientists made essentially the same proclamation, most notably Robert Dahl in his article "The Behavioral Approach in Political Science: Epitaph for a Monument to a Successful Protest." Yet this was some time later; Dahl's epitaph did not appear until 1961.[27]

Lasswell was equally far-sighted in appraising the coming issues of the postbehavioral period. With a view to future directions, he suggested in his 1951 essay that the discipline must now turn its attention to "the choice of significant problems on which to apply and evolve method." [28] He urged political scientists to choose problems "according to their relevance for all . . . goal values." [29] However, Lasswell was not suggesting that relevance and personal-value bias become substitutes for scientific objectivity. On the contrary, he explicitly stated that:

> The place for nonobjectivity is in deciding what ultimate goals are to be implemented. Once this choice is made, the scholar proceeds with maximum objectivity, and uses all available method.[30]

Lasswell made no attempt to conceal his predilections. He thought that political science in the United States would "be directed toward providing the knowledge needed to improve the practice of democracy." [31] He was, however, especially concerned that the discipline attempt to grapple with the difficult question, "Knowledge for What?" Method, however objective, could not in the end be divorced from the human context in which it is developed and applied. Recognizing this, Lasswell indicated that the discipline needed to ask fundamental questions directly relevant to human needs and public policy.

Although some scholars undoubtedly took up Lasswell's challenge by moving toward a more policy-relevant study of politics, the

---

[26] Harold D. Lasswell, "The Policy Orientation," in *The Policy Sciences: Recent Developments in Scope and Method*, ed. D. Lerner and H. D. Lasswell, Stanford University Press, Stanford, 1951, p. 7.
[27] Robert A. Dahl, "The Behavioral Approach in Political Science: Epitaph for a Monument to a Successful Protest," *American Political Science Review*, 55 (December 1961), 763–772.
[28] Lasswell, "The Policy Orientation," p. 7.
[29] Ibid., p. 11.
[30] Ibid.
[31] Ibid., p. 15.

response more frequently was belated. The problems raised by Lasswell did not generally become recognized concerns of political scientists until the mid-1960s.

Events of the intervening years helped convince a substantial number of scholars of the urgency of Lasswell's early appeal. A number of compelling issues—including the civil rights movement, the urban riots in the mid-1960s, a series of assassinations of major American political leaders, the deterioration of the environment, and the growing disenchantment over the Vietnam War—forced many political scientists to ask basic questions about the relevance of their work, the adequacy of their approaches, and the general responsibility of scholars. Many found current approaches lacking. As David Easton pointed out:

> There can be little doubt that political science as an enterprise has failed to anticipate the crises that are upon us. One index of this is perhaps that in the decade from 1958 to 1968, *The American Political Science Review* published only 3 articles on the urban crises; 4 on racial conflicts, 1 on poverty, 2 on civil disobedience; and 2 on violence in the United States.[32]

While more "relevant" articles may have been published elsewhere and these figures may reflect merely the bias of the *American Political Science Review*, the figures are significant: this journal is generally considered the most prestigious in the discipline.

These central failings led to what Easton called the "new revolution in political science," post-behavioralism. Events in the external environment have, to a major extent, provided the impetus for the current reappraisal. We suggested earlier that anomaly and crisis play an important role in changing the scope, methods, and objectives of any inquiry.[33] This general reappraisal in the social sciences manifests itself in the twin guises of questions of relevance and action. As Easton points out, "its objects of criticism are the disciplines, the professions, and the universities." [34] It is a movement of profound potential consequence that raises some agonizingly difficult questions.

---

[32] David Easton, *The Political System: An Inquiry into the State of Political Science*, 2d ed., Alfred A. Knopf, New York, 1971. Reprinted by permission.

[33] Kuhn, *The Structure of Scientific Revolutions*.

[34] Easton, *The Political System*, p. 323. See also *The Post-behavioral Era: Perspectives on Political Science*, ed. George J. Graham, Jr., and George W. Carey, David McKay Company, New York, 1972; Charles A. McCoy and John Playford, *Apolitical Politics: A Critique of Behavioralism*, Thomas Y. Crowell Company, New York, 1967; J. Peter Euben, "Political Science and Political Silence," in *Power and Community: Dissenting Essays in Political Science*, ed. Philip Green and Sanford Levinson, Vintage Books, Random House, New York, 1970, pp. 3–58; and Kenneth M. Dolbeare, "Public Policy Analysis and the Coming Struggle for the Soul of the Postbehavioral Revolution," in ibid., pp. 85–111.

Although the banners of "relevance and action" had been used previously to justify a return to traditional approaches to political inquiry, Easton does not feel the postbehavioral revolution is basically reactionary. We tend to agree with him. For the most part, the redirection implied by the new revolution is future oriented and concerned with questions of scope and objectives. Postbehavioralists do not, as a rule, reject scientific method or strides made in the behavioral period. On the contrary, they point out merely that we have not reached the end of the road. Further problems must be resolved, problems of overriding significance and urgency, problems that concern both scholars and human beings in general. As Easton points out, current postbehavioralists have diverse political and methodological leanings and are drawn from many areas of the discipline. They represent no particular age group—old and young alike are found among these contemporary critics. Their affinity rests on a common commitment to making political science more relevant to current problems and their resolution.

Easton does feel that the current postbehavioral movement is sufficiently well defined to delineate its broad outlines. He calls postbehavioralists' credo the "Credo of Relevance." Its major tenets on the scope, methods, and objectives of the field follow:

1   Substance must precede technique. If one must be sacrificed for the other—and this need not always be so—it is more important to be relevant and meaningful for contemporary urgent social problems than to be sophisticated in the tools of investigation. For the aphorism of science that it is better to be wrong than vague, post-behavioralism would substitute a new dictum, that it is better to be vague than non-relevantly precise.

2   Behavioral science conceals an ideology of empirical conservatism. To confine oneself exclusively to the description and analysis of facts is to hamper the understanding of these same facts in their broadest context. As a result empirical political science must lend its support to the maintenance of the very factual conditions that it explores. It unwittingly purveys an ideology of social conservatism tempered by modest incremental change.

3   [Too much] behavioral research loses touch with reality. The heart of behavioral inquiry is abstraction and analysis and this serves to conceal the crude realities of politics. The task of postbehavioralism is to break the barriers of silence that behavioral language necessarily has created and to help political science reach out to the real needs of mankind in a time of crisis.

4   Research about and constructive development of values are inextinguishable parts of the study of politics. Science cannot be

and never has been exclusively neutral despite protestations to the contrary. Hence to understand the limits of our knowledge we need to be aware of the value premises on which it stands and the alternatives for which this knowledge could be used.

5   Members of a learned discipline bear the responsibilities of all intellectuals. The intellectuals' historical role has been and must be to protect the humane values of civilization. This is their unique task and obligation. Without this they become mere technicians, mechanics for tinkering with society. They thereby abandon the special privileges they have come to claim for themselves in academia, such as freedom of inquiry and a quasi-extraterritorial protection from the onslaughts of society.

6   To know is to bear the responsibility for acting and to act is to engage in reshaping society. The intellectual as scientist bears the special obligation to put his knowledge to work. Contemplative science was a product of the nineteenth century when a broader moral agreement was shared. Action science of necessity reflects the contemporary conflict in society over ideals and this must permeate and color the whole research enterprise itself.

7   If the intellectual has the obligation to implement his knowledge, those organizations composed of intellectuals—the professional associations—and the universities themselves, cannot stand apart from the struggles of the day. Politicization of the professions is inescapable as well as desirable.[35]

While not all the preceding views are endorsed by all postbehavioralists, Easton's listing adequately summarizes the various tenets put forth by these contemporary critics. The first point, for example, is probably most generally accepted, while the last is most debated.

Taken together, the various tenets of the postbehavioral credo suggest a substantial reevaluation of current images of what social scientists do and should do, what priorities should be set, and what aspects should be emphasized. They suggest a need for restructuring much present inquiry and new directions in professional training and competence. The criticisms of postbehavioralists raise a number of difficult questions regarding professional ethics and values, the relations between science and society, freedom of inquiry, and the relation between government and the scholarly community. These problems form the central discussion of Chapter 3.

The current plea for a shift in scope and objectives need not be taken as a call for change in scientific method in the broad sense. We

---

[35] Easton, *The Political System*, pp. 325–327.

view much postbehavioral criticism of the limited scope and objectives as an attack on de facto rather than inherent limitations of political inquiry posed by scientific method. Furthermore, pleas for shift in scope and objectives are not limited to political science; similar demands are heard from varying quarters in all social and natural sciences. The interdisciplinary nature of the postbehavioral ranks is understandable: many of the most urgent social, economic, ecological, and political problems do not fit neatly into one field of inquiry. For this reason Lasswell, Easton, and others suggest the need for broad interdisciplinary work.[36] Easton, in particular, sees systems analysis as an appropriate analytic framework for integrated, interdisciplinary work.

Sociology has perhaps been the field most influenced by the cry for more relevant, action-oriented work. One sociologist, Herbert Gans, suggests that the problem in sociology has not been a neglect of relevant, current problems. On the contrary, Gans claims that sociologists have been quick to climb on "the bandwagon of current social problems."[37] He sees the problem of sociology as a neglect of action-oriented, policy-oriented research.

> Judging by all the anthologies on poverty that have been announced, sociologists seem to be mainly concerned with informing their students about the existence and causes of poverty. I see a much more urgent concern: research to eliminate poverty. A particularly great need is policy-oriented research: for example, studies that evaluate current antipoverty efforts and propose or test alternative solutions.[38]

Gans asserts that precious little work on *any* topic in sociology is explicitly policy oriented. What are the roots of this neglect? He sees them as stemming from several factors: the current time constraints upon scholars, who are first and foremost teachers rather than researchers; lack of research funding; and problems within the disciplines themselves arising from the use of "methods and concepts not easily adapted to the needs of policy."[39]

Similar questioning is taking place in psychology, too. In his article entitled, "Psychology Can Now Kick the Science Habit," David Bakan argues that psychologists frequently fail to recognize that their

---

[36] Ibid. See also Lasswell, *The Future of Political Science* and *Politics and the Social Sciences*, ed. Lipset.

[37] Herbert Gans, "Where Sociologists Have Failed," in *The Values of Social Science*, ed. Norman K. Densiz, Aldine-Transaction Books, New York, 1970, pp. 83–86.

[38] Ibid., p. 83.

[39] Ibid., p. 84.

discipline is not an autonomous field of inquiry and that they can become stultified by adherence to an antiquated model of science.

> They are often unaware of the social and historical forces that have shaped psychology—unaware especially of the ways in which the development of the university, and the natural sciences within it, have shaped their attitudes and interests. This lack of awareness has handicapped the field internally, in its emergence as an authentic discipline, and externally, in its usefulness to society.[40]

Bakan points out that psychology, like other social sciences, was originally "a largely philosophical and moral enterprise, a handmaiden to religion. It purported to raise moral virtue." [41] With the decline of the religious-philosophical dominance, psychology became closely attached to the natural sciences. The German, experimental laboratory model became the predominant antidote to the moral-philosophical model of the past. At approximately the same time, a split occurred within most natural sciences that resulted in a divorce between the process of acquiring knowledge and a concern with its application. Bakan sees World War II as the point at which this two-step process came to fruition:

> The creation of the bomb taught policy makers an important lesson: scientists could contribute significantly without knowing how those contributions would be used. Research could be split up, assembly-line fashion, with someone else responsible for putting the pieces together and using it. This division of labor accorded comfortably with the scientists' belief that they were interested in truth for its own sake.[42]

The 1950s, the Cold War, and the McCarthy period witnessed a continuation of this process of truncated responsibility and resulted in a general ambivalence toward science. At the same time as the American scholarly community was increasingly put under various forms of surveillance to safeguard American scientific knowledge, the Russian satellite Sputnik accelerated governmental interest in scientific research. This period, according to Bakan, saw an emphasis on narrow-gauge research with immediate practical application; exploratory, large-scale humanistic studies had (and continue to have) low priority. This emphasis resulted in a narrowing of focus and a hardening of

---

[40] David Bakan, "Psychology Can Now Kick the Science Habit." Reprinted from *Psychology Today* Magazine (March 1972), 26. Copyright © 1972 Ziff-Davis Publishing Company. All rights reserved.
[41] Ibid.
[42] Ibid., p. 28.

orthodox experimental methodology. Bakan argues that the current priorities are unfortunate because broad empirical work is likely to be more significant and more productive, and the payoffs from narrowly construed experimental research have been small. As he points out:

> We made it to the moon, but did less to improve the earth. . . . Military research produced defoliants, napalm, and poison gases but did not end the conflict in Vietnam. Indeed, the association between the military and science meant that as the prestige of the one fell, so did that of the other. By early 1970 the reaction against science was considerable. The Government, again following the public mood, began to withdraw its previously enthusiastic support for so-called basic research.[43]

Believing that the social sciences can do better, Bakan, like many other contemporary critics within the scholarly community, has called for internal reappraisal:

> Psychology, which once sought to free itself from its philosophic-religious tradition, now has an opportunity to free itself from the natural-science model, to pursue intrinsically relevant goals.[44]

Bakan's explicit conclusion is that social science must commit itself to making a better world. In his words, "the major function of social science, including psychology, should be to make man aware of the forces that operate on him." [45] This calls for a concern with *both* the acquisition and the application of knowledge, a reappraisal of the methods we presently use to acquire knowledge, and a general questioning of the problems we choose to study. Bakan does not suggest that we abandon "science"; his message is not as radical as the title might imply. He, like many contemporary critics, argues for a more relevant science with an emphasis on methods most appropriate to resolution of current societal needs.

Two other points in the postbehavioral credo deserve detailed examination. The first concerns the demands of scientific method in the context of justification; the second involves the place of values in scientific research under conditions of truncated responsibility for the acquisition and application of knowledge. Easton has suggested that overly strict adherence to the tenets of scientific method may help to account for the failure of social science to meet the need for relevant, action-oriented research. Science by definition is a tentative, conservative process of inquiry. The tests of time and replication play important roles in its procedures. Postbehavioralists on the other hand, argue that time is running out and that traditional temporal frames of postponed judgment no longer serve adequately. They contend that

[43] Ibid., p. 87.
[44] Ibid., pp. 87–88.
[45] Ibid., p. 88.

if contemporary social scientists continue to retreat into inaction through reference to the scientific canon of reserved judgment, there may be no world to judge in decades ahead. Our problems simply may outrun our ability to deal with them. The meanings of time and space have changed, and research standards and strategies must take this into account if we are to survive in a decent environment— indeed, if we are to survive at all.[46]

Postbehavioralists also argue that we must learn to recognize and explicate the value judgments that necessarily underlie much research. The recognition that values are an inescapable part of the research process is not, of course, new; Max Weber and Karl Mannheim made essentially the same point some years ago. Many postbehavioralists maintain that the lesson has been imperfectly learned by scholars and laymen alike. The problem is doubly complex because the current division of responsibility for acquisition and application of scientific findings raises the possibility that those who use "scientific results" may fail to recognize the implicit value assumptions underlying any given piece of research. Philip Green, for example, argues that implicit and questionable value judgments underlie application of game theory to problems of nuclear war and deterrence.[47] This problem brings the present division of responsibility into question. Unfortunately, there is no easy answer to this dilemma. Unified responsibility raises equally difficult and dangerous problems.

The problems posed by postbehavioralists are difficult at best. Whether social science will prove equal to their challenge will have vast implications for society at large. As Easton points out:

> We are faced with the question not of a new science but of an appropriate contemporary strategy for science . . . the times now call for dedication in the application of whatever knowledge we may have to transparently critical problems. This does not imply the abandonment of or even a retrenchment in our search for basic understanding. But it does require a re-ordering of our concerns. It imposes on us the obligation to increase greatly the resources to be devoted to meet the needs of the day.[48]

Review questions and exercises

1 Explain the meaning and significance of the following terms:

   a Behavioralism
   b Postbehavioral credo

[46] See for example Alvin Toffler, *Future Shock*, Bantam Books, New York, 1971.
[47] Philip Green, *Deadly Logic: The Theory of Nuclear Deterrence*, Ohio State University Press, Columbus, 1966.
[48] Easton, *The Political System*, p. 377.

    c   The irony of form
    d   Behavioral sciences
    e   The traditionalists' position
    f   Pragmatism
    g   The attack of the political pluralists
    h   The role of anomaly
    i   Scientific revolutions
    j   Questions of scope, method, and objectives

2   What do you see as major weaknesses of the traditionalists' position? Major advantages?
3   What do you see as major advantages and disadvantages of the behavioralists' position?
4   What units of analysis and what types of questions are most appropriate from the various perspectives discussed in this chapter?
5   What problems does the postbehavioral position raise? Analyze any problems you find in each of the tenets discussed in this chapter.

Science is built with facts as
a house is built with stones, but
a collection of facts is no more
science than a heap of stones is
a house.

Henri Poincaré

2
SCIENTIFIC METHOD

Is political science a genuine science? In this chapter we return to the question raised in our discussion of the behavioralist-traditionalist debate. Answers to this question demand two preliminary steps: (1) we must provide an account of what constitutes a genuine science; and (2) we must characterize the methodology suited to political science.

We discuss scientific method in this chapter in order to isolate characteristics that political science must share with natural science if it is to be considered a genuine science. The detailed discussion of specific methodological procedures is relegated to the remaining chapters of this text. Although these problems are closely related, debate about the status of political science has not always made explicit and precise which methods distinguish a genuine science from other methods of inquiry.

The standard view

A principal aim of scientific inquiry is to obtain an *organized* body of *empirical* knowledge. This rough characterization suggests two ways of distinguishing scientific methods. First, scientific conclusions are usually justified by direct or indirect appeal to empirical or observational evidence. Second, scientific inquiries typically organize data provided by direct observation. Crucial, however, is the kind of organization in question; after all, a telephone directory systemizes data obtained by an inquiry into the names and addresses of subscribers, but it is not normally considered science.[1]

Scientific inquiry seeks to go beyond mere collection of facts by producing generalizations from data, but this feature does not of itself distinguish scientific enterprise from various unscientific or pre-scientific practices. Common sense and folk wisdom provide numerous generalizations—for example, that fishing is best just before a storm, or that a shot of brandy relieves a faint. A compendium of such common-sense generalizations—useful though it may be—does not constitute a body of scientific knowledge. It is not that such generalizations are false—modern pharmacological research, for example, has attested to the medicinal value of some folk remedies. Rather, it is that they do not appeal to well-confirmed laws and theories which explain the data observed.[2] To say this much, however, merely sets the problem, because philosophers of both natural and social science have offered conflicting accounts of the roles of law, theory, and explanation in science. One position can lay claim to being the standard view at least in the sense that it serves to focus critical discussion.[3]

According to the standard view, the chief aim of scientific investigation is explanation (and, derivatively, prediction) of observable phenomena. Phenomena are subsumed under and explained by observational or experimental laws, and the laws themselves are justified and explained by underlying theory. Scientific methods are treated fundamentally as means of evaluating arguments put forward to support these experimental laws, scientific theories, and the explanations and predictions they afford. Questions of which laws are well supported, which theories are acceptable, and which explanations are adequate are decided by scientists working in a given field. No general method provides specific answers to scientific questions; the questions require

---

[1] Ernest Nagel, *The Structure of Science*, Harcourt, Brace & World, New York, 1961, p. 3.

[2] Ibid., chap. 1.

[3] Historically what has here been dubbed as the "standard view" is a position that grew out of logical positivism (logical empiricism). It is associated most closely with the work of Carl Hempel and Ernest Nagel, but even they have recognized the need to modify their positions in response to recent criticisms. See for example, Carl Hempel, "On the 'Standard Conception' of Scientific Theories," in *Minnesota Studies in the Philosophy of Science, Volume IV: Analyses of Theories and Methods of Physics and Psychology*, eds. Michael Radner and Stephen Winokur, University of Minnesota Press, Minneapolis, 1970, pp. 142–163. The term "standard view" is used to denote this view by Israel Scheffler, *Science and Subjectivity*, The Bobbs-Merrill Company, New York, 1967, pp. 7–15. The position is also referred to as the "received view," and an extended historical account of its development as well as a discussion of alternatives can be found in Frederick Suppe, *The Structure of Scientific Theories*, University of Illinois Press, Urbana, Ill., 1974, pp. 3–241.

substantive scientific research. Nevertheless, according to the standard view, scientific enterprise may be distinguished from other methods of obtaining knowledge by the *pattern of evaluation* or *justification* appropriate to it.

It is important to note that this view characterizes science according to its *products*, not according to the *process* of scientific inquiry itself.[4] Philosophers discussing the nature or pattern of justification appropriate to scientific laws, theories, and explanation are not concerned with the historical, psychological, or social contexts in which some individual or group first conceived the laws, theories, or explanations. However important the context of discovery might be for the history or sociology of science, the standard view holds that such considerations are essentially irrelevant in considering the nature of science as a product of this context.[5] In particular, the standard view sets aside any consideration of the "logic of scientific discovery" and the conditions of scientific creativity.[6]

The standard view treats the product of scientific inquiry as a body of statements, open to public inspection and evaluation, standing in a certain systematic relationship. As our introductory remarks suggest, this body of statements typically contains three components:

1   Observational (evidence) statements
2   Observational (experimental) laws
3   Theories

The relationship of these components to each other constitutes the two final topics central to the standard view, namely:

4   Explanation of observed phenomena by appeal to laws and theories
5   Evaluation of laws and theories by appeal to observed phenomena

These topics are discussed individually in the following sections.

---

[4] For a discussion of the process-product distinction see Richard Rudner, *Philosophy of Social Science*, Prentice-Hall, Englewood Cliffs, N.J., 1966, pp. 7–8.

[5] For a discussion of the distinction between the context of discovery and the context of justification see Hans Reichenbach, *The Rise of Scientific Philosophy*, University of California Press, Berkeley, 1951, p. 231; also Rudner, op. cit., pp. 4ff.

[6] A brief discussion of some issues raised by neglect of the context of discovery is found in P. B. Medawar, *Induction and Intuition in Scientific Thought*, American Philosophical Society, Philadelphia, 1969. More detailed arguments concerning the importance of the context of discovery for the understanding of science are Karl Popper's classic treatment in *The Logic of Scientific Discovery*, Harper and Row, Publishers, New York, 1968; and N. R. Hanson, *Patterns of Discovery*, Cambridge University Press, Cambridge, England, 1969; Stephen Toulmin, *Human Understanding*, vol. I, Princeton University Press, Princeton, N.J., 1972.

OBSERVATIONAL (EVIDENCE) STATEMENTS

Observational statements are those in which we record data; they justify our generalizations and support our theories. They ascribe the presence or absence of an observable characteristic to some readily identifiable object, person, event, or to a group of such objects, persons, or events.[7] It should be noted that observational statements need not record only observations that have been made; they may also describe observations that could be made in the future or those that could have been made in the past. Furthermore, they may be false or true.

Observational statements are important to science because their truth or falsity can be determined readily when conditions for observation are optimal. They can serve as an evidential base for science because they provide the greatest ground for intersubjective agreement. People are more likely to agree about statements whose truth can be settled by making a few observations, especially if these observations can be made under controlled (laboratory) conditions. In practice, we often are unable to determine whether a member of this privileged class of statements is true or false because of inadequate technology or limitations in time, energy, personnel, or money. This is particularly true in social science, where accurate description or measurement often demands sophisticated techniques of data collection and evaluation.

At first it may appear simple to pick out characteristics that are observable and, hence, statements that are observational. Aren't observable characteristics simply those which we see or hear (and perhaps smell, taste, and feel)? Consider, however, the statement, "John Doe voted in the last Springville city election." Can we *see* that John Doe voted? Or are we limited to saying that all we literally can see is whether John Doe marked his ballot at a specified time in a certain place? Even if we allow that we can observe that a person votes, further complications arise when we consider application of simple mathematical operations to observational data. What, for example, is the status of statements such as, "Of the adults in Springville, 25 percent voted in the last election," or "The 'average' voter in Springville earned less than $5,000 a year." Can we observe that 25 percent of the adults voted? Can we observe the "average" voter?

There are few, if any, terms whose ascription cannot be the subject of disagreement. (Witnesses to a crime may disagree over even the most straightforward physical characteristic of the participants.) Nevertheless, a broad distinction can be drawn between terms that are likely to provoke intersubjective agreement after observation and

[7] Carl Hempel, "Empiricist Criteria of Cognitive Significance," in *Aspects of Scientific Explanation and Other Essays*, The Free Press, New York, 1965, pp. 102–103.

Observational statements characteristically contain terms such as:		Nonobservational statements characteristically contain terms such as:	
red	employed	electric field	Oedipus complex
warm	salivates	electron	virus
left of	has a radio	atom	ego
longer than	marked a ballot	molecule	developing area
hard	answered item	wave function	authoritarian
floats	5 "no"	mass	institution
wood			

Table 2-1

those which can be ascribed only indirectly. The exact line of demarcation is difficult to draw and may be one source of controversy within a science. In psychology, for example, the debate between "behaviorists" and "mentalists" is in part a controversy over whether introspective reports of "mental states" are admissible evidence.[8]

Although there is no general agreement on the principles that distinguish observational and nonobservational characteristics and statements, there is substantial agreement on at least some statements that fall into each category depicted in Table 2-1.[9]

Few psychologists would hesitate to treat the statement, "Fido heard the bell, then salivated,"as a report of observation. Many more would question the status of, "S. F. has an Oedipus complex," by claiming that we cannot directly observe that someone has an Oedipus complex. At best we can observe and interpret individual overt behaviors.

One important way to increase intersubjective agreement is to cast observational statements in precise terms. Thus, for example, we can expect less disagreement over the claim that John Doe answered item 5 "no" than that he reacted unfavorably, since the difference between unfavorable, favorable, and indifferent reactions is often

[8] For discussions of this debate see Noam Chomsky, *Language and Mind*, Harcourt, Brace & World, New York, 1968, especially chap. 1; Jerry A. Fodor, *Psychological Explanation: An Introduction to the Philosophy of Psychology*, Random House, New York, 1968, chap. 2; Jerrold J. Katz, "Mentalism in Linguistics," *Language*, 40 No. 2 (1964), 124–137.

[9] This list has been adapted from Peter Achinstein, "The Problem of Theoretical Terms," *American Philosophical Quarterly*, 2 (July 1965), 193. It should be noted that the question of whether we can precisely delineate a class of observational or evidential terms is the focus of substantial contemporary debate in the philosophy of science. We discuss some aspects of this problem later in this chapter. See also Achinstein's discussion, op. cit., passim.

difficult to detect and may be disputed. A similar rationale may be offered for preferring quantitative to qualitative descriptions. There is less controversy, for example, about whether a person is 5 feet 11 inches in height than whether he is tall.

Observational terms and statements constructed from them bear a twofold relationship to other products of scientific inquiry. First, they serve as instances of scientific hypotheses. Second, they figure into "operational definitions" of nonobservational terms within a scientific theory. We can provide an observational basis and give empirical content to the terms of a scientific theory only by linking them to observation. When this link is missing or obscure, the scientific character of a purported theory is called into question. Unless there are some observational signs closely connected with having an Oedipus complex, for example, there is no basis for agreement about whether a person has one.

Restrictions on the character of operational definitions of theoretical (nonobservational) terms has been the subject of much debate within the philosophy of science. However, there is widespread agreement among proponents of the standard view that not all concepts of a scientific theory can be eliminated in favor of observational concepts, because the meaning of many terms in a scientific theory goes beyond what can be conveyed by the restricted vocabulary of observation. In addition to disputes about the status of observational terms and statements among philosophers, there are discussions within the individual sciences themselves. One important task facing social scientists is the proper formulation of operational definitions. Without a proper connection between theory and observation, scientific theories and hypotheses are untestable.[10]

OBSERVATIONAL (EXPERIMENTAL) LAWS

As the epigraph to this chapter suggests, science is not merely a collection of observational statements. One way in which science moves beyond observation is by producing hypotheses—generalizations put forward for test—that record regularities or correlations among observable characteristics but that go beyond mere enumeration or description of past and present observed instances. They may be treated as generalizations that have observational statements as instances. When these generalizations have been tested adequately, they may be put forward as observational (experimental) laws. They differ in form from the corresponding observational statement by ascribing an observable characteristic not to a single individual,

[10] We examine some of the philosophical problems and practical difficulties surrounding operational definitions and related issues about measurement in Chapter 4.

but to all, most, or a certain percentage of individuals over all temporal instances. The statement, "All [most, 98 percent of people] inoculated with typhoid vaccine remain free of the disease," is a generalization that has as an instance the observational statement, "John Doe was inoculated with the vaccine and remained free of the disease." Sometimes we use statements having the form of a generalization (for example, "All members of the legislature are male") as abbreviations for a conjunction of observation sentences that we could enumerate (by listing all legislators and their sex).

Laws and generalizations that are candidates for the status of law, however, characteristically go beyond observational evidence at hand. This process of going from statements of observational evidence to observational laws is often called "induction." The observations are projected to hitherto unexamined cases, and a claim is made that the observed correlation holds for them as well.

Nevertheless, not all generalizations that project from examined to unexamined cases are laws or even lawlike, that is, candidates for laws; some are "accidental generalizations" that assert "spurious correlations" or mere "constant conjunction" of observational characteristics. It may be true to say of a given room, for instance, that everyone coming into it is less than 6 feet tall. We may advance this generalization on the basis of observing the heights of some people who come into the room on some occasions when it is occupied. Nevertheless, the height of its occupants is nothing more than an accidental or coincidental characteristic of the room or group occupying the room. This situation can be contrasted with that of a lawlike generalization such as, "All samples of pure water at normal atmospheric pressure freeze at 32° Fahrenheit."

Confusion about this distinction is particularly apt to cause problems for beginning students of social science. It might be assumed that because we use a certain sampling technique to obtain "generalizations" ("85 percent of all Americans have radios"), such a statement expresses a law. While it is certainly true that this statement may go beyond the observed evidence, this is not sufficient to qualify the statement as lawlike. Unless such a statement is asserted in a context that gives us reason to suppose the statistic will obtain in the future, it counts merely as a description of a present, perhaps temporary, state of affairs.

The distinction between lawlike and accidental generalizations may be marked in three ways.[11] Lawlike generalizations (1) are con-

[11] A more elaborate discussion of these issues can be found in Carl Hempel, *Philosophy of Natural Science*, Prentice-Hall, Englewood Cliffs, N.J., 1966, pp. 64ff, 85ff; Nelson Goodman, *Fact, Fiction, and Forecast*, 2d ed., The Bobbs-Merrill Company, New York, 1965; and Karel Lambert and Gordon G. Brittan, Jr., *An Introduction to the Philosophy of Science*, Prentice-Hall, Englewood Cliffs, N.J., 1970, chap. 4.

firmed (or falsified) by observation statements which are their instances; (2) figure in explanations; and (3) serve as a basis for prediction.

First, a lawlike statement, unlike an accidental generalization, is a generalization for which observation provides evidence. The observation that the first ten people we meet in a given room are under 6 feet tall, for example, does not itself warrant the claim that everyone who came into the room in the past or who will come into it in the future has a height of less than 6 feet. Our willingness to use past observed instances as evidence is a sign that we are treating a generalization as lawlike. A collection of facts is, as the chapter epigraph suggests, like a heap of stones—unless the statement that generalizes them is at least potentially a law.

Not only do observational statements provide evidence to support observational laws, they also serve to formulate counterexamples that potentially falsify purported laws.[12] A generalization such as "All swans are white" is, for instance, falsified by the observational statement "There are black swans in the Dublin zoo." In practice not all cases are as simple as this example suggests. Consideration of a counterexample does not always lead to rejection of a purported law. Some generalizations are so well entrenched that, whenever an exception is allegedly observed, the observation is cast in doubt sooner than the generalization. It is just in such a case that we are tempted to speak of the generalization as a *law* in the full-fledged sense rather than as a *hypothesis*. But we should remember that, according to the standard view, no matter how well supported a generalization may be, it qualifies as an empirical law *only if it could be falsified* by hitherto unobserved cases.

A second mark of genuine laws is that they figure in explanations in a manner that accidental generalizations do not. The generalization that everybody coming into the room is under 6 feet tall does not help us explain why a given person, for example, is under 6 feet. In con-

[12] Within the standard view of science there continues to be debate about the relationship between observational statements and theories (or laws). One position presses for the development of inductive logic and promotes the concept of "degree of confirmation (or verification)." See Carl Hempel, "Studies in the Logic of Confirmation," in his *Aspects of Scientific Explanation and Other Essays*, pp. 3–51. A second position, identified with the work of Karl Popper, is sceptical about the development of inductive logic and holds that vulnerability to falsification by observation is the crucial factor. See Karl Popper, *The Logic of Scientific Discovery*, Harper and Row, New York, 1968, pp. 251–281; Karl Popper, *Objective Knowledge*, Oxford University Press, Fairlawn, N.J., 1972, pp. 1–33; Imre Lakatos, "Falsification and the Methodology of Scientific Research Programmes," in *Criticism and the Growth of Knowledge*, eds. Imre Lakatos and Alan Musgrave, Cambridge University Press, New York, 1970, pp. 91–195; and Karl Popper, *The Philosophy of Karl Popper*, ed. Paul Schilpp, Open Court, La Salle, Ill., 1974, especially pp. 1013–1080.

trast, we are on our way to an explanation of why a radiator burst by pointing out that it contained relatively pure water (no antifreeze), that the temperature went below 32° Fahrenheit, and that there is a law to the effect that all samples of pure water expand when they are subjected to a temperature below 32° Fahrenheit.

Explanation is relevant to lawlikeness in another way. Part of what renders a generalization a candidate for the status of empirical law depends on whether the concepts it employs and the connections it recognizes have theoretical underpinnings or explanation. Even if astrology, for example, were to produce strong correlations between certain personality characteristics and the position of heavenly bodies, we would be unwilling to honor such generalizations as "scientific law" until we had some suggestion that the relative position of certain heavenly bodies and individual birth dates and times were connected to each other in other ways. It would be better still to have at least the outlines of a theory to explain the connection between changes in the heavens and alterations in human mental states. In practice, full-fledged explanatory theories often are constructed after some empirical generalizations or putative laws have been presented. Since it is often difficult to determine what theoretical concepts and connections are relevant antecedents to the development of a theory, it is often difficult to distinguish relevant from irrelevant correlations, lawlike from accidental generalizations.

Third, lawlike statements provide a ground for prediction. This follows directly from the fact that lawlike generalizations support statements that are subjunctive; they are statements of the form, "If such-and-such conditions *were* to obtain, then such-and-such *would happen*." We are prepared to say of an arbitrary sample of pure water that if it *were* at a temperature of 32° Fahrenheit or below and at one atmospheric pressure, it *would* freeze. We would not be prepared to say of some arbitrary person that if he *were* to come into the room mentioned above, he *would* be under 6 feet tall. Accordingly, a law warrants predicting what will happen if certain conditions obtain in the future, and it permits us to retrodict what did happen, if certain conditions obtained in the past.

Although they offer general guidelines, these three marks of lawlike generalizations do not provide definitive criteria that specify the conditions under which we are justified in treating a generalization as lawlike. Some philosophers maintain that we are *never fully justified* in generalizing from experience.[13] Proponents of the standard view agree with these philosophers insofar as they recognize that not every inductive generalization is a candidate for a law. Science is not merely

[13] David Hume, *An Inquiry Concerning Human Understanding*, Library of Liberal Arts, New York, 1955, sec. VII; see also Nelson Goodman, op. cit., especially chap. III

a matter of collecting as much data as possible, observing correlations, generalizing on observations, and testing generalizations. Not all data are relevant; not all generalizations are lawlike.[14] Nevertheless, according to the standard view, certain generalizations can attain the status of law.

THEORIES

The two previous sections discussed observational statements, which provide evidential foundations for science, and observational laws, which are generalizations closely tied to observation. Scientific theories are a third important product of scientific inquiry. Theories are constructed to provide "deeper understanding" of observed regularities or potential laws. As Carl Hempel suggests:

> Theories . . . are the key to the scientific understanding of empirical phenomena; to claim that a given kind of phenomenon is scientifically understood is tantamount to saying that science can offer a satisfactory theoretical account of it.[15]

A scientific theory may be characterized as "a systematically related set of statements, including some lawlike generalizations, that is empirically testable." [16] The standard view characteristically treats theories as having a twofold relationship to observation. First, theories explain the regularities recorded by observational laws, which in turn explain individual occurrences described by observation statements. Second, theories are in part justified (or falsified) by showing that the regularities and individual occurrences they predict do (or do not) occur. Nevertheless, since the statements of a theory usually are connected only indirectly with observable results, the acceptability of the theory cannot be judged solely in terms of its connection with observation.

Figure 2-1 contains a simplified schematic of these relationships.[17]

---

[14] See Carl Hempel, *Philosophy of Natural Science,* pp. 11–15.

[15] Carl Hempel, "On the 'Standard Conception' of Scientific Theories," p. 142.

[16] Richard Rudner, *Philosophy of Social Science,* p. 5; see also Lawrence Mayer, *Comparative Political Inquiry,* The Dorsey Press, Homewood, Ill., 1972.

[17] The diagram is simplified in two important ways. First, it treats the theoretical statements as discrete elements without indicating that many of the statements in a theory are typically interrelated rather than independent. Second, it abstracts from the actual testing situation in which auxiliary theories may be employed to justify the testing instrument, that is, the observational statements themselves. We discuss these questions further in Chapter 4. See also Hubert M. Blalock, Jr., "The Measurement Problem: A Gap Between the Languages of Theory and Research" in *Methodology in Social Research,* eds. Hubert M. Blalock, Jr., and Ann B. Blalock, McGraw-Hill Book Company, New York, 1968, especially pp. 23–27.

THEORETICAL
STATEMENTS

OBSERVATIONAL
(EXPERIMENTAL)
LAWS

OBSERVATIONAL
STATEMENTS

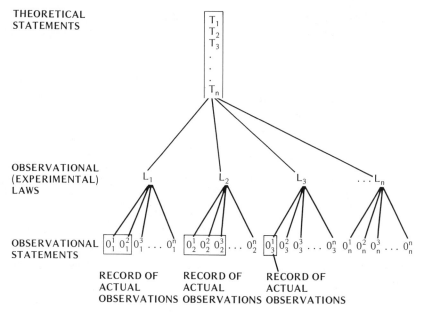

Figure 2–1

In this figure, a theory is supposed to consist of a number of statements containing theoretical terms $T_1, T_2, T_3 \ldots T_n$, some of which are theoretical laws while others of which may be definitions. From the theory we can derive observational (experimental) laws $L_1, L_2, L_3 \ldots L_n$. Each of these observational laws will have observational statements associated with them as instances: $O_1^1, O_1^2, O_1^3 \ldots O_1^n$ with L_1; O_2^1, $O_2^2, O_2^3 \ldots O_2^n$ with $L_2, \ldots$ etc. Only some of these observational statements, however, record actual observations; the others refer to cases in which observation could, but has not, occurred—for example, because no one has taken the trouble to observe, or because the statement refers to some future (predicted) state of affairs.

We shall discuss the relation of explanation and of support or falsification in subsequent sections of this chapter. Here we are concerned with elaborating some features of theories. As an illustration of the relationship mentioned above, consider the following formulation of Durkheim's theory of suicide:[18]

---

[18] Adapted from the discussion in Robert Merton, *Social Theory and Social Structure*, 3d ed., The Free Press, New York, 1968, pp. 150–155, in conjunction with Emile Durkheim, *Suicide: A Study in Sociology*, The Free Press, New York, 1951, pp. 154, 197, and passim. See also Walter Wallace, *The Logic of Science in Sociology*, Aldine-Atherton, New York, 1971, pp. 25–29, for further discussion of Durkheim and theory formation.

Theoretical *statements*	T_1	Social cohesion provides psychic support to group members subjected to acute stresses and anxieties.
	T_2	Suicide rates are functions of *unrelieved* anxieties and stresses to which persons are subjected.
Observational "laws" *or regularities*	L_1	Catholics have lower (recorded) suicide rates than Protestants.
	L_2	Married persons living with spouses have a lower (recorded) suicide rate than single persons living alone.
Observational *statements*	O_1^1	The recorded suicides for Catholics in Austria for 1852–1859 were 51.3 per million persons, and for Protestants 79.5 per million persons.
	O_1^2	The recorded suicides for Catholics in Prussia for 1849–1855 were 49.6 per million persons, and for Protestants 159.9 per million persons.
	O_2^1	The recorded suicides for unmarried men are 975 per million persons.
	O_2^2	The recorded suicides for married men with children are 336 per million persons.

Several important features of theories emerge from this example.

1   The terms or concepts that appear in the theory (social cohesion, suicide rate, anxiety, stress, psychic support, etc.) are *more abstract* (farther *removed from direct observational test*) than those employed either in the statement of observed regularity or in the individual observational statements (married person, recorded suicide, Catholic, Protestant).

While there may be no firm line between purely observational and purely theoretical terms, there is a clear sense in which determination of "religious affiliation" or "death by suicide" is more readily observed and recorded as data than "social cohesion" or "anxiety."

2   A theory has a *broader scope* than the individual regularities used to support it and which it explains.

The theory at hand, for example, when supplemented by the less abstract statement that Catholics have greater social cohesion than

Protestants, helps explain why Catholics have lower suicide rates than Protestants. It explains, as well, why single people tend to have a suicide rate higher than married people and why members of tightly knit families have rates lower than social outcasts. In this way, a theory brings together relatively diverse phenomena and goes beyond the observed regularities that first prompted its formulation to suggest new regularities.[19] This broadness of scope provides grounds for prediction—for example, the prediction that if the social cohesion of Catholics decreases then differential suicide rates between Catholics and Protestants would decrease.

One important reason why theories can be fruitful in this way is that their theoretical terms, such as "social cohesion," are in principle susceptible to a number of different tests or measures. They have an "open texture"; they admit the possibility of finding new applications as a result of further research.

3   A theory consists of systematically related statements from which it is possible to derive empirical, testable consequences.

Proponents of the standard view suggest that in the ideal case a scientific theory is "systematic" because it forms a deductive system. It consists of certain axioms or postulates and theorems, such that the theorems follow deductively (that is, according to the canons of deductive logic) from their axioms or postulates. The first statements in the example from a theory of suicide provide an informal correlate to the interpreted axioms or postulates in a fully formalized theory; whereas the observational laws correspond to theorems derivable from these axioms.

In practice theories are often only partially formalized. Certain presuppositions are taken for granted, and certain deductive steps are not fully spelled out. Often, full formalization is neither fruitful nor feasible. Nevertheless, the standard view holds that a body of statements must *resemble* a deductive system; that is, some observational laws must follow from the basic statements in order to deserve the title "scientific theory."

The deductive relation is important in several respects. In a deductively valid argument, if the premises are true, then the conclusion must be true. Thus, if the observational law that Catholics have a lower suicide rate than Protestants follows deductively from Durkheim's theory of suicide, we know that, if the statements of the theory are all true, the law must be true. Similarly, if the conclusion is false, one premise must be false. Thus, if we found that Catholics actually evidenced higher suicide rates than Protestants, this would imply that at least one theoretical premise was false.

For a set of statements to function usefully in a deductive system,

[19] See Merton, *Social Theory and Social Structure*, p. 151.

it must fulfill at least two requirements. First, the relationships among the terms they contain must be spelled out precisely and explicitly; second, they must be self-consistent. Failure in the first requirement results in a theory that has limited and uninteresting consequences (limited explanatory power). Failure in satisfying the second requisite produces a theory from which we can deduce any proposition whatever. We can satisfy the first requirement by formalizing a theory, that is, by rendering explicit the presuppositions, assumptions, and definitions needed to make it deductively fruitful. In doing so, it is often possible to see whether the second requirement—self-consistency—is satisfied. Robert Dahl, for example, in *A Preface to Democratic Theory*, has displayed some previously unnoticed inconsistencies in (informal) democratic theory by attempting to formalize it.[20]

EXPLANATION

Ideal case   As we mentioned previously, the standard view holds that the basic reason for advancing scientific laws and theories is to provide explanations (and predictions) of observable phenomena. For this reason, an account of scientific explanation is at the core of the standard view. One widely accepted presentation of the ideal or standard for scientific explanation has been offered by Carl Hempel, P. Oppenheim, and Karl Popper. It is known variously as the deductive-nomological, hypothetico-deductive, or covering law model of explanation.[21]

According to this model, scientific explanations are answers to certain kinds of "why" questions: questions about why a particular event occurred, or why a certain kind of regularity obtains. The model is not advanced to answer all "why" questions, for example, "Why should we obey the law?" or "Why are vixens female foxes?" [22] In the case of an ideal and complete scientific explanation, we explain an event, a state of affairs, or a regularity by deducing a statement describing it from a set of premises that contains a description of specific conditions and generalizations where at least one of the generalizations is an empirical law, i.e., either an observational or

[20] Robert Dahl, *A Preface to Democratic Theory*, University of Chicago Press, Chicago, 1956.
[21] Carl Hempel and Paul Oppenheim, "Studies in the Logic of Explanation," in Carl Hempel, *Aspects of Scientific Explanation and Other Essays*; Karl Popper, *The Logic of Scientific Discovery*, pp. 59ff; Karl Popper, *The Poverty of Historicism*, Harper Torchbook, New York, 1964, pp. 120ff.
[22] These questions presumably would be answered, respectively, by appeal to a normative (or ethical) inquiry and an inquiry into the meaning of words. For further discussion of kinds of "why" questions, see R. M. MacIver, *Social Causation*, Harper Torchboook, New York, 1964, p. 24 and passim.

theoretical law, essential to the deduction. A genuine scientific explanation exhibits the following form:

Laws	L_1 & $L_2 \ldots L_n$
Conditions	C_1 & $C_2 \ldots C_n$
Hence	Event or regularity

Suppose, to illustrate, that someone asks why his engine block cracked during the night. If we wish to spell out all painful details, we might offer an explanation along the following lines:

Laws	L_1	(Pure) water turns to ice and expands when it is subject to temperatures substantially below 32° Fahrenheit for a substantial amount of time.
	L_2	The pressure exerted by expanding ice exceeds the ultimate tensile strength of cast iron.
	L_3	Whenever the ultimate tensile strength of a material is exceeded, it cracks (or breaks).
Conditions	C_1	His water-cooled engine was filled with pure water.
	C_2	The temperature in his engine dropped substantially below 32° F for a substantial time.
	C_3	His engine block is made of cast iron.
Hence	E	His engine block cracked.

This model also provides a characterization for certain kinds of *prediction*. If we know that the requisite conditions for an event will occur or already have occurred, then we are in a position to argue that the kind of event to which they are linked by laws will also occur. Unfortunately, we often are unable to predict whether these particular conditions will occur, even though we can explain an event after it happens. To illustrate, it is almost impossible to predict an automobile accident before it happens, even though we often can explain why it happened afterwards. Conversely, we sometimes can predict events without being able to fully explain why they occur—for example, that salmon will return to rivers to spawn.[23]

[23] The relationship between explanation and prediction is a matter of debate among philosophers of science. As the examples indicate, we may have low-level, isolated observational laws that enable us to predict, even if we do not have an adequate explanatory theory. Prediction has greater *practical* significance than our account might suggest, particularly for social science. This springs in part from the close connection between the ability to predict and the ability to influence or control events. For a useful discussion of these issues, see Robert Dubin, *Theory Building*, The Free Press, New York, 1969, pp. 9–25; and Stephen Toulmin, *Foresight and Understanding*, Indiana University Press, Bloomington, 1961.

The above model idealizes explanation. It is not claimed that explanations are actually delivered in a way that formally satisfies the model's requirements. It is suggested, however, that appeal to this model of explanation is necessary in order to characterize explanations. We cannot pick out an incomplete explanation unless we know what a complete or fully drawn-out explanation would be like.

Incomplete explanations Explanations can be incomplete in several ways. First, in many everyday cases we do not explicitly mention a generalization or spell out all conditions, although it is plausible to assume that relevant laws and particular sets can be produced readily. Thus, explanations frequently lurk in the background.

A second kind of incompleteness results in partial explanation. We may attempt to explain why Alice compliments Algernon more now than before, by appeal to the fact that they are seeing more of each other and George Homan's "law" that if the frequency of interaction among persons increases, the degree of their liking of one another will increase and vice versa. Such an appeal does not fully explain why Alice expresses greater affection for Algernon in the way that she does. According to the deductive-nomological model of explanation, such an account must hold the promise that appropriate laws will be discovered to explain the specific form of behavior manifested in this relationship.

Finally, and perhaps most commonly, what is ordinarily offered as an explanation is only an explanation sketch; it provides only "the general outlines of what *might* well be developed by gradual elaboration and supplementation into a more closely reasoned explanatory argument, based on hypotheses which are stated more fully." [24]

Causal explanations Of particular interest are explanations that offer causes. A causal explanation contains a description of the cause of the event or phenomenon to be explained among the statement of conditions, and causal generalization connecting the cause with the effect among the laws. In a causal law the antecedent cause is often referred to as the *"independent variable,"* while the effect is called the *"dependent variable."* As the names suggest, a causal law asserts that the effect depends on the cause, but that the cause is independent of the effect.

Ernest Nagel offers the following characterization of causal laws:[25]

1 The relationship is asymmetrical;

[24] Hempel, *Aspects of Scientific Explanation and Other Essays*, p. 424.
[25] Ernest Nagel, *The Structure of Science*, pp. 73ff.

2   The cause constitutes a necessary and sufficient condition for the occurrence of the effect;

3   The relation holds between spatially contiguous phenomena;

4   The cause and effect are continuous in time; and

5   The relationship between independent and dependent variables is uniform or invariant—"same cause, same effect."

Nagel's account is controversial in a number of ways. First, a practical obstacle to the development of causal laws exists because it is often difficult to determine which variable is independent and which is dependent. Even if it is established that the relationship between a two-party system and a stable democracy is invariable or uniform, it is not yet determined which is the cause and which is the effect.

Second, Nagel's requirements are so strong that they rule out virtually all causal generalizations actually offered in social science. Nagel's model can still be regarded as the ideal; but it is useful to consider a modified characterization of causal laws such as that offered by Hans Zetterberg, since it provides categorizations which are more relevant to social science.[26]

1   A relation may be *reversible* (if X, then Y; and if Y, then X) or *irreversible* (if X, then Y; but if Y, then no conclusion about X).

As Zetterberg points out, reversible propositions are not uncommon in social science, as in the example of Homan's law about the effect of frequency of interaction upon liking. Furthermore, our acceptance of Zetterberg's distinction does not force us to deny Nagel's claim about asymmetry of the relation. In any particular case, either an instance of X caused an instance of Y or an instance of Y caused an instance of X, *but not both*. Particular relationships may be asymmetrical, although the law expressing the relationship may be reversible.

2   A relation may be *sufficient* (if X, then Y, regardless of anything else) or *contingent* (if X, then Y, but only if Z).

Sufficient relations are rare in social science and in ordinary discussions of causation. We may say that a spark caused an explosion, but it would not do so without the presence of explosive material, oxygen, etc. Similarly, although we know that American blacks tend to vote Democratic, the relation is not sufficient because of the influence of other intervening factors (such as a particular candidate) upon which the relation is contingent.

3   A causal relation may be *necessary* (if X, and only X, then Y) or *substitutable* (if X, then Y; but if Z, then also Y).

[26] Hans L. Zetterberg, *On Theory and Verification in Sociology*, Bedminister Press, Totowa, N.J., 1965, pp. 69–79.

Relations in social science are commonly substitutable. This is evident, as Zetterberg points out, in the common phrase "functional equivalence." Two-party competition might be regarded as a condition for electoral choice, but factional competition within one party may be a substitutable condition.

4   A causal relation may be *sequential* (if X, then later Y) or *co-extensive* (if X, then also Y).

The notions of spatial continuity and temporal continuousness offered by Nagel are difficult to make precise. Lazardsfeld's proposition that voters subject to contradictory voting pressures are likely to delay voting is an example of a sequential relation. A coextensive relation, by contrast, makes no reference to the time dimension. A co-extensive relation is illustrated by the proposition, "The higher the rate of social mobility, the less the extent to which the lower classes accept militant class ideology." As Zetterberg points out, no assumption is made about whether mobility occurred before or after militant class ideology.

5   A causal relation may be *deterministic* (if X, then always Y) or *stochastic* (if X, then probably Y).

Although deterministic causal relations are not uncommon in natural science, they are rare in social science.

The importance of Zetterberg's distinctions is obvious in light of the common confusions arising from mistaking one type of relation for another. Zetterberg's discussion of the continuing debate over Max Weber's thesis about a relation between the Protestant ethic and the rise of capitalism demonstrates how confusion can arise from mistakenly construing one type of causal relation for another.

EVALUATION OF SCIENTIFIC CONCLUSIONS

How are scientific conclusions evaluated? In the most straightforward case we can determine that a purported observational law is falsified by finding a counterinstance. Thus the discovery of a black swan falsifies the claim that all swans are white. As indicated above, the failure to find a falsifying instance does not in itself give reason to maintain a purported law; we also need supportive evidence. This procedure, however, does not always uniquely support a single generalization. It always remains possible that the scientist is faced with two hypotheses, both of which are confirmed by the observational evidence accumulated; neither is falsified, but they appear to differ with respect to unexamined cases. Sometimes disputes can be resolved by performing so-called "crucial experiments" to test hitherto unexamined cases. But the notion of a crucial experiment makes sense only when competing hypotheses are put forward in a context where there is substantial agreement about background theory. In cases where there is no such agreement, a given generalization can be maintained in the face of apparently conflicting evidence by making adjustments in the background theory—which suggest that the research design is faulty or that other factors influence results. Furthermore, since lawlike generalizations apply to future as well as past cases, evidence can never exhaustively confirm hypothesis even when no competing generalizations are being considered. As suggested above, one way to justify a generalization that projects from past to future cases is to provide a well confirmed or tested theory that explains the correlations observed.

In this way we move from questions about unfalsified generalizations to questions about the evaluation of scientific theories for which supporting evidence and no falsifying evidence has been found. How then are such scientific theories evaluated? The general criteria are (1) *operational capability*, (2) *logical consistency*, (3) *scope*, and (4) *simplicity*.

Failure to meet the requirement of operationalization means that a theory cannot be tested and results in its being, in an important sense, not empirical. If a theory is not logically consistent, then it is impossible for all the statements it contains to be true, which is grounds for rejecting it. The two remaining considerations—scope and simplicity—loom large in evaluating competing theories that fulfill the other requirements.

Given two theories, both of which explain data, that theory which applies to a wider range of phenomena, which has the larger scope, is preferred. One appeal of Newtonian theory is that it not only applies to the movement of celestial bodies but also explains the laws which govern pendulums and projectiles. Because it applies to these additional cases, it is supported by a wider variety of evidence than an alternative theory more limited in scope. In general, the greater the scope of a theory, the greater its explanatory and predictive powers.

The simpler of two theories should also be preferred. Although the criterion of simplicity is difficult to render precisely, it suggests that we should prefer a theory that includes fewer ad hoc hypotheses (those having little, if any, confirming evidence) and fewer qualifications. A theory that is simpler in these respects is more amenable to falsification because there are fewer ways to explain away apparently disconfirming instances.[27]

None of these considerations provide an error-free method for evaluating attempts at scientific justification. We are forced to recognize that, at best, the claims of scientists are only "probably" true or false. Unfortunately the tentative or hypothetical nature of scientific

[27] Karl Popper, *The Logic of Scientific Discovery*, especially pp. 78–92, 136ff.

conclusions has created doubts about whether there is genuine scientific *knowledge*. If we maintain that the standards of deductive proof from "self-evident" premises provide the only standard of genuine knowledge, the results of scientific enterprise fall short; but so do the results of ordinary observation, since it is not logically impossible or self-contradictory to assert that at any given moment we are suffering from some coherent hallucination. In neither case does the mere possibility that we might have to revise our judgments provide a reason for denying that, at least on occasion, we are justified in claiming to have knowledge.

> If someone asks for evidence for the prediction about the sunrise, we can readily produce it from our records. But if he then asks what makes us think this is evidence, i.e., how any evidence from the past can support predictions about the future still ahead, we can only reply that evidence is simply that material from the past which until now has turned out to be a reliable indicator of the future. And if doubts are raised as to the propriety of so using the term "evidence" (or "grounds," etc.), we can only say, "It does the job: it does connect the key elements in the concept of grounds and evidence; it does identify indicators that lead from truths to further truths: such a use had led to true predictions, does not contradict other uses, and so on." . . .what we are calling evidence is living up to its billing.[28]

Criticisms of the standard view

The standard view has been attacked on a number of points: some criticism concerns matters of detail; other raises more substantial objections. Two grounds of criticism are particularly important: (1) the observational-theoretical distinction and (2) the account given of explanation.

The standard view as described embodies a "two-tier"[29] view of the language of science. On the ground level we have the language of observational statements and their generalization into observational or experimental laws; on the second level we have theoretical laws and other theoretical statements. There is no firm line between observational and theoretical terms and, hence, no final division between the statements that contain them. What counts as a theoretical statement for one area of inquiry may be taken as an observational statement for another.

The relativity of the observational-theoretical distinction, when

---

[28] Michael Scriven, *Primary Philosophy*, McGraw-Hill Book Company, New York, 1966, p. 30.
[29] Israel Scheffler, *Science and Subjectivity*, p. 46ff.

taken seriously, appears to conflict with the position implicit in the standard view that a body of clearly identifiable observational evidence statements serve as the ultimate ground and justification of scientific theories. The implications of this relativity are made manifest in an alternative view which holds that all terms and all statements employed in science are "theory laden." This "one-tier" view of scientific language obliterates the distinction between ultimate evidential statements and the theories they are purported to justify. If the evidence or data we collect is in part dependent on the antecedent theories we have, then two scientists who differ in the theories they hold will not be faced with the same data.

Two scientists, for example, both gathering data about "free elections" may disagree in their generalizations because they do not include the same data in their accompanying body of evidence. It is not at all obvious that two scientists would necessarily be able to resolve such a dispute. This problem is common to both natural and social science. Norwood Russell Hanson has suggested, for example, that when Tycho Brahe (who believed the sun went around the earth) and Kepler (who believed the opposite) saw a sunrise, they observed something different.[30] One observed that the sun was literally rising, the other that the plot of earth he occupied was rotating toward the sun. Must there be some common ground of observation, some neutral way of describing what we observe? Psychological research suggests that, at least in some cases, for example, optical illusions, people may differ radically in what they can and cannot observe. But even if there is some common stock of observational concepts, say, colors, direction of dial indicators, etc., upon which all but a few could agree, it is not obvious that this stock of concepts is rich enough to generate the bodies of data necessary to support interesting scientific conclusions. We need only think of the kinds of presuppositions that go into our accepting the simplest of measurements.

Obviously, there is widespread agreement about the data in many areas of science, though perhaps more so in physical than in social science. Nevertheless, this agreement in itself does not bequeath special status on the concepts employed in recording this data; after all, groups of people have unanimously agreed about what they have seen, and they have been wrong.

The *one-tier view* of scientific language has been supported most influentially by Thomas Kuhn in his book *The Structure of Scientific Revolutions*.[31] According to Kuhn scientific activity can be divided into

---

[30] N. R. Hanson, *Pattern of Discovery*, p. 25 and passim.
[31] In addition to Thomas S. Kuhn, *The Structure of Scientific Revolutions*, 2d ed., University of Chicago Press, Chicago, 1970, prominent advocates of the position are N. R. Hanson, *Patterns of Discovery*, and Paul Feyerabend, "Against Method: An Outline of an Anarchistic Theory of Knowledge," *Minnesota Studies in the Philosophy of Science*, vol. IV.

two kinds: "normal science" and "revolutionary science." During a period of normal science in a given scientific discipline, research is guided by a paradigm, in terms of which problems are stated and results are evaluated. The paradigm effectively determines which observations are significant, and it provides the vocabulary to describe them. The main task of normal science is puzzle-solving. What counts as a genuine puzzle and what counts as its solution are determined by the particular community of scientific specialists in a given discipline. Such a community of scientists is defined by their adherence to what Kuhn broadly calls a "scientific paradigm," or, alternatively, a "disciplinary matrix." It consists of shared symbolic generalizations, shared metaphysical or heuristic models, and shared values.[32] It also consists of paradigms more narrowly construed as shared *exemplars*; these include the kind of concrete problem solutions taught to beginning students of the discipline.[33]

Kuhn argues that it is only through mastery of the methods and standards of problem solution embodied in the paradigm or disciplinary matrix that students gain entry into the scientific community, and it is only by continued adherence to the paradigm that they remain members in good standing within the community.

This characterization, however, applies only to a period of normal science. Before an area of inquiry develops into a full-fledged science, it is characterized by a number of conflicting schools, each of which attempts to develop a paradigm. In this preparadigmatic period each scientist attempts to develop the field anew. More importantly, even in a mature science, there exist periods of extraordinary or revolutionary science in which the dominant paradigm itself is called into question. It is not merely that there is a conflict among competing theories offered as solutions to the same scientific puzzle; such disputes may occur during a period of normal science. Rather, there is a wider crisis that affects not only specific theories but the whole method of characterizing problems and their solutions. Thus, Copernican astronomical theory, Einsteinian mechanics, Bohr's theory of the atom, and Lavoisier's discovery of oxygen marked scientific revolutions.[34] They brought a new range of scientific puzzles to solve and a new method of solution.

[32] Important sources of Thomas Kuhn's views are *The Structure of Scientific Revolutions*, especially "Postscript: 1969"; his essay "Logic of Discovery or Psychology of Research" in *Criticism and Growth of Knowledge*, eds. I. Lakatos and Alan Musgrave, Cambridge University Press, New York, 1970. Kuhn has augmented his discussion in "Second Thoughts on Paradigms" in *The Structure of Scientific Theories*, ed. Frederick Suppe, op. cit., 459–482.
[33] Kuhn, *The Structure of Scientific Revolutions*, p. 250; Lakatos and Musgrave, *Criticism and the Growth of Knowledge*, p. 272.
[34] Kuhn, in Lakatos and Musgrave, *Criticism and the Growth of Knowledge*, p. 251.

The crisis that provokes scientific revolutions does not result merely from the discovery of observations incompatible with a previously held theory. Kuhn maintains that during any period of normal science anomalous data exist which cannot be readily assimilated into existing theories either because they are apparently incompatible or because these theories do not cover them at all.[35] But these anomalies may not be treated as counterinstances to the theories in question; rather, they may be treated as further puzzles for normal science to solve. The moral, according to Kuhn, is that

> no process yet disclosed by the historical study of scientific development at all resembles the methodological stereotype of falsification by direct comparison with nature. . . . The act of judgment that leads scientists to reject previously accepted theory is always based upon more than a comparison of that theory with the world. The decision to reject one paradigm is always simultaneously the decision to accept another, and the judgment leading to that decision involves comparison of both paradigms with nature *and* with each other.[36]

A crisis exists when there is growing recognition of the inadequacy of existing paradigms among members of a given scientific community. The conditions producing scientific revolutions are similar to those producing political revolution: in both cases a certain segment of the community detects fundamental inadequacies in existing practices.[37] And in both cases crisis produces a growing polarization of the community and disputes that cannot be resolved within the context of existing practices.

In the case of a crisis in science, there exists an incommensurability of paradigms in a given field. Since it lacks a neutral standard for uncontroversially adjudicating between them, the shift of paradigms has more in common with a "Gestalt switch" or with a conversion than with the ordered process of confirmation and falsification suggested by the standard view.

> Though some scientists, particularly the older and more experienced ones, may resist indefinitely, most of them can be reached in one way or another. Conversions will occur a few at a time until, after the last hold-outs have died, the whole profession will again be practicing under a single, but now a different, paradigm.[38]

Critics of Kuhn, often proponents of the main outlines of the standard view, have pointed out the difficulties produced by extreme

[35] Kuhn, *The Structure of Scientific Revolutions*, p. 139.
[36] Ibid., p. 139.
[37] Ibid., p. 54.
[38] Ibid., p. 214.

interpretations of his position. If the meaning of terms in two different theories or paradigms are completely independent (incommensurable) and the description of data depends on these theories, then

1   Theories cannot contradict each other;

2   The data explained by different theories will be different and hence no two theories can be alternatives to each other;

3   The statements of theories will become analytic truths, true by virtue of their meaning which cannot be falsified by any data; and

4   The vocabulary of each new theory would have to be learned without appeal to concepts that a learner antecedently possessed.[39]

Kuhn himself sometimes appears to take a more moderate position. He denies, for example, that theory choice is irrational or mystical and merely relative to a scientist's preference.[40] He is not a relativist in the sense that he holds that "one scientific theory is as good as another for doing what scientists normally do."[41] Theory choice is governed by considerations of accuracy, scope, simplicity, and fruitfulness. But though these factors provide reasons for preferring one theory to another, they do not provide criteria for theory acceptance that determine in all cases which of two competing theories it is more rational to accept.

Furthermore, even though what we observe is in part conditioned by education, language, past experience, and culture, it is also true that a wide range of agreement is possible. Similarly, although words change their meanings (including words by which we describe what we observe) in the transition from one paradigm to another, there remains the possibility of partial translation. There is a sense in which proponents of Newtonian mechanics can understand at least part of what relativists are asserting. But it does not follow from this that a perfect translation is possible. In a sense understanding a new paradigm is like learning a new language that is only partially translatable into one's first language; what counts as correct use of the languages depends on the standards of the two different language communities. Thus, the decision to speak a second language is like the decision to adopt a new paradigm in that neither are bound by clear-cut rules.

[39] David Braybrooke and Alexander Rosenberg, "Comment: Getting the War News Straight: The Actual Situation in the Philosophy of Science," *American Political Science Review*, LXVI (September 1972), 823. See also Dudley Shapere, "Meaning and Scientific Change," in *Mind and Cosmos*, ed. Robert G. Colodny, University of Pittsburgh Press, Pittsburgh, 1966, pp. 41–85.

[40] Kuhn in Lakatos and Musgrave, pp. 259ff.

[41] Ibid., p. 265.

Construed in this way, it is not clear that Kuhn's position is at odds with the main outlines of the standard view. He is primarily concerned with the context of discovery rather than the context of justification. With respect to periods of normal science, at least, it remains open to proponents of the standard view to accept much of what he says without giving up the view that science is constructed upon an evidential base, and that it seeks lawlike generalizations which explain it and are in turn confirmed by it.

The second criticism of the standard view approaches it from a different direction by focusing on the deductive-nomological model of explanation. Michael Scriven, for example, offers an alternative analysis:

> What is a scientific explanation? It is topically unified communication, the content of which imparts understanding of some scientific phenomenon. And the better it is, the more efficiently and reliably it does this, i.e. with less redundancy and a higher *over-all* probability. What is understanding? Understanding is, roughly, organized knowledge, i.e. knowledge of the relations between various facts and/or laws. These relations are of many kinds—deductive, inductive, analogical, etc. (Understanding is deeper, more thorough, the greater the span of this rational knowledge).[42]

This characterization of explanation obviously relaxes the requirements of scientific explanation. The ground for such a relaxation is the purported failure of the standard view to account for the actual practice of accepting explanations. The divergencies are seen as manifold. First, not all cases satisfying the model actually satisfy those seeking an explanation. The appeal to the "law"—"All men are mortal" and the condition that "Socrates was a man," does little to bring an understanding of why Socrates died. Second, explanations are accepted even though they do not satisfy the deductive-nomological model. Scientists are willing to accept accounts that cite an antecedent cause or string of causes for a given event, even when they are ignorant of the requisite causal law or some of the attendant conditions. For example, we can explain that Socrates' death was the result of his taking hemlock, even though we do not know all the conditions under which it produced his death. Furthermore, in disciplines such as history, explanations are offered and similarly accepted without meeting the requirements of the deductive-nomological model. The kind of "explaining what happened," for instance, places

[42] Michael Scriven, "Explanation, Predictions and Law" in *Minnesota Studies in the Philosophy of Science*, vol. III, eds. Herbert Feigl and Grover Maxwell, University of Minnesota Press, Minneapolis, 1960.

the events to be explained in larger classificatory schema. But though such concepts apply to recurrent social phenomena, they do not record any lawlike regularities.

The response of proponents of the standard view has been to remind its critics that the deductive-nomological model is an idealization that provides the logic of explanation and serves as a rationale for the practice of actual scientists. They maintain that the question of what produces understanding for a given individual or group is a psychological question. Some people will accept bad explanations; others will reject good explanations. What is important, they insist, is the *pattern* of explanation scientists should accept or strive to attain.

A more important claim for proponents of the standard view is that we cannot understand the behavior of scientists unless we assume that they are implicitly seeking explanations which measure up to this model. In the case of "causal narratives," scientists assume that not all antecedent events are equal candidates for being treated as the cause for an event under consideration.[43] But how, they ask, can we understand this move without assuming the existence of causal laws, linking the genuine cause with the event in a manner not applicable to other antecedent events? Similarly, not all concepts are treated as equally useful in describing historical events. This is often precisely because they do not figure into lawlike generalizations that can be used to deduce empirically verifiable consequences.

This should not suggest that the identification and discussion of purported causal connections is interesting or fruitful only when some generalization is being sought. In this respect historians might be likened to prosecuting attorneys or practitioners of forensic medicine. They seek to discuss specific causal connections and need appeal only to "common-sense" generalizations, if at all. In this they stand in marked contrast to somebody engaged in medical research. But it would be foolhardy to argue that because the standards of justification in the courtroom are rightfully different from those in the laboratory, the standards of explanation used in the laboratory are irrelevant.

A more serious threat to the standard view of explanation results from the fact that both natural and social science contain numerous explanations that appear probabilistic in character rather than strictly deductive. Their premises contain lawlike statements that are not universal in form; that is, they do not state that *all* members of a certain class have a certain property, but rather that *most*, or a certain percentage of, members of a given class have a certain property. For example, we know that the percentage of conceptions experienced by

[43] Alan Ryan, *The Philosophy of the Social Sciences*, Pantheon Books, New York, 1970, pp. 100ff.

women taking birth control pills is quite low, less than 2 percent. Suppose we wish to explain the fact that Mrs. Roe, who is taking birth control pills, has not conceived:

1 The probability of conception for women taking birth control pills is low.
2 Mrs. Roe is taking birth control pills,
_____
Therefore (very probably): Mrs. Roe has not conceived.

The conclusion does not follow deductively from the premises, since it remains logically possible that Mrs. Roe is among the small percentage for whom the pill is ineffective. Nevertheless, we may be willing to accept the explanation as providing an answer to the question, "Why has Mrs. Roe not conceived?"

It is important to note that differences between probabilistic explanations and nonprobabilistic explanations do not reside in the amount of evidence which supports the various generalizations. We may have more evidence to support the claim that there is only a 2 percent conception rate among women taking the pill than for the claim that all cases of paresis of the brain are caused by syphilis, even though the first is probabilistic and the second is universal in form.

There has been substantial disagreement about probabilistic explanations among philosophers (who otherwise accept the central position of the deductive-nomological model) in the explication of the concept of scientific explanation. Three positions may be distinguished:

1 That probabilistic explanations may provide genuine explanations, which though not deductively certain, provide inductive support and hence understanding of why the event described in the conclusion occurred.
2 That probabilistic explanation provides a genuine deductive explanation of why a group has a certain characteristic, but that we cannot explain why a given person has this characteristic.
3 That probabilistic explanations provide only an explanation sketch, which must ultimately be filled out by appeal to laws which are universal in form.[44]

The resolution of this dispute goes beyond the purposes of this chapter, but it is important to note that all three views recognize the importance of probabilistic generalization in science.

[44] Ernest Nagel, *The Structure of Science*, p. 22; May Brodbeck, "Explanation, Prediction and 'Imperfect' Knowledge," in *Readings in the Philosophy of the Social Sciences*, ed. May Brodbeck, The Macmillan Company, New York, 1968, pp. 376–379.

The debate between behavioralists and traditionalists

The discussion of the standard view and the position of its critics presented in the two previous sections suggests that it is possible to set the requirements of a genuine science so narrowly as to rule out all but a few natural sciences or so broadly as to include almost any kind of common-sense speculation. If we count as a science only those areas of inquiry for which we now have *fully formalized theories* providing explanations that are *strictly deductive* in form, our range is too narrow. If we overemphasize the difficulty in obtaining relatively unbiased observational data and underemphasize the importance of lawlike generalizations, it is difficult to exclude a vast array of pre-scientific and philosophical inquiries from our account.

The role of theory is central to the discussion of scientific method in terms of both the standard view and the modifications suggested by its critics; it is on this score that social science has been viewed as most lacking. It has not produced a widely accepted account that can serve as a paradigm for further research. Therefore it has not even produced the grounds for adjudicating the relevance and lawlikeness of empirical generalizations, nor, ultimately, the grounds for explanation of social behavior. Traditionalists have argued that this failure is endemic to political science; that not only has the discipline failed to measure up to the requirements in the past, but there are overriding reasons for holding that it can never satisfy these requirements.

We might construe traditionalists as making the empirical claim that the past history and present condition of political science provides adequate evidence for predicting continued failure to measure up to the requirements of a genuine science. If this is the claim, the traditionalists' position is at best inconclusive. Social scientists have been successful in applying a variety of sophisticated statistical techniques to data, and they have used these techniques to make accurate predictions. Furthermore, empirical theories have been propounded and have gained some measure of support. The traditionalists' denigration of the accomplishments of empirical theorists is plausible only if we expect a "total theory" which does for social science or at least for one of its major divisions what Newton's theory did for physics. It is doubtful, however, whether even contemporary physics has a theory of such global significance. Robert K. Merton has suggested that the proper aim (at least in current conditions) and the proper measure of social science is its success in providing "theories of the middle range."[45] Such theories, he maintains, are more than mere empirical generalizations or summaries of observed uniformities, yet they yield

---

[45] Merton, *Social Theory and Social Structure*, pp. 39–72.

specific, testable assumptions that can be falsified and confirmed by observation. They are midway between isolated observational generalizations and all-embracing, speculative theories. Merton's examples of theories of the middle range include classic accounts, such as Emile Durkheim's theory of suicide and Max Weber's theory of the relationship between Protestantism and capitalism, as well as more recent work in reference-group theory and role-set theory.[46] Given the numerous theories of the middle range, traditionalists' claims about the dearth of theories in social science are hollow.

Even if we were to discount these developments, it remains unclear whether the failure of political science to produce widely accepted and well-established "grand theories" after only thirty years can be used to predict future developments. The history of the development of other sciences suggests that the "gestation" period for a "new" natural science often has been much longer. It is not at all obvious that more manhours have been expended during the last thirty years in political science than were expended in the development of, say, modern chemistry. Think only of the centuries during which human beings engaged in alchemy or primitive metallurgy.

More often traditionalists buttress their claim by appeal to a priori philosophical arguments. In Chapter 1 we mentioned three prongs of the traditionalists' attack in relation to political behavior:

1   That human political behavior involves too many variables, is too complex, to visibly exhibit the regularities necessary for the determination of empirical laws and theories.
2   That the subject matter, human behavior, precludes explanation by empirical laws and theories.
3   That even such laws and theories as might be presented are inevitably biased in such a way as to prevent "scientific objectivity in evaluating them.

Each of these criticisms have been widely challenged. They do not provide the support necessary to establish the strong claim that it is *impossible* for social science to resemble natural science in method. If we adopt a moderate account of the methods of science that avoids the extremes mentioned at the beginning of this section, then the arguments discussed in detail in the remainder of this chapter suggest that traditionalists have not established their case. That is to say, political science properly practiced can be a genuine science. To say this much does not commit us to the view that social science *must* or *will* develop in such a way as to meet the requirements outlined in early sections of this chapter; rather, it maintains that such a goal has not been shown impossible to obtain.

[46] Ibid., p. 68.

THE COMPLEXITY ARGUMENT

The objection that social and political behavior is too complex to be explained in terms of lawlike generalizations resting on adequate empirical theory presents many confusions. Chief among them is a confusion that has been dubbed the *"reproductive fallacy."* [47] This fallacy results from the view that an adequate explanation of a given event must account for that event in *all* its uniqueness. Noting that any event is susceptible of many different descriptions, it is argued that no "complete" description is possible. The notion that our descriptions must somehow capture or reproduce reality is related to the view that language in general is inadequate to capture experience. While it is obviously true that talking about something, that is, describing it, is different from actually perceiving and reacting to it, it does not follow that descriptions are somehow *necessarily* inadequate. Furthermore, social behavior does not differ in this respect from the behavior of inanimate objects; in both cases an adequate explanation of the behavior will be an explanation of the behavior under only one of many possible descriptions.

A second version of this objection points out that the uniqueness governing social behavior is not merely the uniqueness governing all events, but, rather, that the kind of behavior of interest to political scientists is often behavior that does not recur. That is, behavior that interests political scientists as a matter of fact applies to a single instance or at best to a few cases, whereas the descriptions of interest to physicists apply to many more. This, again, is not limited to social science. Geologists and meteorologists are interested in explaining events which are unique in the sense that they can be placed in a special category, for example, the San Francisco earthquake of 1906 or Hurricane Dora. There is a sense in which these sciences have not developed the tools to adequately explain these events. But this in itself does not provide a reason to despair of future success. Nor is this a "failure" of these "young sciences" alone. Physicists can neither predict nor "completely" explain why a given leaf falls to earth exactly where it does. In part this inability may be attributed to lack of knowledge governing which particular conditions the leaf will face or has faced.

More significantly, it may be due to the fact that the kinds of concepts employed by physicists are idealizations that actual physical objects only approximate. Physical laws apply in their purity to "rigid bodies," "objects in a vacuum," "frictionless masses." They can only be made to apply to actual physical objects if we assume that, for the purposes involved, an object is approximately rigid or frictionless or nearly in a vacuum. Even in these cases explanation and prediction

[47] Rudner, *Philosophy of Social Science*, pp. 69–70.

apply to objects and events only when we accept simplifying assumptions that exclude some variables. Similarly, the "rational economic man" is a construct or idealization that involves simplifying assumptions. Although actual economic agents will only approximate this model, it does not follow that we cannot adduce lawlike generalizations which apply to actual economic behavior to the extent that it approximates this ideal.

As Karl Popper points out, one reason for the view that social science deals with phenomena more complex than those investigated by natural scientists is the tendency to compare concrete social or political situations with those found in the laboratory of natural scientists.[48] But the laboratory situation is shaped precisely to limit the effect of certain variables. As mentioned above, when physicists, for example, go outside the laboratory and seek to predict or explain certain concrete physical events, they too are faced with a large number of variables.

Another source of the assertion of complexity, according to Popper, is the belief that social scientists must give an account of social phenomena which somehow includes the mental condition of all participants. This requirement is clearly as unrealistic as demanding that physicists know the behavior of each particular molecule before they can employ concepts like pressure or temperature that relate to collections of large numbers of molecules.

SUBJECT-MATTER DIFFERENCES

The second argument in the armory of traditionalists is the claim that human behavior is *different in kind* from the behavior of inanimate objects because human beings are uniquely conscious of their own behavior. This type of objection has several different forms. In one form, it points out that inanimate objects do not react differently because a theory has been advanced or a prediction made, but human beings can alter their behavior precisely because social scientists have proffered a theory or made a prediction. A more general objection springs from the fact that human beings give meaning to their actions and their institutions, and that no adequate explanation of human political behavior and institutions can be complete unless it takes due account of this factor. Moreover, it is argued that this unique human significance or meaning cannot be understood solely in terms of some theory which abstracts from overt human behavioral responses. Contemporary behavioralism by this accounting misses an entire dimension and the most important dimension of human behavior.

[48] Karl Popper, in *Philosophical Problems of the Social Sciences*, ed. David Braybrooke, The Macmillan Company, New York, 1965, pp. 39–40.

It is undoubtedly true that dissemination of the results of political inquiry may have effects different from the publication of conclusions in natural science. We are at least prepared to consider the claim that publication of preference poll results may affect election outcomes, but nobody expects the publication of tide tables to affect the tides. Nevertheless, this difference between natural and social science is not as great as might be first imagined. For example, the attempt to measure temperature by using a thermometer may affect the temperature of the substance to be measured, however slightly, just as the process of asking for preferences or the practice of publishing the results of preference polls may affect that which they were designed to measure. More importantly, however, the effects of publishing polls are themselves open to empirical study, just as are the effects of using a thermometer. Herbert Simon's work on the bandwagon effect is a good example of how publication of preference polls may be treated as an empirical variable.[49]

A more elaborate defense of the claim that the subject matter of social science enjoins a methodology radically different from that employed in natural science has been offered by Peter Winch in his controversial book, *The Idea of a Social Science*.[50] Winch points out that the description of human behavior as an action, rather than merely as a piece of physical behavior, demands that the actor possess certain concepts in terms of which he views his action. What he does is intimately connected to what he perceives himself to be doing. When we describe a man as voting, we are doing more than saying that he physically moved a lever of certain shape to a certain position on the voting machine. We presuppose that the agent is acting in accordance with the electoral rules and, hence, that he knows at least, implicitly, what these rules are. On a given occasion, he may not realize that he is in fact voting for the wrong party; but even in such a case he possesses the necessary concepts to understand the results of this move. Winch maintains that all meaningful human behavior, and in particular "social behavior," can be adequately described only when it is treated in terms of the rules or concepts which make it the kind of behavior it is. Winch draws two important conclusions from his account of human action. First, human action can only be understood in terms of the concepts the agents actually have. Second, since the ideas and theories of people change and develop, social behavior and social relations are an unsuitable subject for broad generalizations

---

[49] Herbert Simon, "The Effect of Predictions," in *Readings in the Philosophy of the Social Sciences*, ed. May Brodbeck, pp. 447–456.
[50] Peter Winch, *The Idea of a Social Science*, Humanities Press, New York, 1958. For controversy see Alasdair MacIntyre, "The Idea of a Social Science," in *Rationality*, ed. Bryan R. Wilson, Harper & Row, Publishers, New York, 1970, pp. 112ff.

of the type sought by friends of the standard conception of science.[51] As a consequence, social science differs from natural science in two respects. First, criteria for determining evidence are not those of the observer, but those of the observed. Second, the kind of explanation appropriate is not through the subsumption of particular behavior under lawlike generalizations, but rather an understanding of behavior as instances of some social practice or activity. Winch aligns himself with Max Weber against the views put forward by Pareto and Durkheim, who suggested that a vocabulary of recurring observable social features can be developed (at least in principle) suitable for inclusion in scientific generalizations.[52] Social facts, so construed, may describe social behavior in terms radically different from those employed by the actors themselves. Durkheim's concept of anomie as it functions in his discussion of suicide serves as a conspicuous example.

In contrast, Weber and Winch hold that social scientists must attempt to obtain a *Verstehen,* an emphatic or interpretive understanding of human social action.[53] For neither Weber nor Winch is this understanding merely a case of social scientists, attempting to put themselves into the other person's shoes, to "see" the world as the social actor sees it.

Unlike Weber, however, who sees *Verstehen* as a first step in social research to be supplemented by a search for (statistical) generalizations, Winch suggests that social scientists should engage in an inquiry akin to that of philosophers.[54] They should attempt to understand the standards or social rules relevant to the behavior under study that make this behavior intelligible. Thus, for example, we can understand the behavior of a "precinct captain" by seeing it as an attempt to gain a patronage position, and patronage in turn can be understood in terms of the place it has in the precinct captain's political life and battery of political concepts.

Winch no doubt is justified in pointing out the importance of the agent's own account of social and political behavior, and behavioralists can take it into consideration. Normal social and political concepts or categories can provide a focus for investigation, and specific individual explanations can be included as data. And further, behavioralists can take refuge by pointing out that the demand to account for human social behavior in all its uniqueness is another example of the "reproductive fallacy." There is a sense in which we do not fully understand or appreciate bureaucratic behavior unless we see it from the viewpoint of a practicing bureaucrat. Nevertheless, it does not follow that there is no alternative explanation or understanding to be

---

[51] Winch, *The Idea of a Social Science,* p. 133.
[52] Ibid., p. 104.
[53] Ibid., pp. 111ff.
[54] Ibid., pp. 135–136.

gained from subsuming this behavior under lawlike generalizations, even when the concepts employed in framing these generalizations and in describing the specific pieces of behavior are radically different from those that the agent himself would employ. In contradistinction to Winch's position social science has been described as the study of the *unintended* consequences of human action. This description understates the relevance of Winch's argument, while his position neglects this aspect of social inquiry.[55]

Even if we allow that one important task of social science is to characterize the rules which constitute various social practices or activities, we need not accept the suggestion that this is all there is to social inquiry. Such an analysis is conspicuously static; it does not leave room for equally important questions that arise about the origin and development of various practices and activities.

SOCIAL SCIENCE AND OBJECTIVITY

The third objection of traditionalists focuses on the intrusion of values that supposedly prevent social scientists from making objective judgments. We can identify two forms of this objection. First, social science has been indicted by appeal to particular examples in which bias or prejudice is alleged to enter into the collection and evaluation of data, allocation of funds for research, or admission or rejection of certain variables in theories. Even more strikingly, it is claimed that behavioralism or methodism leads to concern with problems which aren't politically relevant; this in turn can be seen as giving at least tacit support to existing political institutions and practices. Second, social science has been indicted as but one instance of a global, philosophical thesis which maintains that all our complex judgments are reflections of ideology and are hence (historically) relative rather than objective.[56]

To answer the first objection, it should be noted that no doubt particular pieces of research have been infected by bias, by an unacceptable intrusion of particular judgments of value, and by points of view. It is also probably true that this happens more often in social science than in natural science. However, empirical evidence does not show that the intrusion of values is unique to social science nor that it cannot be eliminated. The examples discussed in detail in Chapter 3 indicate that judgments of value enter into the evaluation and recep-

---

[55] Alan Ryan, *The Philosophy of the Social Sciences*, pp. 149ff.
[56] A systematic and more detailed discussion of these issues can be found in Ernest Nagel, *The Structure of Science*, chap. 13; and Quentin Gibson, *The Logic of Social Inquiry*, Humanities Press, New York, 1960.

tion of results in natural as well as social science. In this respect social science may be seen as, in principal, no worse off than natural science.

Nor can it be denied that some research in social science has been trivial and irrelevant to immediate social and political problems. In neither respect, however, does social science differ in kind from natural science. It is certainly a misconception of natural science to assume that all or even most investigations are endowed with special significance or scientific importance. Banality in choice of research problems, unimaginative research design, lack of insight into the relationship between particular pieces of research and larger problems in a field, and relative stupidity can produce trivial and uninteresting results in both natural and social science.

The lack of direct relevance or application often besets basic research in natural science as well; theorizing is always some steps removed from practical applications. But a wide degree of latitude is necessary because we are never sure what will lead to a fruitful development, and there is no reason to suppose this is less true of theorizing in social science. It is difficult to see how the demand for "relevance" at the expense of theorizing is different from the charge that a given scientist should turn away from some basic research in biology to study various ways of ameliorating the symptoms of the disease he is studying. Both may be worthwhile (and not necessarily exclusive) undertakings. Nor does it mean that, in particular cases, priorities cannot be established. If funds are limited, we might be more inclined to support research on heart disease than on the common cold, insisting that the first is more important than the second.

Finally, even if biases and different value systems create greater difficulty in social science, it does not follow that they cannot be eliminated. Some critics seem to be able to identify these biases, for example, the application of the "Western developmental model" to the Third World, and this suggests that there is at least a prospect for offering alternatives less nefarious in their intrusion of values into scientific inquiry.

A more sweeping perspective is provided by critics of behavioralism who assert the thesis of relativism. This assertion maintains that social science fails to be objective, that is, truly scientific, because it is but one instance in which human "ideology," our subjective beliefs or social political perspective, intrudes upon our judgments. We are told that, "it is impossible to conceive of absolute truth existing independently of the values and position of the subject unrelated to social context." [57]

Support for this position has been gathered from some critics of

[57] Karl Mannheim, *Ideology and Utopia*, Harcourt, Brace & World, New York, 1965, p. 79.

behavioralism who point to Kuhn's claims in the *Structure of Scientific Revolutions*. They seize upon those passages in which Kuhn talks about replacement of one paradigm by another in natural science as a "Gestalt switch" or "conversion" to reinforce their view. Even in natural science, they say, individual and group prejudices shape judgments; thus there is no objective procedure for ultimately adjudicating various claims.

Several comments are in order. First, such a global indictment does not distinguish the problems faced by social scientists from those faced by natural scientists. Both are tarred with the same brush. Furthermore, behavioralists need not commit themselves to discovering some "absolute truth"; they might seek rather to develop laws and theories adequate to their subject matter in the same sense that laws and theories are adequate in natural science.

Second, such a global relativism generates what is known as "Mannheim's paradox." If all judgments about social life are relative to social and individual perspective and therefore lack objectivity, this judgment itself is relative and lacks objectivity. Further, if relativity and lack of objectivity casts doubts on particular judgments about social life, then doubt is equally cast on the relativity thesis itself.[58]

Third, part of the initial appeal of relativism springs from the identification of "absolute truth" with objectivity. It is assumed that to hold scientific statements as tentative or hypothetical, to acknowledge that they are open to revision, is tantamount to rendering them nonobjective, merely relative. We would argue that such a claim attempts to hold scientific judgments or good evidence to an inappropriate standard.

Questions about objectivity in social science are further complicated by the assumptions that objectivity must entail neutrality. It is not obvious that this is the case. Science can be viewed as providing "institutionalized control procedures" that are necessary precisely because observers and theorizers are not neutral.[59] Seen in this way, redundancy, duplication, and overlap are essential to maintain the integrity of the system of scientific inquiry.[60] If this is the case, then objectivity in science is possible even though people may be conditioned or shaped in various different ways. What is essential is not that scientists claim neutrality, but that they accept responsibility in the joint enterprise of collecting and assessing evidence and of considering and evaluating alternative theories.

---

[58] See Martin Landau, *Political Theory and Political Science*, The Macmillan Company, New York, 1972, pp. 34ff.

[59] Ibid.

[60] See ibid., pp. 43ff; also "Redundancy, Rationality and the Problem of Duplication and Overlap," *Public Administration Review*, 29, No. 4 (1969), 346–358.

Review questions and exercises

1   Explain the meaning and significance of the following terms:

   a   Context of discovery
   b   Context of justification
   c   Observational statement
   d   Observational law
   e   Theory
   f   Observational-theoretical distinction
   g   Explanation
   h   Prediction
   i   Lawlikeness
   j   Falsification
   k   Open texture
   l   Scope
   m   Formalized theory
   n   Logical consistency
   o   Deductive-nomological model
   p   Causal explanation
   q   Crucial experiment
   r   Simplicity
   s   Operational capability
   t   Normal science
   u   Paradigm
   v   Verstehen
   w   Causal narrative
   x   Probabilistic explanation
   y   Theory of the middle range
   z   Reproductive fallacy
   aa   Mannheim paradox
   bb   Neutrality
   cc   Objectivity

2   Discuss some of the connections and differences between scientic theories and observational data.

3   Compare common-sense and scientific explanation or understanding. In what ways are they similar or different?

4   Distinguish Thomas Kuhn's view from the standard view.

5   Discuss the various criteria for evaluating alternative theories.

6   Discuss whether or how the values of social scientists might affect their results.

7   Is objectivity in political science possible?

The scientist, as such, has no ethical, religious, political, literary, philosophical, moral, or marital preferences. . . .

As a scientist he is interested not in what is right or wrong or good or evil, but only in what is true or false.

Robert Bierstedt

The Community . . . with its wider interests, its larger purposes, and its more deliberate aims, surrounds us, encloses us, and compels us to conform, not by mere pressure from without, not by fear of censure within, but by a sense of our interest in, and responsibility to, certain interests not our own.

Robert E. Park

3
ETHICAL CONSIDERATIONS
IN SOCIAL RESEARCH

In addition to the previously mentioned debates about what constitutes a "genuine science," there has been continuing controversy over the place of values in scientific inquiry and over ethical considerations that influence and/or should influence the scientific community. In Chapter 2 we indicated that many problems surrounding the concept of objectivity in social science can be dissipated if we treat science as essentially a community activity providing "institutionalized control procedures." This approach to science suggests that even if we treat the personal biases of scientists and their criteria for problem selection as extrascientific, value considerations still affect scientists *as* scientists. They remain members of a scientific community, and this membership creates obligations and responsibilities.

In this chapter we will consider problems that arise when we attempt to specify the obligations and responsibilities of the scientific community. It should be noted that there are no simple, non-normative solutions to many problems treated here. No formula spells out what conduct scientists should follow in each situation.

Discussion is further complicated because ethical problems may be treated on two levels: either as empirical descriptions of standards that in fact *are employed* by scientists or as normative statements about standards that *should be employed*. The positions exemplified by Park and Bierstedt in the chapter epigraphs can be taken as two different empirical descriptions of the extent to which human beings can separate their various roles. An additional consideration concerns whether this separation is desirable.

Empirical analyses of sociologists and social psychologists often distinguish between the subjective and prescribed aspects of roles. The *prescribed aspect* of roles relates to the general set of norms and expectations attached to most roles that serve as an orienting basis for our behavior. Prescribed aspects point out how we should behave in a given situation. The degree to which these norms are made explicit and enforced will, of course, vary. The norms pertaining to the role of doctor, for example, are more explicit than those relating to the role of friend. The *subjective aspect* of roles refers to an individual's interpretations of these norms and expectations. Individuals actively, consciously and unconsciously, interpret and somewhat redefine prescriptive norms. Thus there is frequently some variance between how individuals actually behave and how they should behave according to prevailing prescriptions. Several positions we examine in the following pages are concerned primarily with prevailing prescriptive norms.

The concept of role is also relational in another sense. Because human beings assume a number of different roles, there is always the possibility that these roles and their attendant norms may conflict with one another. The human situation is thus inherently one of choice among priorities. To a certain extent, ethical questions emerge from the question of priorities. Although various procedural guidelines have been suggested to deal with this problem of choice, they are far from exhaustive.

The roles of social scientists and fiduciary responsibility

A number of scholars have suggested the fiducial model as appropriate for considering ethical questions in science.[1] The fiduciary relationship is one in which an individual or a group holds some endowment in trust for another. The meaning and value of the relationship is in part dependent upon the maintenance of public confidence and support. The trustee is normally considered broadly responsible for the endowment. His duty is not only to conserve and guard that endowment, but also to enhance its value. With regard to the relationship between scientists and the larger society, this conception depicts a scientist as a trustee who

> because of his superior competence and the trust and reliance placed in him, owes a duty of undivided loyalty and devotion to his client, the more so when the fiduciary, like a lawyer or doctor, enjoys as a class certain exclusive privileges to carry on his calling. This model underscores the obligation of full disclosure and the limitations of consent.[2]

Unfortunately the model is vague in certain respects. Who, for example, is the client of the fiducial relationship? What is the meaning of "full devotion and loyalty"? The scientific community does enjoy certain privileges, including academic freedom as well as a large

---

[1] See, for example, Paul A. Freund, *Experimentation with Human Subjects*, George Braziller, New York, 1970, p. xiii; James W. Wiggins, "Fiduciary Responsibility and the Improbability Principle," in eds. Helmut Shoeck and James W. Wiggins, *Scientism and Values*, Van Nostrand, Reinhold Company, New York, 1960.

[2] Freund, *Experimentation with Human Subjects*.

financial endowment. But the nature of that endowment and the purposes it supposedly serves are seldom spelled out.

The relationship within the scientific community can also be depicted as fiducial. Science, as a communal and cumulative enterprise, rests upon certain widely shared beliefs and values:

> Among these are the use of relevant concepts, prediction based on probabilities, a commitment to objectivity, avoidance of value positions, a search for all the evidence, and a public methodology which allows fellow scientists to test conclusions through replication.[3]

These beliefs and values are obviously integral to scientific enterprise, as should be clear from the discussion in Chapter 2. The model does not spell out specific guidelines for the choice of research questions and procedures, however; nor does it suggest that scientists must be ethically neutral, though they clearly must be objective.

While the notion of fiduciary responsibility might serve as a general model, it does not provide concrete answers to specific situations. These more particular judgments must be evolved from the basic principles of the general model. What, for example, is the nature of the endowment of the fiducial relationship? What is the constituency of this relationship? Is it to coincide with national boundaries, or is the scientific community responsible to a larger constituency? The Nuremberg Code and the prosecutions of Nazi leaders and collaborators made on its basis suggest that individual responsibility sometimes overrides national commitments. Nevertheless, practical, political impediments to this interpretation are rather obvious.

In discussing the notion of fiduciary responsibility, it is helpful to center our analysis on the several roles of scientists and on several dimensions of ethical concern. Much of the debate about the ethical responsibilities of scientists rests on different interpretations of the desirability or even the possibility of separating these various roles.

We may view scientists first as producers of social forces. Directly and indirectly, scientific research contributes to the shaping and reshaping of the social order. The end products of science, both constructive and destructive, surround us—from the atomic bomb to atomic energy for power, from the polio vaccine to various forms of lethal germs for potential use in biological warfare. While scientists do not normally endeavor to develop specific technological instruments, their work almost invariably makes such advances possible.

Second, social scientists have a role as experimenters and social thinkers. This role concerns their relationship as scientists to their subject matter, their colleagues, their experimental subjects, and their students.

---

[3] Wiggins, "Fiduciary Responsibility . . . ," p. 100.

Third, scientists may, nonprofessionally, be participants in social action. Their standing in the larger society and their knowledge have some relevance to this role that may or may not give them special privileges and perspectives.

Kelman points out that at least three broad ethical domains cross-cut these various roles. First, the question of values and human relations broadly concerns the implications of various scientific procedures for human relations in general and for specific relations between researchers and subjects. Second, values and societal processes more generally consider the possible uses of scientific research and its procedures. Finally, the dimension of values and the scientific study of human beings refers to "the appropriateness of the social scientist's observational techniques, of his assumptions about scientific methodology, and of his models of man to the nature of the task before him." [4]

As Kelman indicates, much debate over ethical considerations turns on differences of opinion about objectivity and the demands of scientific method. Strict proponents of objectivity construe it to mean neutrality in general. Arguing that science should limit itself to questions of fact, they contend that scientists should not make value judgments because they entail sheer preferences and hence are not subject to rational argument.[5] Strict proponents of this position tend to put aside ethical questions in general, arguing that they cannot be adjudged on scientific grounds. While these proponents would not necessarily deny the relevance of ethical questions in other roles, they argue that a social scientist's role *as* scientist must set aside such considerations. Thus scientists as experimenters and social thinkers and as producers of social forces must minimize personal and general societal values in their scientific work. This means that they have no particular competence as *scientists* for deciding which research is most relevant, useful, or desirable from the standpoint of the larger society. This position postulates strict role differentiation as a necessary part of scientific process. As Bierstedt points out, scientists *as* scientists must have no ethical, religious, political, literary, philosophical, moral, or marital preferences.

Those who endorse this neutralist position criticize some current research and the posture of more action-orientated professional associations by arguing that they violate the fiducial principle. Science, they maintain, has adopted the façade of objectivity only to rationalize

---

[4] Herbert Kelman, *A Time to Speak: On Human Values and Social Research*, Jossey-Boss, San Francisco, 1968, pp. 2–3.

[5] Wiggins, "Fiduciary Responsibility . . ."; Murray Rothbard, "The Mantle of Science," in Shoeck and Wiggins, *Scientism and Values*, pp. 159–180; Ludwig von Bertalanffy, "The Psychopathology of Scientism," in ibid., pp. 202–218.

the erosion of individual responsibility and the adherence to the values of the larger society.[6] Murray Rothbard points out that:

> A façade of the position is now adopted . . . Instead of choosing his own ends and valuing accordingly, the scientist supposedly maintains his neutrality by adopting the values of the bulk of society.[7]

Thus we see larger societal commitments to egalitarianism, for example, leading the scientific community to reject certain concepts, such as *race*, on value-laden grounds.[8] A similar violation of professional commitment to objectivity can be found in the commitment of some scholarly societies to the advancement of certain human values.

Many other scholars, including Herbert Kelman, take a less demanding view of scientific objectivity. Kelman, for example,

> starts with the assumption that, to achieve scientific objectivity, it is neither necessary or sufficient to avoid value-laden problems, to treat the subjects of research in a completely impersonal way, to rely entirely on experimental and quantitative techniques, and to adopt mechanistic models.[9]

The following sections of this chapter consider a number of issues relating to the general positions raised here: first, the question of fiduciary responsibility and research methods and techniques; second, scientific reception systems and the actual ability of the scientific community to be impartial observers; and finally, a general consideration of ethical problems arising from the connection between government and science.

Fiduciary responsibility and ethical considerations in research methods and techniques

There has been increasing concern in recent years over the manner in which research is conducted, and a number of scholars have suggested a need for the consideration of fundamental human values in choosing not only research topics but also research procedures. This concern is manifest in both natural and social science, and it has long been recognized as an important problem in medical research. Recent work with heart transplants, for example, raised a number of questions regarding

---

[6] Rothbard, "The Mantle of Science," p. 173.
[7] Wiggins, "Fiduciary Responsibility . . . ," pp. 100–118.
[8] Ibid.
[9] Kelman, *A Time to Speak*, p. 4.

the application of experimental medical procedures to human beings.[10] The Tuskegee syphilis experiments, medical experimentation on convicts, and similar projects raise a number of related questions. What means of scientific investigation are permissible? When do the ends justify the means? What underlying standards should apply in evaluating the propriety of any research design? What responsibilities do scientists have to their subjects? What is the exact nature of fiducial responsibility? What are the implications of certain research procedures for the scientific community as a whole?

While it is obvious that certain constraints operate on research methods and techniques, it is not always easy to draw the line as to which tactics are permissible and which are not. Nor is the rationale behind such evaluations always made explicit. Scientists are obviously not permitted to reenact urban riots for experimental purposes, however useful the results might be. Nor do we allow wholesale experimentation with the economy or the international political system. Nevertheless, to a certain extent the lines of permissibility are historically and culturally determined. What was legally permissible scientific technique in Nazi Germany is not considered legally or morally permissible in most countries today.

The concepts of "consent" and "harm" are frequently put forth as criteria for determining permissibility, with the general rule being that an experimental subject's consent must be obtained before the experiment and that the subject not be asked to participate in potentially harmful research.[11] The problem with both criteria is that they often are too imprecise to be effective procedural guidelines. The concept of "harm," for example, is fraught with ambiguities. Is the concept to only apply to instances of physical harm, or is it to include psychological harm? If we adopt the broader definition, what constitutes "psychological harm?" Moreover, is it possible to predetermine the potential consequences of an experiment? Several experiments discussed by Herbert Kelman may serve to illustrate this problem:

> For example, a brilliant experiment was recently designed to observe the effects of threat on group solidarity and the need for strong leadership. In this study (one of the very rare examples of an experiment conducted in a natural setting) independent food merchants in a number of Dutch towns were

[10] See *Experimentation with Human Subjects*, ed. P. Freund; W. Goodman, "Doctors Must Experiment on Humans: But What Are the Patient's Rights?" *New York Times Magazine*, July 2, 1967, pp. 12–23, 29–33; and M. M. Katz, "Ethical Issues in the Use of Human Subjects in Psychopharmacologic Research," *American Psychologist*, 22 (1967), 360–363.

[11] See, for example, David D. Rustein, "The Ethical Design of Human Experiments," *Daedalus*, 98, No. 2 (1969), 523–541.

brought together for group meetings and informed that a large organization would soon open a chain of supermarkets in the Netherlands. In a "highthreat" condition, the subjects were told that their towns would probably be selected as sites for such markets, which would cause a considerable drop in their business. On the advice of the executives of the shopkeepers' organizations who had helped to arrange the meetings, the investigators never revealed, even after the experiment was over, that the supermarket threat was a fiction.

I have been worried about those Dutch merchants ever since I first heard about this study. Did some of them go out of business in anticipation of the heavy competition? Do some of them have an anxiety reaction every time they see a bulldozer? Chances are that they soon forgot about this threat (unless, of course, supermarkets actually did move into town) and that it became just one of the many little moments of anxiety that occur in every shopkeeper's life. But do investigators have the right to add to life's little anxieties and to risk the possibility of more extensive anxiety purely for the purposes of such experiments?

Two other recent studies provide further examples of potentially harmful effects arising from the use of deception. In one set of studies, male college students were led to believe that they had been homosexually aroused by photographs of men. In the other study, subjects of both sexes were given disturbing information about their levels of masculinity or femininity, presumably based on an elaborate series of psychological tests they had taken. In all of these studies, the deception was explained to the subjects at the end of the experiment. One wonders, however, whether this explanation removes the possibility of harmful effects. For many persons in this age group, sexual identity is a live and sensitive issue, and the self-doubts generated by this laboratory experience could linger.[12]

The famous Milgram experiments further illustrate the difficulties surrounding the concept of harm. These experiments involved having experimental subjects administer electric shocks to other subjects in what they were told was a learning experiment. The experiment was actually designed to measure deference to authority.

One volunteer was "smiling and confident" when he entered the laboratory. "Within 20 minutes . . . he was reduced to a

[12] Herbert Kelman, "Deception in Social Research," in eds. B. J. Franklin and H. W. Osborne, *Research Methods: Issues and Insights*, Wadsworth Publishing Company, Belmont, Calif., 1971, pp. 60–61. Published by permission of Transaction, Inc., from *Transaction*, July/August 1966. Copyright © 1966 by Transaction, Inc.

twitching, stuttering wreck, who was rapidly approaching a point of nervous collapse." . . . They (the volunteers) were instructed to administer increasingly severe shocks to another person, who after a while began to protest vehemently. In fact, of course, the "victim" was an accomplice of the experimenter and did not receive any real shocks. But in some cases, the experimenter instructed the subject to continue to "shock" the "victim" up to the maximum level, which the subject believed to be extremely painful when the victim writhed in pain and pounded his head against the wall.[13]

The Milgram experiments, like most experimental situations, were followed by a debriefing period in which subjects were informed of the real nature of the experiment. Follow-up interviews with some of the experimental subjects indicated that many felt they had learned a great deal about themselves through the experiments. The experiments were justified on the grounds that they dealt with an important research question and that they provided a learning experience. Many critics of the Milgram experiments questioned whether scientists should make this type of a decision for others. Undoubtedly, some so-called volunteers had considerable doubts about themselves after the experiment. Psychological harm *may* have been or could have been a consequence of this type of research.[14]

The preceding experiments also raise questions about the meaning of "consent" and its usefulness as a criterion for evaluating the propriety of any research design. Consent may obviously be defined in a number of different ways. Is simply using so-called *volunteers* a sufficient interpretation of consent, or must the experimental subject be informed of the nature of the experiment and its potential consequences? Can "consent" mean anything at all when it is given out of total ignorance of the circumstances involved? Are all subjects equally "voluntary," or must special interpretations of "consent" be given in the case of children, prisoners, and others who are under some special constraint?[15]

---

13 Ibid., p. 59.
14 There is a large literature concerning these experiments. See, for example, D. Baumrind, "Some Thoughts on Ethics of Research After Reading Milgram's 'Behavioral Study of Obedience,' " *American Psychologist*, 19 (1964) 421–423; S. Milgram, "Behavioral Study of Obedience," *Journal of Abnormal and Social Psychology*, 67 (1963), 371–378; S. Milgram, "Issues in the Study of Obedience: A Reply to Baumrind," *American Psychologist*, 18 (1964), 848–852; K. Ring, K. Wallston, and M. Corey, "Mode of Debriefing as a Factor Affecting Experiments: An Ethical Inquiry," mimeograph, University of Connecticut, 1967; Stanley Milgram, *Obedience to Authority*, Harper & Row, Publishers, New York, 1973.
15 M. B. Smith, "Conflicting Values Affecting Behavioral Research with Children," *American Psychologist*, 22 (1967), 377–382.

A number of scholars argue that fiduciary responsibility need not entail full disclosure with regard to consent. A certain amount of deception is usually justified on the grounds that full disclosure would either close entry to the researcher or contaminate the results. This is perhaps particularly true in research on deviant behavior. Deception is used in participant observation as well as laboratory experiments. A recent instance involved the researcher's posing as a homosexual in order to study homosexual behavior in public places.[16] The publication of the results of this study raised a storm of protest regarding the propriety of this method. Critics questioned the need for deception and the implications of its use.

Several arguments can be raised against the use of deception in general. Kelman offers three criticisms in particular: its larger ethical implications, the effectiveness of its use, and the consequences of such procedures for scientific research in our society.[17] Kelman points out that researchers frequently justify deception on the grounds that subjects must remain naive about the real purposes of an experiment. Unfortunately, as he notes, it is difficult to continually replenish one's supply of naive subjects. College students, for example, seem to have outlived their usefulness in this respect. This criticism implies that in the long run the technique is self-defeating. Second, it is not always clear that deception is necessarily effective as a research technique; its use often rests on unexamined empirical claims. Perhaps most important, however, are the implications of the widespread use of deception for the scientific community. In the long run, the use of deception may undermine the public's faith in the scientific community and the community's ostensible commitment to open communication. Science will simply become another force contributing to the dehumanization of society. Ironically, while some control over manipulation of human behavior appears necessary for constructive behavior change, it is difficult to determine what is constructive, and the process may easily become destructive of those very values we seek to further.[18] Thus, scientific techniques may present something of a paradox.

The preceding cases raise general questions regarding scientists' responsibility to their subjects and the possible consequences of different research procedures for the integrity of the scientific community and the larger values of society. While there is no widespread consensus within the scientific community regarding most of these issues, there is increasing cognizance of these problems. Various governmental funding agencies now require statements safeguarding

[16] L. Humphreys, "Tearoom Trade: Impersonal Sex in Public Places," *Transaction*, 7 (Jan. 1970), 10–25.
[17] Kelman, "Deception in Social Research," p. 60.
[18] Kelman, *A Time to Speak*, pp. 34–49.

the rights of experimental subjects, and a number of professional organizations have adopted general guidelines regarding professional ethics.

The fiducial relationship within the scientific community: scientific transmission and reception systems

Our preceding discussion suggests that scholars hold a number of different positions as to the roles and responsibilities of scientists and the various means and goals of scientific procedures and inquiry. There is considerably more agreement concerning the ethics of scientific transmission and reception. Most of these ethical positions emerge directly from the communal and cumulative nature of scientific inquiry, and from its tentative status.

Nevertheless, scientific inquiry, the interests of individual scientists, and scientific results are very much a part of the larger social framework in which they are developed. To a variable extent, national and international societal practices impinge on this process. Similarly, the community of scientists may impose its own standards and constraints. As Georges Gurvitch points out in his comprehensive study, *The Social Frameworks of Knowledge,*

> In spite of its pretensions to be "above the melee," i.e. detached from social frameworks, scientific knowledge has but a relative independence, and the great error of positivism was to take these pretensions literally. In all scientific knowledge social correlates intervene. . . .[19]

The following sections of this chapter discuss ethical problems associated with the reception and transmission of knowledge. After initially describing the prescribed ethics of the scientific community in this regard, we turn to an examination of several case studies that exemplify problems in their actual application.

Scientific reception systems: The ideal model

The ideal model of the scientific transmission and reception system can be termed the *rationalist model.* Its norms and criteria correspond to the following categories propounded by Marlan Blissett:

[19] Georges Gurvitch, *The Social Frameworks of Knowledge,* Harper Torchbooks, New York, 1972, p. 33.

1 *Universalism*   The realization that all scientists are obliged to uphold common, objective standards of truth that transcend personal influence or social position.

2 *Communism*   The recognition that effective communication is essential to science and that "property rights" have no place in the dissemination of scientific findings.[20]

3 *Disinterestedness*   Disavowal of personal or material interest in the product of scientific research.

4 *Organized skepticism*   Acceptance of the idea that each scientist is responsible for critically evaluating the work of his peers and for suspending his judgment until "the facts are at hand."

5 *Rationality*   Adherence to objective, consensual standards of proof.

6 *Emotional neutrality*   A prohibition against intense personal commitment to particular ideas or theories to the extent that their truth or falsity might be affected.

7 *Individualism*   Commitment to resist any regulation or control of scientific research.[21]

These seven canons set general standards for judging what is appropriate professional behavior within scientific circles. Nevertheless, it is an ideal model, and scientists in different disciplines and societies adhere to its various strictures to varying degrees. These canons and any communal consensus that surrounds them result largely from the educational process and the socialization of novitiates into the scientific ranks. Thus scientists, like medical doctors, learn what is expected of them in terms of their prescribed role. Unfortunately, political science lacks the clear credo provided by the Hippocratic oath. Instead, social scientists find themselves confronted by a seemingly unsolvable controversy concerning the nature, relevance, and appropriateness of ethical questions. As a result, the communal consensus is perhaps best characterized as a lack of consensus.

There is also great variation in the degree to which these canons are institutionalized, regulated, and protected. For example, the model presupposes that channels of communication among scholars exist and that they operate in an open and impartial manner. Scholarly journals are among the most important channels of communication in this

[20] The term "communism" has become so emotion laden in contemporary times that it might be advisable to substitute "communalism" in its place.
[21] Marlan Blissett, *Politics in Science*, Little, Brown and Company, Boston, 1972, p. 67; see Norman Storer, *The Social System of Science*, Holt, Rinehart and Winston, New York, 1966, for a discussion of some of the inconsistencies in these canons.

respect, yet they vary enormously in structure, influence, and enforced impartiality. Some scholarly journals require authors of articles to pay a standard fee for publication. This requirement has obvious consequences in terms of the distribution of costs and benefits in a society in which not all potential contributors can equally afford to pay the costs. Many scholarly journals attempt to formally ensure impartiality in the consideration of publishable manuscripts by having a number of different readers independently judge manuscripts with no indication of their authorship. This formalized impartiality is not always used, however; and when it is not, established scholars may have an advantage.

Undeniably, disinterestedness and emotional neutrality are crucial for the growth of knowledge in any discipline, but they are often difficult to achieve, particularly in transitional periods of a discipline's development, when far-reaching questions of scope, objectives, and methods are being raised. Furthermore, the need for emotional neutrality is perhaps inevitably contradictory to the very human need for personal emotional commitment.

The canon that science must resist any control or regulation is also an obvious necessity if scientific results are to have the validity and reliability for which they strive, but this particular norm is also difficult to maintain. Increasing governmental involvement in the funding of various scientific projects has important implications in this respect. We consider these in greater detail later, when we examine the relation between government and the scientific community.

To what extent do scholars themselves subscribe to the ethics of the rationalist model? Unfortunately, we have only scattered evidence as a basis for answering this question. Blissett attempted to broach this question in a survey of scientists.[22] As Table 3-1 indicates, he did not find anything approximating universal agreement with these canons. In fact, there was considerable ambiguity regarding several norms, particularly those of universalism, emotional neutrality, and organized skepticism. Blissett's questions do appear to call for two types of answers. Some questions (marked "normative") ask for abstract agreement with the ideal, while others (marked "actual") ask whether the ideal is actually practiced. Generally speaking, there is more consensus on the abstract ideal than on actual practice.

What factors might be related to these ambiguities? Blissett examines several factors including institutional prestige, age, and academic discipline, but none of these proved to be significant. The inconsistencies may imply that scientific norms are changing. Unfortunately, Blissett's evidence as to the determinants of this change is inconclusive.

[22] Ibid.

Scientific reception systems: alternative models

Ambiguities within the canons of the rationalist model and its inability to account for a number of scientific controversies have led to the formulation of several alternative models of the process of scientific reception.

Probably the most obvious rebuttal to the rationalist model would be put forth as a variant of the Marxist thesis that all ideology, consciousness, and formalized ways of learning are manifestations of the economic and political interests of the dominant classes. The Marxist reply would probably fall under the model of scientific reception systems which Alfred de Grazia has termed the dogmatic model.[23] The dogmatic model postulates the existence of a united elite that accepts or rejects scientific results on the grounds of whether they conform to prevailing theories or norms. This unequivocal rejection or acceptance is, moreover, largely predicated on considerations of the enhancement of the power of the given elite. The relevance of the dogmatic model to a given situation can usually be determined on the basis of the character of the "gatekeeping elite" within the scientific community and within the larger society, the nature of the accreditation and selection process, and the type of evaluative grounds used to assess any given work, that is, objective-rationalistic, dogmatic and authoritative, etc.

Related to the dogmatic model is what de Grazia terms the *power model*.[24] This depicts the scientific community as an elite group that seeks to enhance and preserve its power by selectively using the rationalist doctrine. Rather than operating as a universal principle governing the transmission and reception of scientific results, the rationalistic doctrine is largely a stabilizing and rationalizing myth. Democracy and communalism among scientists are myths in the power model. Through their control of conference programs, the important journals and scholarly channels of discourse, occupancy of the highest, most prestigious university positions, and advice on funding, hiring, and promotion, the alleged power elite exercises a subtle but real despotism over the larger scientific community.

Finally, de Grazia offers one other alternative reception system,

---

[23] Alfred de Grazia, "The Scientific Reception System," in eds. Alfred de Grazia et al., *The Velikovsky Affair*, University Books, New Hyde Park, New York, 1966, pp. 216–221. Reprinted by permission.

[24] Ibid., pp. 200–216; for a related analysis especially relevant to political science see Sheldon S. Wolin, "Paradigms and Political Theories," in eds. Preston King and B. C. Parekh, *Politics and Experience*, Cambridge University Press, New York, pp. 134–135.

Norm	Questions
Universalism	"The acceptance or nonacceptance of scientific evidence does not in any way depend upon the social position of the one who submits it (that is, his institutional affiliation—university or lab—his degree of recognition, those under whom he has studied or worked)." (Actual)
	"Scientists must adhere to a common set of objective standards by which proof can be demonstrated." (Normative)
	"Despite different cultural backgrounds and different patterns of belief, scientists (all over the world) can communicate effectively with each other because the terms used for communication have precisely the same meaning to the various members of the scientific community." (Actual)
Communism	"For science to be advanced it is not enough that fruitful ideas be originated, or new experiments developed, or new methods instituted, the innovations must be effectively communicated to others." (Normative)
	"Only those scientists who have high standing, or work or associate informally with those who do, have the kind of information that lies at the cutting edge of inquiry." (Actual)
	"In the area of fundamental research, scientists regard their ideas as common property, they regard suppression of information or scientific discoveries (providing, say national security is not threatened) as unethical." (Actual)
Disinterestedness	"Science differs from other professions (medicine, law, etc.) in that there is less chance that a scientist would take advantage (financial or otherwise) of the layman." (Actual)
Organized skepticism	"Scientists are skeptical even about their own findings until other scientists have evaluated them." (Actual)
Rationality	"Scientists must adhere to a common set of objective standards by which proof may be demonstrated." (Normative)
Emotional neutrality	"Intense personal commitment to ideas or theories is not a proper scientific attitude." (Normative)
Individualism	"The pursuit of science is best organized when as much freedom as possible is granted to all scientists." (Normative)

Table 3-1   Agreement and disagreement on the norms of scientific research

	Percentage response			
Number	Agree	Disagree	Undecided	Total
840	33	60	7	100
832	64	29	7	100
838	72	22	6	100
849	97	1	1	99
831	30	57	12	99
842	82	12	6	100
818	47	30	23	100
819	44	45	11	100
832	64	29	7	100
834	42	50	8	100
835	77	15	7	99

Social parameters of the system

Social norms of research

Source: Marlan Blisset, *Politics in Science*, pp. 72–73. Copyright © 1972 by Little, Brown and Company (Inc). Adapted by permission.

the indeterminancy model:

> The Indeterminancy Model postulates a scientific order that is not replenished according to any scheme that is instrumentally rational. Rather it almost randomly absorbs or refuses. . . . The truth value of the scientist and his product are alleged to have very little to do with their chances of success in being incorporated into science. Nor are they kept out by skillful managers of power and arbiters of claims.[25]

The preceding models of scientific reception systems all have some descriptive utility. Although the rationalist model is usually depicted as the prevailing system, recent history contains numerous examples of its violation in the pure form. The following case studies shed some light on the difficulties with the ideal rationalist system and the human context in which scientific results are judged.

Case studies of ethical controversy in research

THE KAMMERER CASE

> On September 23, 1926, an Austrian experimental biologist named Dr. Paul Kammerer blew his brains out on a footpath in the Austrian mountains. His suicide was the climax of a great evolutionary controversy which his experiments had aroused. The battle was between the followers of Lamarck, who maintained that acquired characteristics could be inherited, and the neo-Darwinists, who upheld the theory of chance mutations preserved by natural selection. Dr. Kammerer's experiments with various amphibians, including salamanders and the midwife toad (*Alytes obstetricans*), lent much weight to the Lamarckian argument and drew upon him the full fury of the orthodox neo-Darwinists. . . .[26]

The debate over Kammerer's experiments and their implications was fought in a venomous atmosphere, with decidedly unscholarly means being employed to discredit his work.

Heading the attack on Kammerer was a British scientist, William

[25] Ibid., pp. 191–200; Chapter 2 discusses the work of Thomas Kuhn and its relevance to this issue in greater detail. His conception of revolutionary sciences does not clearly fit into any of de Grazia's models. See also Stephen Toulmin, *Foresight and Understanding*, Harper & Row, Publishers, New York, 1963; he suggests that the evolution of scientific ideas and their scientific merit is virtually a question of their survival ability and a highly chaotic, almost random process.

[26] Arthur Koestler, *The Case of the Midwife Toad*, Random House, New York, 1971; quoted from jacket description. Reprinted by permission.

Bateson, who hinted that the Viennese's experiments were fakes, but who failed to examine the evidence, including the so-called nuptial pads of Kammerer's last remaining specimen of the midwife toad. It was a young American scientist who delivered the *coup de grace*; on a visit to Vienna, he discovered that the discoloration of the nuptial pads was due not to natural causes but to the injection of India ink. When his findings were published, Kammerer shot himself.[27]

Several points are worth noting with regard to the Kammerer case in addition to those stressed in the above brief abstract from Arthur Koestler's recent investigation. First, Kammerer's suicide was widely construed within scientific circles as an admission of guilt that invalidated his lifetime work. This factor appears particularly unscholarly in light of the fact that Kammerer had brought all his experimental specimens to Cambridge where they had been thoroughly examined by the most eminent men in the field in 1923. There had been no evidence of fabrication at this time, and Kammerer's Cambridge lectures had convinced many of his more sceptical critics of his sincerity if not his thesis.

Second, insufficient efforts were made to replicate Kammerer's experiments, particularly in light of the significance of their implications. Scattered attempts were made at replication, but Kammerer's followers were not apparently as skilled as he, and the specimens did not survive; in other instances, his procedures were not followed accurately.

Third, Kammerer publicly stated that he did not regard his experiments with the midwife toad as the most definitive support of his thesis, and yet he was continually attacked on the weakest case.

The Kammerer case demonstrates that scientists are not the uninvolved, impartial precursors of knowledge we sometimes picture them to be. There is some irony in the fact that Kammerer's most strident and unreasoning opponent, William Bateson, was in his earlier years, also a Lamarckian, but one who had failed in a difficult attempt to gather supporting data. Lest it be thought that such unscholarly treatment was a product of the early years of the twentieth century alone, let us now examine a case more pointed in its implications, more recent in its contest, and more ominous in its apparent disposition.

THE VELIKOVSKY CASE

In 1950, a book called *Worlds in Collision*, by Dr. Immanuel Velikovsky, gave rise to controversy in scientific and intellectual

---

[27] Ibid.

circles about scientific theories and the sociology of science. Dr. Velikovsky's historical and cosmological concepts, bolstered by his acknowledged scholarship, constituted a formidable assault on certain established theories of astronomy, geology, and historical biology, and on the heroes of those sciences. Newton, himself, and Darwin were being challenged, and indeed the general orthodoxy of an ordered universe. . . .

What must be called the scientific establishment rose in arms, not only against the new Velikovsky theories but against the man himself. Efforts were made to block dissemination of Dr. Velikovsky's ideas, and even to punish supporters of his investigations. Universities, scientific societies, publishing houses, the popular press were approached and threatened; social pressures and professional sanctions were invoked to control public opinion. . . .

As it was, the "establishment" succeeded in building a wall of unfavorable sentiment around him: to thousands of scholars the name of Velikovsky bears the taint of fantasy, science-fiction, and publicity.

He could not be suppressed entirely. In the next years he published three more books. He carried on a large correspondence. And he was helped by a very few friends, and by a large general public composed of persons outside of the establishments of science. The probings of spacecraft tended to confirm—never to disprove—his arguments. Eventually the venomous aspects of the controversy, the efforts at suppression, the campaign of vilification loomed almost as large, in their consequences to science, as the original issue.[28]

Beginning in about 1950 with the publication of *Worlds in Collision*, the Velikovsky case continued into the 1960s, ebbing and flowing somewhat in accordance with the publication of Velikovsky's new manuscripts and the accusations and retorts of his critics. Although much of the argumentation was without basis (many of his ardent opponents proudly admitted that they had not read and did not intend to read his work), totally inaccurate, and unreasoned, there was reasoned opposition to his theories as well. Albert Einstein, for example, criticized Velikovsky's thesis but later offered to help Velikovsky arrange for experimentation which would help to validate or falsify it. Although Einstein continued to disagree with many of Velikovsky's ideas, he recognized the increasingly favorable evidence that was then becoming available. Many other colleagues were considerably less gracious, and some of the most unscholarly, strident opposition came from scientists of otherwise high repute. A group of

[28] *The Velikovsky Affair*, pp. 1–2.

these scholars worked to close the scholarly channels of communication to Velikovsky and went so far as to threaten Velikovsky's publisher with academic boycott. Because the normal channels for the dissemination of scientific results were closed to Velikovsky, much of his work appeared in the popular press; this did not further endear him to the scholarly community.

The nature of Velikovsky's work, his thesis, and the methodology and sources he used appeared to call up the prejudices of the scientific community as well. By using a wide variety of sources including literature, mythology, cosmic and ancient political history, and archaeology, Velikovsky had come to the conclusion that there had been a series of catastrophes on earth and in the solar system. As Larrabee noted, Velikovsky broke down the disciplinary boundaries of scholarship in reaching and substantiating this thesis; this approach represented a fundamental threat to contemporary modes of scholarly inquiry.[29] Bruno de Finetti put the matter somewhat more bluntly:

> Scholars refused to discuss the merits of Velikovsky's studies because their attentions were diverted by a more personal issue —the fact that he challenged "the right of their fossilized brains to rest in peace" with the skills and problems already established.[30]

The Velikovsky case[31] is one of the most well documented instances in which many members of the scholarly community failed to live up to the ethics implied by the rationalist model. Strands of all the alternative models are apparent in this instance. Both the Kammerer and the Velikovsky cases demonstrate that scientific research is not always received in a totally open and impartial manner. The methodologies that scientists use, the credentials that they bring to their research, and the research topics themselves may influence the scientific reception process. According to Berkeley Rice, some lines of thought are more acceptable than others in academia.[32] This point was made quite clear in recent debate surrounding the work of Arthur Jensen and William Shockley. Both these men are involved in research on the relationship between race, intelligence, and heredity.

[29] Ibid., p. 56.
[30] Ibid., p. 133.
[31] For a current discussion of this case and recent evidence supporting Velikovsky's work see May 1972 special issue of *Pensee* (P.O. Box 414, Portland, Oreg., Student Academic Freedom Forum). *Pensee* has devoted a half-dozen subsequent issues to this controversy as well.
[32] Berkeley Rice, "The High Cost of Thinking the Unthinkable." Reprinted from *Psychology Today* Magazine, December 1973, 89–93. Copyright © 1973 Ziff-Davis Publishing Company. All rights reserved.

Their conclusions challenge some of the most cherished beliefs of liberals within the academic establishment as well as a number of basic assumptions underlying compensatory education programs.

THE JENSEN AND SHOCKLEY CASES

According to Berkeley Rice's discussion of this controversy,

> The turmoil began in 1969, when the *Harvard Educational Review* published an article entitled, "How Much Can We Boost IQ and Scholastic Achievement?," by Arthur Jensen, a respected educational psychologist at the University of California at Berkeley. . . . His article created a furor for several reasons: he presented evidence that blacks, as a group, score lower on IQ tests than whites; he suggested that heredity may have more effect than environment in determining intelligence, thereby rekindling the long-smoldering "nature-versus-nurture" controversy. . . .[33]

In the period following the publication of the *HER* article, Jensen's view were popularized in stories in *Time, Newsweek, Life,* and other popular, mass circulation magazines. Rice asserts that the popular press simplified the Jensen thesis and played up its controversial racial aspect; the result was that "tentative and qualified hypotheses became hard assertions." [34]

Response from the general public was immediate and heated. Letters to editorial offices denounced Jensen, compared him to Hitler, and urged various punishments "ranging from censure to hanging." [35] On the campus, Jensen was greeted with similar response. Rice indicates that Jensen

> found himself being denounced as a racist by liberal organizations and radical student groups. On the Berkeley campus, the Students for a Democratic Society held anti-Jensen rallies . . . and invaded his classes, forcing him to move seminars to secret meeting places. . . .
>
> Back in Cambridge, the *Harvard Educational Review* received a great deal of mail attacking Jensen and protesting publication of his article. . . . In a belated attempt to limit the furor

---

[33] Ibid., p. 89.
[34] Ibid.
[35] Ibid.

they had wrought, *HER*'s editors decided to halt sales of the Jensen article . . . until it could be sent out with reprints from the following . . . issue, which would contain rebuttals and comments.[36]

When portions of the academic community protested, the *Harvard Educational Review* reversed its position. In the meantime, the Society for the Psychological Study of Social Issues, a division of the American Psychological Association, issued a news release on the Jensen thesis calling its conclusions "unwarranted," but as Rice points out, the condemnation did not specifically indicate

the degree of knowledge that would warrant such views, or who would decide when the correct degree of knowledge had been attained. . . . The SPSSI statement went on to distort much of Jensen's article, and to deny several arguments he never made.[37]

A number of other individuals who have also written on the subject of race, heredity, and intelligence have received treatment similar to Jensen. William Shockley, Stanford physicist and Nobel Laureate, is one such individual. Though untrained in the area, Shockley acquired an interest in racial genetics. According to Rice, Shockley's position differed somewhat from Jensen's:

With a zeal that contrasts sharply with Jensen's cautious, detached approach, Shockley has launched a one-man crusade to warn the country of the evils of "dysgenics," a term he defines as "retrogressive evolution through the disproportionate reproduction of the genetically disadvantaged." Unlike Jensen, Shockley describes blacks as "genetically inferior," and . . . proposes a "bonus sterilization plan" under which blacks, as well as whites, with sufficiently low IQs would receive cash incentives if they agreed to sterilization.[38]

The reaction to Shockley's proposals was heated and abrupt. His classes were disrupted, and finally in the spring of 1972 Shockley's request to teach a regular university course on dysgenics became the focal point of the controversy. To decide the issue a special committee was appointed to advise the dean. By a close vote, the committee ultimately recommended that Shockley be allowed to teach the course, but only on a non-credit basis and only for one quarter. The dean overruled his committee, stating that Shockley's proposed course would be "polemical" and that his qualifications to teach it were subject to

[36] Ibid.
[37] Ibid., p. 90.
[38] Ibid., p. 91.

doubts. The committee itself appeared split on whether the real issue was the controversiality of the subject or the qualifications of Shockley.

Although the dispute focusing on Jensen and Shockley constitutes a single case historically, each man was subjected to substantially separate criticism. Shockley's credentials were called into doubt (he being a physicist, not a geneticist); but more importantly, critics condemned him because he became a self-appointed advocate for a policy about which evidence was inconclusive at best. The challenge to Shockley's qualifications does not of itself undermine his conclusions, but insofar as members of other branches of the scientific community and of the public at large often rely on the disciplinary authority of scientists as a result of their training, a measure of scepticism is justified. Otherwise, difficulty often arises in distinguishing the genius from the crackpot.

Shockley's position is further weakened by his advocacy of not only a "scientific conclusion" but also a particular social policy related to this conclusion. It is questionable whether scientists or other scholars should assume the position of advocate at all. But if we assume that advocacy is in some instances permissible, there are clearly questions that must be answered concerning the causes which such advocacy should serve, the circumstances in which it is desirable, and the degree of evidence which is required to "warrant" advocacy of a given conclusion. The scholarly community is often depicted as a guardian of humanitarian values. Shockley's advocacy of sterilization appears to many to be unhumanitarian, especially when the United States is suffering social tensions because of racial attitudes. Shockley's position appears socially dangerous in such volatile circumstances. Finally, the controversy within the scientific community itself raises questions about whether sufficient scientific evidence exists to warrant Shockley's advocacy of sterilization as a social policy.

The Jensen case raises more complicated problems. His treatment at the hands of the scientific and academic community clearly violates the canons of the rationalistic model. On the surface at least, his case resembles Velikovsky's; both had their publications affected and their views distorted. There is this important difference, however: critics were primarily challenging Velikovsky's "scientific" methodology. For Jensen, the research topic itself and its clash with prevailing values were important factors in explaining its reception by both the scientific establishment and the general public. His critics appear to demand a greater degree of evidential support to "warrant" unorthodox views, particularly if the position clashed with what is accepted by the scientific community and institutionalized in numerous public policies. The sense of "warrant" that is operative here, however, must mean something more than the use of the term in describing a justified but uncontroversial scientific conclusion. The added dimension reflects an ethical consideration that intrudes into the evaluation process itself. Jensen is said to be "unwarranted" in his conclusions[40] because the evidence he has provided is not sufficient to ethically justify his reaching conclusions that have such a direct connection to public policy.

All the preceding case studies question whether the scientific community in fact lives up to the canons of the rationalist model, and they indicate how ethical questions crop up in the evaluation process. They indicate, as Maslow points out, that:

> The path to truth is a rocky one. Full knowing is difficult. This is true not only for the layman but also for the scientist. The main difference between him and the layman is that he has enlisted in this search for truth deliberately, willingly, and consciously and that he then proceeds to learn as much as he can about the techniques and the ethics of truthseeking. Indeed, science in general can be considered a technique with which fallible men try to outwit their own human propensities to fear the truth, to avoid it, and to distort it.[39]

Scientists, as we have seen, do not always succeed in outwitting —or even in recognizing—their human foibles.

Fiduciary responsibility: the relationship between science and government

There is a long and interesting history of the problems surrounding the relationship between science and government, and the politics of science in general. A number of scholars assert that the conception of science as neutral is in itself a distinctly historical and political conception.

> The development of the Western scientific world view and the development of the commercial society proceeded hand-in-hand. Science took its peculiarly "neutral" form in order that it might survive and be allowed to pursue its research, and the Royal Society was allowed to form in London on the specific condition that it refrain from religious and political matters.[40]

The parameters of this neutrality have of course varied. Scientific research into religion, sex, evolution, and other sensitive subjects

---

[39] Abraham H. Maslow, *The Psychology of Science*, Henry Regnery Company, Chicago, 1969, p. 29.
[40] Ernest Becker, *The Structure of Evil*, George Braziller, New York, 1968, p. 275.

is no longer politically taboo in many countries of the world. These parameters also vary from nation to nation. T. N. Madan's fascinating case study, "Political Pressures and Ethical Constraints upon Indian Sociologists," [41] and Pierre L. van den Berghe's study, "Research in South Africa: The Story of My Experiences With Tyranny," [42] provide two interesting comments on varying national constraints. Similar examples could be found for almost any nation of the world.

Much of the literature on science and government is concerned with elucidating the potentialities of cooperation between science and government, with the problems attending current relationships, and with the purposes this relationship entails. As such, much of the literature is normative and prescriptive in intent.

A number of early scholars, such as Auguste Comte, saw the rise of science as a step toward a rationally ordered society, governed according to scientific principles and technology. Others observed that science could accompany, justify, and help maintain the most authoritarian of societies. The writings of Aldous Huxley, for example, suggest the multiple ends that scientific advances can serve.[43] Other social critics see the present political relationships between the scientific community and government as the source of contemporary problems. Speaking through one of his characters, Fred Hoyle comments:

> Politicians at the top, then the military, and the real brains at the bottom. . . . We're living in a society that contains a monstrous contradiction, modern in its technology but archaic in its social organization. . . . We [scientists] do the thinking for an archaic crowd of nitwits and allow ourselves to be pushed around by 'em in the bargain.[44]

It is of course debatable whether scientists are invariably located at the bottom of the pecking order, and some would also question the extent to which scientists are actually heeded, Don Price, for example, has argued that the scientific community has become something of an "estate" occupying an autonomous position in the political system outside the normal channels of political responsibility.[45] J. Bronowski, on the other hand, sees a growing entanglement of science and

---

[41] T. N. Madan, "Political Pressures and Ethical Constraints upon Indian Sociologists," in ed. Gideon Sjoberg, *Ethics, Politics and Social Research*, Schenkman Publishing Co., Cambridge, Mass., 1971, pp. 162–179.

[42] Pierre L. van den Berghe, "Research in South Africa: The Story of My Experiences with Tyranny," in *Ethics, Politics and Social Research*, pp. 183–197.

[43] Contrast, for example, Huxley's later work *Island*, Harper & Row, Publishers, New York, 1972, with *Brave New World*, Bantam Books, New York, 1958.

[44] Fred Hoyle, *The Black Cloud*, New American Library, New York, 1959, p. 87.

[45] Don K. Price, *The Scientific Estate*, Oxford University Press, London, 1968.

politics and a need for the "disestablishment of science."[46] Bronowski argues for the development of moral responsibility within the scientific community commensurate with its increasingly important role in society. In a similar vein, Floyd Matson contends that the "broken image" of the relations among human beings, science, and society must be mended, and science enlisted in the cause of humanity.[47]

While there have been a number of attempts to develop a consensus within the scientific community regarding their responsibility for their work, most scholarly communities are extremely wary of attempts to politicize their organizations.[48] Bronowski notes, for example, that in 1939 Leo Szilard sent a letter to atomic physicists suggesting a voluntary moratorium on new information regarding uranium fusion to forestall any misuse of this information. This moratorium did not crystallize; nor does it appear likely today.

The sensitive account of what the relationship between science and government *should be* must reflect an awareness of current constraints if it is not to be hopelessly naive. These constraints must be taken into account in any discussion of what scientific responsibility is or is not. While individuals may debate endlessly on the definition of the possible, few would hold an individual or group responsible for failing to undertake the impossible. The last few pages of this chapter, we hope, will help to spell out the constraints that affect the relationship between science and government.

One complicating factor in the relation between government and the scientific community is that the two operate to a considerable extent on the basis of different needs and premises. Any student of the political process should be aware that elected officials operate under considerably different pressures, precedents, and premises than does the scientific community. These differences in perspective suggest that governmental relations with the scientific community will raise a number of problems and potential conflicts. There is, for example, a temporal difference between the vistas of politicians and scientists. This factor can help to explain governmental preference for applied over basic research and for relatively short-term projects; there is obviously little political pay-off in a project that comes to fruition twenty years after its instigator leaves office. Unfortunately, many problems cannot be resolved in this short-run fashion. A number of

---

[46] J. Bronowski, "The Disestablishment of Science: I and II," *The New York Times* (Oct. 18, 19, 1971), pp. 37, 43.

[47] Floyd W. Matson, *The Broken Image*, Anchor Books, Garden City, N.Y., 1966.

[48] The McCarthy period in the United States apparently contributed to this caution. For an excellent discussion of this aspect see M. P. Rogin, *The Intellectuals and McCarthy: The Radical Spector*, The M.I.T. Press, Cambridge, Mass., 1967.

critics argue that governmental agencies often terminate programs prematurely.[49] Too frequently, the symptoms of a problem are treated rather than its cause simply because of political expedience. The electoral mechanism, it is argued, reinforces the short-range perspective of politicians. A variety of other structural factors can also raise difficulties in implementing, executing, and developing policy-relevant scientific knowledge. The decentralized nature of American political parties, the federal structure of government, the separation of powers, and other factors contribute to the fragmentary nature of policy responses. Thus scientific conclusions are frequently at variance with institutional constraints.

Problems between government and science also arise from the increasingly complex network of interdependence between the two. Government interacts with the scientific community at a variety of levels. Governmental relations begin with the legal and statutory context they establish for institutions of education, but the financial context of educational teaching and research operates in a multiple governmental matrix in both direct and indirect ways. For example, the government interacts fairly directly with the scientific community through its own research and development programs. In some cases, governmental research monies are allocated to scholars after the given agency has essentially developed the research design; in other cases, individuals are granted funding on the basis of their own design. A variety of different institutions perform the actual execution of various governmental projects—some are fairly autonomous of governmental agencies, some are semi-autonomous, and others are directly within governmental agencies and departments. In spite of disclaimers to the contrary, there does appear to be a feeling among university scholars that the university setting provides a degree of independence from political constraints and prejudices that is not available in research units which are more directly dependent upon governmental agencies. On the other hand, the past decade has witnessed considerable reaction—at least among students—against government-funded research at universities. To an extent, much current debate involves two separate but confounding issues: should some existing research be undertaken at all; and if so, what is the best locus for such research? Unfortunately, the problem of governmental involvement in scientific research is difficult to resolve. While many large-scale research projects cannot be undertaken without governmental support, such support raises problems of considerable import. Can scientists satisfactorily combine the ethical canons of scientific method with

[49] For case studies relevant to this point see *Social Science and National Policy*, ed. Fred Harris; and *The Values of Social Science*, ed. Norman K. Denzin (both Transaction Books, 1970); and *Ethics, Politics and Social Research*, ed. Gideon Sjoberg, Schenkman Publishing Co., Cambridge, Mass., 1967.

the political demands of various governmental missions? Does not governmental funding raise the possibility of censorship and control on nonscientific grounds?

The following case study highlights some problems associated with government-sponsored research. While the publicity surrounding Project Camelot makes it somewhat atypical, the problems it raises are by no means unique.

PROJECT CAMELOT

Project Camelot was a large-scale social science research project sponsored by the United States Army in 1965. It aimed to measure and forecast the causes of revolution in underdeveloped parts of the world, hopefully to yield information that would help eliminate the revolutions and insurgencies endemic to underdeveloped countries. The project was cancelled abruptly in its initial developmental stages when it became a hot political issue in certain Latin American countries and within various governmental agencies in the United States. Chile and other Latin American nations became concerned about how information generated by Project Camelot might be used, and there was general concern about the possible implications of army sponsorship of a project of this type. Was the project actually a legitimate research project, or was it a cover for army planning overseas?

In his excellent summary of the controversy Irving Louis Horowitz discusses the motivations of the men and women working on Project Camelot.[50] His collective portrait is that of individuals committed to their profession and to the social relevance of their work. Although the staff had some misgivings about military sponsorship, there was widespread recognition of the need for a large-scale project of this type. Only government sponsorship provided ample funding for an investigation of this size. The professional staff was also highly idealistic according to Horowitz. They saw themselves as playing an important role in preventing destructive revolutions.

Others were less sanguine about Project Camelot. A number of critics expressed misgivings on scientific and ethical grounds, but the project's termination was primarily the result of political considerations. The project opened a full-scale rift between the State Department and the Department of Defense about who had ultimate authority in foreign affairs. The United States Congress said little about the scientific merit of the project and appeared primarily interested in ensuring the current equilibrium in foreign alliances.

[50] Irving Louis Horowitz, "Life and Death of Project Camelot," *Transaction*, 3 (Nov./Dec. 1965), 3–7, 44–47.

Academics, on the other hand, reacted with prejudice and institutional jealousy and argued that research was best left to universities, where it would be free from political ties and influences.

Ultimately, Project Camelot was cancelled under presidential directive. In its wake it left suspicion in Latin America, diminishing research monies for social science research, intragovernmental hostility, and indications of growing governmental censorship. Horowitz contends that the "cancellation came as an act of government censorship, and an expression of the contempt for social science so prevalent among those who need it most." [51] He warns that such cases destroy science and foretell of times when science will serve to satisfy the "policy needs—or failures—of the moment." [52]

Review questions and exercises

1   Explain the meaning and significance of the following terms:

    a   Fiduciary responsibility
    b   Subjective role
    c   Prescribed role
    d   Scientific reception systems
    e   The rationalist model
    f   The power model
    g   The indeterminancy model
    h   The dogmatic model

2   Critically analyze the quotations by Park and Bierstedt at the beginning of the chapter.

3   In Chapter 2 the *context of discovery* was distinguished from the *context of justification*. The former is considered the proper subject of the psychology or sociology of science, while the latter is the basis on which conclusions are to be evaluated. On the basis of the case studies outlined in this chapter, discuss whether the two contexts can be sharply separated.

4   What would you suggest as appropriate standards or guidelines for determining "acceptable" research methods and techniques? How might these be institutionalized? What factors might make this institutionalization difficult?

5   There is much controversy about using prisoners for medical and pharmaceutical research. Survey the major arguments supporting and opposing this practice and indicate the major ethical questions that arise.

[51] Ibid.
[52] Ibid.

6   Critically analyze the canons of the rationalist model suggested by Blisset. Are they at all inconsistent? Are they psychologically naive?

7   Do the considerations raised in this chapter make the idea of objectivity in science impossible? Why or why not?

"I only wanted to see what the garden was like, your Majesty—"

"That's right," said the Queen, patting her on the head, which Alice didn't like at all: "though, when you say 'garden'—I've seen gardens, compared with which this would be a wilderness."

Alice didn't dare to argue the point, but went on: "and I thought I'd try and find my way to the top of that hill—"

"When you say 'hill,'" the Queen interrupted, "I could show you hills, in comparison with which you'd call that a valley."

"No, I shouldn't," said Alice, surprised into contradicting her at last: "a hill can't be a valley, you know. That would be nonsense—"

The Red Queen shook her head. "You may call it nonsense if you like," she said, "but I've heard nonsense, compared with which that would be as sensible as a dictionary!"

Lewis Carroll, from
Through the Looking Glass

4
SOCIAL MEASUREMENT
AND RESEARCH DESIGN

One major reason why scientific method is considered an optimal procedural base for social research is that it provides guidelines for establishing criteria by which reality may be conceived and explained with the smallest amount of disagreement. What Alice and the Red Queen lack in their interchange is precisely this basis, and the result is that they continually talk past one another. Their dispute in part is definitional; they cannot agree on common meanings of such terms as "hill," "garden," and "wilderness." Obviously a set of definitions is needed that will establish criteria for judging reality on a more common basis. In the parlance of scientific method, what they require is a set of operational definitions that make adjudication of every future perception unnecessary. As it stands, meaning is hopelessly idiosyncratic for Alice and the Red Queen, and the Red Queen clearly recognizes its conditional nature. The debate between the Red Queen and Alice suggests that meaningful communication is possible only if both parties agree in the application of language in straightforward observational situations. Common meanings are obviously crucially important. Without them, discourse is impossible.

In recent years social scientists have become highly aware of the difficult problems arising from the conditional nature of meaning. The questions of whether a concept adequately reflects the properties of the object that it purports to reflect and how one justifies a given label or measure have received much attention. Although the problem of meaning is of continual philosophical interest,[1] the practical solution that most social researchers have reached is to demand precision in definition and explicit delineation of the criteria underlying the application of a given term.[2] These scientists demand precise operational definitions.

---

[1] See, for example, Israel Scheffler, *Science and Subjectivity*, The Bobbs-Merrill Company, Indianapolis, 1967.
[2] See, for example, Arnold Brecht, *Political Theory: The Foundations of Twentieth Century Political Thought*, Princeton University Press, Princeton, N.J., 1967, especially pp. 1–117.

Measurement and operationalism

OPERATIONAL DEFINITIONS: CHARACTERIZED

As you might imagine from our discussion of the debate between the Red Queen and Alice, the concerns of operationalism lie at the point of contact between our theoretical concepts and the empirical world. Both Alice and the Red Queen obviously have some general notion about what constitutes "hills" and "valleys," "a garden" and "a wilderness" (we could call this an informal theory); but they do not agree either in the verbal explication they give of these concepts nor in whether a particular entity constitutes a "hill" or a "valley."

To avoid this type of confusion, some scientists and philosophers of science recommend that all concepts employed in scientific theories be connected with observational tests that describe operations for precisely determining whether a given object falls under the concept or not. Operationalizing a concept or giving it an operational definition simply means providing a set of instructions to indicate exactly how you propose to measure, label, or otherwise designate a given concept. The operational definition can be regarded as a recipe or set of instructions. The key properties of properly framed operational definitions are that they add precision to concepts and make them publicly testable; this makes replication possible.

If Alice had indicated she was designating as a "hill" any land mass rising at an angle greater than 25° to a height of at least 30 feet above the surrounding terrain, then the Red Queen would have known more exactly what Alice meant when she referred to a hill. Furthermore, such a characterization suggests a method of directly testing whether an object is a hill, namely, by measuring its height and the angle of its sides. To offer such an operational definition does not foreclose all controversy—Alice and the Red Queen might still disagree about the choice of this particular operational definition—but the Red Queen would at least be able to see how Alice arrived at the conclusion that the given entity was a hill.

Proponents of operationalism differ on how to interpret the fundamental operationalist principle that the terms of a scientific theory must have operational definitions.[3] In its strongest form, oper-

---

[3] The discussion of operationalism among social scientists can be traced back to the work of the physicist and philosopher of science, P. W. Bridgeman, *The Logic of Modern Physics*, The Macmillan Company, New York, 1972; also "Operational Analysis," *Philosophy of Science*, 5 (April 1938), 114–131. A discussion of the history of this debate among philosophers of science can be found in Carl G. Hempel, "Operationism, Observation, and Theoretical Terms," in *Philosophy of Science*, eds. Arthur Danto and Sidney Morgenbesser, Meridian Books, 1960, pp. 101–120; and Frederick Suppe, *The Structure of Scientific Theories*, University of Illinois Press, Urbana, Ill., 1974, pp. 3–241.

ationalism demands that *every* theoretical concept be directly operationalized and that each testing operation be related to a *separate*
theoretical concept. Critics have pointed out that this requirement is
too simple (and demanding) to become actual accepted scientific practice. As a consequence, philosophers and many practitioners of natural
and social science have given up the demand for operational definitions
in this form.

It is more common to have operationalism characterized as the
demand that at least *some* concepts in a scientific theory can be connected, either directly or indirectly, to an operation or empirical test,
while at the same time recognizing that the most interesting concepts
in a scientific theory are susceptible to multiple tests and can be
operationalized in several ways. So construed, operational definitions
need not be true definitions. That is, they need not provide necessary
and sufficient conditions for the application of a theoretical term;
instead they may be treated as partial definitions.

As we pointed out in Chapter 2, some theoretical terms have
clearer (in the sense of generally recognized) operational definitions
than others. It is easier, for example, to come up with a generally
accepted way of operationally defining and measuring "temperature"
than "legitimacy." [4] Similarly, it is perhaps easier to operationally
define an individual's "partisan identification" than his or her feeling
of "political efficacy."

One reason why concepts vary in clarity of operational definitions is because they differ in susceptibility to direct measurement.
With many concepts, indirect indicators are needed, and some indirect
indicators are more indirect than others. There is substantial disagreement among social scientists and particularly among psychologists, over the relative merits of different indicators of behavior and
attitudes. Some researchers prefer to deal only with concepts for
which easily quantified direct indicators are readily available. [5] The
beauty of direct measures is that they require less inference to determine their "meaning."

In cases where indicators are indirect, a scientist often employs
(or presupposes) an auxiliary theory separate from the main theory
to support the use of these indicators. This is most obvious when
physical measuring instruments are used.

---

[4] Even the operations used for determining temperature have their limitations.
Used as an instrument for measuring temperature, the human body has a very
limited range and is not very precise. Even more precise instruments like the
mercury thermometer have a limited range of application. These limitations
become particularly obvious when we think of possible tests (operations)
adequate for determining the "temperature" at the point of atomic fusion
reactions in the interior of stars. See Martin K. Barnett, "The Development of
Thermometry and the Temperature Concept," *Osiris*, XII (1956), 269–341.

[5] Behaviorism in psychology is especially noted for this position.

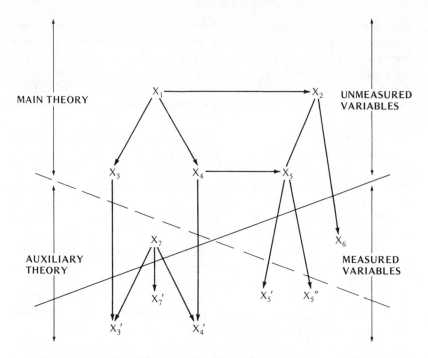

Figure 4-1 Model involving distinctions between (1) main and auxiliary theories and (2) measured and unmeasured variables

Source: Hubert M. Blalock, Jr., "The Measurement Problem: A Gap between the Languages of Theory and Research," in *Methodology in Social Research,* eds. Hubert Blalock, Jr., and Ann Blalock, p. 25. Copyright 1968 McGraw-Hill Book Company. Used with permission of McGraw-Hill Book Company.

The role of operational definitions and theories is illustrated in an informative way by Hubert Blalock in Figure 4-1.[6] This diagram indicates a pattern of interrelationships among possible concepts or variables, $x_1, x_2, \ldots$. The variables or concepts at the top of the diagram represent elements in a scientific theory that are connected to each other as suggested by arrows. They are separated by the dashed line from more observable concepts or variables falling below the line. This distinction roughly corresponds to the distinction between variables that can be directly tested or measured and variables that cannot be measured directly or cannot be measured at all. Cutting across this distinction is the distinction between those concepts or variables within the main theory (above the dashed line) and those in the auxiliary theory (below the dashed line).

[6] Hubert Blalock, "The Measurement Problem: A Gap between the Languages of Theory and Research," in *Methodology in Social Research,* eds. Hubert Blalock and Ann Blalock, McGraw-Hill Book Company, New York, 1968, p. 25.

Figure 4-1 illustrates a number of the possible techniques of operationalization:

1   A variable in a theory, such as x_6, might be directly measurable.
2   It may be connected by an operational definition to a variable that is directly measured, for example, x_2.
3   It may be defined in terms of two or more separate measurable variables connected to each other as part of an auxiliary theory (x_5).
4   It may be defined in terms of a variable that is itself part of an auxiliary theory (x_3 and x_4).
5   It may not be operationalized at all, and only be defined within the theory (x_1). When physical scientists, for example, use an ammeter to measure amperage, they are making certain presuppositions about the operation (not only of the particular instrument used) and, more importantly, about measuring devices of that kind.

OPERATIONAL DEFINITIONS: QUALITATIVE AND QUANTITATIVE MEASURES

Operational definitions can be thought of as yielding qualitative or quantitative measurement. Falco argues that "the distinction between quality and quantity is the difference between different levels of operationalization and measurement—of more or less meaning." [7] She argues that the two should be thought of as lying on a continuum:

> Concepts at the qualitative end of the continuum are vague, more complex, perhaps, but harder to measure, and hence less "meaningful" than those at the quantitative end. Qualities may not be any less abstract than quantities but we are less certain of their meaning. In some ways they may be closer to the "inchoateness" or "ineffableness" of raw experience than they are to the precision and clarity of knowledge. We have not yet agreed upon the indicators to be used and the scales or indexes to be devised by which to operationalize and measure them. [8]

Classification schemes abound in social science, and many are cast in the form of qualitative measures. Max Weber, for example, provided a typology for the various bases of legitimacy in a political system: charismatic, traditional, and rational-legalistic. To the extent

---

[7] Maria J. Falco, *Truth and Meaning in Political Science: An Introduction to Political Inquiry,* Charles E. Merrill Books, Columbus, 1973, p. 78.
[8] Ibid., p. 79.

that these general categories are not more specifically operationalized, we have a qualitative measure of "legitimacy." Classification schemes vary, however, and some are more quantitative than others. Weber's typology could be cast in terms that require less individual judgment in placing a given system in one category or another by giving more precise meaning to "charismatic," "traditional," and "rational-legalistic." The scheme would be more "meaningful" if we could establish a metric for the various categories.

OPERATIONAL DEFINITIONS AND VARYING LEVELS OF MEASUREMENT

Extending our discussion of the distinction between qualitative and quantitative measurement, we can further distinguish among quantitatively measured variables. When we measure something, we assign labels or numerals to it according to the rules provided by the operational definition.[9] Operational definitions search for systems that "can do three kinds of things: name, order, and specify intervals."[10] Qualitative measures normally provide only names, sometimes order, but, infrequently, intervals.

Characteristically, when we set up a measurement scale as part of a research design, we attach numbers to observable items so that relationships between numbers on our scale correspond to (or parallel) empirical relationships observed between these items.[11] Since a primary consideration in choosing an operational definition is that it provide a meaningful means of locating the object or event relative to others, the more precisely it does so, the better (more meaningful) it is. A researcher must thus ask, "Does the operational definition and prescribed measurement process enable me to interpret the object as fitting or not fitting a given categorization or as high, medium or low on a given property?" There are various levels of measurement in this respect.

The *nominal level of measurement* provides only discrete cat-

[9] E. Terrence Jones, *Conducting Political Research*, Harper & Row, Publishers, New York, 1971, p. 30.
[10] Ibid., p. 33
[11] The classic paper on measurement and a source for much of the subsequent discussion is Patrick Suppes and Joseph L. Zinnes, "Basic Measurement Theory," in *Handbook of Mathematical Psychology*, vol. I, eds. R. D. Luce, Robert Bush, Eugene Galanter, John Wiley & Sons, New York, 1963. More recent discussion can be found in Blalock, "The Measurement Problem," pp. 5–27; and Clyde Coombs, Robyn Dawes, and Amos Tversky, *Mathematical Psychology*, Prentice-Hall, Englewood Cliffs, N.J., especially chap. 1.

egories and constitutes the simplest measurement. Dividing political systems into democratic/nondemocratic, partisan affiliations into Republican/Democrat, or race into white/nonwhite would constitute a nominal measurement of the variables race, partisan identification, and type of political system. There is no metric or order in nominal data—simply categories.

The *ordinal level of measurement* categorizes *and* orders. Sometimes ostensibly nominal data can be treated as ordinal data. If you were to argue, for example, that an ideological ordering is attached to the partisan categories of Democrat and Republican, you could argue that ordering also exists in the data and that the individuals could be ordered as well as categorized along a liberal/conservative dimension. The more-than and less-than ordering notion is the essential ingredient of the ordinal level. Because the ordinal level goes beyond mere categorization, it is considered a higher and more meaningful level of measurement; it yields more precise information than nominal categorization. But although ordinal measurements yield a rough ordering, they lack a precise metric. We cannot, for example, assume that a liberal Republican is *twice* as liberal as a conservative Republican; all we can say is that a liberal Republican is more liberal than a conservative Republican.

The *interval level of measurement* is characterized by a precise and constant metric or interval.[12] Since the interval is constant, the difference between different points can be determined. Age, weight, height, and income form natural interval scales. Mathematically, we can say precisely what the difference is between someone earning $5,000 and $10,000. Similarly, education can be considered to be an interval measurement. Although the question can be asked whether a person with four grades of education has twice as much knowledge as a person with two grades, the important point is that mathematically 4 is twice as much as 2. From a statistical point of view, the interval level of measurement is the most desirable. Mathematical statisticians have developed powerful techniques to use with interval-level data.

Thus, operational definitions vary in terms of "meaningfulness" and precision. The qualitative-quantitative distinctions touch on one difference, and the varying levels of measurements attained touch a related distinction. Operational definitions also vary in how they are derived. As we pointed out before, some operational definitions are based upon more direct indicators than others. The procedures by which they are derived often influence their overall adequacy and meaningfulness.

---

[12] The ratio scale actually provides the highest level of measurement. The ratio scale involves interval-level data with a standardized zero point. Ratio scales are rare in social science.

OPERATIONAL DEFINITIONS: CLASSIFIED BY
DERIVATION PROCEDURES

Cook and Selltiz distinguish five different types of measurement that
have been used as a basis for making inferences about attitudes:

1   Measures in which the material from which inferences are drawn
     consists of self reports of beliefs, feelings, behavior, etc., toward
     an object or class of objects
2   Measures in which inferences are drawn from overt behavior
     toward an object
3   Measures in which inferences are drawn from the individual's
     reactions to, or interpretation of, partially structured material
     relevant to the object
4   Measures in which inferences are drawn from performance on
     objective tasks where functioning may be influenced by disposi-
     tion toward the object
5   Measures in which inferences are drawn from physiological
     reactions to the object.[13]

1   Self-reports probably constitute the most commonly employed
means of ascertaining individual attitudes. Questionnaires are a type
of self-report. When this procedure is used, it is assumed that the self-
report is a valid indicator of the attitude. Thus, to operationally define
people's partisan orientations, we might simply ask them to fill out
questionnaires and define themselves in partisan orientation. Similarly, we could ask them whether they are prejudiced and to
what degree.

It is also the major problem with self-reports appears to be the tendency
of respondents to attempt to present a favorable image of themselves
and to respond in a socially desirable way. Individuals who are prejudiced against blacks, for example, might not admit their prejudice
because they feel this attitude is at variance with prevailing social and
cultural mores. In this circumstance, the self-report may not provide
an accurate indication of attitude because the individual is responding
to the questions on the basis of extraneous factors. While sophisticated
questionnaire design procedures may lessen the likelihood of response
on extraneous grounds, the problem of inferring the coincidence of
the self-report with the real attitude remains.

It is also questionable whether reported attitudes coincide with
real behavior. While theoretically related, there is no necessary coincidence. La Piere's early study on the discrepancy between the actual

---

[13] Stuart Cook and Claire Selltiz. "A Multiple-indicator Approach to Measurement," in *Attitude Measurement*, ed. Gene Summers, Rand McNally & Company,
Chicago, pp. 25–26.

behavior of motel owners and their reported response to a questionnaire as to whether they would accept Chinese guests is a classic investigation of this question.[14]

2   Because self-reports are not necessarily accurate indicators of
attitudes and behavior, some have argued that it is preferable to rely
upon observations of overt behavior. As Cook and Selltiz point out,
three approaches have been used to develop behavioral measures
of attitude.[15]

First, staged situations are sometimes created in which subjects
are led to believe that they are participating in a situation unrelated
to the actual attitude being studied.

> For example, subjects may be asked to sign a petition on behalf
> of an instructor about to be discharged for membership in the
> Communist party, to contribute money for the improvement
> of conditions for migratory workers, [or] to indicate whether
> they would be willing to have a Negro roommate.[16]

Second, subjects have been asked to participate in admittedly
staged situations where they play a certain role. The role-playing
situation is structured to elicit information about the relevant attitude
on the basis of participants' performances.

Third, attitudes have been inferred from choice situations involving factors relevant to the attitude being studied:

> Early applications of this technique to the study of intergroup
> attitudes were made in studies by Moreno . . . and Criswell . . . in
> which patterns of choices by school children were analyzed in
> terms of development of cleavage along racial lines.[17]

3   A third type of attitude measure infers attitude from subjects'
responses to partially structured material presented in an impersonal
context. Subjects may be asked to describe something—a scene, a third
person, an instance of certain behavior. The subjects' attitudes are
inferred from the description they give. Most projective techniques
rely upon this procedure. It is assumed that depersonalizing the situation will result in less distortion and less desire to present a favorable
image of oneself.

4   Attitudes can also be inferred from how a task is performed. For
example, we know that people most readily receive and remember
information congenial to their own attitudes. A researcher might then

[14] R. T. La Piere, "Attitudes vs. Actions," *Social Forces*, 14 (1934), 230–237.
[15] Cook and Selltiz, "A Multiple-indicator Approach . . . ," pp. 30–31.
[16] Ibid., p. 30.
[17] Ibid., p. 31.

ask subjects to memorize some material and then assess their retention. Memory retention is then taken as an indication of the subjects' own attitudes. Similarly, people could be asked to listen to a political speech that contains favorable and unfavorable material on a candidate, and retention could be taken as an indication of the subjects' attitudes toward the candidate. A variety of tasks could be constructed to indirectly measure subjects' attitudes.

5 Finally, attitudes can be directly inferred from physiological responses. Because physiological responses are not subject to conscious control, they have been regarded as least subject to distortion. Lie detector tests are an example of this technique. They are based upon physiological responses such as changes in pulse rate, galvanic skin response, and vascular constriction.

For purposes of social research, physiological responses can be measured to any verbal or nonverbal stimuli.[18] Unfortunately, there is now considerable evidence that physiological response measures can be effectively employed to measure arousal, interest, and attentiveness, but they do not effectively distinguish positive or negative affective states. Thus, while we could measure arousal from a subject's physiological responses to a candidate's picture for example, we could not determine whether the subject was positively or negatively disposed toward the candidate.

With various derivation procedures available, the obvious question is "Which procedure yields the most meaningful measure?" A good measure of a variable is obviously one that reflects the property which it purports to reflect. But, as we have seen, there are often numerous ways of measuring a variable. We choose one procedure over another on the assumption that it better reflects the variable and therefore is more adequate. Although the question of adequacy can never be answered definitively, some measures are obviously better than others. The self-report technique is considered inadequate because it often is subject to response bias and distortion. As such, self-reports frequently constitute *reactive measures.*[19] Reactivity is commonly regarded as one major source of measurement error. Since reactivity stems from the measurement procedure itself, it may be difficult to control. Measurements based upon physiological responses, by contrast, are not highly reactive in this sense. Unfortunately, they suffer

[18] See, for example, Robert E. Rankin and Donald T. Campbell, "Galvanic Skin Response to Negro and White Experimenters," *Journal of Abnormal and Social Psychology,* 51 (1955), 30–33; and Daniel J. Mueller, "Physiological Techniques of Attitude Measurement," in Summers, *Attitude Measurement,* pp. 534–552.
[19] E. J. Webb, D. T. Campbell, R. D. Schwartz, and L. Sechrist, *Unobtrusive Measures: Nonreactive Research in the Social Sciences,* Rand McNally & Company, Chicago, 1970.

from an inability to readily differentiate negative and positive affective orientations.

In recent years a variety of measurement procedures have become available, and each has its strengths and weaknesses. No single method is invariably superior. At the same time, we would agree with Boring that multiple measures are better than single measures. In 1953 he wrote:

> As long as a new construct has only the single operational definition that it received at birth, it is just a construct. When it gets two alternative operational definitions, it is beginning to be validated. When the defining operations, because of proven correlations, are many, then it becomes reified.[20]

Webb argues that the most "persuasive evidence and the strongest inference comes from a triangulation of measurement process." [21] A variety of scholars now suggest that the appropriate strategy is one of *methodological triangulation*. Multimethod operational definitions are an important component. "The combination of multiple methods, data types, observers and theories in the same investigation is termed multiple triangulation." [22]

The call for multiple triangulation is a plea for more sophisticated research methodology with more valid and reliable results as its goals. In the next section we shall discuss the two major considerations in assessing the adequacy of a given measure—reliability and validity.

Reliability and validity

Although researchers enjoy wide latitude in the choice of operational definitions and measurement procedures, they should demonstrate the procedure's adequacy. They do so by indicating the measure's reliability and validity.

First, researchers must ask whether the procedures they employ are repeatable, whether they will yield similar readings on repeated applications. This consideration is the question of *reliability*.[23] Secondly, they must ask, "Does the measurement procedure reflect

---

[20] E. G. Boring, "The Role of Theory in Experimental Psychology," *American Journal of Psychology*, 66 (1953), 169–184.

[21] Eugene Webb, "Unconventionality, Triangulation, and Influence," in *Sociological Methods: A Sourcebook*, ed. Norman Denzin, Aldine Publishing Company, Chicago, 1972, p. 450.

[22] Ibid., p. 472.

[23] Jum C. Nunnally, Jr., offers a good discussion of reliability in *Tests and Measurements: Assessment and Prediction*, McGraw-Hill Book Company, New York, 1959.

the properties and relations that it purports to reflect?" This is the question of *validity*.[24] The question of validity most properly arises when two different measurable variables are in question. In such a case, questions about validity can be converted into questions about the correlation between these two variables. Such a correlation exists (roughly) in the case of measuring temperature by means of felt heat, a mercury thermometer, and a properly instrumented thermocouple. If in a theory we were to have an isolated variable that was not itself directly measured and was operationalized in terms of a single variable, questions of validity arise only in terms of potential alternative operationalizations which may be applied in the future. There is no direct way to examine whether such a theoretical concept applies without asking whether the observational term that operationally defines it applies. Thus, there is no question in this degenerate case of whether this measure is valid. The case is special and unusual because it is characteristic of concepts in a scientific theory that they can be measured at least potentially by more than one means, introducing again questions of validity.

A large number of procedures are available for determining the reliability and validity of a measure, and we shall cover only some more common measures here.[25] Other reliability and validity measures are discussed later in the text.

If measurement procedures aim at adequately defining and locating relevant characteristics of the entity they purport to describe, they must obviously do so on a continuing basis. To be effective, a given measure of "partisan identification" must continually and repeatedly differentiate proponents of the various parties. General synonyms for reliability are "dependability, stability, consistency, predictability, accuracy." [26] Two distinct elements of reliability are *stability* and *dimensionality*.

"In dimensionality, the concern is with the purity of the measure: is a single property expressed in the scores resulting from the measure-

---

[24] See Fred Kerlinger, *Foundations of Behavioral Research*, 2d. ed., Holt, Rinehart and Winston, New York, 1973, for an extended discussion of validity.

[25] See, for example, James A. Wiggins, "Hypothesis Validity and Experimental Laboratory Methods," in *Methodology in Social Research*, eds. H. Blalock and A. Blalock, McGraw-Hill Book Company, New York, 1968, pp. 390–427; C. Selltiz, M. Jahoda, M. Deutsch, and S. Cook, *Research Methods in Social Relations*, Holt, Rinehart and Winston, New York, 1959, chap. 5; Murray Sidmar, *Tactics of Scientific Research*, Basic Books, New York, 1960, chap. 1–6; Jum C. Nunnally, Jr., *Tests and Measurements*, chap. 4–6; *Research Methods in the Behavioral Sciences*, eds. L. Festinger and D. Katz, The Dryden Press, New York, 1953; Brent Rutherford, "Dilemmas in Construct Validation: An Integration of Measurement Criteria in Political Science," paper delivered at the 1970 annual meeting of the Midwest Political Science Association.

[26] F. N. Kerlinger, *Foundations of Behavioral Research*, Holt, Rinehart and Winston, New York, 1964, p. 429.

ment process?" [27] Later, in Chapter 7, we discuss Guttman scalogram analysis, which is directed specifically toward answering this question of dimensionality. The need for considering dimensionality is rather obvious if you recall that the basic purpose of measurement is to develop adequate means of *defining* concepts and variables. When a given measure lacks dimensionality, it is difficult to interpret, and its meaning is unclear.

Dimensionality is sometimes determined by the congruency of several indicators, the extent to which they measure the same thing. In this case a variety of different indices of the same variable are employed and reliability is assumed if they prove to be largely redundant in effect. *Internal consistency* is the test here. If we were interested in establishing the reliability of a given measure of partisan identification, for example, we could use a number of indicators. We could ask individuals about their partisan identification (the self-report), their voting intentions (self-report), their previous presidential vote (self-report behavior); or we might use any combination of measurement procedures discussed in the last section of this chapter. Together these questions provide a multiple set of measurements for gauging partisan affiliation.

Stability is another consideration of reliability, for we are interested in employing measures that reflect the constancy of the property they purport to measure over time.[28] There are several ways to assess a measure's reliability from the standpoint of stability. One means is simply to readminister it at different points in time; this is called the *test-retest procedure*. Consistency in response is the crucial factor here. If responses are highly similar, we can assume that the measure is reliable from the standpoint of stability. Unfortunately, we must also assume that circumstances have not changed which might also account for changes in response. Test-retest procedures are thus useful *only* when we can assume that circumstances have not changed. The test-retest procedure essentially measures the constancy of a measure over time on a single individual. The constancy of a measure across judges is another measure of reliability from the standpoint of stability.

While reliability is a necessary component of validity, a reliable measure is not necessarily valid. Validity, you will recall, has to do with whether an indicator actually reflects the property that it purports to reflect. The question of validity asks, "Is a given measure or indicator an accurate measure of the concept?" When we use indirect indicators rather than direct measures, the question of validity becomes very important, and this is the rule rather than the exception in social science. As we pointed out in Chapter 2, the conclusion "Fido salivated

[27] Rutherford, "Dilemmas in Construct Validation . . . ," p. 11.
[28] Ibid., pp. 11–12.

when he heard the bell" would pose no great problem from the standpoint of validity because direct measures of the "ringing of the bell" and the "salivation of Fido" can be provided. More frequently, we employ indicators or indirect measures of a phenomena, and then the problem of validity is important. When we ask subjects a question about their attitudes toward school segregation, we want to know their *real* attitudes; and when we ask them whether they voted for the President in the previous election, we want to know whether they actually voted. The validity of data from surveys is limited by the extent to which people tell the truth.

Steps we can take to establish the validity of our measures involve preparing arguments that the measures are *concurrent* and/or *predictive.* Concurrent validation involves correlating values obtained by a given measure with those obtained by other well-established indicators of the variable. The usual problem for social scientists is that there are few established benchmarks against which we can establish concurrent validity.

Predictive validation involves assessing the consistency of behavior with that which would be expected from previous measurement of the variable. For instance, if a researcher theorized that registration with a particular party plus a belief in democratic processes plus an expressed intention to vote would provide a score which would predict that a person would vote (voting-intention scale), the predictive test would be whether voting actually occurred. If one found that a high voting-intention score is associated with a high rate of voting, the measure would be considered to have good predictive validity.

Many factors may lead to invalidity and unreliability. Table 4-1 outlines studies of four general sources of bias.[29] In all cases nonrelevant factors were examined for their effect on a measure's validity.

Research design

THE EXPERIMENTAL RESEARCH DESIGN: THE IDEAL MODEL

The experimental research design is generally regarded as the model of scientific method since it embodies the principle of controlled observation more fully than any other procedure. The principle of controlled observation means that procedures are embodied in the research design so that the effects of possible confounding variables are eliminated. As a result, a researcher can have a relatively high degree of confidence in concluding that any observed difference is, in fact, the result of the

---

[29] For a good critical discussion of the pitfalls of social research see Derek L. Phillips, *Knowledge from What?* Rand McNally & Company, Chicago, 1971.

Sources of bias	Specific factor	Study[30]
Attributes of experimenter/ interviewer	Race	Katz (1964); Rankin and Campbell (1955); Hyman (1954); Athey (1960); Summers and Hammonds (1966); Williams (1964); Welch, Comer, and Steinman (1973)
	Sex	Binder et al. (1957); Friedman (1967); Sarason and Harmetz (1965); Stevenson and Allen (1964); Stevenson and Odum (1963); Benney and Associates (1956); Hanson and Marks (1958)
	Age	Erhlich and Riesman (1961); Benney and Associates (1956); Hanson and Marks (1958)
	Religion	Robinson and Rohde (1946)
	Social status	Rosenthal (1966); Lenski and Leggett (1960); Katz (1942); Riesman (1958); Dohrenwend (1968); Williams (1964, 1968)
	Personality characteristics	Cleveland (1951); McGuigan (1963); Winkel and Sarason (1964); Mulry (1952); Sarason (1962); Mulry (1962); Luft (1953); Sampson and French (1960)
Subject and respondent attributes	Need for social approval	Crowne and Marlowe (1964); Rosenberg (1965, 1969); Riecken (1962)
	Aquiescent response set	Bass (1955); Messick and Jackson (1961); Couch and Keniston (1960); Wells (1963); Rorer (1965)
	Social desirability	Edwards (1959); Maccoby and Maccoby (1954)
Physical setting	Location of experiment	Maslow and Mintz (1956); Mintz (1956)
Expectancy and modeling effects		Rosenthal (1966); Rosenthal and Fode (1963); Harvey (1938); Wyatt and Campbell (1950); Friedman (1967); Barber and Silver (1968); Rosenthal (1968); Rice (1929); Hanson and Marks (1958)

Table 4-1   Factors affecting validity of surveys and experiments

[30] K. Athey, "Two Experiments Showing the Effects of the Interviewer's Racial Background on Responses to Questionnaires Concerning Racial Issues," *Journal*

variable under investigation. In the classic experiment a researcher observes the relationship between two variables by deliberately manipulating one variable to see whether this produces a change in the other. The variable which is manipulated is referred to as the *independent variable* because it is independently manipulated by the researcher. The variable examined for the effects of the manipulations is conventionally referred to as the *dependent variable*.

of Applied Psychology, 44 (1960), 244–246; T. X. Barber and Maurice J. Silver, "Fact, Fiction, and the Experimenter Bias Effect," Psychological Bulletin Monograph, 70 (1968), 1–29; and "Pitfalls in Data Analysis and Interpretation: A Reply to Rosenthal," Psychological Bulletin Monograph, 70 (1968), 48–62; B. M. Bass, "Authoritarianism or Acquiescence?" Journal of Abnormal and Social Psychology, 51 (1955), 616–623; M. Benney, David Riesman, and S. Star, "Age and Sex in the Interview," American Journal of Sociology 62 (1956), 143–152; A. D. Binder, D. McConnell, and N. A. Sjoholm, "Verbal Conditioning as a Function of Experimenter Characteristics," Journal of Abnormal and Social Psychology, 55 (1967), 309–314; S. Cleveland, "The Relationship between Examiner Anxiety and Subjects' Rorschach Scores," Microfilm Abstracts, 11 (1951), 415–416; A. Couch and K. Keniston, "Yeasayers and Naysayers: Agreeing Response Set as a Personality Variable," Journal of Abnormal and Social Psychology, 60 (1960), 151–174; D. P. Crowne and D. Marlowe, The Approval Motive, John Wiley & Sons, New York, 1964; Barbara S. Dohrenwend, J. Colombotos, and Bruce Dohrenwend, "Social Distance and Interviewer Effects," Public Opinion Quarterly, 32 (1968), 410–422; E. L. Edwards, "Social Desirability and Personality Test Construction," in Objective Approaches to Psychology, eds. B. M. Bass and I. A. Berg, Van Nostrand Reinhold Company, New York, 1959, pp. 101–116; J. Ehrlich and D. Riesman, "Age and Authority in the Interview," Public Opinion Quarterly, 23 (1961), 39–56; J. J. Feldman, H. Hyman, and C. W. Hart, "A Field Study of Interviewer Effects on the Quality of Survey Data," Public Opinion Quarterly, 15 (1951), 734–761; Neil Friedman, The Social Nature of Psychological Research, Basic Books, New York, 1967; S. M. Harvey, "Preliminary Investigation of the Interview," British Journal of Psychology, 28 (1938), 263–287; Herbert Hyman, Interviewing in Social Research, University of Chicago Press, Chicago, 1954; D. Katz, "Do Interviewers Bias Poll Results?" Public Opinion Quarterly, 28 (1964), 248–268; Irwin Katz, "Body Language: A Study in Unintended Communication," unpublished doctoral dissertation, Harvard University, 1964; R. Hanson and E. Marks, "Influence of the Interviewer on the Accuracy of Survey Results," Journal of the American Statistical Association, 53 (1958), 635–655; G. Lenski and J. Leggett, "Caste, Class, and Deference in the Research Interview," American Journal of Sociology, 65 (1960), 463–467; J. Luft, "Interaction and Projection," Journal of Projective Techniques, 17 (1953), 489–492; E. Maccoby and N. Maccoby, "The Interview: A Tool of Social Science," in Handbook of Social Psychology, vol. 1, ed. Gardner Lindzey, Addison-Wesley Publishing Company, Reading, Mass., 1954; A. Maslow and N. Mintz, "Effects of Esthetic Surroundings: 1. Initial Effects of Three Esthetic Conditions upon Perceiving 'Energy' and 'Well-being' in Faces," Journal of Psychology, 41 (1956), 247–254; F. Guigan, "The Experimenter: A Neglected Stimulus Object," Psychological Bulletin, 60 (1963), 421–428; S. Messick and Douglas Jackson, "Desirability Scale Values and Dispersions for MMPI," Psychological Reports, 8 (1961), 409–414; N. Mintz, "Effects of Esthetic Surroundings: II. Prolonged and Repeated Experience in a 'Beautiful' and 'Ugly' Room," Journal of Psychology, 41 (1956),

In the classical experimental design, two groups are generally used: an *experimental group* that is exposed to the stimulus or independent variable and a *control group* that is identical to the experimental group in all other respects except it is not exposed to the independent variable. The two groups are generally compared before and after the administration of the stimulus (independent variable).

459–466; R. C. Mulry, "The Effects of the Experimenter's Perception of His Own Performance in a Pursuit of Rotor Task," unpublished master's thesis, University of North Dakota, 1962; R. Rankin and D. Campbell, "Galvanic Skin Response to Negro and White Experimenters," *Journal of Abnormal and Social Psychology*, 51 (1955), 30–33; S. Rice, "Contagious Bias in the Interview: A Methodological Note," *American Journal of Sociology*, 35 (1929), 420–423; H. W. Riecken, "A Program for Research on Experiments in Social Psychology," in *Decisions, Values, and Groups*, vol. 2, ed. N. F. Washburne, Pergamon Press, New York, 1962, pp. 25–41; D. Riesman, "Interviewers, Elites, and Academic Freedom," *Social Problems*, 6 (1958), 115–126; J. Robinson and S. Rohde, "Two Experiments with an Anti-Semitism Poll," *Journal of Abnormal and Social Psychology*, 41 (1946), 136–144; L. Rorer, "The Great Response-Style Myth," *Psychological Bulletin*, 3 (1965), 129–156; M. Rosenberg, "When Dissonance Fails: On Eliminating Evaluation Apprehension from Attitude Measurement," *Journal of Personality and Social Psychology*, 1 (1965), 28–42; and "The Conditions and Consequences of Evaluation Apprehension," in *Artifact in Behavioral Research*, eds. Robert Rosenthal and R. Rosnow, Academic Press, New York, 1969; Robert Rosenthal, *Experimenter Effects in Behavioral Research*, Appleton Century Crofts, New York, 1966; and "Experimenter Expectancy and the Reassuring Nature of the Null Hypothesis Decision Procedure," *Psychological Bulletin*, 70 (1968), 30–47; Robert Rosenthal and K. Fode, "Psychology of the Scientist: V. Three Experiments in Experimenter Bias," *Psychological Reports*, 12 (1963), 491–511; E. E. Sampson and J. French, "An Experiment on Active and Passive Resistance to Social Power," *American Psychologist*, 15 (1960), 396; I. Sarason, "Individual Differences, Situational Variables, and Personality Research," *Journal of Abnormal and Social Psychology*, 65 (1962), 376–380; I. G. Sarason and M. Harmatz, "Test Anxiety and Experimenter Condition," *Journal of Personality and Social Psychology*, 1 (1965), 499–505; H. W. Stevenson and S. Allen, "Adult Performance as a Function of the Sex of Experimenter and Sex of Subject," *Journal of Abnormal Psychology*, 68 (1964), 214–216; H. W. Stevenson and R. D. Odum, "Visual Reinforcement with Children," unpublished manuscript, University of Minnesota, 1963; Gene F. Summers and Andre Hammonds, "Effect of Racial Characteristics of Investigator on Self-enumerated Responses to a Negro Prejudice Scale," *Social Forces*, 44 (1966), 515–518; William Wells, "How Chronic Overclaimers Distort Survey Findings," *Journal of Advertising Research*, 3 (1963), 8–18; S. Welch, J. Comer, and M. Steinman, "Interviewing in a Mexican-American Community: An Investigation of Some Possible Sources of Response Bias," *Public Opinion Quarterly*, 37 (1973), 115–126; J. A. Williams, Jr., "Interviewing Respondent Interaction: A Study of Bias in the Information Interview," *Sociometry*, 27 (1964) 338–352; and "Interviewer Role Performance: A Further Note on Bias in the Information Interview," *POQ*, 32 (1968), 287–294; G. H. Winkel and I .G. Sarason, "Subject, Experimenter, and Situational Variables in Research on Anxiety," *Journal of Abnormal and Social Psychology*, 68 (1964), 601–608; D. F. Wyatt and D. Campbell, "A Study of Interviewer Bias as Related to Interviewers' Expectations and Own Opinions," *International Journal of Opinion and Attitude Research*, 4 (1950), 77-83.

This design enables a researcher to develop three crucial types of evidence relevant to the test hypothesis:

1   Evidence of concomitant variation between the dependent and independent variables which suggests that they are or are not associated
2   Evidence that the association is temporally continuous and that the dependent variable did not occur *before* the causal variable
3   Evidence that other factors (such as the measurement process itself, other characteristics of the subjects, etc.) are not the actual determining conditions of the dependent variable

Almost all research designs allow a researcher to offer evidence that the dependent and independent variables are related, but only the ideal experimental model provides evidence on all three factors. As Anderson points out, the ideal experiment can be contrasted with the natural experiment. In the natural experiment, all variable are free to vary; if controls are employed, they are generally introduced one variable at a time. In the ideal experiment, by contrast, all variables are controlled; any variation is introduced by the experimenter, one factor at a time.[31]

Anderson's simple example makes the superiority of the experiment strikingly clear. Suppose you are interested in testing the hypothesis that not eating breakfast makes one irritable. One procedure that could be employed would be to take a poll of people in the street— who had and had not eaten breakfast—to see if they differed in irritability. While you might find that, indeed, those who had not eaten breakfast were more irritable, it would still be difficult to accept the initial hypothesis, since you have no evidence that other factors might not be affecting the relationship. As Anderson indicates, the subjects who skipped breakfast might have done so "because they were irritable in the first place; or because their wives had decided to sleep late that morning, and that made them irritable; or because they were out of breakfast food, and that made them irritable." [32] The controlled experiment would not raise these problems since *only* the breakfast factor would be varied. Unfortunately, the pure experimental model *is only* an ideal. Actual research designs only approximate it. As a result, actual research designs differ in the extent to which various factors that threaten the study's validity are controlled. An examination of several different research designs will, perhaps, make these distinctions clearer.

[31] Barry Anderson, *The Psychology Experiment: An Introduction to the Scientific Method*, Wadsworth Publishing Company, Belmont, Calif., 1966; reprinted in *The Conduct of Political Inquiry*, eds. Louis Hayes and Ronald Hedlund, Prentice-Hall, Englewood Cliffs, N.J., 1970, pp. 127–132.
[32] Ibid., p. 129.

	Prestest experiment P	Uncontrolled events U	Posttest T	
Experimental group	X	E	X′	$d = X' - X$
Control group	Y		Y′	$d' = Y' - Y$

Table 4-2   Two-group experimental design

THE CLASSIC TWO-GROUP EXPERIMENTAL DESIGN

The classic design is the two-group design.[33] In Table 4-2 the experimental group is denoted the X group. Prior to receiving the experiment they are tested; this is the pretest (P). These same individuals are given the experiment (E) and then tested. The second testing is the posttest (T). The experimental group is tested before (X) and after (X') the experiment.

The control group (Y), is identical to the experimental group (insofar as possible), but it will not receive the experimental stimulus.

.   *Matching* or *randomization* is usually employed to assign individuals to the experimental and control groups. Randomization is simply a way of assigning individuals to the groups in such a way that the two groups will be quite similar. Randomization is achieved by an assignment process that gives each individual an equal chance of being assigned to either group. The implications of the randomization process are discussed in greater detail in Chapter 5, but it is important to recognize that its significance is far-reaching. "It achieves a matching of the two groups on all variables, with an estimated degree of error. This degree of error can be reduced by increasing the size of the experimental and control groups." [34]

Matching procedures involve matching individuals in the experimental and control groups on only a limited number of factors that are considered important for the experiment.[35] In either case, the goal is to create comparable groupings so that a researcher can measure the influence of only one variable—the experimental variable.

[33] John Ross and Perry Smith, "Orthodox Experimental Designs," in *Methodology in Social Research*, eds. Blalock and Blalock, pp. 355–358; Donald T. Campbell and Julian C. Stanley, *Experimental and Quasi-experimental Designs for Research*, Rand McNally & Company, Chicago, 1963, pp. 13–24. A simple but classic article on designs is Samuel A. Stouffer, "Some Observations on Study Design," *American Journal of Sociology*, 40 (January 1950), 355–361.

[34] Bernard S. Phillips, *Social Research*, 2d ed., The Macmillan Company, New York, 1971, p. 108.

[35] Ibid., pp. 105–112, provides a good discussion and comparison of various randomization and matching procedures.

The control group (Y) is also tested before (Y) and after (Y'), and both groups are tested at the same time to control a wide variety of uncontrolled events (U) common to both groups. As indicated in Table 4-2, two sets of different scores can be calculated; the first set (d) results from subtracting the pretest scores (X) from the posttest scores (X') for the experimental group. From the control group, the second set of difference scores (d') results from subtracting the pretest scores (Y) from the posttest scores (Y'). We have scores, for example, for person A (and other persons) in the experimental group. For person A, the pretest score on a test is subtracted from the posttest score on the same test. These scores summarize the performance of the two groups. On the basis of our hypotheses, we expect a significant difference between the experimental group (d) and the control group (d').

FOUR-GROUP EXPERIMENTAL DESIGN

All designs are subject to a series of threats to the validity of the statement that the "experimental stimulus has caused the performance of the experimental group to exceed that of the control group." These events and circumstances, designated in Table 4-2 as U, arise with both the classic experiment and the more natural quasi experiment.[36]

The classic four-group design, depicted in Table 4-3, is considered a strong research design because it controls many problems and clearly treats a most significant threat—the effect of testing itself.[37] One of the best examples of this problem occurred in the Hawthorne studies.[38] In this study, a variety of working conditions were manipulated to see how they affected workers' productivity. Much to their surprise, the researchers found that output rose under almost all the varied conditions, both good and bad. The researchers concluded that the testing situation itself had led to a change in social relations within the plant which in turn led to increased productivity.

The testing effect is a product of the pretest and the interaction with the experimental stimulus. The pretest problem occurs when the experiment or the posttest or both follow too closely to the pretest. As outlined in Table 4-3, the four-group design allows testing for these effects because the combination of X' and V' provides an estimate of

---

[36] A full list of threats, both internal and external, are discussed in Campbell and Stanley, *Experimental and Quasi-Experimental Designs for Research*, pp. 5–6.

[37] The design is also known as the Solomon four-group design. For further discussion see Campbell and Stanley, *Experimental . . .* , pp. 24–25; and Ross and Smith, "Orthodox Experimental Designs," pp. 360–366.

[38] G. Homans, "Group Factors in Worker Productivity," in *Basic Studies in Social Psychology*, eds. H. Proshansky and B. Seidenberg, Holt, Rinehart and Winston, New York, 1965, pp. 592–604.

	Pretest P	Experiment	Uncontrolled events U	Posttest T
Experimental group 1	X	E		X'
Control group 1	Y			Y'
Experimental group 2		E		V'
Control group 2				W'

Table 4-3   Four-group experimental design

the main effect of the experiment when compared with Y' and W'. If everything goes right, X' and V' are equal, and Y' and W' are equal; and the measures, when combined, would show the grouping of X' and V' to be greater than the group of Y' and W'.

To test for the effect of the pretest, you can combine X' with Y' and V' with W', and the resulting combinations should be equal. If the X' and Y' combination show a higher performance than the V' and W' there is evidence that pretesting had some effect on the final results— the posttest scores. The four scores (X', Y', V', W') could be tested against each other to look for interactions between pretest and the experiment.[39]

The preceding experimental designs are not commonly used in social science, but in recent years there has been increasing work in the area of *quasi-experimental* design. These procedures are a hybrid of experimental laboratory procedures and nonexperimental procedures. As Caporaso and Roos indicate:

> This approach is characterized by an effort to use the logic of experimentation in situations which are not truly experimental; in such situations the investigator cannot randomly assign individuals to groups and cannot control the administration of the treatment or stimulus.[40]

The final sections of this chapter examine some common quasi-experimental design procedures.

[39] Among works which treat in detail the analysis, see E. F. Hindquist, *Statistical Analysis of Experiments in Psychology and Education*, Houghton Mifflin Company, Boston, 1953; B. J. Winer, *Statistical Principles in Experimental Design*, McGraw-Hill Book Company, New York, 1962; Roger E. Kirk, *Experimental Design: Procedures for the Behavioral Sciences*, Brooks/Cole Publishing Company, Belmont, Calif., 1968.

[40] *Quasi-experimental Approaches*, eds. James A. Caporaso and Leslie Roos, Northwestern University Press, Evanston, Ill., 1973, p. xvii.

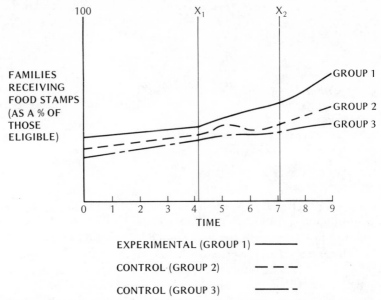

Figure 4-2   Time series design Some possible outcomes from the introduction of experimental variables at points X_1 and X_2

INTERRUPTED AND CONTROL TIME SERIES DESIGN

The time series design is employed when we have data across time, and when there is reason to believe that the introduction of some event will alter behavior of the series. To employ this design, it is thus necessary to have data over time, with the event occurring within the time series, and with measurement taking place both after and before the event.

For example, let's assume that under a new program the federal government provided 50 percent of the cost of administering food-stamp programs at the county level. We have data on the number of families receiving food stamps at nine different points in time, as indicated in Figure 4-2. The funds for the new program became available at time 4. Our basic problem is to determine whether federal support made any difference in the number of families receiving food stamps.

We can think about the quasi experiment in the following manner:

1   We check to see if the number of families receiving food stamps has significantly increased after time 4. A first check is to compare the number of families who received food stamps before time 4 with the number of families who received food stamps after time 4. Thus, the same counties, measured before and after time 4, provide the experimental group, group 1.

2   Since county participation in the new program is optional,

counties that did not choose to participate in the federally supported food-stamp program, provide a useful control group. This enables us to use the *control series design,* an extension of the interrupted time series design, employing a parallel control group. In this case, we might check whether the number of families receiving food stamps in these counties is appreciably different from the number of families receiving food stamps in counties that joined the federal program. The control group provides some assurance that the new program itself and not some extraneous factor accounts for the change.

3   Finally, let's assume that a second program providing 100 percent of the administrative costs to food-stamp programs goes into effect at time 7. Counties that had not participated in any federal programs now split into two groups. In addition to the initial control group, we now add another control group that has consistently declined to participate. The consistent decliners are the second control group (group 3) in Figure 4-2.

FIELD STUDIES AND FIELD EXPERIMENTS

The *field study* is often thought of as lying at the opposite pole from the laboratory experiment in terms of degree of closure achieved over variables other than the one(s) being investigated.[41] Kerlinger characterizes the *field study* as an ex post facto research design aimed at discovering relationships among factors.[42] Field studies may be further differentiated in terms of whether they are primarily exploratory or hypothesis testing. Used for exploratory purposes, field studies can be highly suggestive. Phillips suggests, in fact, that they are perhaps *most* useful in the context of discovery.[43] The weaknesses of the field study derive from its ex post facto character, uncontrolled variance, and weak measurement. It is a relatively imprecise design compared with experimental methods in the laboratory.

The *field experiment* can be thought of as lying midpoint in precision between the laboratory experiment and the field study. Kerlinger defines the field experiment as a situation in which "one or more independent variables are manipulated by the experimenter under as carefully controlled conditions as the situation will permit."[44]

A researcher thus proceeds through various steps raising questions at each point in the research design. At the operational-measurement stage various questions must be raised about the adequacy of a

[41] Phillips, *Social Research,* p. 124.
[42] Fred Kerlinger, *Foundations of Behavioral Research,* 2d. ed., Holt, Rinehart and Winston, New York, 1973, p. 405.
[43] Phillips, *Social Research.*
[44] Kerlinger, *Foundations . . . ,* p. 401.

given measure and its general meaningfulness. A researcher must ask about the measurement procedure, the level of measurement, and whether validity and reliability are indicated. If the measure proves to have a low level of reliability and little validity, the measure must be discarded and another, more meaningful measure found. But as we have indicated in this chapter, measurement is only one important aspect of the overall problem of research design. The ideal research design reduces the various problems of validity and reliability through procedures of strictly controlled observation. In Chapter 5 we examine another aspect of measurement and design—sampling—in greater detail.

Review questions and exercises

1   Explain the meaning and significance of the following terms:

    a   Validity
    b   Reliability
    c   Measurement
    d   Operational definition
    e   Internal consistency
    f   Concurrent validity
    g   Predictive validity
    h   Stability
    i   Nominal level of measurement
    j   Ordinal level of measurement
    k   Interval level of measurement
    l   Dimensionality
    m   Methodological triangulation
    n   Acquiescent response set
    o   Social desirability effect
    p   Expectancy and modeling effects
    q   Controlled experiment
    r   Dependent variable
    s   Independent variable
    t   Intervening variable
    u   Experimental group
    v   Control group

2   Select several of the following concepts and indicate ways of operationally defining them and how their reliability and validity might be ascertained.

    a   Legitimacy
    b   Political participation

    c   Alienation
    d   Political efficacy
    e   Power
    f   Consensus
    g   Compliance
    h   Influence
    i   Equality
    j   Conservative
    k   Radical
    l   Violence
    m   Freedom
    n   Effectiveness
    o   Party
    p   Justice

3 Devise alternative measurement designs for the following topics and discuss the advantages and disadvantages of each:

    a   Racial prejudice
    b   Tolerance
    c   Political participatory orientation
    d   Partisanship
    e   Alienation

4 Select one of the topics listed below and read at least three articles or chapters listed under each. On the basis of your reading, write a four- to six-page essay that (*a*) very briefly summarizes each article; (*b*) explicitly identifies the dependent, independent, and control or intervening variables discussed in each article and the operational definition of each; and (*c*) summarizes the state of our knowledge of the subject on the basis of what each article states.

Party Identification and Voting Behavior

    a   Wayne Shannon, "Electoral Margins and Voting Behavior in House of Representatives" *Journal of Politics*, 30, No. 4 (November 1968), 1028–1045.
    b   David E. RePass, "Issue Salience and Party Choice," *American Political Science Review*, LXV, No. 2 (June 1971), 389–400.
    c   Paul Sinderman, "Psychological Sources of Political Beliefs: Self-esteem and Isolationist Attitudes," *American Political Science Review*, LXV, No. 2 (June 1971), 401–417.
    d   Angus Campbell, Philip Converse, W. Miller, and D. E. Stokes, "The Impact and Development of Party Identification" in *American Party Politics,* eds. D. G. Herzberg and G. Pomper, Holt, Rinehart and Winston, New York, 1967, pp. 365–377.

Personality and Attitudes

e   Charles P. Farris, "Selected Attitudes on Foreign Affairs as Correlates of Authoritarianism and Political Anomie," *Journal of Politics*, 22, No. 1 (February 1960), 50–67.

f   Morris Rosenberg, "Some Determinants of Political Apathy," *Public Opinion Quarterly*, 18, No. 1 (Winter 1954–1955), 349–366.

g   Herbert McClosky, "Conservatism and Personality," *American Political Science Review*, LII (March 1958), 27–45.

h   Bernard Hennessy, "Politicals and Apoliticals: Some Measure of Personality Traits," *Midwest Journal of Political Science*, III (November 1959), 336–355.

Political Development and Stability

i   Ernest Duff and John McCamant, "Measuring Social and Political Requirements for System Stability in Latin America," *American Political Science Review*, LXII, No. 4 (December 1968), 1125–1143.

j   Robert D. Putnam, "Toward Explaining Military Intervention in Latin America," *World Politics*, 20, No. 83 (October 1967), 110.

k   Ivo Feierabend, R. L. Feierabend, and B. A. Neavold, "Social Change and Political Violence: Cross National Patterns," in *Political Development and Social Change*, 2d ed., eds. Jason Finkle and Richard Gable, John Wiley & Sons, New York, 1971, pp. 569–604.

l   Edward Mitchell, "Inequality and Insurgency: A Statistical Study of South Vietnam," *World Politics*, 20, No. 3 (April 1968), 421–438.

5   Write up a research design for investigating the effects of some of the factors listed in Table 4-1 on a topic of your choice.

Teratology, the study of exceptions
and of "marvels" . . . is of no great
scientific interest except as it
teaches more about the "normal"
processes.

Abraham Maslow

5

SAMPLING IN
SOCIAL SCIENCE RESEARCH

As we pointed out in Chapter 2, science is concerned mainly with
generalization. In recent years social scientists have been interested
particularly in searching for regularities and trends in human behavior
with a goal of developing general empirical theories. In spite of their
interest in general empirical theories, social scientists seldom study
the entire population in which they are interested. Time, money, and
other resource constraints frequently demand that scholars focus their
research on a sample rather than on the larger population. The interest
in the population remains, but findings are generalized from the
sample rather than based upon a total enumeration.

In this chapter we discuss the various procedures used in social
research to select or sample objects or units from some universe or
population. Sampling theory provides relatively objective guidelines
for this purpose. Its increasing use in political science is a mark of the
growing maturity of the field. As Cochran points out:

> The purpose of sample theory is to make sampling more efficient.
> It attempts to develop methods of sample selection and of estima-
> tion that provide, at the lowest possible cost, estimates that are
> precise enough for our purpose. This principle of specified pre-
> cision at minimum cost recurs repeatedly in the presentation
> of theory.[1]

[1] W. Cochran, *Sampling Techniques*, John Wiley & Sons, New York, 1963, p. 5.

Sampling: basic terms

The term "population," as we have used it in the above paragraphs, does not correspond to its everyday usage. The distinction is important and should be thoroughly understood. You will find the terms "universe" and "population" used synonymously in the literature; they are essentially interchangeable. There are an infinite number of possible "populations"—human and nonhuman—in the world of a scientist. A *population* might be defined as "a collection of measurements about which we wish to make an inference." [2] The term is partly one of definition, depending upon the interest of a researcher. An alternative definition might be that a population refers to the aggregate of all cases that conform to some designated specifications. [3] Thus by the specification "people residing in the United States" we define a population of all persons residing in the United States regardless of age and former or present nationality. The population specification "persons holding an elected governmental office" would include all persons holding elected governmental positions—state, local, county, city, and federal—but it would not include appointed governmental officials. Similarly, the population specification "legislators in the United States" would include state as well as national legislators unless otherwise designated. It is important to recognize that one's population must thus be defined in terms of content, units, extent, and time. The preceding example is incomplete in that it fails to include a *time* designation, and we have no way of determining whether the specified legislators are only those for a specific year, a decade, or whatever. *Extent* is indicated by the designation including national and state levels. *Unit* specification is not applicable in this instance but might include housing units in another population designation. Although designation of the relevant population is at least partially definitional, it is important that a researcher have a clear designation in mind. If we were interested in expenditure patterns in the American states and analyzed all fifty states, we might be taking a census of the entire population. An analysis of all fifty states might, on the other hand, be considered a *sample* of state expenditure patterns at a given time. As this example should indicate, clarity of research purpose is of utmost importance.

"Population" is essentially an aggregate term. When we refer to a single member of the population, we call it a *population element*. If we have a population with an aggregate membership of 210 million

[2] William Mendenhall, Lyman Ott, and Richard Schaeffer, *Elementary Survey Sampling*, Wadsworth Publishing Company, Belmont, Calif., 1971, p. 20.
[3] Claire Selltiz, Marie Jahoda, Morton Deutsch, and Stuart Cook, *Research Methods in Social Relations*, Harper & Row, Publishers, New York, 1959, p. 509.

people, we have 210 million elements in that population. Frequently, we are interested in knowing how certain opinions, attitudes, preferences, and characteristics are distributed in a population. Some of the various polls you see in your newspaper, for example, are interested in ascertaining the distribution of opinion with regard to the President's performance and his handling of domestic and foreign affairs.

If we wanted information on all elements in the population on some question or characteristic and polled the entire population, we would be conducting a *census* of the population, a total enumeration of all constituent elements.

Whether we wish to study the total population or only part of it, we need some means of enumerating the population. The enumeration source is frequently referred to as the *sampling frame*. Few sampling frames are totally accurate from the standpoint of being current and including all possible elements. As we shall see in subsequent sections of this chapter, some sampling frames are more adequate (inadequate) than others.

Frequently, we cannot gather information on all elements of our population, because it is too costly or they are inaccessible. We might then use what is termed a *sample* of the population, hoping to learn something that we can generalize from a smaller number of elements to the larger population. We hope to find that what is true for our sample is also true for the larger population. This may or may not be the case; whether it is or not will depend largely on how we collect the sample.

Figure 5-1 depicts the relationship among the terms discussed in this section.

Historical development of modern sampling: a brief review

Sampling is not particularly new. In fact, if we use the broadest and least rigorous definition of the term, sampling probably has existed since prehistoric times. Numerous human activities involve, in one way or another, making generalizations to some larger population on the basis of a more limited sample. As Frederick Stephen has pointed out in his survey of the history of modern sampling:

> All empirical knowledge is, in a fundamental sense, derived from incomplete or imperfect observation and is, therefore, a sampling of experience. An unusually interesting example, not unrelated to modern population research, can be found in Halley's selection of mortality statistics in Breslau to form the basis of his life

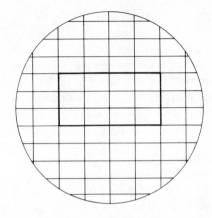

POPULATION: Children in the United States currently enrolled in the third grade.

ELEMENT: Each child in the United States currently enrolled in the third grade.

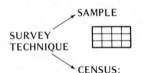

SAMPLE Selected children in the United States currently enrolled in the third grade.

SURVEY TECHNIQUE

CENSUS: Total enumeration of all children in the United States currently enrolled in the third grade.

FRAME: U.S. Department of Education lists of number of children in primary school, by grade and state, private and public schools.

Figure 5-1   Basic terminology of sampling

table. From this sample of one city he drew general conclusions pertaining to "the mortality of mankind." This was in 1693.[4]

Sampling was used occasionally in the eighteenth and nineteenth centuries in agriculture, commerce and industry, and public health, but the goal was more frequently to obtain a total enumeration of the

[4] Frederick F. Stephen, "History of the Uses of Modern Sampling Procedures," *Journal of the American Statistical Association*, 43 (1948), 13.

population. At that time a census appeared to be the only means of securing reliable information. Needless to say, a census was tremendously costly and not always reliable; enumeration and location difficulties, and time lags in the collection process, often led to unreliable results. Some public opinion polling was done at the beginning of the twentieth century, but sampling was not used in this connection to any great extent. For the most part, early sampling efforts were fairly crude in light of current standards. However, as Stephen points out, "the problems of observing and recording data were almost always far more serious than the problem of sampling." [5]

The apparent crudity of early sampling is somewhat surprising in light of the fact that the theory of probability, which underlies contemporary probability sampling methods, was well established in the eighteenth century. Nevertheless, for the most part, its applications to sampling practice were not noted until the twentieth century. Tippett's publication of his table of random numbers in 1927 facilitated the development and widespread use of random sampling.

In the twentieth century great strides were taken in the direction of more sophisticated sampling procedures. The Great Depression and World War II significantly accelerated these developments. They created a need for current reliable, large-scale statistical information, and they also drew large numbers of talented scientists and statisticians into government work in this area. During this period the United States government established numerous bureaus and departments specializing in the collection and dissemination of statistical data and information.

Sampling has now burgeoned into a field of considerable sophistication. A variety of sampling techniques and methods are now available, and various problems associated with each are fairly well understood.

Sampling in political science: a brief overview

Political scientists have used relatively sophisticated sampling procedures since the 1940s. The most consistent usage has probably been in the area of public opinion research, particularly with regard to voting preferences. The Survey Research Center at the University of Michigan is especially well known for the presidential election studies it has conducted since 1952.

One of the earliest efforts to apply sampling theory to political phenomena was in the voting study *The People's Choice*.[6] Similar in

[5] Ibid., p. 20.
[6] P. Lazarsfeld, B. Berelson, and H. Gaudet, *The People's Choice*, Columbia University Press, New York, 1948.

methodological procedures to a subsequent study, *Voting*,[7] *The People's Choice* used probability sampling procedures and repeat interviews to determine influences on and changes in voting preferences in presidential elections. While opinion change has been investigated occasionally, cross-sectional analysis of public opinion is the more common procedure among academic sociologists and political scientists. Longitudinal analysis is extremely costly and often difficult to execute. Other notable early studies that delved into public opinion more generally include the work of Samuel Stouffer[8] and Hadley Cantril,[9] among others.

Sampling theory has not been as extensively applied in most other areas of political inquiry, but its use is increasing. Almond and Verba's classic five-nation study, *The Civic Culture*, is one notable early study in comparative politics based upon probability sampling procedures.[10] With the exception of its use in connection with content analysis, there has been little use of survey research and probability sampling procedures in international relations. In the area of legislative behavior, efforts have most frequently been directed toward total enumeration rather than sampling among states. Both *The Legislative System* (Eulau, Buchanan, Ferguson, and Wahlke, 1962) and *Lobbying* (Zeigler and Baer, 1969) were based upon data drawn from four states. In both instances the authors made an attempt to interview all legislators in those states. Whether the findings of these studies can be generalized to other state legislatures is, of course, an empirical question. As the authors themselves point out, there is no reason to assume so from the standpoint of sampling theory, since the states were not randomly selected.

The discipline's uneven record in using sampling theory can be traced to a number of factors. First, in many areas of political science there is considerable difficulty associated with the development of an adequate sampling frame. Second, there is some disagreement within the discipline about whether we have sufficient exploratory studies to proceed to a more general level of analysis. In some cases it is not clear whether the authors are interested in testing generalizable hypotheses

[7] B. Berelson, P. Lazarsfeld, and W. McPhee, *Voting*, University of Chicago Press, Chicago, 1954.

[8] Samuel Stouffer, *Communism, Conformity and Civil Liberties*, John Wiley & Sons, New York, 1966; Samuel Stouffer et al., *The American Soldier*, Princeton University Press, N.J., 1949.

[9] Lloyd A. Free and Hadley Cantril, *The Political Beliefs of Americans: A Study of Public Opinion*, Clarion Books, New York, 1968; and Hadley Cantril, *The Pattern of Human Concerns*, Rutgers University Press, New Brunswick, N.J., 1965.

[10] Gabriel A. Almond and Sidney Verba, *The Civic Culture*, Little, Brown and Company, Boston, 1965. For a good summary of other recent cross-national work see *Cross-National Micro-Analysis: Procedures and Problems*, eds. John C. Pierce and Richard A. Pride, Sage Books, Beverly Hills, Calif., 1972.

or whether they are interested in making generalizations limited to their particular case studies. From the standpoint of the methodology employed, most studies would have to fall into the latter category. It is equally clear, however, that the discipline must work toward better sampling procedures if its goal is the development of systematic, *general* theory.

Political leadership studies[11] have been criticized particularly on a number of grounds that relate to the general applicability of their conclusions. Critics argue that the criteria governing the choice of (1) leaders, elites, or decision-makers; (2) decisions; and (3) locale or cities to be studied not only bias the results but also invalidate any attempt to generalize their conclusions to other elites, decisions, or locations.

Studies of community power have probably been criticized most heavily for subjectivity in their manner of selecting leaders. The reputational approach is used frequently in this connection. In this case, a number of "informed persons" are asked to list individuals who make decisions in a given city. This approach is sometimes supplemented with a listing of titular leadership. An alternative approach involves ex post facto procedures whereby leaders are selected on the basis of whether they participated in decisions already made. Random selection procedures are not normally used with either procedure simply because the number of leaders is usually small enough to interview the entire population.

One of the most pointed criticisms of the existing leadership studies is made by Bachrach and Baratz, who argue that "nondecisions" carry an explicit bias in terms of political power and public policy.[12] This criticism suggests that analysis must be directed toward nondecisions as well as decisions and toward non-decision-makers as well as decision-makers if the question of who governs is to be satisfactorily answered.

While there is certainly some merit in the various criticisms of community power studies, the points raised by Bachrach and Baratz are not without their own methodological difficulties. Some problems with previous community power studies may eventually be resolved simply by rewording research questions into more generalizable forms. A recent study of decision-making and non-decision-making with regard to air pollution by Matthew Crenson[13] is a rather exceptional

[11] See, for example, Floyd Hunter, *Community Power Structure*, Doubleday Anchor Books, New York, 1963; and Robert Dahl, *Who Governs?* Yale University Press, New Haven, Conn., 1961.

[12] Peter Bachrach and Morton S. Baratz, *Power and Poverty: Theory and Practice*, Oxford University Press, New York, 1970, especially chap. 1. The concept of "nondecisions" is regarded as a philosophical monstrosity by some critics, however.

[13] Matthew A. Crenson, *The Un-politics of Air Pollution*, Johns Hopkins Press, Baltimore, 1971.

approach to the question "Who governs?" Crenson samples a number of different cities with substantial air pollution and asks whether there are any particular structural characteristics associated with different decision-making patterns and policy responses. The objective problem becomes the constant in Crenson's study. This provides a new way of broaching an old question, but in a manner that may be more meaningful in the long run. Wording the question as Crenson does facilitates the application of sampling theory in a way that the old approaches did not. It is also more likely to lead to generalizable findings.

Other reasons why sampling theory has not been applied more frequently in political science include the skills and training of scholars. Work in statistics and sampling theory has not been a required part of the training of political scientists until recently. Cost is often an additional constraint in this regard. In many instances only scholars with governmental or private research funds can afford the high costs associated with probability sampling and professional interviewing.

Finally, a number of areas of political science are simply not raising questions that facilitate and/or necessitate the incorporation of sampling procedures into their research methodology. In comparative politics, for example, the case-study approach is still very much alive. Its proponents argue that there is a need for more detailed analysis of individual countries before we attempt to develop generalizations about some features they have in common.

The remaining sections of this chapter outline various types of sampling procedures. An understanding of the purposes of sampling procedures combined with some idea of the goals of political science should enable you to assess more directly the usefulness of these methods to the various areas of political science.

Nonprobability sampling

One basic distinction in sampling is between probability and non-probability sampling. The concept of "representativeness" underlies this distinction. When, for purposes of economy, researchers decide to sample a portion of a population, they want to know whether they can generalize findings to the larger population. They are interested in determining, in other words, the degree to which their sample is "representative" of the larger population. Only probability sampling procedures allow researchers to state with a specifiable degree of confidence the amount of error involved in sampling only a portion of a population and the actual variance between the sample's values and those of the population. Nonprobability sampling methods, by contrast, embody no procedures that allow one to ascertain the representativeness of the sample. Strictly speaking, nonprobability sampling procedures can be employed only to test hypotheses pertaining to the sample itself. It is, therefore, important that a researcher clearly articulate the purpose of the study before choosing sampling methods.

The principal advantages of nonprobability sampling methods are economy and convenience. In some instances, these advantages will outweigh the additional costs associated with probability sampling techniques. Nevertheless, nonprobability sampling methods do have distinct characteristics and drawbacks that should be kept in mind. In the following parts of this chapter we discuss three major types of nonprobability sampling: the accidental sample, the purposive or judgmental sample, and the quota sample.

THE ACCIDENTAL SAMPLE

Accidental sampling involves precisely what the term implies—more or less accidental choice of a sample, usually on the basis of immediate availability and convenience. If you were to walk out on the street and interview the first hundred people you met, you would probably draw an accidental sample of the residents of your city. A number of factors might make it more or less accidental, including the time of day you interview people, the street you select, and others. Similarly, if your instructor were to interview the members of this class, he or she probably would draw an essentially accidental sample of the population of college students. If you were to interview the first fifty persons walking into your student union at dinner time, you also might draw an accidental sample of students at your college or university.

The essential feature of the accidental sample is that there is no means for determining the degree to which it approximates the true values of a specific population. No criteria are built into the selection process to ensure representativeness. In the final analysis, this usually means that results are biased in unascertainable ways, and the researcher, therefore, has no reliable basis for making inferences to the larger population. The best one can hope for is a rough approximation. Realistically speaking, it is generally best to avoid accidental sampling altogether. If this technique must be used, it is best to limit one's discussion and findings to the sample itself rather than to attempt generalizing about the larger population on a faulty basis.

THE PURPOSIVE, OR JUDGMENTAL, SAMPLE

Purposive samples are usually drawn on the assumption that a combination of good judgment and a well-defined purpose can yield an adequate sample. Purposive sampling is frequently combined with random, probability sampling in two-stage designs. If researchers decided to study consumer spending in cities having populations of 20,000 or more and preselected fifty cities for this purpose, and then later sampled random houses or family units within these cities, they would be employing this two-stage design. The process of initially choosing the cities in this example would be essentially based upon purposive or judgmental criteria rather than upon considerations of random approximation of the total population of cities in this bracket. Frequently, this preselection is necessary because of other considerations such as access to data, transportation costs, and costs in time and personnel.

Purposive sampling is also used frequently in forecasting trends. Certain states, for example, have shown a remarkably high degree of fit in the past with presidential election returns. For this reason, these states have frequently been taken as barometers of national preference. Televised early election returns and projections are frequently based upon a sampling of a small number of districts that have proved to be "good indicators." As Selltiz and her associates point out, however, forecasting probably could be done as efficiently on the basis of past returns for the entire nation or state if the political climate has not changed substantially. On the other hand, if the political climate has changed substantially, we would need to know how the changes were affecting the selected districts or states relative to other districts or states. In either case, the sampling design would be inadequate.[14]

Statisticians have little respect for the purposive method of sampling, since it has the same shortcomings as an accidental sample. Nevertheless, it may be more economical than conducting a total enumeration, as required for a random sample, and especially when selected access is necessary because of resource constraints. On occasion it has been used with a high degree of sophistication. Nevertheless, shortcomings of the method should be borne in mind, particularly when attempting to generalize to a larger population from a sample collected in this manner. As Parten points out, the principal disadvantages of the method are the following:

1 To be reliable, a considerable knowledge of the population must be available in advance of the sample;
2 The controls are often not effective; and
3 The estimate of sampling error rests upon hypotheses which are seldom if ever met in practice.[15]

[14] Selltiz et al., *Research Methods in Social Relations*, pp. 520–521.
[15] Mildren Parten, *Surveys, Polls and Samples: Practical Procedures*, Harper & Row, Publishers, New York, 1950, pp. 237–238.

QUOTA SAMPLING

Quota sampling is a type of nonprobability sampling that was used frequently in past social science research. Quota sampling has the advantage of being able to ensure the inclusion of the proper proportion of elements from various specified strata in the population, but it remains essentially a nonprobability method of sampling. The basic goal of quota sampling is to secure a reliable replica of the population with reference to certain predefined criteria. The nature of a research project will determine which particular criteria are used for selection. Demographic and stratification characteristics such as age, place of residence, education, and income are used frequently as quota criteria. This type of sampling depends upon a certain familiarity with the characteristics of the larger population since this information provides the basis for the inclusion of approximately proportionate numbers in the sample.

The essential procedures involved in quota sampling are quite simple. The quota criteria are first selected, the proportion of the population falling into each category on these criteria is determined, and then proportionate numbers are included in the sample on these dimensions. If we were conducting a quota sample survey using sex as a quota criterion, we might, for example, instruct our interviewer to draw a sample in which 50 percent of the respondents are male and 50 percent female, the same proportion of males and females that exists in our population. Any number of characteristics can be used as the basis of a quota sample, with the proportion always being gauged to its known representation in the larger population. Obtaining quotas proportionate to those in the population is not difficult with a small number of criteria. The number of defining criteria is, of course, practically infinite, and the more quota criteria employed, the more difficult it becomes to find approximate proportions. The advantage of defining the sample on a large number of criteria is to make it a more approximate representation of the population, but this advantage must be weighed against the additional costs of obtaining the increasingly elusive cases in the sample.

When using the quota sampling method, it is best to define the requisite quotas explicitly and to provide the interviewer with standard forms to fill out as the various categories are obtained. Table 5-1 is a suggested format for this purpose. Notice that the table defines the criterion variable (education); each of the categories (0–8 years formal education, 9–12 years, 1–4 years college, and formal education beyond the 4-year college course); the known proportion of the general population located in each category (15 percent, 50 percent, 20 percent, and 15 percent, respectively); the requisite sample size (100 cases); and the number in the sample to be obtained in each category. The final

Categories	Percent in population*	Expected number in sample	Number obtained in sample
0–8 years education	15	15	14
9–12 years education	50	50	49
1–4 years college	20	20	22
Postcollege education	15	15	15
Totals	100	100	100

*Source of population values should be given.

Table 5-1   Quota sampling coding form   Quota criterion: education

column is provided for the interviewer to record the number or percentage obtained in each category; this makes underrepresentation or overrepresentation immediately visible. Quota sampling does make it possible to locate any variance between the obtained and expected sample. Underrepresentation or over representation can then be noted and/or corrected through weighting or some other means. In Table 5-1, for instance, the first three categories show slight variance between expected and attained numbers in the sample.

In spite of the fact that quota sampling appears to be more accurate than either purposive or accidental sampling, it remains a nonprobability method of sampling. As such it is subject to essentially the same limitations inherent in those methods. Although quota sampling will yield an approximate representation of the population (in numerical terms) on the specified criteria, it nevertheless constitutes an essentially accidental sampling of these strata. In the preceding example we have an approximately proportionate, but accidental, sampling of those individuals who have had 0 to 8 years of formal education, 1 to 4 years of college, etc. We may have obtained a highly unrepresentative sample of these educational groupings. We will never know. Quota sampling provides no way to ascertain the representativeness of proportionate groupings.

THE 1936 LITERARY DIGEST POLL

Throughout this chapter we have indicated that the major disadvantage of nonprobability sampling is that it fails to provide an adequate basis for generalizing results to the larger population. This means that we can only apply the findings to the sample itself. Nonprobability methods fail primarily because they do not embody procedures that ensure independence of events. Through its assurance that every element in the population has an equal chance of being included in the sample, the random sample ensures independence of events—at least theoretically, if not always in practice. Nonprobability sampling methods lack this essential feature.

The now-famous story of the 1936 presidential poll conducted by *Literary Digest* demonstrates this central problem of nonprobability sampling techniques. In 1936 *Literary Digest* conducted a presidential preference poll based on a large sample of nearly ten million voters, nearly one out of every four voters in the United States at that time. On the basis of this poll, *Literary Digest* predicted that Alfred Landon would win the Presidency with 60 percent of the popular vote. In fact, Landon received only 38 percent of the popular vote.

What was wrong with the poll? Did the discrepancy simply result from the fact that a large number of respondents lied to the pollsters, or did they change their minds at the last minute? Gallup and others have indicated that timing may have contributed to the inaccuracy of the prediction, since the poll was taken several months before the actual election. Size of the sample was certainly no problem. A more central failing of the poll stemmed from the fact that its sampling procedure and particularly its sampling frame were inadequate from the standpoint of generalizing about the American voting population. The sample, large as it was, did not represent the American electorate, mainly because it was not randomly selected. *Literary Digest* drew its sample from enumerations of the population in telephone directories and automobile registration lists. In 1936 automobiles and telephones were not as common among American voters as they are today. Sampling on the basis of these sources resulted in a sample that was disproportionately upper class and pro-Landon. As Gallup points out in his discussion of this major polling disaster:

> From the point of view of cross section this was a major error, because it limited the sample largely to the upper half of the voting population, as judged on an economic basis. Roughly 40% of all homes in the United States had telephones and some 55% of all families owned automobiles. These two groups, which largely overlap, constitute roughly the upper half or upper three-fifths, economically, of the voting population.[16]

Independence of events—presidential preference and likelihood of being included in the sample—was not secured by the sampling techniques underlying the *Literary Digest* poll.

[16] George Gallup, *A Guide to Public Opinion Polls*, Princeton University Press, Princeton, N.J., 1948, p. 73. For discussions of the methods currently used by commercial pollsters see Charles W. Roll and Albert H. Cantril, *Polls: Their Use and Misuse in Politics*, Basic Books, New York, 1972; George Gallup, *The Sophisticated Poll Watcher's Guide*, Princeton Opinion Press, Princeton, N.J., 1972; Harold A. Mendelsohn and Irving Crespi, *Polls, Television, and the New Politics*, Chandler Publications, San Francisco, 1970; and Frederick Mosteller et al., *The Pre-election Polls of 1948*, Social Science Research Council, New York, 1949.

Probability sampling methods

THE SIMPLE RANDOM SAMPLE

The simple random sample is the basis of all the various forms of probability sampling. The most basic feature of the random sample—in all its various forms—is that it is drawn in such a way so as to ensure that every element of the population has an equal chance of being included in the sample. Statisticians have demonstrated that random selection procedures usually result in a preponderance of samples closely approximating the true population values when the sample size is greater than thirty.[17] If we were to randomly draw thirty samples of thirty states from a list of fifty states in terms of voting turnout rates in presidential elections and list the mean turnout rate in each sample, the distribution of sample means would approximate the shape of a normal curve. The theoretical sampling distribution of the means depicted in Figure 5-2 indicates that most of the sample means lie close to the mean value for the population, with a small number located at the extremes.[18] This regularity in the behavior of sampling means allows us to have relative confidence that our sample is likely to lie within close approximation of the population's mean value.

After discussing the physical process of drawing different types of probability samples and the characteristics of each, we shall return to the characteristics of probability samples in our discussion of sample size and sampling error.

The simple random sample requires and uses only minimal knowledge of the larger population in its selection procedures. Nevertheless, a finite listing of the population is required as a basis for selecting the sample. This listing will constitute the sampling frame.

Physically drawing a random sample is not difficult, and a variety of procedures are available for this purpose. One of the simplest means of achieving a random selection is with the assistance of a table of random numbers such as the one included in Appendix D. Many computer centers also have programs to generate random digits. When using a table of random numbers, the first step is to assign each element of the population a unique number. Second, determine the number of cases you wish to include in your sample. Finally, select

[17] This general rule is based upon the law of large numbers "which demonstrates that increasing the sample size causes the sampling distribution of the mean to tend toward the normal." Dean Champion, *Basic Statistics for Social Research*, Chandler Publishing Company, Scranton, Pa., 1970, p. 89.

[18] It can be demonstrated on the basis of the central limit theorem that if repeated samples are drawn from a normal population, the sampling distribution of sample means will be normal. For a good discussion of the central limit theorem and the law of large numbers see Hubert Blalock, *Social Statistics*, 2d ed., McGraw-Hill Book Company, New York, 1972, pp. 177–184.

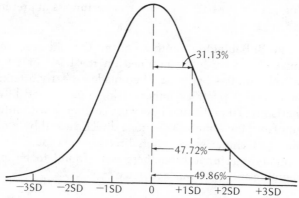

Figure 5-2 Theoretical sampling distribution of mean

the cases by matching randomly chosen numbers with previously assigned case numbers. If, for example, you have a finite population of 1,000 elements, and you wish to draw a sample of 100 cases, you would first number all the elements of the population from 1 to 1,000. You select the first case by letting your pencil fall randomly on any row or column in the table of random digits. All subsequent cases are chosen by continuing down that row or column (omitting cases with duplicate numbers) until you have the requisite 100 cases. The table of random numbers listed in Appendix D contains five-digit numbers. Since your population includes a maximum four-digit number, you consistently drop either the first or last digit in selecting cases. If, for example, your pencil fell on the entry "04805" in the second row of the table, this would indicate that the element numbered "480" would be the first case in your sample, number "489" the second case, and so forth.

There has been some controversy as to whether Tippett's table does in fact constitute a listing of truly random digits. Various attempts have been made to assess the degree of bias incurred with this and other procedures for drawing random integers. With the exception of computer-assisted randomization procedures, mechanical procedures for obtaining random numbers are generally recognized as unsatisfactory.

Dice-throwing, for example, to give random series of the integers 1 to 6, notoriously results in bias. Nor are roulette tables much better. Karl Pearson has shown by analysis of the gaming results at Monte Carlo that the odds against the absence of bias are exceedingly large. The source of the bias is not altogether clear, but if we exclude the possibilities of deliberate falsification, it would appear to arise from small imperfections in the roulette wheel which direct the ball into some compartments in preference to others.[19]

M. G. Kendall and B. Babington Smith point out that the randomness of numbers must ultimately be determined on the basis of whether they yield relatively unbiased results. They made an early attempt to assess the reliability of Tippett's numbers using a variety of different tests and comparisons. Tippett's numbers were compared with integers drawn randomly from the London telephone directory and by a mechanical randomizing machine. The London directory was found to yield highly biased numbers. Tippett's numbers were found to be locally random, although the entire set was not tested.[20]

SYSTEMATIC SAMPLING

Systematic, or interval, sampling is a frequently used variant of the simple random sample. It has several advantages. First, it is usually easier to perform and less subject to interviewer and clerical errors. Second, it often provides more information for the same cost than does the simple random sample. When sampling elements are arranged in a natural and easily obtainable list or sequence, it is frequently simpler to select the cases at a fixed interval rather than individually.

The systematic sample is drawn by randomly selecting the first case of the sample and then sampling on the basis of some predetermined interval. If the population contains N (for example, 100) elements and the sample size is n (20), we would compute the *sampling interval* on the basis of the ratio N/n (100/20), in this case selecting every fifth element. As in the case of the simple random sample, a listing of the population elements must be available, and unique labels distinguish the elements. A table of random numbers is used for selecting the first element.

Systematic sampling provides a relatively representative sample if the values are randomly distributed throughout the initial population listing. Unfortunately, many sampling frames are ordered or incomplete in one way or another. A sample drawn from a telephone directory, for example, may be biased because of unlisted phones and listings in husbands' names. The bias results in these instances from the incompleteness of the population listing rather than from the procedure of systematic sampling. Systematic sampling itself will only produce biased results when the population listing manifests periodicity (such as listing congressional representatives by state). On the other hand, systematic sampling of cities listed alphabetically would

[19] M. G. Kendall and B. Babington Smith, "Randomness and Random Sampling Numbers," *Journal of the Royal Statistical Society*, 101 (1938), 156.
[20] Ibid., pp. 157–163.

probably not result in an unrepresentative sample of cities in terms of socioeconomic factors. Systematic sampling of court cases in terms of their positions on court dockets might also be an economical method of obtaining a representative sample.

CLUSTER SAMPLING

Cluster, or area, sampling is frequently used when no definitive listing of the population is available. It also is employed when resources are limited and sampling units are geographically defined. The population is divided naturally into a number of clusters such as states, counties, regions, precincts, clubs, factories, etc. Through these clusters it is possible to identify the individuals we are interested in sampling. Unfortunately, cluster sampling tends to be the least efficient probability sampling procedure from the standpoint of sampling error; relatively larger samples are necessary for the same degree of precision.

Cluster sampling is essentially a two-stage sampling method. It is accomplished by first specifying the clusters to be employed and then sampling among them. A complete count is then usually taken of the elements within the randomly selected clusters. If systematic sampling is combined with cluster sampling, a partial count is taken among the selected clusters.

If the clusters are defined as geographic units, as is often the case, the designated area (city, county, state, etc.) is divided first into clusters of *relatively equal size*. A city, such as that depicted in Figure 5-3, is first marked off into clusters with industrial areas and other places of low residential population made into somewhat larger units to compensate for the greater number of elements in strictly residential areas. The clusters are then numbered. After deciding how many clusters to sample, the numbers are selected on the basis of a table of random digits, matching the cluster numbers with the random numbers. All or some elements within the selected clusters are then interviewed.

As Mueller, Schuessler, and Costner point out, the physical and mechanical convenience of cluster sampling is frequently purchased at a price in quality:

> Generally, to a degree, it lacks the very characteristic which is the objective of good sampling: typicality and representativeness. ... Sampling within clusters understates the dispersion (within the population) and provides unnecessary duplication (with regard to the typical).[21]

[21] John Mueller, K. F. Schuessler, and H. L. Costner, *Statistical Reasoning in Sociology*, Houghton Mifflin Company, Boston, 1970, p. 358.

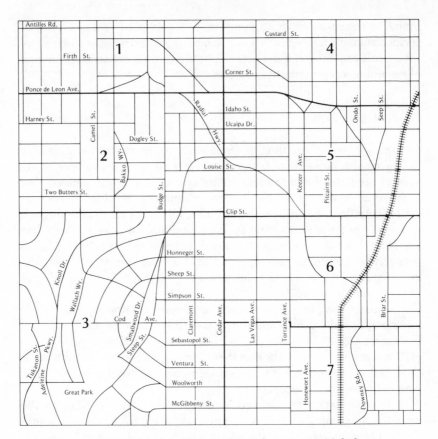

Figure 5-3   Cluster sampling, division of city into initial clusters

For this reason, it is frequently preferable to use a number of small clusters rather than fewer, larger ones. Diversity and heterogeneity are usually better tapped using this procedure. Simon suggests that cluster sampling is most useful in situations of geographic dispersion and heterogeneity within clusters, since it will then lower the cost per interview while preserving the population's heterogeneity. He feels that the utility of cluster sampling will depend almost exclusively upon these two factors.[22]

Initial cluster sampling is frequently combined with systematic sampling in political science and sociology. Samuel Stauffer's classic study, *Communism, Conformity and Civil Liberties,* was based upon this procedure, as was *Voting,* by Berelson, Lazarsfeld, and McPhee.

---

[22] Julian L. Simon, *Basic Research Methods in Social Science,* Random House, New York, 1969, pp. 260–261.

STRATIFIED RANDOM SAMPLING

Stratified sampling is another two-stage probability sampling procedure that bears a certain resemblance to quota sampling in that the population is first divided into two or more strata. It differs from quota sampling in that it uses random procedures for sampling within strata. In some cases, stratified sampling will be the most efficient way to isolate relatively homogeneous classes within populations and ensure that sufficient numbers are included from each strata. When strata are relatively homogeneous, stratified sampling is useful. Nevertheless, it makes little difference whether stratification is introduced at the sampling or analysis phase of research design.

The procedures for drawing the stratified random sample should be apparent at this point. The strata you are interested in sampling are specified first. The various elements within the strata are numbered, the sample size within each strata is determined, and then the selection is made by random means within each strata. The subsamples selected for each strata then are joined together to form the larger sample.

Stratified sampling requires relatively more information about the population since it presupposes a finite listing of the various population elements on a number of criteria. This requirement often raises difficult questions regarding the adequacy of sampling frames. It is important to consider both the currency and the inclusiveness of the sources of stratification information.

In addition to the probability methods that we have discussed, a number of other multiple-stage sampling methods and various combinations of the preceding procedures are available. Ackoff's summary of various sampling designs in Table 5-2 briefly outlines these variations as well as the major features of the methods covered in this chapter. A number of good sampling texts cover these methods in greater detail.[23]

DETERMINANTS OF SAMPLE SIZE

As our previous discussion indicates, a number of factors must be taken into account in determining the size of a sample for any given study. While it is true that the more closely the sample size approximates that of the larger population, the closer the values of the two are apt to be; size—in and of itself—is not the determining factor for

[23] See, for example, Leslie Kish, *Survey Sampling*, John Wiley & Sons, New York, 1965; Cochran, *Sampling Techniques*; Mendenhall, Ott, and Schaeffer, *Sampling Techniques*; Morris H. Hansen, William N. Hurwitz, and William G. Madow, *Sample Survey Methods and Theory*, vols. I and II, John Wiley & Sons, New York, 1962.

Table 5-2 Sampling chart

Type of sampling	Brief description	Advantages	Disadvantages
A *Simple random*	Assign to each population member a unique number; select sample items by use of random numbers	1 Requires minimum knowledge of population in advance 2 Free of possible classification errors 3 Easy to analyze data and compute errors	1 Does not make use of knowledge of population which researcher may have 2 Larger errors for same sample size than in stratified sampling
B *Systematic*	Use natural ordering or order population; select random starting point between 1 and the nearest integer to the sampling ratio (N/n); select items at interval of nearest integer to sampling ratio	1 If population is ordered with respect to pertinent property, gives stratification effect, and hence reduces variability compared to A 2 Simplicity of drawing sample; easy to check	1 If sampling interval is related to a periodic ordering of the population, increased variability may be introduced 2 Estimates of error likely to be high where there is stratification effect
C *Multistage random*	Use a form of random sampling in each of the sampling stages where there are at least two stages	1 Sampling lists, identification, and numbering required only for members of sampling units selected in sample 2 If sampling units are geographically defined, cuts down field costs (i.e., travel)	1 Errors likely to be larger than in A or B for same sample size 2 Errors increase as number of sampling units selected decreases

	Description	Advantages	Disadvantages
1 With probability proportionate to size	Select sampling units with probability proportionate to their size	1 Reduces variability	1 Lack of knowledge of size of each sampling unit before selection increases variability
D *Stratified*			
1 Proportionate	Select from every sampling unit at other than last stage a random sample proportionate to size of sampling unit	1 Assures representativeness with respect to property which forms basis of classifying units; therefore yields less variability than A or C 2 Decreases chance of failing to include members of population because of classification process 3 Characteristics of each stratum can be estimated, and hence comparisons can be made	1 Requires accurate information on proportion of population in each stratum, otherwise increases error 2 If stratified lists are not available, may be costly to prepare them; possibility of faulty classification and hence increase in variability
2 Optimum allocation	Same as 1 except sample is proportionate to variability within strata as well as their size	1 Less variability for same sample size than 1	1 Requires knowledge of variability of pertinent characteristic within strata
3 Disproportionate	Same as 1 except that size of sample is not proportionate to size of sampling unit but is dictated by analytical considerations or convenience	1 More efficient than 1 for comparison of strata or where different errors are optimum for different strata	1 Less efficient than 1 for determining population characteristics, i.e., more variability for same sample size

Table 5-2 (Continued)

Type of sampling	Brief description	Advantages	Disadvantages
E *Cluster*	Select sampling units by some form of random sampling; ultimate units are groups; select these at random and take a complete count of each	1 If clusters are geographically defined, yields lowest field costs 2 Requires listing only individuals in selected clusters. 3 Characteristics of clusters as well as those of population can be estimated 4 Can be used for subsequent samples, since clusters, not individuals, are selected, and substitution of individuals may be permissible	1 Larger errors for comparable size than other probability samples 2 Requires ability to assign each member of population uniquely to a cluster; inability to do so may result in duplication or omission of individuals
F *Stratified cluster*	Select clusters at random from every sampling unit	1 Reduces variability of plain cluster sampling	1 Disadvantages of stratified sampling added to those of cluster sampling 2 Since cluster properties may change, advantage of stratification may be reduced and make sample unusable for later research

Type	Description	Advantages	Disadvantages
G Repetitive: multiple or sequential	Two or more samples of any of the above types are taken, using results from earlier samples to design later ones, or determine if they are necessary.	1 Provides estimates of population characteristics which facilitate efficient planning of succeeding sample, therefore reduces error of final estimate 2 In the long run reduces number of observations required	1 Complicates administration of field work 2 More computation and analysis required than in nonrepetitive sampling 3 Sequential sampling can only be used where a very small sample can approximate representativeness and where the number of observations can be increased conveniently at any stage of the research
H Judgment	Select a subgroup of the population which, on the basis of available information, can be judged to be representative of the total population; take a complete count or subsample of this group.	1 Reduces cost of preparing sample and field work, since ultimate units can be selected so that they are close together	1 Variability and bias of estimates cannot be measured or controlled 2 Requires strong assumptions or considerable knowledge of population and subgroup selected
1 Quota	Classify population by pertinent properties; determine desired proportion of sample from each class; fix quotas for each observer.	1 Same as above 2 Introduces some stratification effect	1 Introduces bias of observers' classification of subjects and nonrandom selection within classes

representativeness. *Variability* is the most important determinant of representativeness. If there is no variability within the population on the dimension you are interested in, a sample of one element will be sufficient. Therefore, the more homogeneous the population is on the dimensions you are studying, the smaller your sample can be without loss of accuracy. Unfortunately, it is often difficult to predetermine the exact degree of homogeneity in a given population. For this reason, we frequently draw a sample that is larger than might be required otherwise.

A second factor that affects sample size is the type of sampling procedure employed. Generally speaking, for the same degree of precision, a stratified sample requires the smallest number of cases, a simple random sample somewhat more, and a cluster sample the greatest number of cases.

Third, available resources in terms of time, money, and personnel affect sample size. The increased costs associated with a simple random sample in terms of identifying each element of the population and sampling across widely dispersed geographic areas sometimes makes cluster sampling a more economical design in spite of the fact that it requires a larger number of cases. Fairly lengthy interviews, on the other hand, which are professionally executed, cost over \$35 per interview. This figure suggests that increasing precision through enlarging the sample size is a rather costly process.

Fourth, with a sizable number of categories, a larger sample is needed. This observation again relates to our discussion of variability within the population. It is difficult to set a hard-and-fast rule on requisite numbers of cases, but Galtung suggests that sample size should be related to the number of variables and values examined.[24] A minimal frequency in a cross-tabulation is about ten and preferably twenty. Thus if we were interested in three variables each having three values and a minimal frequency of twenty, the number of cases for the sample required would be $3^3 \times 20 = 540$. Statistical requirements offer further guidelines. For example, one statistic which we shall discuss later, chi-square, cannot be used with any degree of confidence in a tabulation that has less than five cases in any one cell. When a large number of categories and controls are used, it is often difficult to meet this minimum—even with a sample of 400 cases.

Finally, the overall consideration to take into account in determining sample size is the degree of accuracy and precision required. Accuracy requirements depend partly on the purpose for which a given study is undertaken and the significance of results. Government census statistics—which are used to allocate various state, local, and federal funds—obviously should set stringent requirements on accuracy. On

[24] J. Galtung, *Theory and Methods of Social Research*, Columbia University Press, New York, 1967, p. 60.

the other hand, studies of less general significance can afford to be more lax.

ESTIMATING ERROR

There are two major types of error: (1) that arising from *nonsampling error*, or bias; and (2) *sampling error* arising from random error. While either error may contribute to an unrepresentative sample, the causes and methods of dealing with each type differ. *Nonsampling errors* are errors in measurement. Nonresponse can be a major source of non-sampling error when nonresponse patterns are biased in some systematic way. Studies involving questionnaires always include a certain amount of nonsampling error. Our later discussion of questionnaire design will outline some common procedures for limiting nonsampling errors.

Sampling error refers to the difference between results obtained by sampling and those which would have been obtained if the entire population had been interviewed. Since the main purpose of sampling is to make generalizations to the larger population, determining the amount of tolerable error is an important consideration in evaluating any research. Sampling error also is present to a greater or lesser extent in all studies. In some cases, it arises primarily from failure to meet minimal size requirements.

The problem is that a high degree of either kind of error invalidates the results of a study; and while the sources of error differ, overall error cannot be reduced substantially unless both sources are controlled. If nonsampling errors are large, simply increasing the size of the sample will not help. Normally, researchers decide how much sampling error they reasonably can tolerate before they begin the physical process of drawing a sample. This decision is based on the aforementioned criteria: sampling procedure, population variability, purpose of the study, available resources, and others.

When population values are known, sampling error can be determined easily and directly. If, for example, you survey twenty cities and obtain a mean presidential voting turnout rate of 73.6 percent, and you know the true mean turnout for the population, the two figures simply are subtracted to obtain the sampling error. More often the true population value is not known. Fortunately, it is possible still to make fairly precise estimates of sampling error.

Recall our previous discussion of the simple random sample. We pointed out that the means of a large number of random samples would take on the characteristic normal curve with most of the sample means approximating the true population value. Since the sampling error is simply the difference between the sample's value and the true population value, the distribution of sampling errors also would assume the normal distribution. The distribution of sampling errors again illustrates the regularity in the behavior of samples. It indicates that approximately 68 percent of the samples would be in error by less than plus or minus one standard error or standard deviation; 95 percent of the samples would be within two.

To estimate the precision of a sample statistic without knowing the true population value, we use three pieces of information that we already have or can derive:

1   *The point estimate*   This single value serves as an estimate of the parameter. A mean sample score or a percentage for the sample are used frequently.

2   *The standard error*   An estimate of the errors to which such point estimates are subject, or the average by which all samples deviate from the unknown parameter.

3   *The confidence interval*   Derived on the basis of the foregoing pieces of information, the confidence interval specifies a range of values having a specified probability of including the parameter.

The standard error is computed on the basis of some point estimate. A percentage or a sample mean (average) can be used for this purpose. In principle the procedures are the same, so we shall discuss only the relevant procedures for computing the standard error of the mean. Assuming that we have computed the mean for our sample, the question then becomes, "Where does our particular sample mean lie relative to the population mean?" Although we know that sampling errors tend to resemble the normal distribution, we do not know where our sample's mean is located in this distribution.

The formula for determining the estimated standard error of the mean is as follows:

$$s\overline{X} = \sqrt{\frac{\sum (x_i - \overline{X})^2}{n(n-1)}}$$

where $s\overline{X}$ = standard error of the sample mean
$\overline{X}$ = mean of the sample
x_i = individual observed score
n = sample size

The formula for the computation of the standard error reflects two properties that are major determinants of sampling error: the size of the sample and the scatter, or variance, in the values. These two factors, of course, are related integrally. As sample size approaches that of the population, standard errors will be reduced. When sample size equals the population, there is, of course, no variance in sampling distribution. Degree of scatter in a sample and universe also has some bearing. If there is no variance in a universe, then a sample of one will be sufficient to approximate a population's value. As degree of scatter increases, sample size must similarly increase to reflect adequately scatter in the population.

73	72	66	71	62	54
58	75	61	64	60	68
62	62	61	64	72	67
69	65	45	62	53	68
55	59	56	61	59	63
63	68	52	69	53	68
59	58	78	59	54	57
60	68	62	70	71	64
22	64	58			

Table 5-3 Percentage of Republican vote for President, 1972 Fifty states plus District of Columbia

Let us assume that we have the data depicted in Table 5-3 on the percentage of Republican vote for President in 1972 for the fifty states and the District of Columbia. We want to draw a sample from this population to use as a basis for making inferences about the population. We decide to draw a random sample of thirty cases for this purpose. This can be done through simple random sampling procedures or systematic sampling. The second step in our procedure involves computing the sample mean ($\overline{X}$), which is simply the sum of the individual means divided by the number of cases. Assume in this case that the mean is computed, and $\overline{X} = 60.2$. Third, the standard error of the sample mean is computed:

$$s\overline{X} = \sqrt{\frac{\sum (x_i - \overline{X})^2}{n(n-1)}} = \sqrt{\frac{2493}{(30)\,(29)}} = 1.69$$

While we now know the standard error, or the average deviation of all samples from the population value, we still do not know how well our value approximates the true population value. We would like a means of being able to say that our sample figure is probably approximate in 95 of 100 samples or 99 of 100 samples. Since the actual population value is unavailable, we can only derive an *estimate* of the standard error and not the actual standard error. The actual standard error can be calculated only when the actual population values are known. Nevertheless, an estimate provides a basis for calculating whether the odds are on our side. To construct a more certain basis for determining the level of approximation, we establish a *confidence interval* or an interval which is likely to contain the true mean over the long run. The confidence interval is based upon the sampling distribution of sample means. In effect we estimate the range within which the largest proportion of sample means is likely to lie. We know from our previous description of the normal curve that the greatest proportion of sample means lie within one or two standard errors of the actual population mean.

Confidence level	Standard errors
.99	2.58
.95	1.96
.90	1.64
.80	1.28

Table 5-4 Standard errors associated with different levels of precision

Table 5-4 shows the proportion of sample means that probability theory says will fall within the indicated number of standard errors on either side of the true population mean. Thus, if an infinite number of samples of equal size were drawn from some population, 99 percent would have means within 2.58 standard errors of the true population mean. We can use this information to estimate a range of values within which a population mean should fall when the only information we have is that obtained from a single random sample. If it is true that any single sample mean has a 99 percent chance of being within 2.58 standard errors of the population mean, then it is also true that the population mean has a 99 percent chance of being within 2.58 standard errors of any known sample mean. Hence, if we wished to have a 99 percent chance of being correct in estimating a range within which the true population mean actually falls, we would specify an interval ranging from 2.58 standard errors below our sample mean to 2.58 standard errors above it. If we were willing to run a greater risk of being wrong for the sake of reducing the range of our estimate, we might select the .90 confidence level (meaning that there is a 90 percent chance that the population mean is within our estimated interval) and estimate the population mean to be within 1.64 standard errors of the sample mean.

To adjust for the agreed-upon confidence level and the standard error of the sample mean, we then multiply the standard error of the sample mean by the number of standard errors chosen for a certain confidence level. If, for example, we chose the 95 percent interval, we would multiply the standard error of the sample mean by 1.96. Using our previous example:

$$1.96 (s\overline{X}) = 1.96 (1.69) = 3.3$$

Finally we would add and subtract this value from our initial estimate:

$$\overline{X} \pm 1.96(s\overline{X}) =$$
$$\overline{X} \pm 3.3 =$$
$$60.2 + 3.3 = 63.5$$
$$60.2 - 3.3 = 56.9$$

Thus, we now have an upper and lower limit and a range within which the true population mean is likely to be located in 95 of 100 samples.

Standardized tables of sampling errors present the average sampling errors associated with different percentages in random samples of various sizes. These tables are reproduced in Appendix D for the .95 confidence level.

Choosing the appropriate confidence interval is largely a matter of individual judgment. The 95 percent confidence interval frequently is chosen by convention, but if great precision is required, a higher level is acceptable.

In addition to sampling error, a number of other sources of error may affect the results of a study. Nonsampling sources of error include bias in nonresponse, clerical error, mechanical error, interviewer bias, and similar factors. These errors usually can be minimized by employing complex checking procedures and extensive training, but, again, costs increase in personnel, training, equipment, and time.

Russell Ackoff has employed the term *populationing* to refer to illegitimate generalization, a common error in social research. Populationing results from inadequate means of selecting representatives from the larger population and from inadequate knowledge of that population.[25] It frequently arises from an inadequate understanding of sampling theory itself. The error is inherent in sampling with non-probability methods, and this is the major reason why these methods should never be use to test hypotheses generalizable to the larger population.

Johan Galtung has pointed out an additional problem of generalization that is associated with all sampling procedures (and with most research procedures, for that matter). Most social research essentially constitutes sampling within space but not within time. Thus, most social research is synchronic. Galtung argues that there is lack of sophistication in social science research in this respect:

> Just as for sampling in space, sampling in time can be argued on the basis of our lack of knowledge of the variability of the units. . . . Thus, the respondent may be more conservative at home than at work. . . . But this is hardly ever taken into account, by sampling from different points in time. Nor is it customary to see specifications of the time-cut—there seems often to be an underlying doctrine of uniformity of nature.[26]

This is a problem of generalization and representativeness that is presently beyond most current research design. It nevertheless demon-

[25] Russell L. Ackoff, *The Design of Social Research*, University of Chicago Press, Chicago, 1965, pp. 122–123.
[26] Galtung, *Theory and Methods . . .* , p. 65.

strates the continuing difficulties and perhaps the increased awareness of social scientists as they recognize these problems in their quest for empirical generalized knowledge.

Review questions and exercises

1   Explain the meaning and significance of the following terms:

a   Population, or universe
b   Sample
c   Population element
d   Census
e   Sampling frame
f   Nonprobability sampling
g   Quota sample
h   Accidental sample
i   Purposive sample
j   Probability sampling
k   Random sample
l   Stratified sample
m   Systematic sample
n   Sampling error
o   Nonsampling error
p   Populationing
q   Cluster sample
r   Confidence level
s   Synchronic
t   Standard error
u   Point estimate

2   Critically compare the relative merits of several sampling designs covered in this chapter for one or more of the following topics:

a   A project designed to ascertain whether home owners differ significantly from renters in their involvement in local politics.
b   A study attempting to determine relative awareness within your community of public facilities and the factors associated with differential awareness.
c   A study attempting to ascertain what personality factors, if any, are related to long-term nonvoting.
d   A project to study the political participation patterns of the elderly.

3   Critically analyze the sampling procedures used in some social science literature on a subject of your choice.

4   What major factors must be taken into account in deciding which sampling design is best in a given research situation?

5   What do you see as major problems involved in synchronic social research? How might social research be made less synchronic?

6   What, if any, are necessary preconditions for stratified sampling procedures?

7   What units might be used to define clusters in cluster sampling?

8   What factors make stratified, cluster, or systematic sampling procedures preferable to a simple random sample?

9   Using the table of random numbers in Appendix D, draw two samples of thirty cases from the data presented in Table 5-2.

    a   Compute the standard error of the mean for each sample.

    b   Compare the sample means with the true mean for the population.

    c   Why are the sample means and sample errors different for the two samples?

    d   In what range would the true mean lie in 95 percent of the samples for each of your selected samples?

> Those [polls] that come out good
> for you, those are the good polls;
> those that come out bad for the
> candidate, those are the unscien-
> tific ones: so saith the politicians.
>
> Hubert Humphrey

6

SURVEY RESEARCH IN
POLITICAL SCIENCE

Most people today are familiar with the results of survey research
primarily through the popular press. Rarely will a week pass without
the opinions of a sample of the American public, as measured by the
Gallup or Harris polls, being brought before the country as a whole.
The poll may measure confidence in the Presidency, current voting
margins for political candidates, or attitudes toward unemployment.
Often these responses will be divided into categories of age or political
affiliation which allow an analyst to state that disenchantment with
the Presidency is most prevalent among those who are registered
Democrats under forty years of age. While most people are familiar
with end results or outcomes of these polls, they often are unfamiliar
with procedures employed. It is the purpose of this chapter to examine
the steps taken to reach this end and the problems that may be encountered in the process. After a brief description of the appropriate
application of the survey as a research technique, the chapter delineates
major considerations in design and execution from conceptualization
through analyses. While the limitations of an introductory text in
methods does not permit a detailed and elaborate treatment of procedures involved, this overview should provide students with tools
necessary to pursue any aspects of particular interest.

The technique

The survey is a technique widely used in social science in which interviews are conducted with selected respondents to gather information. Because the costs involved are often substantial,[1] the first question to be faced is whether this particular technique is most appropriate to gather what are deemed necessary data to examine the question at hand.[2] If, for example, the topic involved the examination of roll-call voting patterns in the United States Senate, the data would be available through personal interviews with Senate members. However, these same data would be available also through copies of actual voting records and at a cost significantly less than that involved in personal interviews. An equally important question is whether the persons to be interviewed have the information that researchers desire.[3] If the incidence of Tay-Sachs disease among children of Jewish descent were under investigation, for example, personal interviews may not yield results that might be gained by a screening clinic. As Cannell and Kahn point out, however, "if the focal data for a research project are the attitudes and perceptions of individuals, the most direct and often the most fruitful approach is to ask the individuals themselves." [4] If, after careful examination of all alternative sources, a survey appears the most appropriate method to gather relevant data, then deliberate execution of subsequent stages is the best way to ensure the success of a project.

The survey research procedure has been developed through the use of techniques in a number of disciplines.[5] The personal interview itself was used in psychology and anthropology, for example, as an information gathering device as well as a diagnostic tool; sociology and psychology have been sources of various methods of measurement, and agricultural economics has provided sampling techniques.[6]

---

[1] For a text relating specifically to cost aspects see Seymour Sudman, *Reducing the Cost of Surveys*, Aldine Publishing Company, Chicago, 1967.

[2] Angus Campbell and George Katona, "The Sample Survey: A Technique for Social Science Research," in *Research Methods in the Behavioral Sciences*, eds. Leon Festinger and Daniel Katz, Holt, Rinehart and Winston, New York, 1965, p. 16.

[3] Ibid., p. 16.

[4] Charles F. Cannell and Robert L. Kahn, "The Collection of Data by Interviewing," in Festinger and Katz, *Research Methods . . .* , p. 330.

[5] For a brief history of modern survey development, see Mildred Parten, *Surveys, Polls and Samples: Practical Procedures*, Harper & Row, Publishers, New York, 1950, chap. 1.

[6] Campbell and Katona, in *Research Methods . . .* , p. 15.

The components of survey design

Most experts dealing with the technique of survey research break the process down into several components dealing with various phases of the project. While this is helpful in defining the progressive steps, it is important to note that the steps are not as discrete as this breakdown suggests; decisions made at one point may eliminate options in another phase of the process. A decision, for example, to do a longitudinal survey that measures the impact of some external event implies the necessity to sample the population at least twice, at two different times. Similarly, a survey dealing with attitudes of high school students will determine the universe from which the sample is drawn. Careful framing of the research questions, the first step in survey planning, can minimize expensive mistakes, such as those involved in drawing an inappropriate sample that may invalidate conclusions drawn from the analysis. As Campbell and Katona point out:

> As in any other research, the specific characteristics of any survey will be determined by its basic objectives. The statement of the essential questions which the research is intended to investigate delineates in large part the universe to be studied, the size and nature of the sample, the type of interviewing to be used, the content of the questionnaire, the character of the coding, and the nature of the analysis. Specific survey methods vary according to specific survey objectives.[7]

Bearing these facts in mind, a project using survey research can be viewed as going through several stages, as delineated by Backstrom and Hursh in Table 6-1.[8] The remainder of this chapter examines these phases in detail.[9]

PROJECT PREPARATION

This phase involves all aspects of planning from conceptualization through funding. Hypothesizing, the first step listed by Backstrom and Hursh, actually involves several related activities that result in the formation of hypotheses to be tested. The first is the formulation of the problem: exactly what is going to be investigated? In his comprehensive work *Survey Design and Analysis*,[10] Herbert Hyman relies on

[7] Ibid., p. 17.
[8] Charles H. Backstrom and Gerald D. Hursh, *Survey Research*, Northwestern University Press, Evanston, Ill., 1963, p. 19. Reprinted by permission.
[9] Also see Earl R. Babbie, *Survey Research Methods*, Wadsworth Publishing Company, Belmont, Calif., 1973, particularly chap. 7.
[10] Herbert Hyman, *Survey Design and Analysis*, The Free Press, New York, 1955.

A Project preparation	1	Hypothesizing: deciding what it is you want to study
	2	Designing: establishing the procedures and methods to use
	3	Planning: figuring materials and personnel needed
	4	Financing: arranging support for the survey
B Sampling	5	Sampling: choosing which people are to be interviewed
C Questionnaire construction	6	Drafting: framing the questions for use in the field
	7	Constructing: planning the format of the questionnaire
D Field work	8	Pretesting: determining whether the questions elicit the data desired
	9	Training: teaching interviewers how to gather information correctly
	10	Briefing: showing interviewers how to use the questionnaire
	11	Interviewing: securing data from respondents
	12	Controlling: seeing that the interviewing gets done
	13	Verifying: assuring that the collected data are accurate
E Data processing	14	Coding: preparing the data for analysis
	15	Processing: organizing data mechanically or electronically
	16	Analyzing: interpreting the data
	17	Reporting: sharing the new knowledge

Table 6-1

a number of basic studies to illustrate various points, and in his description of each survey, the problem to be studied is stated. Some studies and their objectives are given below.[11]

Survey 1: Industrial Absenteeism   The purpose was to establish certain facts about the nature and extent of industrial absenteeism in the war industry and to determine some factors leading to such absence.

Survey 2: Prejudice and Personality   A study oriented to the basic proposition that certain factors in the personality of modern

[11] For additional studies relating to cross-national surveys, see the annotated bibliography contained in part II of Stein Rokkan, Sidney Verba, Jean Viet, and Elina Almasy, *Comparative Survey Analysis*, Mouton and Company, The Hague, Paris, 1969.

human beings predispose them to hostility to racial and religious groups.

Survey 3: American Sexual Behavior   A study to collect sufficient information to describe American sexual behavior and to establish what factors account for individual differences in sexual behavior and for group differences among various major segments of the population.

Survey 4: Class Consciousness   The theory to be tested stated: "A person's status and role with respect to the economic processes of society imposes on him certain attitudes, values and interests relating to his role and status in the political and economic sphere." [12]

Once the area has been defined, a researcher usually conducts a search into work that has already been done in the area. This allows familiarity with theoretical constructs as well as the identification of variables that, according to previous research, have been proposed or shown to be related (or not related) to the topic under investigation. Interaction with interested colleagues may help to further define the problem and the parameters of inquiry. This is one of the most creative and critical periods of any research design and may determine whether a piece of research is first rate or mediocre.

Options relating to the design of the survey are under consideration at this time as well. There are basically two types of surveys, descriptive and explanatory, and surveys can be longitudinal or cross-sectional. In addition there are several ways to gather desired information: personal interview, mail questionnaire, telephone interview, and self- and group-administered questionnaires. There are advantages and disadvantages to each type and method, and a brief explanation and description will illuminate these considerations.

Hyman defines a *descriptive survey* as one in which "the focus of such analysis is essentially precise measurement of one or more dependent variables in some defined population or sample of the population." [13] The analysis attempts to measure and correlate rather than determine causes; that is, researchers attempt to determine to what extent certain variables exist. The analysis usually measures the existing state of affairs.

A descriptive survey can be used to examine population characteristics and the extent to which certain values correlate. While it often is used to describe the population, an analysis can be quite elaborate, and because of the broad scope, preliminary findings often point to further avenues of inquiry. Random sampling is usually employed, making results generalizable to other populations.

[12] Ibid., pp. 10–15.
[13] Ibid., p. 68.

A *cross-sectional explanatory survey* attempts to explain attitudes and behavior on the basis of measurements taken at one point in time. It usually includes a variety of variables and groups which permits a researcher to make inferences about the relationship between variables on the basis of comparisons across groups. Though technically unjustifiable, it usually is assumed that differences across groups are also differences across groups over time. Thus researchers interested in the impact of group cohesion on the incidence of suicide could survey, using the cross-sectional procedure, a number of people in circumstances evidencing different types and levels of group cohesion (marital status, religious ties, etc.) and reach some conclusions about the relationship of group cohesion to suicide. Their survey might reveal that married Catholics with children have lower suicide rates and different attitudes toward suicide than unmarried, nonreligious individuals. In this case the inference of a relationship between group cohesion and suicide would be based on cross-sectional comparisons of different groups. Most social science survey research is in fact based upon the cross-sectional method.

Explanatory surveys can also be longitudinal, which means that they are actually administered at different times. The advantage of a longitudinal survey can readily be seen in its attempt to establish the incidence, strength, and direction of causal relations and to deal with change in attitudes and behavior. Questionnaires dealing with preferences for political candidates often will sample the population several times as the election draws closer. The major distinction in a longitudinal survey is whether a sample will be drawn anew each time or the same respondents will be reinterviewed. When respondents are reinterviewed, the survey is called a *panel study*. It is particularly useful in measuring where change occurred. The costs are higher due to the work necessary in contacting the same respondents again; the sample generally dwindles over time because some respondents may not be available or no longer eligible; and the probability of contamination through repeated contacts increases. Nonetheless, the research question may dictate the use of a longitudinal design.

An *experimental survey* is one in which researchers intentionally manipulate some independent variable(s) and observe and measure change in the dependent variable(s). While a descriptive survey can accomplish its purpose through measurement at one point in time, an experimental survey needs at least two: one measurement prior to the introduction of change and another afterward to measure its impact. An experimental survey may include a separate sample, known as a *control group*, in which the experimental variable has not been introduced. A control group is measured in the before-and-after sequence as well, in order to determine changes that otherwise might be attributed falsely to the independent variable in the experimental group. Evaluation of social action programs, for example, often samples the population before the program begins and then at various points in its duration. If the program is citywide, a control city is often chosen with approximately the same population parameters, and the control city is sampled simultaneously. This procedure has the additional advantage of determining whether the activities of the program are responsible for changes or whether some changes have occurred naturally over time.

Thus cross-sectional, longitudinal, experimental surveys are explanatory in purpose, but the basis of the inference is somewhat different. Longitudinal and experimental surveys obviously are best suited to deal with questions of change.

Surveys also may be classified according to how data are collected. There are basically five data gathering methods in which an interview is used: personal interview, mail questionnaire, telephone interview, self-administered questionnaire, and group-administered questionnaire.[14] The advantages and disadvantages of each method are examined below.

In a *personal interview* the actual questionnaire is administered by a trained interviewer who records the respondent's answers. Its major disadvantage is cost: it is the most expensive type of survey to conduct. Another consideration is the possibility of interview bias, both in how a question is asked and how an answer is recorded. The advantages of a personal interview, however, are numerous. This situation allows the use of a fairly lengthy interview, and much information may be gathered. A personal interview is the most flexible survey technique; although each interviewer begins with the same questionnaire, probes of previous responses are often done. In the case of an unclear question, explanations may be given to ensure that the question asked is the question being answered. To ensure the representativeness of the sample, callbacks usually are incorporated into the design to minimize the possibility of a biased sample.

A *mail questionnaire* involves (1) posting the interview schedule to the selected sample, (2) recording of answers by respondents, and (3) return of the schedule to the researcher. Its major advantage is low cost: it does not require trained personnel, and recording and coding can be done by a small staff. The major disadvantage of a mail questionnaire is its low return rate, which strongly increases the possibility of sample bias. A mail questionnaire must be short (to increase return probabilities) and simple (to attempt to eliminate translation problems). Because of its relatively low cost, however, this technique often obtains a larger sample; but because of its low return rate, a greater sample must be chosen initially. Many methods to increase the return rate have been tried. (See Table 6-2, which gives these

[14] A. N. Oppenheim, *Questionnaire Design and Attitude Measurement*, Basic Books, New York, 1966, pp. 30–37.

Method	Possible increase of total % of returns	Optimal conditions
Follow-up*	40%	More than one follow-up may be needed. If possible, returns may be increased by using double postcards with the most important questions on follow-ups. The telephone can often be used effectively for follow-up. Researchers should find out if respondent needs another copy of the questionnaire (which he may have destroyed or misplaced). Sewell and Shaw report a 87.2% return on 9007 from parents of Wisconsin high school students using 3 waves of mailed questionnaires and final telephone interview. *American Sociological Review*, 33 (April, 1968), p. 193.
Sponsor	17%	John K. Norton found that people the respondent knew produced the best results. A state headquarters received the second best rate. Others following in order were: a lower status person in a similar field, a publishing firm, a college professor or student, and a private association or foundation.

* The Bureau of Social Science Research, Inc., 1200 Seventeenth St. N.W., Washington, D.C., 20036, has compiled completion rates in mail surveys undertaken by B.S.S.R. Data compiled by Lenore Reid. They report as many as four follow-ups. Covering letter from institutional sponsor is believed very important.

Table 6–2   Techniques for increasing percentage of returns

Source: Copyright © 1964, 1970 by the David McKay Company, Inc. From the book *Handbook of Research Design and Social Measurement* by Delbert C. Miller. Published by the David McKay Co. Inc., reprinted with permission of the publishers.

methods as well as the percentage increase in returns each is likely to produce.)

In a *telephone interview,* a trained interviewer calls selected respondents on the telephone, asks the questions, and records the answers. If done on a local basis, the cost per interview *obtained* can rival that of a mail questionnaire, with a minimization of sample bias.

Method	Possible increase of total % of returns	Optimal conditions
Length	22%	If a questionnaire is short, then the shorter the better. A double postcard should produce the best results. However, if the questionnaire is over 10 pages at the minimum, length may cease to be a factor. Sewell and Shaw used a double postcard in the study reported.
Introductory letter	7%	An altruistic appeal seems to have better results than the idea that the respondent may receive something good from it.
Type of questions	13%	Questionnaires asking for objective information receive the best rate and questionnaires asking for subjective information receive the worst.
Inducements	33%	Shuttleworth found that a questionnaire containing a quarter produced better results than one without. However, the population and the type of questionnaire could make such inducements unnecessary. Consider promise of report to respondent.
Method of return	Not known	A regular stamped envelope produces better results than the business-reply envelope.
Time of arrival	Not known	The questionnaire, if sent to the home, should arrive near the end of the week.

Table 6-2 (cont.)

However, the sample will contain the additional bias of excluding those who do not have telephones or who have unlisted numbers. In a mobile society the outdatedness of telephone directories can be serious. Another disadvantage of a telephone interview is its length: it must be short and direct and is therefore limited in scope. To "test the waters" for political candidates, to determine the use of certain products, or to examine information levels on specific issues, a telephone interview can be most useful.

In *self-* and *group-administered questionnaires*, the interview

Method	Possible increase of total % of returns	Optimal conditions
Format	Not known	Sletto found a need for an esthetically pleasing cover, a title which would arouse interest, an attractive page format, a size and style of type easily readable under poor illumination and by people with poor vision, and photographs to illustrate the questionnaire. 1 Non-readers and non-writers are excluded from participation. 2 Interest in, or familiarity with, the topic under investigation is a major factor in determining the rate of return. 3 The better educated are more likely to return questionnaires. 4 Professionals are more likely to return questionnaires.
Selection of respondents	Respondent selection can rarely increase returns to above a total of 80%	One of the highest returns reported in the research literature is that by Rensis Likert. In a study of the League of Women Voters (commissioned by the League) a cross sectional sample of 2,905 League members and officers showed the following percent of return: 79% of members 95% of board members 100% of chapter presidents (Rensis Likert, *New Patterns of Management*, p. 145).

Table 6-2 (cont.)

schedule is given either to an individual or to a group, is filled out by the respondent(s), and is returned to the administrators. In the case of ambiguous questions, assistance is available for explanation. This method is usually used in groups assembled for a specific purpose (evaluation after a formal presentation, for example) or to gather information in a specific situation (hospital admittance).[15] The sample is usually quite specific (sixth-grade students) and generalizable only

[15] Ibid., p. 36.

to that population. In these cases, respondents usually come to the administrators for specific purposes, and these often will define population parameters.

When these preliminary questions have been answered—what is to be studied and how—staff and materials can be considered. In all instances, a project director must be chosen to be responsible for total coordination and then, according to the type of survey selected, the availability of interviewers, or information on telephone rates, printing costs, coders, computer time, etc., must be examined. When these needs are estimated, a budget can be drawn up. The costs of survey research usually prohibit financing by individual researchers, and outside sources often are sought to provide the needed assistance. Government and private agencies with research interests within the scope of the proposed inquiry are contacted, and proposals are submitted. Once appropriate financing has been obtained, and the necessary skilled personnel have been acquired, sampling, questionnaire construction, interviewing—the actual execution of the survey—can begin.

SAMPLING

The integrative nature of the survey technique was stressed at the beginning of this chapter, and while the actual selection of sampling method is logically treated here, it should be obvious that the type of universe sampled will be dictated largely by the subject and scope of the inquiry. While the most familiar survey (Gallup and Harris) usually relies on samples of the general population, this may not be the most appropriate group to examine. While the universe may be defined in an obvious way in the research question (a survey of doctors' attitudes toward socialized medicine, for example, would define the population to be interviewed), in others the universe may not be discerned so readily. Oppenheim describes a commercial survey that illustrates the problem of which population should be sampled:

> In the commercial field, one is often asked to design a survey among the users of Product P. On inquiry, it may turn out that the researcher has two distinct purposes: first, to expand the market for Product P and second, to make current users buy Product P more often. A survey among the users may well suggest ways in which they could be persuaded to buy Product P more frequently, but it is unlikely to help us meet the first purpose, namely, to sell P to nonusers. It now becomes clear that we need two samples and two questionnaires—one for users and one for nonusers; other samples, such as one for ex-

users, might be added. Again, it is essential to clear our minds before we start.[16]

Campbell and Katona state: "Many surveys take the national population as their universe because the nation is a basic political and economic unit"[17]; but they also cite surveys whose basis may be geographically defined (city-wide), occupationally defined (house-keepers, doctors, lawyers, and Indian chiefs), or defined by common behavior or experience (veterans, college graduates, etc.). Additionally, the sample may deal with a demographic characteristic (blacks, women) or be selected on the basis of a "screening survey," which is used "whenever the universe in question has some specific character-istic which is not closely associated with particular localities or is not otherwise identifiable."[18]

When the universe has been defined, the design of the sample is then determined. Various sample designs and their implications were discussed in Chapter 5. Again, it cannot be stressed enough that these decisions are based upon the nature, scope, and objectives of the inquiry and considerations of time and cost. While, for example, stratified samples may require the least number of cases and therefore lower interviewing costs, it presupposes sufficient available informa-tion on selection of strata and the number of cases required within each sampled population. A look to future analyses may also dictate the minimum size of a particular subpopulation in a design that uses a simple random sample: multivariate analysis often requires a minimum number of cases per cell before a statistical technique can be employed. This further illustrates the overlapping nature of the steps involved in the design, execution, and analysis of a survey.

THE QUESTIONNAIRE

The desired information, of course, is defined broadly by the research questions and proposed hypotheses to be tested. Within this broad framework, a questionnaire must elicit quantitative responses to answer research questions that begin initially as conceptually related phenomena. A crucial phase of survey research involves the transla-tion of concepts into operational definitions that in turn may be defined and quantified by an interview schedule. The type of informa-tion that is requested falls into several categories: demographic, level of information, behavioral, opinions and attitudes, motivations, etc.;

[16] Ibid., p. 7.
[17] Campbell and Katona, in *Research Methods* . . . , p. 13.
[18] Ibid., pp. 19–20.

it is important to note that some information gained through the interview technique is more reliable than other information. Questions on race, sex, marital status, or demographic characteristics are less likely to produce unreliable results than those which concern sexual behavior or explore attitudes toward racial integration. Even on factual questions, however, the likelihood of a truthful response is greater with a question on marital status than with one concerning household income.

In all likelihood a researcher will include several questions from each question type when the interview schedule is being constructed, as each type gathers different information needed in analysis. Demographic or personal data such as age, income, education, religion, and party affiliation often are used to break the sample into subgroups to establish behavior and attitude patterns within and among these divisions. In a checklist of demographic characteristics, which should "at least be considered," Backstrom and Hursh list these eighteen items:[19]

1   Home ownership
2   Mobility
3   Marital status
4   Household composition
5   Education
6   Occupation
7   Chief wage earner
8   Union membership
9   Group membership
10   Ethnic background
11   Political affiliation
12   Voting record
13   Religion
14   Income
15   Race
16   Sex
17   Age
18   Name, address, and phone number

Behavioral data concern actual activity that respondents have engaged in; political surveys usually include questions regarding voting, campaign work, letter writing, demonstrations, and political contributions, to name a few. An investigation of the literature often reveals scales of political activity that a researcher might incorporate into a questionnaire.

Opinions and attitudes deal basically with the psychological predisposition of a respondent. Opinions deal with feelings about

[19] Backstrom and Hursh, *Survey Research*, p. 97.

a particular subject, while attitudes attempt to tap underlying psychological phenomena in an effort to develop a basic personality orientation.[20]

A researcher may take past behavior and present predispositions together to indicate certain concepts such as "prejudice," or political "conservatism." Again, an examination of the literature may reveal an already constructed index that attempts to measure a phenomenon appropriate to the inquiry.

Questions concerning motivation are often probe questions that ask the "why" of a previous response. The question, "How do you feel about socialized medicine?" may be followed by a probing "Why?" which asks respondents to list objections or benefits they feel may ensue. "Who did you vote for in the last election?" may be followed by "Why?" in an effort to gauge candidate or party appeal.

Level of information regarding political issues may range from those which ask whether respondents can name their state senators to whether or not they have ever heard the term ERA, what it stands for, what its provisions are, whether the resident's state has had a vote yet, the results if so, etc. Political awareness may then be cross-tabulated with education (a demographic variable), political activity (a behavioral variable), or feelings of political efficacy (an attitudinal response) in an effort to determine which variables relate to high and low levels of political information.

Up to this point the research endeavor usually will have narrowed the scope of inquiry so that specific areas and topics can be isolated and the questionnaire can be blocked out into sections dealing with related phenomenon. Now the actual questions can be formulated.

The matter of question wording contains two parts: how the question itself is to be asked and how the answer is to be treated. Aside from interviewer bias (which is considered next), it is important that the wording of a question make it understandable, that it elicit the type of response desired, that it contain all information needed to make an appropriate response, and that it not contain unnecessary information that may bias respondents.

Cannell and Kahn discuss several considerations in formulating questions:

1   *Language*   "The language of the questionnaire must approximate the language of the respondent."

2   *Frame of reference*   "The questionnaire must introduce each topic in a form which ties into the perceptions of the respondent and is consistent with the respondent's notion of what is and what is not salient to the topic under discussion."

[20] Ibid., p. 71.

3   *Information level*   "No unrealistic assumption should be made about the expertness of the respondent or the amount of information he possesses."

4   *Social acceptance*   "No question should confront the respondent with the necessity of giving a socially unacceptable response."

5   *Leading questions*   "Questions should be phrased so that they contain no suggestion as to the most appropriate response."

6   *The single idea*   "Questions should be limited to a single idea or single reference."

7   *Question sequence*   "Questions should be so arranged that they make the most sense to the respondent, that is, the sequence of ideas in a questionnaire should follow the logic of the respondent." [21]

Aside from the actual phraseology used in posing questions, questions themselves may be classified according to particular purposes. Some "special use" questions, according to Backstrom and Hursh, "are not important as separate question types, but for the reasons they are used. . . . A filter question is used to determine whether a respondent qualifies to answer a succeeding question series." [22] *Filter, funnel* or *contingency questions* essentially will dictate whether the immediate successive questions will be asked or a series will be skipped. They determine their applicability to respondents. In the previous discussion of information level, for example, if a respondent answered that he or she had not heard of the ERA, the succeeding questions regarding its meaning, content, etc., would not be asked. If a question asks whether a respondent voted in the last election for President and the answer was "No," succeeding questions about presidential choice would be skipped.

"A second special use item is the *why* question used to elicit the reasons for a particular answer." [23] These questions usually attempt to tap motivation or underlying dimensions in a previous answer. After naming their chosen candidate, respondents may be asked "why" that candidate was chosen; or after their attitudes toward legalized abortion are determined, respondents may be asked "why" they are opposed to or in favor of legalized abortion.

"Probe questions are used after, say, a 'why' question to induce the respondent to elaborate on his initial remarks: 'Are there any other reasons?' " [24] For example, when a respondent is asked whether he has heard of a campaign to combat drunk driving (a filter question)

---

[21] Cannell and Kahn, in *Research Methods . . .* , pp. 342–350.
[22] Backstrom and Hursh, *Survey Research*, p. 82.
[23] Ibid., p. 82.
[24] Ibid., p. 82.

and he answers affirmatively, the interviewer then may ask where he has heard of it. If the respondent answers "On TV and radio," the interviewer may probe and ask, "Anywhere else?" to see if he adds local newspapers and discussions with friends.

"The *intensity question* attempts to determine the strength with which people have a particular point of view." [25] When a respondent answers "Democrat" to a question regarding party affiliation, the respondent quite frequently is asked whether he considers himself a strong, moderate, or weak Democrat.

"*Sleeper questions* are seemingly innocuous requests for information, actually designed to check on the veracity of the respondent." [26]

In addition to the types of information a question elicits and the specific use of the answer, questions may be classified according to the type of response that is given. The two basic types of responses are (1) those which are closed, structured, or limited, in which a specific answer is anticipated or a choice is given and then recorded; and (2) those which are open, unstructured, or unlimited, in which a respondent may answer freely and the response is recorded as given. A researcher should consider the pros and cons of each question type.

Open-ended questions, which allow respondents to answer freely, in their own words, and to touch on whatever aspects they think appropriate, are useful in topic areas where researchers are attempting to explore new fields and responses cannot be predicted. They are also useful when in-depth responses are desired or when responses are expected to cover a wide range. Disadvantages of open-ended questions are the greater amount of time they require, the greater amount of space needed on the questionnaire, and their relative difficulty in coding for analysis.

Structured, or *closed, questions* are used more frequently; they anticipate specific responses through either their wording or their presentation of fixed alternatives. Closed questions require considerably less time to ask and record than open-ended ones, and they can be handled more easily at the analysis stage. They do, however, diminish the richness of responses and can place respondents in a situation of equally undesirable alternatives. In many situations alternative responses to a question are well defined—"Did you vote in the last presidential election?" requires a "Yes," "No," or "Don't Know" —and there is no loss of information. Cannell and Kahn list three questions in which closed-response questions are used: "(1) there is only one frame of reference from which the respondent can answer the question; (2) within this single frame of reference, there is a known range of possible responses; and (3) within this range, there are clearly

[25] Ibid., p. 82.
[26] Ibid., p. 82.

defined choice points which accurately represent the position of each respondent." [27] Closed questions may be used to gather many of the kinds of data discussed earlier, and "structured" questions may offer many types of response.

These responses may be *dichotomous* (only two alternatives are available) or *multiple choice* (offering several options) and may ask respondents to indicate a choice among alternatives, to express intensity of feeling, or to rank-order given alternatives. Several basic types of response categories are used to achieve specific objectives in a questionnaire. It has been found, for example, that a broad question concerning political behavior may not be answered completely if a respondent is asked, "In what types of political activity do you engage?"—either because he cannot recall, or does not, in his mind, classify certain activities as political. In this case it might be wiser to show the respondent a list of these activities and have him indicate the ones in which he has participated: "Never," "Seldom," "Often," or "Very Often." The type of question that presents a list and requests a specific response is called an *inventory*.

Another type of question might present respondents with several names, for example, of prospective candidates for the Presidency, and respondents are asked to place the names in an order of preference, listing first choice, second, etc. This is called *ranking* and may cover many subjects (from the political candidacy ranking above to the selection of sites for a new playground). A variation of ranking is found in the use of *paired comparison*, in which several pairs of alternatives are presented and respondents are asked to indicate their ranking of each pair. Republican candidates may be listed as "Rockefeller vs. Reagan," "Reagan vs. Ford," "Rockefeller vs. Ford," etc., and respondents indicate their preference within each pair. This type of question requires that each single alternative be placed against every other, and the resulting number of "pairs" can be quite numerous. If the number of alternatives is lengthy, this procedure may not be feasible or desirable.

Checklists are questions that ask respondents to indicate their feelings about a particular subject according to a list which is presented to them. The interviewer may present a respondent with a list of attributes describing professional politicians, and the respondent will be asked which attributes he regards as important. Responses may range from "Honesty" and "Integrity" to "Ambition," and the respondent will indicate whether he regards each particular attribute as "Very Important," "Important," or "Not Important" until the list has been completed.

Ratings ask respondents to indicate their depth of feeling or opinion along a particular dimension. Opposing points are usually

---

[27] Cannell and Kahn, in *Research Methods . . .* , p. 350.

indicated, as well as steps. The rating may indicate "Very Important" to "Unimportant," "Generous" to "Selfish," or "Fast" to "Slow." A visual method used to determine intensity is the *feeling thermometer* —literally a picture of a thermometer on which respondents are requested to mark their answers at or between the extreme points. Responses in intensity questions are often given a weighted numerical rating, and previous research is used to determine the approximate distance between various responses.

In addition to how individual responses are indicated and coded, a researcher may also take the responses of several questions and compose an "index." An index is a single coded variable that actually is based on several combined responses. Indices of political activity may be developed based upon the frequency indicated for each separate item. Indices of poverty, of sociability, or of many other concepts may be constructed through the use of several different questions that attempt to tap the same dimension.

Once questions are formulated and the way in which responses will be recorded is determined, the final construction phase of the questionnaire is done: the questions are given an order. The aims of question ordering are to ensure a natural flow from one subject to the next, to place more personal items in the latter part of the questionnaire, to ensure as much as possible that interview rapport will have been established, and finally, to write letters of introduction or to structure introductory remarks that will lend authority to the enterprise and set respondents at ease.

FIELD WORK

The first step in the actual field work of a survey is to pretest the interview schedule as it is presently constructed. Pretesting involves going into the field with the questionnaire, interviewing the same type of respondents as those who have been selected in the sample, and conducting interviews with them. The purpose of this phase is to assess any difficulties that might be involved in introductory remarks, question format, or question construction. Ambiguous or awkwardly worded questions can be rephrased, and any other problems can be rectified before the instrument is used in the field. The importance of this phase of survey research cannot be underestimated. If there are problems, the time to correct them is now, rather than after the schedule has been used to interview hundreds of people. The instrument should be looked upon as flexible until this phase has been completed. Attention to remarks made by the interviewer and respondents at this time can provide invaluable aid to researchers in making the study easier to administer, code, and analyze. These remarks will be used also in the instructions given to interviewers to familiarize them with potential difficulties that cannot be rectified. Now the researchers will correct or modify potential trouble spots. Before printing the questionnaire, appropriate spacing of questions and responses must be considered, adequate instructions for interviewers at decision points must be given (skip to, probe, etc.), and spacing of identification numbers (for respondents, card numbers, study numbers, etc.) and variable spacing, or column placement, must be assigned. (See Chapter 10 for a full discussion of computer cards.) The questionnaire now can be duplicated for the actual sample.

The next phase of the project concerns *training the interviewers.* This may involve training persons who have never interviewed before, or it may be a briefing to familiarize trained interviewers with the survey instrument. It is always stressed that the purpose of the interviewer is to elicit an appropriate response without bias either in asking a question or in reacting to and recording respondents' answers. An interviewer's manner must be pleasant and nonthreatening, and respondents must be properly motivated to answer all questions as honestly as possible.

The physical appearance of interviewers and their initial contact with respondents are often crucial considerations, for this first meeting often can set the stage for cooperation and rapport. Experience has indicated that middle-aged female interviewers are least likely to evoke adverse reactions from respondents and are also less likely to be regarded suspiciously by females in the sample. If racial or ethnic considerations must be taken into account, it is often helpful to coordinate interviewers and respondents as nearly as possible in order to avoid potential uncooperativeness or possible bias resulting from either interviewer or respondent. Interviewers must look and act like the professionals they are in all phases of the interview, from the introduction through a polite word of thanks.

Introductory remarks should contain the name of the research agency, briefly explain the subject of the study and how respondents were chosen, and ensure the confidentiality of responses which are given. The introduction must be natural, brief, and to the point. If a specific household member has been assigned to the interviewer (youngest female over eighteen, for example), the interviewer should request to speak to her at that point. If necessary, the introduction should be repeated, and when cooperation has been established, the interview can begin. Many books have been written about interviewing techniques and solutions to problems that regularly arise in interview situations. Techniques have been developed that can persuade reluctant respondents to participate, elicit responses to personal questions, or probe more deeply into a given response. Through training, interviewers should be exposed to as many of these techniques as possible in order to be prepared for almost any situation.

When interviewers have achieved an appropriate posture and attitude, it will be necessary to familiarize them with the details of specific questions asked in the survey. They should understand the instrument sufficiently to answer any ambiguity that respondents express; they should be cued on contingency questions; and they must be given careful instruction about coding. All questions should be answered fully in the briefing session, and experienced interviewers may be able to spot potential difficulties that have gone unnoticed to this point. Interviewers should not be told to expect any given response to a particular question, however, as this confounds the possibility of bias. It may be necessary to give specific sampling instructions, and interviewers should clearly understand any selection they must make of both households and respondents. Through pretesting, it should be possible to instruct interviewers on the approximate total time for the interview, the number of interviews they are expected to complete, and the deadline for completion. They should be given necessary identification, letters of introduction, and informational material. The interviewers then are sent into the field.

Controlling the interview involves a checklist by which the project director can determine the rate of interview completion from particular interviewers, provide that all assigned areas are adequately covered, and check refusal rates either in a given area or with a given interviewer. This checklist allows the director to keep close watch on the progress of the survey and to head off difficulties that may arise.

When the completed interviews are returned, it is common practice to personally contact every nth respondent to verify that the interview was conducted and completed. If irregularities are discovered with a specific interviewer, all schedules from that person usually are verified. If personal verification with respondents is not possible, interviewers usually are asked questions about the respondents and the interview situation. In addition, addresses often are checked, and respondents can be contacted by mail with a return postcard sent to the director. Once it has been determined that the data have been collected correctly and completely, preparation of the data can begin.

DATA PROCESSING

During questionnaire construction, it was determined that many responses could be precoded; that is, responses were given numerical equivalents at the time of the interview. Open-ended questions, however, still must be assigned numerical codes in preparation for analysis. Usually a large sample of responses for these questions is examined, listed, and grouped into broad categories that cover most answers given. The responses remaining are then placed in these categories.

Variable	Column	Question	Text and code
	1–4	2	Respondent ID number (code entire number)
	5–6	3	Deck number Code = 01
	7	4	Interview number 1 = Emerton 2 = Brown 3 = Morgan 4 = Lausten 5 = Marsh 6 = Hill 7 = Hickman 8 = Curran 9 = Kaultenback & Connors
001	8–9	5a	County (check I.D. code with county designation) 11 = Blaine 12 = Loup 13 = Garfield 14 = Wheeler 15 = Custer 16 = Valley 17 = Greeley 18 = Sherman 21 = Howard 22 = Merrick 23 = Hall 24 = Hamilton
002	10	5b	Region 1 = Counties 11–18 5 = Counties 21–24
003	11	6	Sex 1 = Male 2 = Female
004	12	7	Where are you now living? 1 = county seat 2 = other city in county 3 = other city out of county 4 = rural address in county

Table 6-3   Master code for citizen consolidation study

When more than one coder is used, questionnaires usually are exchanged to determine the extent of "intercoder reliability"—the extent to which the same items are coded similarly by all individuals. Then coded responses to all questions are placed by their assigned position in the questionnaire (or may be transferred to an eighty-column sheet), and the instrument is given to a keypuncher for transferral to punched cards.

When all coding has been completed, from response assignment to variable number assignment in columns, the entire questionnaire with its original questions and coded responses is placed in "codebook" form. The codebook (see Table 6-3 for an example) is the index used by analysts to determine the placement of all variables and their appropriate values on punched cards. It contains the card and column to which the variable has been assigned as well as all legitimate codes.

The use of "canned" programs (which do not require a computer programming background) has greatly simplified the next step in data processing. Researchers usually will have several programs at their disposal to "set up" the data. These programs contain "subroutines" that can label, manipulate, transform, and statistically analyze data according to requests which are made. The first request of many researchers is to obtain "marginals." *Marginals* list all variables and the breakdown for all responses. Most programs will not only list the number (N) of responses but will also give the percentages. Table 6-4 is an example of marginals obtained for this type of request. Researchers will examine these breakdowns and acquire their first feeling for the survey. They can scrutinize responses and determine recoding and/or collapsing, and they may see obvious initial cross-tabulations and attempt to scale responses along a particular dimension. While data that have been collected contain a finite amount of information, how the information is arranged is not limited to the number of variables in the survey. New variables—scales, factors, scores—can be created from manipulation of existing information. Additionally, marginals from certain demographic variables are often compared with outside data sources to determine sample validity. This preliminary scan of data is then followed by more elaborate stages of analysis.

The hypotheses originally put forward in the conceptual stages of the project are tested to determine the extent to which the data will support or disprove them.[28] Often, however, in the course of this analytic phase, new avenues of investigation may appear, and re-

---

[28] Many statistical techniques are used to test hypotheses and readers may wish to examine statistical handbooks that indicate the purpose and procedure of these tests. See Chapter 9 for introductory statistics as well as references for texts on statistical methods.

Variable 032: Attend political meetings

Value	Absolute frequency	Relative frequency (percent)	Adjusted frequency (percent)	Cumulative adjusted frequency (percent)
0.0	59	55.1	55.1	55.1
3.00	1	0.9	0.9	56.1
4.00	1	0.9	0.9	57.0
5.00	1	0.9	0.9	57.9
6.00	1	0.9	0.9	58.9
7.00	1	0.9	0.9	59.8
9.00	43	40.2	40.2	100.0
Total	107	100.0	100.0	100.0

Variable 067: Read professional journals

Value	Absolute frequency	Relative frequency (percent)	Adjusted frequency (percent)	Cumulative adjusted frequency (percent)
0.0	22	20.6	20.6	20.6
1.00	52	48.6	48.6	69.2
5.00	33	30.8	30.8	100.0
Total	107	100.0	100.0	100.0

Table 6-4   Sample marginals

searchers may attempt to follow them up. Unexpected results are obtained often, and alternative hypotheses may be put forward and tested as well. This period can often be exciting, as certain assumptions are called into question and new explanations are advanced. The broad nature of a descriptive survey often allows the retesting of hypotheses from other research endeavors, and this retesting can support these results or call them into question. While the analysis of a body of data may continue for months, at some point researchers usually desire to put forward their results to be scrutinized and critiqued by professional peers. Criticism may lead to further refinement of the ideas, and the result is usually submission to a professional journal for publication.

REPORTING

Dissemination of knowledge is one professional responsibility of researchers. The contribution of scholars in various fields adds to the growing body of knowledge in any discipline and leads to the development of new theoretical constructs that guide future inquiry. Researchers must provide all relevant information to colleagues— information concerning design, sampling, analysis—so that findings may be judged accordingly and duplicated if desired. This exchange of new theories and research information permits investigators' work to be evaluated by professionals within the discipline who judge both its theoretical and methodological soundness as well as its relevancy to the discipline. It is an essential endeavor both for researchers, who benefit from valid criticism that allows refinement and expansion, and for their colleagues, who learn about research activities that will broaden their scope and perhaps contribute additional knowledge to research interests of their own.

Review questions and exercises

1   Explain the meaning and significance of the following terms:
   a   Universe
   b   Sample
   c   Explanatory survey
   d   Panel study
   e   Longitudinal
   f   Cross-sectional
   g   Demographic characteristic
   h   Screening survey
   i   Contingency questions
   j   Codebook

2   Give examples, other than those listed in the text, in which survey research would *not* be the most appropriate method of inquiry.
3   List the ways in which survey information may be gathered and explain the advantages and disadvantages of each method.
4   Under what circumstances would a longitudinal survey be desirable? What are the types?
5   What are the purposes of random sampling?
6   What is a control group, and why is it used in survey research?
7   Why do most questionnaires include questions concerning demographic characteristics?
8   Construct a short questionnaire including at least ten questions relating to a concept (prejudice, conservatism, etc.) or topic (government spending, political corruption, etc.) of your choice. Use several of the question types discussed in this chapter.
9   Administer the questionnaire to twenty people. With half the

sample, structure the responses; with half, keep the interview free flowing and probing. Note the differences, if any, and then write or report the results.

10 From the experience gained in the above exercise, write a short essay about which answer type you would choose for each question if you were administering the test to a sample of 800. Give reasons for your preference.

> Scientific measuring instruments are not passive blotters; but neither are they so disturbing that they churn subject matters like eggbeaters.
>
> Norwood Russell Hanson

7

SCALING TECHNIQUES
FOR SOCIAL RESEARCH

In the preceding chapters we discussed scaling briefly and indicated that a *scale* is a series of ordered items. In our discussion of survey design (Chapter 6), we provided several examples of self-administered scales in the form of rating charts and checklists. When these procedures are employed, respondents place themselves directly on a scale that has been predefined by the researchers. The types of scaling procedures discussed in this chapter also aim at placing individuals, states, groups, or any other units at various positions on an ordered variable, but the procedures discussed are considerably less direct and more complex.

Many concepts in social science cannot be measured readily in natural units or by direct indicators or single questions. The concepts of political efficacy, alienation, legitimacy, and power are all important to political scientists, and yet they are not quantified easily. A multiplicity of operational indicators could be used with each of these concepts. It might be argued, in fact, that such concepts deal with multi-faceted phenomena which *should* be measured in a multi-dimensional way. Scaling procedures provide a way of dealing with the variety of operational indicators and a means of ascertaining whether and/or how different aspects of a phenomenon "hang together."

Perhaps most importantly, scaling procedures achieve this in an empirically justifiable manner that is objective and readily interpretable. A problem with simple self-administered scales is that they are frequently difficult to interpret. If we were interested in ranking respondents in terms of their perceptions of themselves as "democratic-nondemocratic," we could ask them simply to check the appropriate category on a rating list. Similarly, we might easily ask respondents to rate themselves in terms of self-perceived tolerance or prejudice. Unfortunately, the exact meaning of both responses is unclear. Because researchers have predefined response categories in a general but ambiguous manner, it is not clear if respondents understand the concepts or interpret them as the researchers do. Thus, an alternative, and probably more meaningful, measure would attempt to ascertain some components of a concept and factors that form a basis for a given response. We want to know, in other words, what the terms "democratic-nondemocratic" mean to our subjects. All terms have certain implied meanings: the problem is to determine just what they are. A simple checklist provides no means of ascertaining the ancillary meanings of a term. As such it is of unknown validity.

Thus the scaling procedures discussed in this chapter are considered generally superior to simple untested scaling procedures in terms of determinacy and universality and validity and reliability.

We suggested in Chapter 4 that numerical language is superior to verbal language because it is more determinant in meaning. Durkheim, among others, criticized everyday language because it is always susceptible of more than one meaning.[1] Wallace made essentially the same point when he indicated that connotative richness is vital to poetry but mortal to science.[2] A central problem of simple rating scales is that the assumption must be made that the language is determinant; but this assumption is untested and often unwarranted. Validity—the assumption that a measure indicates what it purports to—is presumed. Thus, in the preceding example, we assume that a respondent understands the concepts of democracy or prejudice in the same manner as do researchers and other respondents. If we did not make this assumption, the various responses would not be comparable.

Universality is really another dimension of determinacy, but here the requirement is that the language or concept be as unequivocally and widely understood as possible. A scale should not be culture bound. A simple self-rating scale usually assumes validity in this respect also.

Thus we should recognize that scaling is simply another aspect of measurement, a more complex measurement process. We use scal-

---

1 Emile Durkheim, *Suicide*, The Free Press, New York, 1951, p. 41.
2 Walter Wallace, *The Logic of Science in Sociology*, Aldine Publishing Company, Chicago, 1971, p. 116.

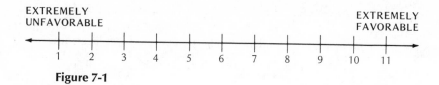

Figure 7-1

ing procedures because they frequently yield *more adequate* measures of important concepts and variables. We chose among scaling techniques on the assumption that some procedures are more adequate than others.

Thurstone equal-appearing interval scale

While most scaling procedures yield an ordinal level of measurement, the Thurstone scaling procedure aims at achieving an interval level of measurement. One of the most frequently used types of Thurstone scales is the *equal-appearing interval scaling procedure*.[3] Like other scaling procedures discussed in this chapter, this technique results in an ordered measure with varying degrees of intensity.

To construct a Thurstone scale, a number of items thought to be relevant to a given variable are first collected. Second, a large number of judges, representative of the target population, then independently order the items into one of eleven categories (see Figure 7-1) in terms of the degree to which they feel the item indicates favorability and unfavorability. Because the Thurstone scaling procedure uses judges to determine the degree of favorability implied in an item rather than inferring favorability from the manner in which they place *their own* attitudes, the procedure has sometimes been termed "judgmental" rather than response-inferred.

Third, the scale value of each statement is determined by the median position (or category) to which it has been assigned by the group of judges. The median is simply the middle category or value that divides any distribution of scores or ranks into two equal parts or proportions. Now scale values have been assigned to each item, and thirty or forty items may remain within each category. At this point we must choose the *best* items to represent each point on the scale. Thurstone proposes the *criterion of ambiguity* for this purpose. Ambiguity is measured by the variation in the judges' rankings. State-

[3] Louis Thurstone and E. J. Chave, *The Measurement of Meaning*, University of Chicago Press, Chicago, 1929.

Category number	Number of judges	Cumulative percentage of placements
1	0	0%
2	25	25
3	25	50
4	25	75
5	25	100
6	0	100
7	0	100
8	0	100
9	0	100
10	0	100
11	0	100

Table 7-1   Category placement for one item with 100 judges*

* Median Category $= 3.5$.

ments that have too broad a scatter or variation among the rankings of different judges are discarded on the assumption that they are either ambiguous or irrelevant.

To judge variation in the rankings of the judges, the *interquartile dispersion value*, or the standard deviation, of the items is used. Computation of the standard deviation is explained in Chapter 9, and here we will only discuss computation procedures for interquartile dispersion. Looking at Table 7-1, we can see the category placements for one item using 100 judges. All the judges (100 percent) ranked the item between categories 2 and 5. The dispersion in values is determined by dividing the category placements into quartiles in terms of the cumulative percentage of placements. The *quartile dispersion* is the difference between the category including 75 percent of the rankings and the category including 25 percent of the rankings. In our example, the quartile dispersion is $4 - 2 = 2$. All other statements are measured similarly in terms of the dispersion in the judges' rankings. The median category placement for the item in our example is 3.5. If this item has the lowest quartile dispersion of the statements with this median value, this item is chosen for inclusion in the final scale.

The Thurstone scale purports to include not only nonambiguous items but also only items that are *relevant* to the concept being measured. It assumes that an individual's actual position on the variable being measured is indicated by his scale score. Thus, a given scale item is likely to be endorsed by individuals with the same position on the variable. Thus, as depicted in Figure 7-2, a person with a scale score of 6 has a low probability of endorsing items at either extreme and an

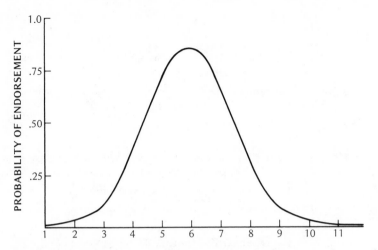

Figure 7-2   Theoretical probability of item endorsement for a subject with a scale score of 6.0

increasingly high probability of endorsing items closest to his actual scale value.[4] Depending upon the scale value for any individual, different curves could be drawn to demonstrate the theoretical probability of endorsement. Practically, this is determined by assessing whether persons with similar scale values exhibit similar endorsement patterns.

The final Thurstone scale is then a series of statements, usually at least twenty,[5] and the position of each item on the scale has been defined in terms of the judges' classification. Items have been chosen with low internal dispersion, and they have been chosen so that they spread out evenly among the categories so that relevant variations in attitude can be ascertained. The final scale might be familiar to that depicted in Table 7-2.

When the scale is administered to actual subjects, numerical values are not shown on the questionnaire, and the items usually are ordered randomly. Subjects are asked to check items that correspond most closely to their own position. The mean or median value of the items chosen will be the basis for assigning subjects a relative position on the variable being measured. Theoretically, an individual should check only items that, in the judges' classification, were immediately

[4] See Allen L. Edwards, *Techniques of Attitude Scale Construction*, Appleton Century Crofts, New York, 1957, pp. 83–119.

[5] Some research suggests that fifty items are needed for a Thurstone scale to be as reliable as a Likert scale with twenty-five items. See Lauren H. Seiler and Richard L. Hough, "Empirical Comparisons of Thurstone and Likert Techniques," in *Attitude Measurement*, ed. Gene F. Summers, Rand McNally & Company, Chicago, 1970, pp. 159–173.

Scale value	Scale item
1.0	There are too many local governments that seem to be duplicating each other.
2.0	Governmental services would probably be better if some local functions were merged.
3.0	A lot of government boundaries are artificial.
	* * *
8.1	Even if services are not what they could be, government at the local level should remain small.
9.0	Government is getting too removed from the people.
10.0	The local community is the backbone of America.

Table 7-2   Hypothetical Thurstone scale and scale values

contiguous. If subjects do not choose contiguous items, it is usually taken to indicate that they have no attitude on the subject, that they have an unorganized attitude, or that the items measure more than one variable.

A scale's reliability can be assessed through *test-retest* proce-dures, or through the use of *parallel forms*. With test-retest procedures, the scale is judged reliable if the same individual gets similar scale values on repeated applications. *Stability* is the main consideration here. Unfortunately, lack of stability is not always a true indication of the scale's lack of reliability. Instability might be a result of changed circumstances.[6] Furthermore, stability does not always indicate reliability; it may result from other factors such as a desire to be consistent.

Because of the difficult assumptions underlying test-retest procedures, *parallel forms* are sometimes used. In this case, two nearly identical scales are constructed, and both are administered to the same individuals. The difference between the scores on the two scales provides the measure of reliability. A high correlation between the two scores is assumed to indicate that the scales are reliable. A somewhat intermediate procedure, which does not involve constructing two separate forms, involves correlating the scores between different parts of the same scale; this procedure is known as *split-half reliability*.[7]

There have been a number of criticisms of Thurstone scaling pro-

---

[6] See George W. Bohrnstedt, "Reliability and Validity Assessment in Attitude Measurement," in Summers, *Attitude Measurement*, pp. 80-99.
[7] Ibid.

cedures. One is that the procedure is time consuming. Although as many as 300 judges frequently were used in initial constructions of this type, subsequent experimental work suggests that the number of judges need not be this large. Both Edwards and Kenney and Uhrbrock found very high correlations between scales using 72 and 300 judges, on the one hand, and two groups of 50 judges on the other.[8]

More serious questions have to do with the use of judges at all.[9] Unlike other scaling procedures discussed in this chapter, Thurstone scaling asks judges to determine the favorability implied in a statement rather than asking them their own attitude toward an item. There is some indication that items with greater specificity in terms of self-references yield more reliable measures.[10] While this implies that variations in judges' rankings are likely to be high simply because of this lack of specificity, the question can also be raised whether the judges' attitudes influence their ratings. This is largely an empirical question open to experimental inquiry. Findings reported by Garson, Beyle, and Hinckley suggest that rankings of items are largely independent of judges' own attitudes.[11] Whether this is true on all questions is unclear. The question is probably best treated as an open one—one to be tested rather than assumed.

An additional criticism of Thurstone procedures is that the individual scale scores which are derived are difficult to interpret.[12] Since an individual scale score is the median or mean of all his or her responses, individuals with very different response patterns can have similar scores. As we pointed out previously, the criterion of relevance theoretically assures selection of contiguous items, but the scale value nevertheless lacks the direct meaningfulness that some scaling procedures yield. This criterion can be levelled at all summated scales, including the Likert scale discussed next.

---

[8] A. L. Edwards and Katherine C. Kenney, "A Comparison of the Thurstone and Likert Technique of Attitude Scale Construction," *Journal of Applied Psychology*, 30 (1946), 72–83; and R. S. Uhrbrock, "Attitudes of 4430 Employees," *Journal of Social Psychology* (1934), 365–377.

[9] Ibid. At present this criticism must be taken into account, pending further empirical investigation.

[10] Charles R. Tittle and Richard J. Hill, "Attitude Measurement and Prediction of Behavior: An Evaluation of Conditions and Measurement Techniques," *Sociometry* (June 1967), 30.

[11] G. David Garson, *Handbook of Political Science*, Holbrook Press, Boston, 1971, p. 114; H. C. Beyle, "A Scale for the Measurement of Attitude toward Candidates for Elective Governmental Office," *APSR*, 26 (1932), 527–544; E. D. Hinckley, "The Influence of Individual Opinion on Construction of an Attitude Scale," *Journal of Social Psychology*, 3 (1932), 283–296.

[12] Claire Selltiz, Marie Jahoda, Morton Deutsch, and Stuart Cook, *Research Methods in Social Relations*, Harper & Row, Publishers, New York, 1959, p. 363.

/ 1	2	3	4	5 /
Strongly agree	Agree	Undecided	Disagree	Strongly disagree

1. "Local government is simply too small to provide the kinds of services that most citizens demand."

/ 1	2	3	4	5 /
Strongly agree	Agree	Undecided	Disagree	Strongly disagree

2. "Even if the services of local government are not as good as they could be, government at the local level should remain small."

/ 1	2	3	4	5 /
Strongly agree	Agree	Undecided	Disagree	Strongly disagree

3. "If I had my choice, I'd rather spend a little more to keep government small and close to the people."

Table 7-3   Likert-scale sample questions

Likert scaling procedures

The *Likert scale*, somewhat similar to the Thurstone scaling procedure, is generally simpler to construct.[13] It results in an ordinal level of measurement. It has been considered a preferable empirical scale because it does not involve the use of judges to evaluate the degree of favorability or unfavorability in an item. The basic procedure also aims at providing a relative ordering, and subjects representative of the projected population are used for this purpose. The adequacy of scale items is indicated by their sensitivity to differences among subjects.

First, researchers initially select a number of representative subjects and a sample of statements; researchers determine whether a given statement is favorable or unfavorable. Subjects are then asked to rank statements into five categories *in terms of the extent to which they themselves agree or disagree with a given statement.* The five categories provide a roughly neutral middle position. (See Table 7-3.) Numbers are not indicated on the questions; only categories are. After all statements have been ranked, they are assigned the numerical values given in the previous example, and average values for all sub-

---

[13] Rensis Likert, "A Technique for the Measurement of Attitudes," *Archives of Psychology*, 22 (1932), 1–55.

Subject	Score on item
Smith	5 Upper quartile
Jones	4
Winter	3
McCarthy	3
Steinman	2
Miller	2
Dunklau	1 Lower quartile
Shocket	1

Table 7-4   Ranking of subjects on question 1

jects are calculated for each statement. Items for inclusion in the final scale are selected by the following means:

1. On the basis of his response, each subject is given a score for each item.
2. The subjects are then ranked by their scores and divided into quartiles.
3. The items for inclusion in the scale are then chosen on the basis of their ability to discriminate between the subjects in the upper and lower quartile.

The ranking of the subjects in quartiles might be similar to that outlined in Table 7-4.

After subjects have been ranked on each item and divided into quartiles, the *discriminating power (DP)* of each scale item is calculated as outlined in Table 7-5.[14] Similar computations are made for each possible scale item. Items are then selected for inclusion in the final scale on the basis of their discriminating power. Items with large *DP* scores are included in the final scale, since those items best distinguish subjects in extreme quartiles. It is assumed that items with large *DP*s meet the Likert criterion of internal consistency by demonstrating the ability to distinguish favorable and unfavorable responses. A substantial difference in the mean item scores (the *DP*s) of the two extreme quartiles demonstrates this. Low *DP*s, on the other hand, usually indicate ambiguity in the item and/or the irrelevance of the item to the factor being analyzed.

An alternative procedure for calculating the Likert scale, which is frequently used when computers are employed to execute the computations, involves summing each subject's individual item scores to derive an overall *attitude score*. If, for example, 200 items were chosen

[14] Garson, *Handbook of Political Science*, uses this format.

(1)	(2) Number of subjects in quartile	(3) Item responses 1 2 3 4 5	(4) Weighted total (response value time frequency)	(5) Weighted mean (4)/(2)
Group				
Top 25%	30	0 2 10 9 9	0 + 4 + 30 + 36 + 45 = 115	115/30 = 3.83
Lower 25%	30	6 24 0 0 0	6 + 48 + 0 + 0 + 0 = 54	54/30 = 1.80
Discriminative Power of one item		$DP = 3.83 - 1.80 = 2.03$		

Table 7-5   DP computing table for one-scale item

Source: G. David Garson, *Handbook of Political Science*, Holbrook Press, Boston, 1971, p. 119. Reprinted by permission.

for analysis, the maximal favorable attitude score would be 1,000. Items are then chosen for inclusion in the final Likert scale by correlating individual item responses with the overall attitude score.

The number of items included in the final scale is somewhat arbitrary, but existing research suggests that twenty or twenty-five items are usually sufficient. This same research suggests that a Thurstone scale requires about fifty items for the same reliability.[15]

Because the Likert scale is constructed on the basis of upper and lower quartiles, it may not be very sensitive to moderate responses.[16] Whether this is an important consideration is largely a function of the type of data with which one is working. As with other scaling techniques, there is no guarantee that the scale and the constituent items are *valid* measures. Means of assessing the validity and reliability of the scale are still necessary. These, you will recall, were discussed at length in Chapter 4 and briefly in our discussion of Thurstone scaling procedures.[17]

Finally, since initial subjects play such an important role in the selection of scale items, it is important to ensure that they are typical of the target population. In other words, it should not necessarily be assumed that a scale composed of items with proven discriminating power on one set of subjects will also discriminate among other subjects. Since the main purpose of constructing the scale is to come up

[15] See footnote 3.

[16] Garson, *Handbook of Political Science*, p. 120.

[17] Many empirical studies compare the different scaling techniques. For a review, see Selltiz et al., *Research Methods* . . . , pp. 368–369; Tittle and Hill, "Attitude Measurement . . ."; and Seiler and Hough, "Empirical Comparisons. . . ."

Instructions: Thinking of the concept of Local Government, rate it on the scales appearing below.

Local Government

	−3 :	−2 :	−1 :	0 :	+1 :	+2 :	+3*	
bad	:	:	:	:	:	:		good
close	:	:	:	:	:	:		distant
rigid	:	:	:	:	:	:		flexible
dishonest	:	:	:	:	:	:		honest
responsive	:	:	:	:	:	:		unresponsive
dirty	:	:	:	:	:	:		clean
active	:	:	:	:	:	:		passive
fast	:	:	:	:	:	:		slow
strong	:	:	:	:	:	:		weak

* Numbers do not appear on the scale to be administered.

Table 7-6   **Sample semantic differential bipolar adjective items for use in measuring attitudes toward local government**

with a discriminating measure for other subjects, this is an important consideration.

Osgood's semantic differential

Although Osgood's semantic differential was originally developed for the measurement of meaning rather than attitudes, it has been frequently used for measuring attitudes.[18] Osgood viewed the verbal response to an object or concept as an appropriate measure of the object's meaning for an individual.

Procedurally, the semantic differential relies upon a series of adjective pairs as the major means of eliciting meaning. As Osgood and his associates have pointed out, the use of the semantic differential is analogous to the game "Twenty Questions."[19] Successive questions and alternatives define the meaning of a concept, and an overall understanding is gradually attained. Similarly, with the semantic differential a large number of adjective parts are administered to subjects in conjunction with a specified concept or object, and subjects are asked

[18] C. E. Osgood, P. H. Tannenbaum, and G. J. Suci, *The Measurement of Meaning*, University of Illinois Press, Urbana, 1957. See also J. Snider and C. Osgood, *The Semantic Differential: A Sourcebook*, Aldine Publishing Company, Chicago, 1968.

[19] Osgood, et al., *The Measurement of Meaning*.

Semantic differential item	Local government	State government	National government
good (bad)	2.13	1.13	−2.13
close (distant)	2.42	1.03	−2.43
responsive (unresponsive)	2.02	0.89	−2.89
honest (dishonest)	0.92	−1.53	−2.03
active (passive)	1.32	1.57	−1.63
fast (slow)	1.62	0.93	−1.98
rigid (flexible)	−1.76	0.95	−1.83

Table 7-7   Citizen evaluation of different levels of government in mean scores

to rate the concept or object on a 7-point scale. The 7-point scale allows for varying intensity and direction, with the middle point providing a neutral position. A sample list is provided in Table 7-6. A more extensive listing of adjective pairs is found in Appendix C. The order of some items is conventionally reversed to ensure that respondents are reading each question and not simply responding to the initial ordering.

There are a number of different ways to use information derived from semantic differential scales. One might, for example, administer the same items to one's sample, asking first about local government and then about state and national government. The mean value for each level could then be computed, and scores for each level of government could be compared. This would provide one means of testing the hypothesis that individuals' attitudes vary toward the different levels of government. For this purpose, one's data might appear as in Table 7-7. These data indicate clear differences in attitudes toward the different levels of government. Citizen evaluations are generally most positive toward local government.

Another way of interpreting the data is to look upon the various items as indicators of different dimensions of a given attitude. Osgood has indicated that the semantic differential frequently measures three dimensions: the evaluative dimension, the potency dimension, and the activity dimension.[20] Cross-cultural studies indicate this also occurs with languages other than English.[21] Specific adjective pairs apparently

[20] Factor analysis is normally used to isolate the various dimensions in the data. For a good review essay see David R. Heise, "The Semantic Differential and Attitude Research," in Summers, *Attitude Measurement*, pp. 235–253.

[21] See C. E. Osgood, "Semantic Differential Technique in the Comparative Study of Cultures," *American Anthropologist*, 66 (1964), 171–200; and "Cross-cultural Comparability in Attitude Measurement via Multilingual Semantic Differentials" in *Current Studies in Social Psychology*, eds. I. D. Steiner and M. Fishbein, Holt, Rinehart and Winston, New York, 1965, pp. 95–107.

are geared more to one dimension than to another. Heise points out that the following adjectives tend to be associated with the different dimensions:

1 Evaluative nice-awful, good-bad, sweet-sour, helpful-unhelpful

2 Potency big-little, powerful-powerless, strong-weak, deep-shallow

3 Activity fast-slow, alive-dead, noisy-quiet, young-old[22]

There initially was hope of deriving a number of adjectives that would consistently tap evaluation, activity, and potency regardless of the concept to which they were applied. This obviously would make the technique of high general applicability. Unfortunately, the items on the evaluative dimension appear to be somewhat dependent on the concept employed. Thus the "hard-soft" item may relate to the evaluative dimension for person concepts, but it may correlate with the potency dimension for concepts such as "war." This concept dependency has been termed *concept-scale interaction* by Osgood and his associates.[23] This phenomenon precludes the use of select semantic differential items across concepts. Instead of assuming that items previously shown to be associated with the evaluative dimension will show similar patterns when applied to a different concept, each analysis must identify anew the set of items that best reflects the different dimensions of a concept.

Although the semantic differential has been used for some time in psychology, it has not been used widely in political science. But its use is increasing. It is a promising, economical, and relatively flexible measure that can be used in a number of ways.

The Guttman scaling procedure

Unlike the Thurstone and Likert procedures, the Guttman procedure is designed to measure whether a number of items form a *cumulative scale*. Operationally this means that items must be ordered in terms of difficulty, and responses must be consistent. Unlike the Thurstone and Likert scales, the Guttman scale score has direct meaning; it is a direct indication of the overall response pattern. In addition, the Guttman procedure provides a means of analyzing the interrelation among items, and it rejects those which do not appear related to the underlying concept. This property of selecting only items that form a single

[22] Heise, "The Semantic Differential . . .," p. 237.
[23] Osgood et al., *The Measurement of Meaning.*

Scale types	Items* a	b	c	d	e	Individual scale score
5	1	1	1	1	1	5
4	0	1	1	1	1	4
3	0	0	1	1	1	3
2	0	0	·0	1	1	2
1	0	0	0	0	1	1
0	0	0	0	0	0	0

* Where 0 = disagree or failing an item, and 1 = agree or passing an item.

Table 7-8   Various scale types with five items

dimension is called *unidimensionality*. Both these properties are determined empirically on the basis of the subjects' responses.

The determining factor is the extent to which responses are patterned in accordance with theoretical expectations. If, for example, subjects were asked to agree or disagree about five items or statements, the item that most respondents agree with can be taken as least difficult. The item most respondents disagreed with can be taken as most difficult. Intermediate items can be obtained similarly. Theoretically, a number of scale types can be obtained, as indicated in Table 7-8. The scale types in Table 7-8 show a pattern forming a perfect Guttman scale. An individual's scale score, if computed by adding 1 for each item passed, would yield a perfect prediction of his pattern of response. All individuals who failed the easiest item, failed all the more difficult ones; and all individuals who passed the most difficult items, passed all the easier items.

In actual practice, data seldom fit this ideal pattern exactly. The test of reproducibility is designed to measure the degree of deviation and indicates the actual error involved in predicting a person's response pattern for his scale score. Obviously, if a scale yields too many errors or inconsistencies, it is not a useful measure. A coefficient of .90 (or allowing one error in ten responses) is often used as a tolerable error level.[24] The coefficient of reproducibility is often interpreted as a measure of the scale's overall acceptability. It is, in fact, a measure of the predictability of response patterns. The coefficient of reproducibility is defined as follows:

$$CR = 1.00 - (e/r)$$

where e = errors in response patterns
$\quad\quad r$ = total number of responses (number of subjects times number of items)

[24] Actually Guttman proposed .85 as an appropriate level. This is largely a matter of individual judgment and the relative need for precision.

When the coefficient is low, it is generally assumed that the scale is not unidimensional. While items may be dropped to raise the coefficient, this constitutes redefining the attitude being measured. Strictly speaking, the Guttman procedure provides a means of testing the cumulativeness and unidimensionality of a series of items, not a means of selecting appropriate items. Nevertheless, this practice is followed frequently. Unfortunately the coefficient of reproducibility is strongly affected by response categories. By definition the number of errors cannot exceed the number of responses in the least numerous category.

Because the coefficient of reproducibility is affected by response-category frequencies, the *coefficient of scalability* often is employed, too. It varies between 0 and 1, and it is equal to 1 minus the number of errors divided by the number of errors that would be expected by chance. A coefficient of scalability of .60 or better is conventionally considered adequate.

$$Cs = 1 - e/x$$

where Cs = coefficient of scalability

e = number of errors

x = errors expected by chance

$= C(n - T_n)$

C = chance of getting any choice by chance alone (.50 if there are only two options in response categories)

n = number of choices of any type

T_n = number of choices in the most numerous response category for each item

To continue our previous example, let's assume that we have the six items from Table 7-2 and ten subjects. We want to determine whether the items constitute a cumulative and unidimensional scale. We would first take the individual responses of each of the items and order them from least difficult to most difficult in terms of the number of respondents passing (or agreeing with) the respective items. This procedure is depicted in Table 7-9.

We first list the item with which most respondents agreed, and then other items are listed in descending order in terms of subject agreement. The first individual listed is either the subject who agreed most with the items or the subject who agreed least with the items. In either case, the patterning of responses becomes clear. The overall response pattern of individuals indicates which item is most difficult (and inferentially, most favorable) and which is least difficult (least favorable), with intermediate points in between. In Table 7-9 it appears that item 6 is most difficult, and item 1 least difficult. There are two errors in the responses to these items, one from subject 2 and one from subject 3. These are errors in the sense that their error responses

	Subjects									
Item	1	2	3	4	5	6	7	8	9	10
1 There are too many local governments that seem to be duplicating each other.	+	+	+	+	+	+	+	+	+	+
2 Governmental services would probably be better if some local functions were merged.	0	0	+	+	+	+	+	+	+	+
3 A lot of government boundaries are artificial.	0	0	0	0	+	+	+	+	+	+
4 Even if services are not what they could be, government at the local level should remain small.	0	0	(+)	0	0	0	+	+	+	+
5 Government is getting too removed from the people.	0	(+)	0	0	0	0	0	0	+	+
6 The local community is the backbone of America.	0	0	0	0	0	0	0	0	0	0

+ = agree
0 = disagree
(+) = error
$CR = .97$
$C_s = .72$

Table 7-9 Scale items and response patterns for six items and ten subjects on attitudes toward local government

(in parentheses) do not fit the overall pattern as they theoretically should if the scale is cumulative and unidimensional. Errors are computed to minimize their occurrence by assuming that subject 2, for example, was inconsistent with item 5 and not with items 2 through 4.[25]

In evaluating the scale one should consider not only errors but also variations in responses. A scale composed of items with no variation is not an adequate measure. Also, several considerations should be taken into account in examining the pattern of errors. First, if one item has a high proportion of errors, this item usually is assumed to be primarily responsible for the apparent lack of cumulativeness and single dimensionality. Second, if most errors fall on one subject, this may indicate that the individual has no organized attitude on the subject. The procedure, in other words, seeks consistency and organization which sometimes may be lacking. Furthermore, it is important to

[25] Errors are not always computed in this manner, however. An alternative method is used in the Statistical Package for the Social Sciences (SPSS), a frequently employed computer package. For a discussion of alternate procedures see Allen L. Edwards, *Techniques of Attitude Scale Construction*, Appleton Century Crofts, New York, 1957, pp. 184–188.

recognize that a given scale may be unidimensional for one group of subjects but not for another. Unidimensionality is a function of the response patterns, not of the measurement procedures.

The Guttman scaling technique is used widely and is included in most statistical packages discussed in Chapter 10. It should be noted that Guttman scalogram analysis can be applied to many types of data. For example, McCrone and Cnudde used Guttman scaling procedures to describe variations in the civil rights orientation of the American states. Their scale is reproduced in Table 7-10. In this case a scale of the American states was derived on the basis of their records in anti-discrimination legislation in a number of different areas. Guttman scaling has also been frequently used in political science to analyze legislative voting.[26] For this purpose it can be employed to characterize the voting of individuals or groups or to characterize votes themselves. Principal advantages of the method are its versatility and applicability to various types of data. In the final section of this chapter we discuss cluster bloc analysis, an alternative manner of analyzing legislative voting.

Cluster bloc analysis

Cluster bloc scaling constitutes one of the earliest and simplest forms of scaling used in political science. It dates back to the 1920s, when Stuart Rice and Herman Beyle used it to analyze legislative voting.[27] It is primarily employed to characterize the voting of groups of legislators and determine issues on which bloc voting appears evident. Like most scaling techniques, cluster bloc analysis allows researchers to rank individuals and group them on some criterion, in this case similarity of voting on selected issues.

Suppose, for example, that we were interested in ascertaining whether voting on a sample of thirty education votes appears to be along party lines. We might hypothesize, for example, that Republicans and Democrats vote as blocs on issues related to educational funding, with one party more favorable to increased funding. Cluster bloc analysis provides a crucial intermediate step toward testing this hypothesis by providing a means of empirically defining voting blocs. It does this by calculating agreement scores between all possible pairs of legislators and then grouping them.

[26] For a good summary of the techniques available for the analysis of legislative voting see Lee F. Anderson, M. W. Watts, Jr., and Allen Wilcox, *Legislative Roll-call Analysis*, Northwestern University Press, Evanston, Ill., 1966.
[27] See Stuart A. Rice, *Quantitative Methods in Politics*, Alfred A. Knopf, New York, 1928; and Herman C. Beyle, *Identification and Analysis of Attribute-Cluster-Blocs*, University of Chicago Press, Chicago, 1931.

State	Public accom- modations	Employ- ment	Education	Private housing	Score
Colorado	+	+	+	+	4
Connecticut	+	+	+	+	4
Massachusetts	+	+	+	+	4
Minnesota	+	+	+	+	4
New York	+	+	+	+	4
Oregon	+	+	+	+	4
Pennsylvania	+	+	+	+	4
Idaho	+	+	+	−	3
Illinois (error)	+	−	+	−	3
Indiana	+	+	+	−	3
Michigan	+	+	+	−	3
New Jersey	+	+	+	−	3
Rhode Island	+	+	+	−	3
Washington	+	+	+	−	3
Wisconsin	+	+	+	−	3
Alaska	+	+	−	−	2
California	+	+	−	−	2
Delaware (error)	−	+	−	−	2
Kansas	+	+	−	−	2
Missouri (error)	−	+	−	−	2
New Mexico	+	+	−	−	2
Ohio	+	+	−	−	2
Iowa	+	−	−	−	1
Maine	+	−	−	−	1
Montana	+	−	−	−	1
Nebraska	+	−	−	−	1
New Hampshire	+	−	−	−	1
North Dakota	+	−	−	−	1
Vermont	+	−	−	−	1
Wyoming	+	−	−	−	1

Table 7-10   A scale of anti-discrimination legislation in the American states

Source: United States Commission on Civil Rights, 1961 Report, vol. 1, "Voting" (Washington, 1961), pp. 208–210. Reprinted in Donald J. McCrone and Charles F. Cnudde, "On Measuring Public Policy," in Robert E. Crew, Jr., *State Politics*, Duxbury Press, Duxbury, Mass., 1968.

1   The first step in a cluster bloc analysis involves selecting votes to analyze. Votes are chosen on the basis of their relevance to the selected problem. Usually some minimal level of contest is an additional criterion. Obviously, issues on which there is unanimous agreement tell us nothing about differences in voting.

State	Public accom- modations	Employ- ment	Education	Private housing	Score
Alabama	—	—	—	—	0
Arizona	—	—	—	—	0
Arkansas	—	—	—	—	0
Florida	—	—	—	—	0
Georgia	—	—	—	—	0
Hawaii	—	—	—	—	0
Kentucky	—	—	—	—	0
Louisiana	—	—	—	—	0
Maryland	—	—	—	—	0
Mississippi	—	—	—	—	0
Nevada	—	—	—	—	0
North Carolina	—	—	—	—	0
Oklahoma	—	—	—	—	0
South Carolina	—	—	—	—	0
South Dakota	—	—	—	—	0
Tennessee	—	—	—	—	0
Texas	—	—	—	—	0
Utah	—	—	—	—	0
Virginia	—	—	—	—	0
West Virginia	—	—	—	—	0
Total	28	21	15	7	

Score	Scale distribution Frequency	Percentage	
4	7	14	Coefficient of
3	8	16	reproducibility = .985
2	77	14	
1	8	16	Coefficient of
0	20	40	scalability = .954
	50	100	

Table 7-10 (cont.)

2 After choosing the issues, agreement scores are calculated for all pairs of legislators. The simple index of agreement is used for this purpose, and it is defined as follows:

$$IA = \frac{f}{t} \times 100$$

where f = number of agreements between each pair of
legislators
t = total number of votes on which both legislators in a
pair voted

Legislators	Agreement score
1, 11	.40
1, 2	.81
1, 4	.62
1, 3	.59
1, 5	.43
etc.	etc.

Table 7-11   Agreement scores for pairs of legislators

Thus, if legislator X voted "Yes" on all of the bills analyzed, and legislator Y also voted "Yes" on all measures, the index of agreement would be 1.0. If they voted exactly opposite, the index would be 0.

One troublesome problem encountered in roll-call analysis in general is that legislators usually are absent on a number of votes. If researchers discard legislators who have been absent, they usually will end up with a small sample. On the other hand, it is difficult to justify inferences about how legislators *would have voted* had they been present. Although one way of treating absences is to ignore any votes on which one legislator in the pair was absent, another way is to add a correction factor to the formula. The latter alternative is particularly justifiable if there is some reasonable basis for making an inference of "likely vote" or some reason to believe that absences are not random but actually reflect some position on the measure. (It is not uncommon, for example, for legislators to abstain deliberately from voting as a part of a compromise.) If this alternative is chosen, then the usual procedure is to compute the index of agreement on the basis of actual votes with an addition of some fraction for partial agreements in those cases on which actual voting did not occur. In this case the formula might be

$$IA = \frac{f + \frac{1}{2}g}{t} \times 100$$

where g = partial agreements

After computing the index of agreement for each pair of legislators one would end up with a tabulation sheet resembling Table 7-11 which lists the agreement scores for each pair of legislators.

3   The next step in the analysis is to take the agreement scores and form the cluster bloc. This will display any bloc voting graphically. The formation of the cluster bloc is usually best achieved by taking the agreement scores, listing the legislators down the side and across the top, and listing first the pair with the highest agreement score. Next list the individual with the next highest agreement score with

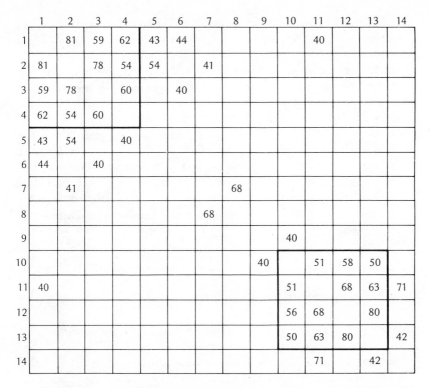

	1	2	3	4	5	6	7	8	9	10	11	12	13	14
1		81	59	62	43	44					40			
2	81		78	54	54		41							
3	59	78		60		40								
4	62	54	60											
5	43	54		40										
6	44		40											
7		41						68						
8							68							
9										40				
10									40		51	58	50	
11	40									51		68	63	71
12										56	68		80	
13										50	63	80		42
14											71		42	

Figure 7-3   Cluster bloc matrix showing two blocs in which the index of agreement is .50 or higher for any pair

one of the members of the first pair, and so forth. This procedure will order legislators into the most inclusive blocs. All agreement scores may be listed, or only high ones. In Figure 7-3 we have included only pairs in which the index of agreement is .40 or higher.

4   Finally, researchers determine the cutoff point for inclusion in the final blocs. In our example the cutoff point is .50. To be included in the indicated blocs, a legislator had to have an agreement score equal to or greater than .50 *with every other legislator in the bloc.* Thus legislator 14 is not included in the bloc in the lower right quadrant because, although he had a high agreement score with some members of the bloc, he does not have sufficiently high scores with all members.

We are now in a position to return to our initial hypothesis. Voting blocs have been empirically defined, and we now will look at additional data on party identification of individual legislators. If we found that all members of the upper bloc are indeed Republicans, and all the legislators in the lower bloc Democrats, we could say that voting does appear to follow party lines. At this point we would want to explain why six legislators do not fit neatly into either bloc.

It should be apparent that cluster bloc analysis is a tedious way of empirically defining voting blocs. It can be employed simply for a *description* of voting blocs, but its real utility lies in explanatory purposes. In use with select independent variables, it can provide a means of testing hypotheses about factors that might explain the dynamics underlying a given configuration. Any number of factors could be used in this respect—party, constituency differences, factional affiliations, and others. This type of analysis can also be applied in many settings other than legislatures. It could be employed to analyze voting in the United Nations, city councils, and in numerous other settings.

Calculating agreement scores for a large number of individual pairs is a tedious process, however, and we generally recommend using available computer programs when the number of pairs is large. In any given sample the number of pairs is $n(n-1)/2$ or 4,950 for 100 Senators.

General considerations in scaling

This chapter has elaborated upon our previous discussion of measurement. Scaling procedures should be undertaken with the same considerations involved in any measurement process. Again, the main considerations are *validity* and *reliability*. In preceding discussion we discussed several means of assessing a scale's reliability in addition to those outlined in Chapter 4. All *good* research contains precise information for evaluative purposes.

Robinson, Rush, and Head suggest three major evaluative criteria for scale assessment:

1 *Item construction criteria* (sampling of relevant content, wording of items, and item analyses)

2 *Response set criteria* (controlling the spurious effects of acquiescence and social desirability on responses to items)

3 *Psychometric criteria* (representative sampling, presentation of proper normative data, test-retest reliability, item homogeneity, discrimination of known groups, cross-validation, and further statistical procedures)[28]

Chapter 6 reviewed some pitfalls of questionnaire design; here we will repeat the basic point that a good scale depends upon adequate

---

[28] John P. Robinson, J. G. Rush, and K. B. Head, *Measures of Political Attitudes*, Institute for Survey Research, Ann Arbor, Mich., 1969, p. 4. This volume is an excellent compendium of major scales used to measure political attitudes. It includes information useful for assessing each scale on the aforementioned criteria. See also the American Psychological Association publication, *Technical Recommendations for Psychological Tests and Diagnostic Methods, Psychological Bulletin Supplement*, 51, No. 2 (1966).

sampling of content. The scaling procedures discussed in this chapter all depend upon a researchers' ability to locate "good" initial questions. Theoretically, a variable or concept measured by scaling procedures is a set of interrelated actions bound together by conceptual definitions that justify the inclusion of certain items as relevant to a given concept and exclude others. Empirically, a given measure is a consistent attitude or behavior found through some scaling or measurement procedure in the responses (and, inferentially, the minds) of subjects. In the happiest of scholarly worlds, the empirical dimension approximates the theoretical concept. The scale procedures outlined in this chapter are designed to measure the degree of approximation. One way that they do this is by helping to locate ambiguous and irrelevent items.

Most of the procedures discussed are *response-inferred scaling techniques* that permit subjects to empirically define the scale values and the items. This helps to avoid the problem of imposing researchers' preconceptions and subsequently of ascertaining whether respondents have responded to an item in the manner in which it was conceived initially. This is one principal advantage of these scaling methods; they do provide empirical measures of *subjects'* perceptions of the apparent relation between various items. Too often, scaling procedures simply assume that subjects will perceive items to be related simply because researchers do. Response-inferred scaling procedures avoid this considerable difficulty.

Sometimes it is not considered sufficient to show that items are perceived by subjects to be related to one another. Rather, we wish to demonstrate that the measure is also a *valid* measure of the underlying variable. As we pointed out in Chapter 4, other criterion variables frequently are used to assess the overall validity of a measure. If, for example, we derived a Likert-type political participation scale, we might compare its results with those for a number of behavioral criterion variables to see if they were highly interrelated. If various measures are highly related, we could have confidence that our scale is a valid measure of "political participation."

Guards against response set usually are also built into scaling procedures. We pointed out item reversal in our discussion of the semantic differential. The main consideration is to guard against response set, which indicates that respondents are not directly responding to an item.

The third major evaluative criterion for judging a scale's adequacy is based upon certain normative information. Minimally, as we have repeatedly pointed out, researchers should indicate their sampling design and the validity and reliability procedures employed. These factors are not self-evident. Adequate scale construction relies upon all the factors discussed. Sampling design, questionnaire construction, and scaling procedure all are related integrally. Creative researchers combine the best procedural guidelines with insight and imagination

—creative theorizing, conceptualization, operationalism, and explanation. Creativity and imagination distinguish truly outstanding research from research that is merely procedurally adequate.

Review questions and exercises

1 Explain the meaning and significance of the following terms:

   a Thurstone scaling
   b Guttman scaling
   c Cluster bloc analysis
   d Likert scaling
   e Test-retest procedures
   f Split-half reliability
   g Parallel forms reliability
   h The coefficient of reproducibility
   i Interval scale
   j Ordinal scale
   k The interquartile dispersion value
   l Criterion of relevance
   m Criterion of ambiguity
   n Discriminating power of an item
   o Semantic differential
   p Concept-scale interaction
   q Cumulative scale
   r Unidimensionality
   s The index of agreement
   t Response-inferred scaling techniques
   u Coefficient of scalability

2 Gather voting information about six or more bills on a subject of your choice. (The *Congressional Quarterly* is useful for this purpose.) Then determine whether voting appears to be on the basis of party lines or some other factor. Use cluster bloc analysis or Guttman scaling.

3 As a class project, gather fifty items relating to some subject and then construct a Thurstone and Likert scale of these items using procedures outlined in this chapter. Compare the results of the two scales in terms of their reliability and validity. It will be useful to employ some behavioral indicators for concurrent validation.

4 Discuss the major assumptions, advantages, and disadvantages of the scaling techniques covered in this chapter.

5 Review the literature that compares scaling techniques dis-

cussed in this chapter and write a summary essay and critical comparison.

6   Review the types of scales used in some prominent journals over the last five years. Are some procedures used more than others? How would you rate the scales on the basis of the assessment criteria discussed in the last part of this chapter?

7   Devise a project in which the semantic differential could be used and write up a research design for this purpose.

It is discourse or conversation
which makes the human image
public in a way that the image of
no lower animal can possibly be.
The term, "universe of discourse,"
has been used to describe the
growth and development of
common images in conversation
and linguistic intercourse. There
are, of course, many universes of
discourse. . . .

Kenneth Boulding

8

CONTENT ANALYSIS

Social scientists attempt to study and understand human behavior in its numerous aspects from a variety of vantage points. As we pointed out previously, some research techniques use direct behavioral measures, whereas others rely upon indirect measures of behavior.

In recent years there has been increasing attention to human discourse, that is, to written and spoken language, as a source of basic data regarding human behavior. In this chapter we discuss content analysis, one research tool used in this connection.[1] It differs from other techniques in its data and its procedures.

After defining content analysis and discussing its various uses, we provide a brief history of this technique. The remaining sections of this chapter discuss some common methods of content analysis and various problems associated with these methods.

[1] This chapter is heavily indebted to Ole R. Holsti, who has written extensively on the technique.

The meaning and purpose of content analysis

Content analysis has been defined in a number of ways. Berelson suggests that: "Content analysis is a research technique for the objective, systematic, and quantitative description of the manifest content of communication."[2] Other scholars question the quantitative component of this definition and argue that qualitative description often is more important than purely quantitative description. There is also debate about which type of quantitative description is most appropriate. Various forms of quantitative analysis are discussed later in this chapter. Further contention centers on whether content analysis must limit itself to the manifest content of documents.[3]

There is, however, general agreement that content analysis should be executed on a systematic and objective basis. The *objectivity* stipulation requires that the analysis be done employing explicit rules which would enable other researchers to arrive at the same results; this factor differentiates content analysis from ordinary perusal of documents. *Systematization* requires consistent application of categories for including and excluding content. This rule ensures unbiased selection of data.

Content analysis is employed for a variety of purposes. Table 8-1 summarizes some different purposes of content analysis studies, the types of questions they seek to answer, and the research problems posed in each case. As Ole Holsti notes in his excellent introductory text on content analysis, the variety of research designs corresponds roughly to the questions, "Who says what, to whom, how, and with what effects?"[4]

CONTENT ANALYSIS: A BRIEF HISTORICAL OVERVIEW

The systematic use of content analysis dates back to the beginning of the twentieth century, but there have been marked variations in application, purpose, basic data, and degree of technical precision and sophistication.

[2] Bernard Berelson, *Content Analysis in Communication Research*, The Free Press, New York, 1952, p. 18.
[3] See, for example, H. D. Lasswell, D. Lerner, and I. de S. Pool, *The Comparative Study of Symbols*, Stanford University Press, Stanford, Calif., 1952; A. Kaplan and H. M. Goldsen, "The Reliability of Content Analysis Categories," in *The Language of Politics*, eds. H. D. Lasswell, N. Leites, et al., George W. Stewart, New York, 1949, pp. 83–112; P. F. Lazarsfeld and A. H. Barton, "Qualitative Measurement in the Social Sciences, Classification, Typologies, and Indices," in *The Policy Sciences*, eds. D. Lerner and H. D. Lasswell, Stanford University Press, Stanford, Calif., 1951, pp. 180–188; W. Stephenson, "Critique of Content Analysis," *Psychological Record*, 13 (1963), 155–162.
[4] Ole R. Holsti, *Content Analysis for the Social Sciences and Humanities*, Addison-Wesley Publishing Company, Reading, Mass., 1969.

Purpose	Branch of semiotics
To describe characteristics of communication	Semantics (sign/referent)
To make inferences as to the antecedents of communication (the encoding process)	Pragmatics (send/sign)
To make inferences as to the effects of communication (the decoding process)	Pragmatics (sign/receiver)

Table 8-1   Content analysis research designs

Source: Ole R. Holsti, *Content Analysis for the Social Sciences and Humanities,* Addison-Wesley Publishing Company, Reading, Mass., 1969, p. 26. Reprinted by permission.

In terms of emphasis, the use of the technique can be understood in the context of larger societal resources and constraints. Initially the technique was applied almost exclusively to American news sources, and the studies were largely media inventories and journalistic studies. Coincident with the increasing sophistication in social science, content analysis was used for historical, sociological, and political research in the 1930s. Harold Lasswell was a pioneer in this and many other

Types of communications	Questions	Research problem
Message source A 1 Variable x across time 2 Variable x across situations 3 Variable x across audience 4 Variables x and y within same universe or document	What?	To describe trends in communication content. To relate known characteristics of sources to the messages they produce. To audit communication content against standards.
Messages source type A Message source type B	How?	To analyze techniques of persuasion. To analyze style.
Messages/standard 1 A priori 2 Content 3 Noncontent	To whom?	To relate known characteristics of the audience to messages produced for them. To describe patterns of communication.
Messages/nonsymbolic Behavioral data 1 Direct 2 Indirect	Why?	To secure political and military intelligence. To analyze psychological traits of individuals. To infer aspects of culture and cultural exchange. To provide legal evidence.
	Who?	To answer questions of disputed authorship.
Sender messages/recipient Messages Sender messages/recipient Behavioral data	With what effect?	To measure readability. To analyze flow of information. To assess responses to communication.

Table 8-1 (cont.)

fields. During World War II, the technique was used extensively in concert with the war effort, and propaganda analysis became a major concern of content analysts.[5]

In the last twenty years content analysis has been extensively used for testing hypotheses on a wide variety of materials and in a number of disciplines. Political scientists, for example, have employed content analysis to assess the impact of constituency on legislative

[5] For an example of this type of analysis see Alexander George, *Propaganda Analysis: A Study of Inferences Made from Nazi Propaganda in World War II,* Row, Peterson & Company, Evanston, Ill., 1959.

behavior,[6] to determine some causes of belligerent behavior,[7] and to assess the relative importance of role and personality factors in explaining the behavior of United States Senators.[8] Michael Malec used content analysis to test the hypothesis that shifts in intellectuals' attitudes are precursors to larger societal revolutions or social movements.[9] Content analysis of the NAACP publication *Crisis* provided a means of testing this particular hypothesis with regard to the black civil rights movement in the United States. Content analysis has also been used to describe individual belief systems and national images; Ole Holsti's case study of John Foster Dulles is an excellent example of this type of work.[10] The most famous application of content analysis is probably the study of the 1914 prewar crisis.[11] Similar work by some of the same authors focuses on events that are more current, the 1962 Cuban Missile Crisis.[12]

Most of the preceding studies were designed specifically to test hypotheses. Content analysis is also used in social science for exploratory and descriptive purposes. A recent example of the descriptive use of this technique is Robert Burrowes' and Douglas Muzzio's study, "The Road to the Six Day War: Aspects of an Enumerative History of Four Arab States and Israel, 1965–1967."[13]

While early content analytic studies relied upon natural, existing data sources such as newspapers and diplomatic reports, current research has progressed beyond these conventional sources of communication. Sociologists and psychologists now are investigating pictoral communications, bodily gestures, facial expressions, vocal tones, and

---

[6] Helen Ingram, "The Impact of Constituency on the Process of Legislating," *Western Political Quarterly*, 22, No. 2 (June 1969), 265–279.

[7] See, for example, Dina A. Zinnes, "The Expression and Perception of Hostility in Prewar Crisis 1914," in *Quantitative International Politics*, ed. J. David Singer, The Free Press, New York, 1968, pp. 85–119; Ole R. Holsti, Richard A. Brody, and Robert C. North, "Perception and Action in the 1914 Crisis," in ibid., pp. 123–158.

[8] James N. Rosenau, "Private Preferences and Political Responsibilities: The Relative Potency of Individual and Role Variables in the Behavior of U.S. Senators," in Singer, *Quantitative International Politics*, pp. 17–50.

[9] Michael A. Malec, "Some Observations on the Content of *Crisis*: 1932–1962," *Phylon*, 28, No. 2 (1967), 161–167.

[10] Ole R. Holsti, "The Belief System and National Images: A Case Study," *Journal of Conflict Resolution*, 6 (1962), 244–252.

[11] Ole R. Holsti, "The 1914 Case," *American Political Service Review*, IIX (1965), 365–378. See also references in footnote 7.

[12] Ole R. Holsti, Richard A. Brody, and Robert C. North, "Measuring Affect and Action in International Reaction Models Empirical Materials from the 1962 Cuban Crisis," reprinted in *International Politics and Foreign Policy*, rev. ed., ed. James N. Rosenau, The Free Press, New York, 1969, pp. 679–696.

[13] Robert Burrowes and Douglas Muzzio, "The Road to the Six Day War: Aspects of an Enumerative History of Four Arab States and Israel, 1965–1967," *Journal of Conflict Resolution*, 16 (1972), 211–226.

dreams as basic communication data. Lawrence Streicher's study, *The Broadsword and the Rapier: An Approach to the Analysis of National Style in Political Caricature,* is an example of some new data sources of content analysts. This extension of inquiry beyond verbal expressions is in keeping with current suggestions that "communication" should be broadly defined to include more than its verbal aspects. Current work with content analysis is employing generated data also: survey research questions, psychiatric interviews, and verbal communication resulting from group interaction and from simulated group experiments are providing new data sources for content analysts.[14]

In addition to these changes in emphasis in the use of content analysis, the technique is being employed with increasing frequency and proficiency. Holsti notes that during the first two decades of the twentieth century only about 2.5 content analysis studies appeared each year. In the period from 1950 to 1958, by contrast, the annual average was 96.3. While early studies were largely descriptive, recent work tends to be explanatory, empirical, and/or methodological in focus.[15] Technological developments also have aided content analysts in recent years. Special computer programs have been designed for content analysis, and a number of standardized manuals and dictionaries provide aid in the categorization of communication content.

> At present most computer content analyses fall into one of two categories. Those of the first type are essentially word count programs. . . . The second type of computer program is characterized by a dictionary system in which text words are looked up in the dictionary and automatically coded with information representing the investigator's frame of reference and assumptions.[16]

A widely used program of the second type discussed above is the "General Inquirer Program." [17]

Which disciplines use content analysis? Holsti indicates that three areas account for approximately 75 percent of all empirical studies: sociological-anthropological (27.7 percent), general communi-

---

[14] Holsti, *Content Analysis* . . . , pp. 22–23.

[15] Ibid., pp. 15–17; for a good survey of recent emphases see Robert Edward Mitchell, "The Uses of Content Analysis for Explanatory Studies," *Public Opinion Quarterly,* 31 (1967), 230–241.

[16] Holsti, *Content Analysis* . . . , p. 86.

[17] See Philip J. Stone et al., "The General Inquirer: A Computer System for Content Analysis and Retrieval Based on the Sentence as a Unit of Information," *Behavioral Scientist,* 7 (1962), 484–498; and Ole R. Holsti, "An Adaptation of the 'General Inquirer' for the Systematic Analysis of Political Documents," *Behavioral Science,* 9 (1964), 382–388; and *The General Inquirer: A Computer Approach to Content Analysis in the Behavioral Sciences,* ed. Philip J. Stone, M.I.T. Press, Cambridge, Mass., 1966.

cations (25.9 percent), and political (21.5 percent). In terms of focus of inquiry, appproximately three-fifths of the empirical studies deal with the following areas: social values, propaganda analysis, journalistic studies, media inventories, and psychological-psychoanalytical research.[18] Within political science the most extensive use of content analysis is in international relations. Part of the reason for its frequent use in this area is undoubtedly the scarcity of alternative data sources.

BASIC RESEARCH DESIGN IN CONTENT ANALYSIS

The basic procedures involved in planning and executing a content analysis study involve essentially six related steps:

1 Formation of the research question and hypotheses
2 Sampling of the selected data sources
3 Defining categories to be used in the analysis
4 Reading the selected sample documents, coding, and condensing the relevant content
5 Scaling items by frequency, appearance, intensity, or some other criteria
6 Interpreting data in light of initial hypotheses and theory

1 We have stressed throughout this text that there is no way of ensuring a "good" research question. Indeed, it is difficult to establish criteria for judging the significance of a question. Usually, close perusal of existing literature, common sense, past experience, and imagination play important roles in generating initial research questions.

2 Because it often is not feasible to analyze the entire population of available documentation on a given topic, sampling is frequently used with content analysis. Of course, the choice of sample documents should be made explicit, and this choice should be justified. In addition to sampling *among* sources, one may sample *within* sources. Again the overriding consideration is to obtain a representative sample. Availability, quality, and other considerations affect this decision.

3, 4 The third and fourth steps in the analysis involve categorizing and coding data.

> Coding is the process whereby raw data are systematically transformed and aggregated into units which permit precise description of relevant content characteristics. Coding rules serve as the operational link between the investigator's data and his theory and hypotheses.[19]

---

[18] Holsti, *Content Analysis* . . . , p. 21
[19] Ibid., p. 94.

Coding rules are a basic part of research design. At this juncture decisions are made about categories, units of content, and system(s) of enumeration.

The number and types of categories that might be used in content analysis are almost infinite. They might include persons, groups, traits, policies, ideas, targets, values, methods, and others.[20] Important considerations in selecting categories include ensuring that they are definitive, mutually exclusive, and systematically applied throughout the analysis.

A further aspect of the coding stage is the selection of units of content. A number of units are available, including the article, the single word or symbol, the theme, the paragraph or sentence, and designated characters or specific items. A small number of experimental studies have attempted to determine the most economical recording units. This usually is accomplished by comparing two different recording methods on the same data. These studies generally indicate that larger recording units, while faster to work with, are often too gross for effective differentiation. Nevertheless, since these studies are based only upon several media, their conclusions, for the most part, are not generalizable. Different units are appropriate to different data and research purposes.[21]

5   In addition to choosing categories and content units, researchers must decide what system of enumeration to employ in quantifying data. Here again a number of alternatives are available.

Space or *time* allotted to a given subject in terms of lines, size of print, column inches, and/or page placement have been used to determine relative emphasis in newspapers and other printed media. If we wish to determine whether newspapers with a national circulation differ in focus and emphasis from newspapers with only local circulation, we might use some measure of space allocation as a basis for quantifying "differences in focus and emphasis." This method is relatively straightforward and simple to execute. Nevertheless, it does have limitations:

> The limitations of space-time units derive mostly from a lack of sensitivity to other than the grossest attributes of content. In general, such measures are most appropriate for descriptions of mass media, but are too imprecise to index attitudes, values, style, and the like.[22]

[20] Ibid., pp. 94–116, provides a good review of some of the possibilities in this connection.

[21] L. Schneider and S. M. Dornburch, *Popular Religion: Inspirational Books in America*, University of Chicago Press, Chicago, 1958; and H. D. Lasswell et al., "Recording and Context Units: Four Ways to Coding Editorial Context," in *Language of Politics*, George W. Stewart, New York, 1949, pp. 113–126.

[22] Holsti, *Content Analysis . . .* , p. 121.

	New York Times	Washington Post	San Francisco Chronicle	Chicago Tribune
Favorable	43.7%	35.3%	50.0%	12.5%
Neutral	46.9%	53.1%	33.3%	12.5%
Unfavorable	9.4%	11.6%	16.7%	75.0%
*Support ratio**	4.7	3.0	3.0	.17

* Support ratio = number of positive editorials divided by the number of negative editorials.

Table 8-2   Editorial support of administration positions on Vietnam during selected periods

Source: Susan Welch "The American Press and Indochina, 1950–1956," in *Communication in International Politics*, ed. Richard Merritt, University of Illinois Press, Urbana, 1972. Reprinted by permission.

Frequency is another common basis of enumeration. In this case, emphasis is determined on the basis of the number of times specified symbols, words, or references appear in the communication.[23] Welch used a frequency count to determine variations in press support for administration positions on Indochina. The unit of content, in this case, was the newspaper editorial. Newspaper editorials were placed in three categories: favorable, neutral, or unfavorable to administration policies. As Table 8-2 indicates, Welch found substantial support for administration policies except for the *Chicago Tribune*.

The actual frequency count is a relatively simple process if categories have been well defined. Category definition is a problem with almost all content analysis procedures. The shortcomings of the frequency-count measure should also be borne in mind. Its assumptions may not be tenable in some research situations.

> First, [the content analyst] assumes that the frequency with which an attribute appears in messages is a valid indicator of some variable such as focus of attention, intensity, value, importance, and so on. Second, he assumes that each unit of content —word, theme, character, or item—should be given equal weight with every other unit, permitting aggregation or direct comparison.[24]

[23] Pitirim A. Sorokin's massive study of social and cultural changes in Western Europe rests partly upon frequency content analysis of this type. The influence of great thinkers was determined partially by the number of special monographs devoted to them. See Pitirim A. Sorokin, *Social and Cultural Dynamics (1937–1941)*, 4 vols., Bedminster Press, Englewood Cliffs, N.J., 1962. See also Charles A. McClelland, "Access to Berlin: The Quantity and Variety of Events, 1948–1963," in Singer, *Quantitative International Politics*, pp. 159–186.

[24] Holsti, *Content Analysis . . .* , p. 122.

In addition to space and frequency analysis, a variety of scaling techniques are designed specifically to measure intensity in an attempt to overcome some shortcomings of these other methods. The following sections of this chapter discuss three major scaling techniques used with content analysis. Each of these techniques, as you will see, has its own characteristics. Choosing a proper scaling technique will rest primarily upon a thorough understanding of the data and research purpose.

Scaling techniques in content analysis

THE Q-SORT METHOD

The Q-sort method is one of the most common methods of scaling intensity.[25] It provides a means of scaling some universe of statements on a particular variable. We may, for example, be measuring the hostility content of a given universe of statements and wish to scale them from low to high hostility content with intermediate points on the continuum.

The Q-sort scale uses a forced-distribution 9-point scale similar to the one represented by the first row in Table 8-3. If, in the above example, we were designing a hostility scale, category 1 would represent the lowest degree of hostility, and category 9 the highest degree of hostility. The figures given in the second row of Table 8-3 indicate the percentage of statements that should fall into each category. In this case the percentage equals the number of statements, since we have assumed that we are scaling 100 statements. It is a simple matter to compute the requisite number of statements for any particular sample size on the basis of these percentages.

The prescription of a 9-point scale with requisite percentages means that the Q-sort scale has the characteristic of providing a *forced distribution*. In examining Table 8-3 you will note that the number of statements placed in each category is not constant. The Q-sort distribution is based on the assumption that the universe of statements is roughly equivalent to a normal distribution, with the greater number of statements reflecting moderate rather than extreme positions on the variable being measured. Whether this assumption is tenable in all situations is dubious. The 9-point scale, together with forced distribution, does, however, have the advantage of forcing one to make fine distinctions.

[25] For a good early discussion of the Q-sort technique see William Stephenson, *The Study of Behavior: Q Technique and Its Methodology,* University of Chicago Press, Chicago, 1953; see also Jack Block, *The Q-sort Method in Personality Assessment and Psychiatric Research,* Charles C. Thomas, Publisher, Springfield, Ill., 1961. For examples of the use of the Q-sort method see Holsti et al., "Measuring Affect and Action. . . ."

Category (y)	1	2	3	4	5	6	7	8	9	(Value)
Percentage (x)	5	8	12	16	18	16	12	8	5	(Number)

Table 8-3   The Q-sort scale and category distribution

Judges usually are used to place selected items in categories provided by the scale. Generally a fairly large number of judges are employed on the assumption that random errors on the part of individual judges will cancel out those of others in the group. It is also advisable to use trial runs to pretest judges and, in some cases, items. A pretest helps to isolate judges who have systematic difficulties in categorizing items and helps distinguish items that are overly ambiguous. It also serves the useful function of providing some gauge on the concentration powers of judges.

A number of problems are associated with the use of judges in categorizing items for intensity. One significant question relates to the *reliability* and *validity* of their classifications. As you recall from Chapter 4, the question of reliability concerns the degree to which a measurement (in this case their placements) is repeatable. The question of validity, on the other hand, relates to the degree to which the variable measures what it is intended to measure.

Certain procedural guarantees should be used to ensure reliability. *Intercoder reliability* is one such guarantee; it consists of testing for the agreement among a number of judges using the same items after having independently categorized them. If the judges' placements appear to be in substantial agreement, we have a relatively high degree of confidence in the reliability of the analysis. Frequently a mean classification figure is used in the final analysis to refer to the average classification among a number of different judges. If, on the other hand, the categorizations vary widely, the item normally is deleted on the assumption that it is too ambiguous to be meaningful.

Intracoder reliability, on the other hand, tests the stability of a single coder's classification over time through test-retest procedures. The major difficulty with this procedure is that it is difficult to determine what constitutes a sufficient test-retest time period, and the stability assumption in some cases is hard to justify. In addition to the prospect that a judge may consciously be attempting to maintain consistency rather than responding directly to an item, it is always possible that intervening factors may account for differential responses.

The problems associated with the use of judges are not, of course, limited to the Q-sort method. Unfortunately, we cannot resolve all the methodological issues raised in this connection, and only limited experimental work is available to guide us. It would be interesting to see more experimental work done on methodological lines. What influence, if any, does a judge's familiarity or lack of familiarity with a given issue have on the categorizations? Are personality factors related to classification patternings? To what extent are classification patternings related to cultural, socio-economic, or other such factors? Garson indicates that empirical studies have shown that white Southerners do not rank civil rights items much differently from blacks, which suggests that cultural and racial differences are not as pervasive as they might otherwise be expected.[26] These factors may be more important in cross-cultural and cross-national research.

PAIR-COMPARISON SCALING

Pair-comparison scaling is another technique for producing a relative scale of intensity among items, but it does not involve a forced distribution. Intensity scaling by pair-comparison analysis involves pairing all selected items into all possible pairs, selecting which statement of each pair represents the most intense statement on the variable, and then tallying the items for the number of times they were graded most intense among all possible pairs. This totaling will yield a relative scale among all items. Evaluating intensity by pairs is sometimes easier for judges to perform in a discerning manner.

Although pair-comparison scaling is relatively simple to execute on a small number of items, the task becomes onerous when the number of items is large. If, for example, we wish to conduct a paired-comparison scaling on 16 items, we will be considering 120 pairs of statements. If a number of different judges are used—as is normally the case—time and personnel costs rise rapidly. Determining the number of pairs for a given number of statements is relatively simple on the basis of the following formula, where n equals the number of items or statements we wish to pair for scaling:

Number of pairs generated for a given number of statements
$$= \frac{n(n-1)}{2}$$

To execute a paired-comparison analysis, we begin by numbering all statements consecutively, assigning each item a unique number. Then we pair all items on a tabulation sheet as depicted in column 1, Table 8-4. The second step of the analysis will involve asking judges to independently select the statement in each pair which constitutes the most intense statement on the designated variable. A judge will

[26] G. David Garson, *Handbook of Political Science*, Holbrook Press, Boston, 1971, p. 114. Guido H. Stempel, "Increasing Reliability in Content Analysis," *Journalism Quarterly*, 32 (1955), 449–455, indicates that coder performance in one type of coding is unrelated to performances with other types.

Statement pairs	Most intense
1-2	1
1-3	1
1-4	4
2-3	2
2-4	4
3-4	4

Table 8-4   Pair-comparison analysis format sheet

indicate his or her choice in the second column of Table 8-4. The final stage of the analysis involves tallying "votes" for intensity to arrive at the final ordering among items. This is accomplished by counting the number of times each statement was considered most intense among all pairs; the item most frequently cited will constitute the highest degree of intensity. In the preceding example, statement 4 was the most intense overall item, and item 3 the least intense; item 4 was cited as the most intense statement among pairs three times, while statement 3 was not accorded intensity over any other item.

Normally a number of judges are used in pair-comparison analysis with the same considerations and constraints pertaining to their use in Q-sort scaling. The final intensity scaling among items in pair-comparison scaling with a number of judges is normally an average of the figures arrived at independently by the judges. Items with extreme variation are discarded.

Dina Zinnes' study, "The Expression and Perception of Hostility in Prewar Crisis: 1914," provides a good example of an alternative use of pair-comparison analysis when the number of statements is large.[27] Professor Zinnes was interested in the determinants of belligerent behavior and

> the extent to which a state's behavior is a function of its perception of a hostile environment, and the accuracy of the proposition that the more hostility a state perceives, the more hostility it will express.[28]

After coding the material for perceptions of hostility, she determined that frequency counting was unsuitable for ascertaining intensity, and that pair-comparison scaling of more than 2,000 statements would be too costly. Instead, 11 random samples of the statements were taken, and the sample statements were then scaled for intensity using pair-comparison scaling. Later the subsamples were joined together to form

[27] Zinnes, "The Expression and Perception of Hostility . . . ."
[28] Ibid., p. 85.

a general yardstick against which all other hostility statements then could be analyzed. In Professor Zinnes' study, pair-comparison scaling provided a means for constructing a relatively objective initial scale which she then used to analyze a larger number of statements.

EVALUATIVE ASSERTION ANALYSIS

Evaluative assertion analysis is another type of intensity scaling that was developed by C. E. Osgood and his associates.[29] It involves translating messages into one of two common assertion formats and assigning numerical values to the constituent elements. The two assertion formats initially used are

> *Form A*   Attitude   Object₁   (AO_1) / Verbal   Connector   (c) /
> Common Meaning Term (cm)
> *Form B*   Attitude   Object₁   (AO_1) / Verbal   Connector   (c) /
> Attitude Object₂ (AO_2)

Attitude objects normally refer to nouns. In the case of AO_1 we are isolating the subject of the phrase or sentence, whereas AO_2 will refer to the noun found in the predicate of the phrase or sentence. Verbal connectors simply locate the verbal components of the phrase or sentence, and common meaning terms usually isolate adjectives. The following example from Holsti may help to clarify the application of the above format:[30]

> *Sentence example*   "The treacherous American aggressors are abetting the corrupt ruling circles of Japan."

This sentence can be broken into four phrases and placed in the proper assertion formats:

1	Americans (AO_1)	are (c)	treacherous (cm)	*Form A*
2	Americans (AO_1)	are (c)	aggressors (cm)	*Form A*
3	Americans (AO_1)	are abetting (c)	Japanese ruling circles (AO_2)	*Form B*
4	Japanese ruling circles (AO_1)	are (c)	corrupt (cm)	*Form A*

After categorizing all phrases or sentences into the proper assertion formats, the next step is to assign numerical values to the constituent parts. Values are assigned to the verbal connectors and to

[29] C. E. Osgood, S. Saporta, and J. C. Nunnally, "Evaluative Assertion Analysis," *Litera*, 3 (1956), 47–102.
[30] Ole R. Holsti, "Evaluative Assertion Analysis," in *Content Analysis*, eds. Robert C. North et al., Northwestern University Press, Evanston, Ill., 1963, pp. 94–95.

1	2	3	4	5	6	7
Source	AO_1	c	Value column	cm or AO_2	Value column	Product column (column 4 × column 6)
Jen-min Jih-pao	Jap. ruling circles	are	+3	corrupt	−3	−9

Table 8-5   Coding format for evaluative assertion analysis

Source: Robert North, Ole Holsti, M. George Zaninovich, and Dina Zinnes, *Content Analysis*, Northwestern University Press, Evanston, Ill., 1963, p. 95. Reprinted by permission.

the common meaning terms for both *valence* or direction (+ or −) and *intensity* (1, 2, 3). The valence of the verbal connector is determined on the basis of whether the expressed relationship is associative or dissociative, and the valence of the common meaning term is determined by whether it lies on the positive or negative side of a neutral scale.

Intensities, on the other hand, range from 1 to 3, with the designation based on the following rules:

1   Most unqualified verbs in the present tense are given the maximal value of ±3 largely on the logic that they are unconditional and immediately relevant.
2   Verbs with auxiliaries are given a ±2 since they contain qualifications.
3   Verbs implying only hypothetical relationships are assigned a value of ±1.

The assignment of values to common meaning terms corresponds roughly to the categorical intensities of "Extremely," "Moderately," or "Slightly." The overall intensity value given to each assertion is the product of the verbal connector and the common meaning term or Attitude Object₂.[31]

Standardized formats are generally best for computing and recording intensity values. These can be referred to later for rechecking and replication. For this task Holsti suggests the format shown in Table 8-5.

Evaluative assertion analysis is a fairly reliable type of intensity scaling. Nevertheless, as Holsti points out, although coders can be rapidly trained to achieve a high degree of intercoder reliability,

[31] Ibid., p. 94.

the method is too laborious to be used for large volumes of data, and it can be uneconomical if only gross measures of attitude (e.g. pro or con) are required. It is probably most useful when the analyst requires precise data on only a limited number of attitude objects. . . ."[32]

Problems of content analysis

THE DATA BASE

One major problem with content analysis concerns the data base. Researchers should consider three aspects of their data: reliability, comprehensiveness, and overall quality. It is important to recall that we seldom have all relevant documentation on any given topic at our disposal. On the other hand, frequently we cannot use all available documentation because of time and resource constraints. Usually, some informed selection among sources must occur. The question then becomes, "Is available documentation sufficient as a basis for generalizing about a given topic or for merely accurately investigating a given question?" This question is difficult to answer definitively, and this is one reason why the conclusions of all scientific inquiry are inherently tentative.

In determining the reliability of available documentation, it is generally useful to consider the following factors: (1) the apparent motivation for the publication of the document; (2) the author's reputation for reliable scholarship and his access to relevant materials; and (3) the period of publication. It is normally not enough to determine a document's authenticity of authorship. As Dina Zinnes and Howard Koch have pointed out, problems frequently arise in connection with war documents.[33] The French Yellow Book, issued at the beginning of World War I, was a genuine government document, but it was full of events that were dubious. Like many documents issued at that time, the French Yellow Book was designed to justify entry into the war and to absolve the French of war guilt.

In selecting a sample of documents from a larger universe of available materials, researchers also must make further judgments about the comparative merits of various sources. In studying inter-

[32] Holsti, "Evaluative Assertion Analysis." Holsti points out that this method was used to assess news magazines' treatment of presidential candidates in 1960, editorial treatment of India in the *New York Times*, and John Foster Dulles' attitude toward the Soviet Union among others.

[33] Zinnes with the collaboration of Howard E. Koch, Jr., "Documents as a Source of Data," in North et al., *Content Analysis*, pp. 19–20; see also related comments on documentation difficulties in Edward Azar, et al., "The Problem of Source Coverage in the Use of Events Data," mimeograph, Michigan State University; and Robert Burrowes et al., "Sources of Middle East International Event Data," *Middle East Studies Association Bulletin*, 5 (1971), 54–71.

national situations, for example, numerous sources might be employed, including consular reports, diplomatic reports, memoranda, and communications between heads of state. It is important to recognize that researchers make certain fundamental decisions in choosing some sources over others. In making these choices, they often effectively decide where the locus of decision-making lies and which levels of informed opinion are most authoritative.

Determining a relative ordering of authoritativeness and quality is not unique to international situations. In our own research the same problem was encountered in content analysis of American newspapers for information on urban riots in the mid-1960s. In this particular instance, we used the *New York Times* as the basic source; local newspapers served as secondary sources. On occasion the reports of the several sources conflicted on basic information regarding damage reports, number of arrests, and other factors. Not surprisingly, local papers often described events in greater detail and in more dramatic terms. In this particular instance, time lags in reporting impeded the research process. Injury and fatality reports were often inaccurate immediately after the disturbance, and extensive follow-ups on the statistics proved necessary.

THE PROBLEM OF RELIABILITY

As we have pointed out in discussing other research methods, reliability is a major concern in all social research. Critics suggest that content analysts are particularly negligent in attempting to assess the reliability of their procedures. Nevertheless, formal attempts to ascertain reliability appear to be increasing. Reliability is a function of the overall design of the study—its sampling and counting procedures as well as coder and category reliability. Intercoder and intracoder reliability are two methods previously discussed to deal with the problem of coder reliability.

Category reliability is, of course, integrally related to the problem of coder reliability. *Category reliability* refers to the degree of repeatability in the placement of data into various categories. When categories are sufficiently well defined, a high degree of agreement should exist among different judges using the same data and categories. As stated previously, pretesting categories and measuring the differences across judges' placements provides one means of assessing clarity of definitions. A number of other approaches also have been developed to deal with the problem of category reliability. These alternative procedures are well outlined in Holsti's summary essay and citations, and we only briefly cover them here.[34]

---

[34] Holsti, *Content Analysis* . . . , pp. 135–149; and H. D. Lasswell et al., "The Reliability of Content Analysis Categories," in *Language of Politics*, pp. 83–112.

Exhaustive definition of categories is probably the most definitive answer to the problem of category reliability. Cues for content placement can be provided through the use of a dictionary or similar reference guide. Unfortunately, it is often difficult to reduce category placement to a clerical task in this manner. Moreover, this assumes that the reference guide is correct.

A third procedure to increase category reliability is to introduce additional judges. Unfortunately, this particular solution raises the cost of the project and does not necessarily solve the problem unless low reliability is more related to systematic errors among the existing judges than to the categories themselves.

In some cases low reliability results because categories have been over defined and the number of distinctions is too great. In this instance collapsing categories may help to resolve the problem.

Finally, categories sometimes yield low reliability because the categorization involves making a number of confounding decisions simultaneously. Thus, if a coder is asked to code items in terms of locational categories (urban, rural, foreign, domestic, historical, contemporary), he could not do so because some categories overlap and an item could fit into several categories. This problem could be resolved by truncating the choices in the form of dichotomies, thereby enabling the coder to focus on one decision at a time.

The problem of category reliability pervades content analysis studies. Unfortunately, there appear to be unavoidable trade-offs between reliability and differentiation. Reliability usually decreases as the number of categories increases. Determining the proper balance between category simplification (for maximal coder and category reliability) and differentiation (for maintaining meaningful distinctions in the data) is a difficult but important decision in the research process.

To a certain extent solving the problem of low reliability is a process of trial and error. Thus Zinnes reports that several different methods of categorization were tried before the final method was selected.[35] In most cases, insufficient methodological work exists to establish general guidelines in this regard. Scores of intercoder agreement are often used as a basis for determining the adequacy of one method over another.

When sampling is used in content analysis, the sampling procedures also affect a study's reliability. If nonprobability methods are employed without clear criteria for inclusion and exclusion of information, the study can be expected to yield a low (and unknown) level of reliability.

It is important that research present clear information relevant to its reliability. *Minimal* coverage includes a specification of the sampling procedures and the measures of coder and category reliability

[35] Zinnes, "The Expression and Perception of Hostility . . . ," pp. 90–91.

used. When this information is lacking, it is difficult to evaluate the study, and it is not open to general public examination, as it should be.

THE PROBLEM OF VALIDITY

Validity is the other major concern in executing and evaluating research. As previously defined, *validity* refers to whether a given research instrument actually measures what it purports to measure. Relevant questions in this regard include: Does the content analysis actually describe the behavior it is intended to describe? Does the perceptual measure have any relation to actual behavior? Can perceptions of increasing hostility, for example, be taken as an indication of actual increasing hostility and tension? The question of validity raises profound questions regarding the use of communications information in general and the use of certain content analysis techniques in particular. There has been a great deal of criticism of content analysis because much of it lacks formal validation procedures. Too frequently, validity simply is assumed to be self-evident.

Assessing the validity of a measuring device is often difficult. Some scholars, adopting a strict position on the problem of validity, argue that we must use only direct measures of behavior which do not raise questions of validity. Thus, sign-vehicle analysis, which deals *only* with the actual presence or absence of a given sign (such as references to "party" or "constituency") raises no problems of validity. Similarly, radical behaviorists attempt to circumvent the problem of validity entirely by only direct measures in the laboratory setting.

More frequently content analysts must consider the problem of validity, because they do not use direct, self-evident measures. Instead they might employ certain cues that purportedly measure hostility or friendliness, for example, or they assume that the frequency of certain references indicates priorities. In the latter case, while the signs might be unambiguous direct measures, they are not treated as such in a strictly descriptive sense. The more complex types of content analysis, such as evaluative assertion analysis, raise even more complex problems of validity, since they involve assumptions about the meaning, implied direction, and force of certain statements.

Unfortunately, as Irving Janis points out, the problem of validity raises something of a paradox in content analysis; by increasing the validity of an analysis through the use of only direct measures, we risk trivializing our findings and diminishing the overall significance of our research.[36] A great deal of useful work in content analysis might

---

[36] Irving L. Janis, "The Problem of Validating Content Analysis," in Lasswell et al., *Language of Politics*, pp. 55–82.

be lost if we insist on strict interpretations of validity. To resolve this problem, Janis suggests a compromise whereby we attempt to indirectly validate the measure through consideration of what he terms "productivity." *Productivity* refers to the degree to which a given study's results serve as good indicators of other related behaviors or variables.[37]

Janis' suggestion is similar to the validation procedure known as concurrent validation discussed in Chapter 4. This procedure, you will recall, uses correspondence with other measures as the criterion for validity. Studies using concurrent validation rest on both logical and empirical grounds. Some logical justification usually underlies the choice of independent measures, but validation rests on the empirical correlation actually obtained. Thus in their 1914 prewar crisis study, Holsti, Brody, and North demonstrate a relationship between their perceptual measures of increasing hostility and financial measures of this tension, such as fluctuations in the flow of gold and the price of securities.[38]

Predictive validity is another validation procedure frequently employed. In this case, the validity of a study is assessed on the basis of its correspondence with future events or, more generally, on the basis of its predictive powers. Propaganda analysis and most other content analyses used for forecasting purposes usually are adjudged on this basis. A study that attempted to determine whether it was possible to infer real intentions and motivations from published communication was conducted by Eto Shimkichi and Tatsumi Okabe, on statements made by the People's Republic of China regarding Japan. These authors' findings indicated that the inference was justified in this case.[39]

Construct validation is the most demanding procedure, since it attempts to validate not only the measure itself but also the theory underlying the measure or concept. Examples of attempts at construct validation include studies that have attempted to validate the concept of "need achievement" and the theory underlying that concept. These studies have usually inferred validity from the theory's ability to discriminate between groups.[40] Some critics argue that attempts at construct validation must aim also at predictive validity. In other words, the continuing ability of the measure to discriminate between groups must be assessed.

The question of validity is obviously related to the problem of reliability. Nevertheless, the two do not always accompany one

---

[37] Ibid., pp. 64–82.

[38] Holsti et al., "Measuring Affect and Action. . . ."

[39] Eto Shimkichi and Tatsumi Okabe, "Content Analysis of Statements in Regard to Japan Made by the People's Republic of China," *Developing Economics*, 3 (1965), 48–72.

[40] See D. C. McClelland, *The Achieving Society*, Van Nostrand, Reinhold Company, New York, 1961.

another. While a study will always be invalid if its procedures are unreliable, reliability will not necessarily guarantee validity. If social science is to progress toward its goal of systematic, generalizable knowledge, both problems will have to be taken seriously. Content analysis, like the other procedures we have discussed, embodies a number of important procedural checks that aim at maximizing objectively and intersubjective transmissability. But like any research technique, it is not without its limitations. The larger problem of meaning surrounding all social science research is summarized by Lewis Carroll in *Through the Looking Glass,* in an exchange between Humpty Dumpty and Alice. Humpty comically but succinctly insists on an idiosyncratic approach to meaning:

> "When I use a word," Humpty Dumpty said, in a rather scornful tone, "it means just what I choose it to mean—neither more nor less."
>
> "The question is," said Alice, "whether you can make words mean so many different things."
>
> "The question is," said Humpty Dumpty, "which is to be master."

Like Alice, social scientists proceed on the assumption that human behavior, in its linguistic manifestations and other forms, does contain generalizable meaning.

Review questions and exercises

1   Briefly define the meaning and significance of the following:

    a   Content analysis
    b   Systematization
    c   Objectivity
    d   General inquirer programs
    e   Coding rules
    f   Categories
    g   Units of content
    h   Enumeration systems
    i   Space-time units
    j   Frequency enumeration
    k   Intensity units of enumeration
    l   Q-sort method
    m   Pair-comparison analysis
    n   Evaluative assertion analysis
    o   Intercoder reliability
    p   Intracoder reliability
    q   Valence

r   Category reliability
s   Predictive validity
t   Concurrent validity
u   Construct validity

2 Read some of the bibliographic sources on the qualitative-quantitative debate in content analysis. On the basis of this reading, define and critically discuss the major issues raised by both sides.

3 What topics or general questions do you feel can be dealt with most successfully and least successfully by using content analysis?

4 On the basis of a sound sampling design, attempt to ascertain trends in formal reliability and validity procedures in content analysis studies over the past twenty years.

5 There has been some debate in recent years over the manner in which the press reports major news. Some observers have charged that the press is biased in its presentation. Draw up a research design for investigating this charge on the basis of content analysis.

6 Sample a number of different newspaper editorials on attitudes toward the Equal Rights Amendment and compare the results that would obtain in using a simple frequency count, paired-comparison analysis, and the Q-sort method. Discuss the differences.

7 Take the data generated in problem 6 and see whether differences in editorial position are related to certain demographic features of the cities, such as income, size, percentage of women in work-force, etc.

8 Outline the assumption, advantages, and disadvantages of the following methods for quantifying data and scaling intensity: space-time allotment, frequency count, paired-comparison analysis, the Q-sort method, and evaluative assertion analysis.

Designers of statistics are indeed
philosophers, however unwilling to
claim the name, and are fully
aware that different aspects of
reality can be lit up if alternative
sets of concepts are used.

Bertrand de Jouvenel

9

STATISTICS: A SMALL SET

The two major tasks of this chapter are to provide you with a simple
set of statistics and to convince you that the statistical enterprise is a
worthy one.

Why is an understanding of statistics important? What is the
purpose of using statistics? There are three main purposes for using
statistics in social research. First, statistics frequently are used for the
sake of parsimony in the general description of one's data. Various
descriptive statistics are employed, for example, to summarize observations on a single variable. We hear reports of the median family
income, the average level of employment or unemployment. A summary statistic such as the average or the median provides a convenient
way to summarize a large number of individual bits of information.

Statistics also can be used for other purposes, however. They
frequently are used to describe associations between two or more variables. We develop and analyze a small set of these measures in this
chapter. Controversies usually arise over the third major purpose of
statistics, which is to make inferences about the population on the
basis of a sample. When using sample statistics for the purposes of
making inferences to the larger population, it is important to recall
that many statistics assume that (1) a random sample is drawn with

each individual having an equal (independent) chance of being drawn (2) from a normally distributed population.[1]

These two conditions are major parts of the assumptions that relate sample statistics to a population. When the assumption is that the parameters of a population are fixed and yet unknown, we begin drawing samples from this population and making decisions about the fixed characteristics of the population. The statistics based on these assumptions of fixed parameters are known as *parametric statistics*.

Whether or not the population is normally distributed is always questionable. A way out of the population dilemma is to use distribution-free statistics. In a real sense, this latter tactic is the plan for the nonparametric statistics used with nominal- and ordinal-level data.[2] While most nonparametric statistics have a distribution counterpoint, they are free of the initial normal distribution assumptions associated with interval data and parametric statistics.[3] Statistics, based on parametric or nonparametric assumptions, offer (1) a sounder basis than common sense for stating the degree of relationship between variables and (2) a statement about the probability that an association is a chance or random event. Statistics help answer several questions, including the following:

1   Is there a relationship among several variables?
2   How strong is that relationship?
3   How much confidence can we have that the relationship is true rather than accidental?

The following sections of this chapter examine a variety of statistical measures useful in social research. Table 9-1 lists data for unemployment compensation and public welfare payments to the fifty states in 1971 from the federal government.[4] These data provide examples for our basic statistics. We first examine descriptive statistics; these include the mean, the median, and the standard deviation.

[1] Denton E. Morrison and Ramon E. Henkel, "Significance Tests Reconsidered," *American Sociologist*, 4 (May 1969), 134; Margaret Hagood and Daniel Price, *Statistics for Sociologists*, Holt, Rinehart and Winston, New York, 1952, pp. 193–195, 287–294, 419–423; Hubert Blalock, *Social Statistics*, McGraw-Hill Book Company, New York, 1960, p. 270; and D. Gold, "Statistical Test and Substantive Significance," *American Sociologist*, 4 (February 1969), 46.

[2] For a more detailed discussion of these distinctions, see Sidney Siegel, *Nonparametric Statistics for the Behavioral Sciences*, McGraw-Hill Book Company, New York, 1965, pp. 2–3; and Myles Hollander and Douglas A. Wolfe, *Nonparametric Statistical Methods*, John Wiley & Sons, New York, 1973.

[3] Nonparametric tests are backed by binomial, multinomial, and chi-square distributions, to name a few. These distributions are analogous to the parametric, continuous distributions, Siegel, 32.

[4] Department of the Treasury, *Federal Aid to States: Fiscal Year 1971*, Government Printing Office, Washington, 1972 (GPO922-788).

State	Public welfare	Unemployment compensation
Alabama	$ 188,258	$ 9,034
Alaska	6,814	4,253
Arizona	29,839	8,426
Arkansas	90,117	6,036
California	1,682,651	86,827
Colorado	107,661	6,926
Connecticut	112,641	15,251
Delaware	17,035	1,711
Florida	178,434	15,089
Georgia	251,080	10,421
Hawaii	28,108	3,390
Idaho	20,498	4,195
Illinois	424,474	34,074
Indiana	101,492	9,992
Iowa	71,376	6,454
Kansas	76,379	6,253
Kentucky	148,104	7,289
Louisiana	201,230	10,272
Maine	52,106	3,714
Maryland	135,053	11,221
Massachusetts	380,178	26,023
Michigan	356,929	34,998
Minnesota	172,840	10,692
Mississippi	107,545	6,304
Missouri	174,510	13,614

Table 9-1   Unemployment compensation and public welfare payments* to the states from the federal government

*Rounded to nearest $1,000; full variable titles are (1) Department of Health, Education, and Welfare, Social and Rehabilitation Service, Public

Descriptive statistics

MEAN

The *mean*, a summary statistic for interval data, is the average value for a series of numbers.[5] As Example 9-1 indicates, adding up the numbers 1, 2, 3, 4, 5 and dividing by the number of numbers (N) would give us a mean of 3. Stated more rigorously, sum the numbers (x) and denote this by the symbol $\sum X$, divided by total numbers (N), and you have the mean denoted by $\overline{X}$. For the variables used in Table 9-1, the

[5] Terrence Jones, *Conducting Political Research*, Harper & Row, Publishers, New York, 1971, pp. 101–103; William L. Hays, *Statistics*, Holt, Rinehart and Winston, New York, 1963, pp. 161–176.

State	Public welfare	Unemployment compensation
Montana	20,193	2,904
Nebraska	43,596	3,352
Nevada	13,280	4,740
New Hampshire	19,408	3,276
New Jersey	279,946	31,103
New Mexico	48,852	4,103
New York	1,499,532	100,184
North Carolina	173,929	13,043
North Dakota	22,270	2,664
Ohio	243,326	28,879
Oklahoma	175,356	8,344
Oregon	88,254	9,012
Pennsylvania	480,116	39,225
Rhode Island	48,755	5,463
South Carolina	60,353	6,793
South Dakota	23,668	2,497
Tennessee	143,865	8,850
Texas	436,593	28,268
Utah	40,752	7,390
Vermont	24,924	2,475
Virginia	117,834	7,802
Washington	158,358	19,331
West Virginia	69,279	5,380
Wisconsin	164,367	13,176
Wyoming	6,427	2,140

Assistance, and (2) Department of Labor, Unemployment Compensation and Employment Service Administration (trust fund).

Source: Department of the Treasury. *Federal Aid to States: Fiscal Year 1971.*

mean for unemployment compensation is $14,256.95, and $190,371.31 is the mean for public welfare payment.

The mean provides a convenient place for dividing a series of

Example 9-1

$x_1 = 1$ Mean $(\bar{X}) = \sum X/N$
$x_2 = 2$
$x_3 = 3$ $\bar{X} = 15/5$
$x_4 = 4$ $\underset{=}{X = 3}$ (mean)
$x_5 = 5$
$\sum X = 15$
$N = 5$

numbers into a high group and a low group; when the variable is divided into two categories, even if the mean is not used, we have a dichotomous variable.

Extreme cases (extra large or very small) skew the distribution and may result in a mean that is exceptionally high or low with only a few cases above or below the mean. When the numbers for extreme cases are large or very small, the mean does not provide a good description of the data distribution. One way to check on the amount of distortion is to calculate the amount of skewness by first finding the median.

MEDIAN

The *median* (*Md*) can be used with ordinal or interval data and is defined as the middle value.[6] Half the cases (50 percent) are below the median, and half are above it. In Table 9-1, the median for public welfare is $107,603, and $8,073.996 is the median for unemployment compensation. If the distribution for the variables is perfectly symmetrical, the median and the mean will have exactly the same value. When the distribution is highly skewed or asymmetrical, the median is preferable to the mean as a summary statistic.

The mean and the median are two commonly employed measures of *central tendency*, locational indicators of values at the center of an array of numbers. Other measures are also available; these are depicted in Table 9-2 and are discussed in most statistics textbooks.

Often researchers are interested in describing data not only in terms of central tendency but also in terms of variation, spread, or dispersion. A number of measures of variability or dispersion are available to describe scatter or variation in the values of a variable. The measures appropriate to different types of data are also outlined in Table 9-2. In the following section we discuss the most prominent measure of dispersion, the standard deviation.

STANDARD DEVIATION

The *standard deviation* (*S*) is formally defined as the square root of the variance (S^2).

> *Variance*, the measure of this spread around the central tendency, is based on how much each unit (each person's age, for example) deviates from the mean (the mean age, for example).[7]

---

[6] The median is discussed in Jones, *Conducting Political Research*, pp. 99–100; and G. David Garson, *Handbook of Political Science Methods*, Holbrook Press, Boston, 1971, p. 75.
[7] Garson, ibid., p. 95.

Level of measurement	Measures of central tendency	Measures of variability
Nominal level	Mode Frequency distribution	Variation ratio
Ordinal level	Median	Decile range Range
Interval level	Mean Median	Standard deviation Variance

Table 9-2   Summary table on descriptive statistics

Variance is calculated by taking the sum ($\sum$) of squared differences (which provide all positive differences) between each number and the mean divided by the total number of numbers (N). The calculation follows the form below and is the squared unit's measure of deviation from the mean. When the square root of the variance is taken, the deviation from the mean is in terms of the original measures and is called the standard deviation.

X	$X - \overline{X}$	$(X - \overline{X})^2$
1	-2	4
2	-1	1
3	0	0
4	1	1
5	2	4
15		10

$$\overline{X} = 15/5 = \underline{\underline{3}} \qquad S_x^2 = \frac{\sum (X - \overline{X})^2}{N} = \frac{10}{5} = \underline{\underline{2}} \text{ (Variance)}$$

$$S_x = \underline{\underline{1.414}} \text{ (Standard deviation)}$$

Thus the variance of the series of numbers equals 2, and 1.414 equals the standard deviation. From the series of numbers used in the example we know that the mean equals 3 and that the median equals 3. If the "sample" of numbers forms a normal distribution, we also know that about two-thirds of the numbers will be within one standard deviation from the mean (actually 68.26 percent of the cases); 95 percent of the cases within two standard deviations; and 99 percent of the cases within three standard deviations. Further, if there is no skewness in the distribution, skewness will be 0. (Because the distribution is discussed in terms of three standard deviations, skewness can range from -3 to $+3$.) Looking at our example, 1.414 standard deviations either

Public welfare
  Mean $(\overline{X})$ = $190,371.31
  Median (Md) = $107,603
  Standard Deviation (S) = $66,516.19
  Skewness = 3.733

Unemployment compensation
  Mean $(\overline{X})$ = $14,256.95
  Median (Md) = $8,072.99
  Standard Deviation (S) = $5,887.62
  Skewness = 3.151

Table 9-3 Distributional statistics for unemployment compensation and welfare payments to the states from the federal government

side of the mean $(\overline{X} = 3)$ would include about two-thirds of the cases $(3/5 = 60$ per cent; 2, 3, 4). The general formula for skewness is

$$\text{Skewness} = \frac{3(\overline{X} - Md)}{S_x}$$

For the set of numbers shown earlier, skewness is

$$\text{Skewness} = \frac{3(3 - 3)}{1.414}$$

$$\text{Skewness} = \frac{3(0)}{7.414} = 0$$

No skewness occurs within our series of numbers. No large numbers exist in the series to draw the mean to the high side (in which case the skewness would lean toward +3), and no very small numbers exist to draw the mean to the low side (in which case the skewness would lean toward −3). In Table 9-1 though, we can see that some very large numbers exist in the unemployment compensation series and in the public welfare series; the means are considerably larger than the medians, and skewness measures exceed 3.

Another way to split up variables would be to use the median or the mean plus or minus one standard deviation. The median would ensure you that an even number of cases could be found above and below the cutoff point. The mean plus and minus one standard deviation would theoretically ensure that the normal majority in the middle of the sample was separated from extremes at either end. Naturally, dividing the series into thirds, fourths, and so on, are other ways to ensure this, but they have no distributional reference. As indicated earlier, dividing a variable in two pieces forms a dichotomous variable; a variable divided into three parts is a trichotomous variable.

Table 9-3 summarizes the distributional statistics discussed in this section using our initial data on public welfare and unemployment compensation expenditures.

Relationships between variables

In addition to describing the distributional characteristics of single variables, there are statistics to measure the relationship between two variables. In the following sections, common measures of association will be discussed. Table 9-4 summarizes the statistical measures appropriate to different types of data. The level of measurement indicates the *minimum* requisite. Any statistics could be used with interval data, but only nominal-level statistics could be used with nominal data.

CHI-SQUARE (χ^2)

The *chi-square* (χ^2) statistic measures the differences between observed values and those that would obtain if there is no relationship between variables. It essentially is a test of a hypothesis that tells whether or not cases are distributed in a random fashion throughout a table. This nominal statistic only tacitly tells whether one variable is related to another, and it does not tell anything about the direction (positive or negative) of whatever pattern may be observed between variables.

The formula for chi-square is

$$\chi^2 = \sum \frac{(FO - FE)^2}{FE}$$

where FO = observed frequencies
FE = expected frequencies

When the differences between expected and observed frequencies divided by expected frequencies are summed $(\sum)$ and the sum is very large, chi-square will be large. It has a possible range from 0 to infinity. The actual calculation procedures for χ^2 are outlined below. Note that this statistic is computed on the basis of *actual* frequencies, not percentages.

Table 9-5 depicts a cross-tabulation between our two variables, unemployment compensation and public welfare expenditures. A statement that there is no relationship between two variables (or two groups) is known as a *null hypothesis*. The null hypothesis is really a straw man because we know that we are more likely to find a difference or a relationship than we are not to find one. The null hypothesis, therefore, is that essentially no relationship exists between expendi-

Level of measurement	Appropriate statistics to measure association and for hypothesis testing
Nominal	Chi-square Lambda Goodman and Kruskal's Tau Cramer's *V*
Ordinal	Spearman's Rho Gamma Kendall's Tau *B* and Tau *C*
Interval	Correlation ratio Pearson's product-movement correlation

Table 9-4   Statistics appropriate with different levels of measurement

tures for the two programs. The alternative substantive hypothesis is that the distribution patterns for the two programs are highly similar.

1   It is convenient to begin the calculation procedure by labeling each cell *a, b, c, d,* etc., as indicated in Table 9-5.

2   Next, set up a worksheet with a column for cells, observed frequency (*FO*), expected frequency (*FE*), observed frequency minus expected frequency (*FO − FE*), the difference squared (*FO − FE*)^2 = D^2, and the difference squared divided by the expected frequency (*D^2/FE*). These features are outlined in Table 9-6.

3   For each cell calculate the expected frequency (*FE*). The row total is multiplied by the column total appropriate for that cell. For example, in Table 9-5, cell *a*'s expected frequency is the row total of *a* and *b*, which is *e* multiplied by the column total of *a* and *c*, which is *g*. This multiple is then divided by the total number of cases involved in the table (*T*). Cell *a*'s expected frequency is equal to *eg/T*.

4   Subtract the expected frequency (*FE*) for each cell from the observed frequency (*FO*) of each cell. To follow through on the example from the second point, cell *a*'s observed frequency (you might also call it the "real" count) is 22, and 12.5 was the expected frequency for cell *a*. The difference is 9.5, which might also be called *D*.

5   The difference is then squared. For cell *a*, 9.5 squared is equal to the 90.25 noted in Table 9-6.

6   The squared difference is divided by the expected frequency to form the individual cell chi-square (*D^2/FE*).

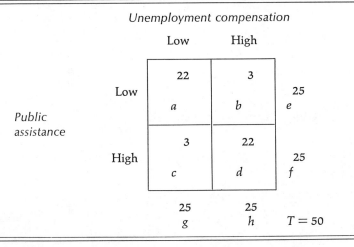

Table 9-5 Cross-tabulation of unemployment compensation and public welfare (Dividing the original variables at the median)

7 These individual chi-squares (D^2/FE) are summed $(\sum)$ to form the total chi-square for Table 9-6 ($\chi^2 = 28.88$).

8 Calculate the *degrees of freedom* in the table. The degrees of freedom for Table 9-6 are equal to the number of rows minus 1 $(r - 1)$ multiplied by the number of columns minus 1 $(C - 1)$. For this particular example, $(r - 1) = (2 - 1) = 1$, and $(C - 1) = (2 - 1) = 1$, and $(1) \times (1) = 1$. Thus, there is 1 degree of freedom in the above example. The number of degrees of freedom tell you how many cells must be filled before all other entries are fixed. To reject the null hypothesis, the chi-square must be larger the greater the number of degrees of freedom.

9 Finally, the last step is to determine how often a given chi-square could be obtained merely by chance. If our chi-square is very large and unlikely to be a chance occurrence, then we can reject the null hypothesis fairly confidently. For this step, refer to Appendix E. In Table 4 there is a p column. This column means that the probability of this happening by chance is only a certain percent. Assuming that we already have picked a rejection level, we then look at the rows of Table 4 (Appendix E) where the degrees of freedom are located. The intersection of the appropriate row and column indicates the chi-square that our statistic must equal or exceed for rejection of the null hypothesis. In our example a chi-square of 28.88 exceeds the 10.83 from Table 4 needed to be significant at the .001 level for 1 degree of freedom.

Cell	FO	FE	FO — FE	$(FO — FE)^2 = D^2$	D^2/FE
a	22	$ge/T = 12.5$	9.5	90.25	7.22
b	3	$he/T = 12.5$	—9.5	90.25	7.22
c	3	$gf/T = 12.5$	—9.5	90.25	7.22
d	22	$hf/T = 12.5$	9.5	90.25	7.22

Table 9-6   Computation of chi-square

$$X^2 = \Sigma \ (D^2/FE) = 28.88$$
$$Df = 1$$
$$\text{sign} = .001$$
$$\text{corrected chi-square } (X^2) = 25.92 \quad Df = 1$$
$$\text{sign} = .001$$
$$\text{uncorrected chi-square } (X^2) = 28.88$$

A good rule is to have more than five cases per cell and absolutely no cell without cases.[8] If fewer than five expected cases occur, a *Yates' correction formula* frequently is employed to correct for distortion of the statistic due to small frequencies. In essence, the Yates' correction formula steals half a case from all the wealthier neighbors and gives it to the poor cell (with fewer than five cases). The example in Table 9-5 had two data-poor cells. As the results in Table 9-6 indicate, the corrected value of chi-square differs from the uncorrected version. The corrected chi-square will be more modest, and unless we have an extremely low number of cases per cell (one or two) or a large number of low-case cells (more than two) or empty cells, the corrected chi-square will be dependable.

It is usually desirable to know *how much* association exists between two variables. One would like to be able to say, "So much of X is explained by Y," or, simply, "X is associated strongly with Y." Obviously there is a problem of deciding at what point an association is strong, weak, or nonexistent. We will make some suggestions about this division after presenting the following measure of association.

CRAMER'S V

The measure of association that we recommend as the most general is *Cramer's V* because it always ranges between 0 (indicating complete independence) and 1 (indicating complete dependence).[9] Cramer's *V*, like many other measures of association, is based upon chi-square

[8] Reasons for these figures are stated in Siegel, *Nonparametric Statistics . . .*, pp. 178–179. The debate about the uses of chi-square are discussed in *Readings in Statistics for the Behavioral Scientist*, ed. Joseph A. Steger, Holt, Rinehart and Winston, New York, 1971, pp. 52–156.

[9] Hays, *Statistics*, p. 606; Blalock, *Social Statistics*, p. 230.

(x^2).[10] Cramer's V is the square root of the chi-square divided by the number of subjects multiplied by the minimum of either the number of columns minus 1 $(c - 1)$ or the number of rows minus 1 $(r - 1)$.

$$V = \sqrt{\frac{\chi^2}{N(M - 1)}}$$

where M = minimum value of columns or rows
χ^2 = chi-square
N = number of subjects

Using the same data from our chi-square example,

$$\text{Cramer's } V = \sqrt{\frac{28.88}{50(2 - 1)}} = \sqrt{\frac{28.88}{50(1)}}$$

$$\text{Cramer's } V = \sqrt{.5776} = .76$$

In this example, we might say that the association between payments for unemployment compensation and public welfare was strong.

We should, however, provide some evidence of how strength was determined. One way would be to provide a footnote indicating how to interpret the measure of association. For example, this could be based on the following specifications:

Cramer's V range	Interpretation
0–.25	Weak
.26–.50	Moderate
.51–.75	Moderately strong
.76–1.00	Strong

On the basis of this specification we would have a precise meaning for the statement, "There is a strong association between unemployment compensation payments and public welfare payments." This statement is made because the Cramer's V was .76, and we stated in our specifications that all associations based on a Cramer's V between .76 and 1.00 will be called strong.

A second way to decide the strength of the measure of association involves averaging the various numbers of measures of association to find the relative mean point for the data. The data may normally provide a high measure of association; this effect may be due to well-known patterns among the variables.

In other words, all our reading about this subject might say there should be a strong association between the two variables. Hence, with the expectation about a strong association between two variables, we should adjust the text description to reflect this expected pattern. We

[10] Most famous is the coefficient of contingency (C); others are Kendall's Q; phi, which equals the simple correlation coefficient (r) in certain cases; and Tschuprow's T. A good source for these is Blalock's *Social Statistics*, pp. 229–232.

just calculated one Cramer's V using the dichotomous variables based on the unemployment compensation and public welfare variables; if we had calculated a series of Cramer's V from chi-square (χ^2) results and the series of Cramer's V appear to be consistently high, we make adjustments when reporting the associations.

If Cramer's V series averages, say, .75, we might have to state that one standard deviation on either side of .75 is a normal or expected association and the lower one standard deviation to 0 is weaker than expected (or weak) and plus one standard deviation to 1.0 is more than expected (or strong). Hence, while readers can quibble, we would be consistent when talking about the meaning of a measure of association, and this is most important.

Lambda is another nominal-level statistic that can be used to judge how much predictability can be found within a table.

LAMBDA (λ)

The *lambda* (λ) statistic allows us to make a bet on the variables. Most important, by knowing something about one variable, call it A, when we look at each category of A (Aj, where $j = 1, 2, 3, \ldots n$) to predict something about B. William Hays points this out in the following remark:

> This index shows the proportional reduction in the *probability* of error afforded by specifying Aj. If the information about the A category does not reduce the probability of error at all, the index is zero, and one can say that there is no predictive association. On the other hand, if the index is 1.00, no error is made given the Aj classification, and there is complete predictive association.[11]

Using the earlier example, lambda should give us some idea about how well we can predict public welfare expenditures if we know what the state received for unemployment compensation; that is, by knowing something about one variable and predicting what another variable is likely to be, we have an asymmetric prediction. The formula for this lambda is

$$\lambda B \text{ (lambda asymmetric)} = \frac{fm - fd}{N - fd}$$

where fm = maximum cell frequency found within each column

fd = maximum frequency found in the marginals of the rows (dependent variable)

N = total number of cases

---

[11] Hays, *Statistics*, p. 608.

Example 1   Unemployment compensation
                                                 (independent variable *A*)

Public welfare
(dependent variable *B*)

22	3	25
3	22	25

$$N = 50$$

$$\lambda B = \frac{(22 + 22) - 25}{50 - 25} = \frac{44 - 25}{25} = \underline{.7600}$$

Example 2   Unemployment compensation
                                                 (independent variable *A*)

                                              Low   Medium   High

	Low	Medium	High	
Low	14	2	0	16
Medium	2	12	4	18
High	0	4	12	16

Public welfare
(dependent variable *B*)

$$N = 50$$

$$\lambda B = \frac{\sum fm - fd}{N - fd}$$

$$\lambda B = \frac{(14 + 12 + 12) - 18}{50 - 18} = \frac{38 - 18}{32}$$

$$\lambda B = \frac{20}{32} = \underline{.625}$$

Table 9-7 Lambda Formulas and Examples Using unemployment compensation and public welfare grants

In Table 9-7, our previous materials are used to demonstrate the lambda asymmetric. The asymmetric lambda states that we are predicting B from what we know of A.[12] Hence, we have assumed, theoretically or by hunch, that A is the independent variable and that B is dependent upon A.

Neither small nor zero cells seriously distort lambda, and it can be used legitimately when chi-square cannot. In interpreting lambda in the first example in Table 9-7, we could say that 76 percent of the errors in predicting public welfare could be eliminated if we knew whether the unemployment compensation paid to a state was above or below the mean. Simply by viewing the distribution we could say intuitively that by knowing a state was below the mean (low) in terms of unemployment compensation, it was probably also low (below the mean) on public welfare receipts. The second example in Table 9-7 shows the same trend, though the index of predictive association λB is only 62.5 percent.[13]

As a modest judgment, a researcher can say that the association between unemployment compensation and public welfare is strong and that the relationship is nonrandom (through the chi-square). Whether there is a theoretical reason for the relationship, or a defensible causal relationship between variables, is the continuing problem the researcher must confront.

Thus far we have analyzed the data with statistics appropriate to nominal-level variables. Next we shall analyze the data using gamma, a statistic appropriate to ordinal data. For both nominal and ordinal statistics we speak of association rather than correlation (or even relationship), because we do not make the strong statistical assumptions necessary when using interval data.[14]

GAMMA (γ)

Gamma (γ) is a measure of association between two ordinal variables.[15] To make the unemployment compensation and public welfare variables ordinal, they can be divided mathematically at their means to provide

[12] An alternative way of treating lambda is to make no choice about whether A or B is the dependent variable and thus calculate the symmetric lambda; see Hays, *Statistics*, pp. 609–610.

[13] See also examples in L. C. Freeman, *Elementary Applied Statistics*, John Wiley & Sons, New York, 1965, pp. 74–78.

[14] Although we do have a lot going for us, the best statements for analysis at these levels are found in Siegel, *Nonparametric Statistics.* . . .

[15] Among the other measures of association with ordinal-level data are the Kendall's Tau, B and C, Somers' D, Eta, one ordinal and one interval, Spearman's rho, p. See, as examples, Siegel, *Nonparametric Statistics*, 200–223; Freeman, *Elementary Applied Statistics*, 210–214; and Gene V. Glass and Julian C. Stanley, *Statistical Methods in Education and Psychology*, Prentice-Hall, Englewood Cliffs, N.J., 1970, pp. 172–179.

dichotomous variables, or they then can be divided further into tri-chotomous variables. Other divisions are possible, of course, if the-oretically desirable. Again, a fairly firm rule is that we want at least five cases in each cell.

Gamma measures the predictability of the order on one vari-able from the order on a second variable. The general formula for gamma is

$$\gamma = \frac{\sum fa - \sum fi}{\sum fa + \sum fi}$$

where fa = frequency of agreements
fi = frequency of disagreements (or inversions)

The calculation for the second example from Table 9-7 is

$$\gamma = \frac{[14\,[(12 + 4) + (4 + 12)] + 12(12) + 2(16) + 2(16)] - [(4)(4) + 2(2)]}{656 + 20}$$

$$\gamma = .9408$$

The American states in the upper left-hand cells are positively paired with the states in the lower right-hand cells.[16] Thus, for the example,

$$fa = 14\,[(12 + 4) + (4 + 12)] + 12(12) + 2(16) + 2(16)$$

The negatively paired states are those in the upper right-hand cells paired with those in the lower left-hand cells. For this example,

$$fi = 0\,[(12 + 2) + (4 + 0)] + 4(4 + 0) + 2(2 + 0) + 12\,(0)$$
$$fi = 16 + 4 = 20$$

The assumptions for testing the statistical significance of gamma are (1) that there are no ties and (2) that the chance of randomly choosing a negative pair is the same as randomly choosing a positive pair. The fa and fi are our calculations for determining the chances of drawing positive and negative pairs.

> Summarizing the properties of gamma, first, it can range from −1 (a high value on one scale is always associated with a low value on the other scale) through 0 (no association) to +1 (a high value on one scale is invariably associated with a high value on the other scale); second, it has a probabilistic interpretation in-volving the comparative likelihood of randomly selecting positive and negative pairs; and third, the coefficient does not take into account the number of tied pairs.[17]

[16] Other writers use their own terms. Some examples: (1) "inversion"—Freeman, *Elementary Applied Statistics*, pp. 80–87; (2) "negative pairs"—Jones, *Conducting Political Research*, pp. 121–123; (3) "discordant pairs"—Garson, *Handbook of Political Science Methods*, p. 161.
[17] Jones, *Conducting Political Research*, p. 123.

To interpret gamma, James A. Davis has stated that although there is no set standard, an arbitrary set may be suggested for consistency.[18]

A gamma with an absolute value over 0.7 will be said to indicate a very strong association; one from 0.5 to 0.69, a substantial association; 0.3 to 0.49, a moderate one; 0.1 to 0.29, a low one; 0.01 to 0.09, a negligible association; and zero, of course, no association.[19]

A word of warning: it should be noted that gamma tends to overstate the strength of the relationship. The statistic is particularly misleading when a high number of ties exist in the ordering of values. With no adjustment for ties, gamma may result in an optimistic estimate. Thus, we suggest that you temper the gamma enthusiasm when presenting the results; that is, use other measures as you become familiar with them, see how close the χ^2 was to random, and check on the strength of association offered by the Cramer's V and the lambda.

SIMPLE CORRELATION

The *simple correlation* is an appropriate measure of relationship between two variables meeting interval assumptions.

In Figure 9-1 a line runs from the bottom left-hand corner to the upper right-hand corner. That line is a linear guide to the relationship between the unemployment compensation and public welfare variables. If the two variables were perfectly correlated, as we discuss in more detail shortly, all the states would lay along the line.

If all the states lay along the line, each increase in one variable would mean an equal increase in the other variable. We spend more time in this chapter with correlation; yet, regression is complementary to correlation, and regression is the extension of correlation that attempts to fit a line through data to minimize the distances from the line for all points.[20] Now we simply seek to demonstrate that as one variable increases, the other variable increases similarly. Indeed, the simple correlation statistic measures the amount of linear congruence between any two variables. If the variables varied such that the best fit for a line would be a curve of some sort, the correlation coefficient

---

[18] James A. Davis, *Elementary Survey Analysis*, Prentice-Hall, Englewood Cliffs, N.J., 1971, p. 49.

[19] Davis, ibid., p. 49.

[20] Regression is covered in almost every text we use as references. A good introduction to the techniques is Blalock, *Social Statistics*, pp. 273–299; and a book that builds a system around regression concepts is Gudmund K. Iverson, *Applied Statistics*, Inter-University Consortium for Political Research, Ann Arbor, Mich., 1974.

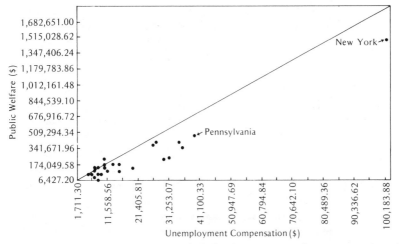

Figure 9-1   Scattergram of federal grant-in-aid program for the American states

would be a poor representative of the relationship; we still could calculate a simple correlation, though its meaning would be questionable. For the simple correlation, the formulas are[21]

Definitional

$$r = \frac{\sum (x - \bar{x})(y - \bar{y})}{\sqrt{\sum (x - \bar{x})^2 \sum (y - \bar{y})^2}}$$ (Formula 1)

Computational

$$r = \frac{N \sum (xy) - (\sum x)(\sum y)}{\sqrt{[N \sum x^2 - (\sum x)^2][N \sum y^2 - (\sum y)^2]}}$$ (Formula 2)

The numerator measures the deviation of the x and y scores from mean $\bar{x}$ and $\bar{y}$ (. . .). When the data form a straight line, points with high x deviations (high $x - \bar{x}$) will also have high y deviations; those with low x deviations will have low y deviations.[22]

A scattergram (or scatterplot) is one way to visualize this relationship. In Figure 9-1 unemployment compensation is displayed as running from left (lowest numbers) to right (highest numbers), while public welfare flows from the bottom (lowest numbers) to the top (highest numbers). States are located where two numbers intersect in the scattergram. New York, for instance, received $100,184 for unemployment compensation and $1,499,532 for public welfare; and

21 Garson, *Handbook of Political Science Methods*, p. 172.
22 Ibid., p. 172.

Pennsylvania garnered \$480,116 for public welfare and \$39,225 for unemployment compensation. Looking at the array we see that the more money a state received for one program, the more likely it was to receive more money for the other program. The simple correlation statistic measures how close the receipts from these two programs relate.

For now, let an example show how this statistic is calculated. Earlier, some distribution statistics were calculated on a series of numbers—1, 2, 3, 4, 5. For the moment consider a few other series found in Table 9-8. Further observe in Table 9-8 how r can be calculated between these numbers. The first r between series x_1 and *series* x_2 show a perfect positive correlation ($r = +1.0$); indeed as the one variable increases, the other variable increases. The opposite trend occurs between x_1 and x_3, in that as the one variable (x_1) increases, the other variable (x_3) decreases; these trends explain the strong (perfect) negative correlation ($r = -1.0$). The final correlation shows the situation where there is little correlation (r between x_1 and $x_4 = -.10$ or 0) and little pattern between the two variables.

To summarize, the Pearson product-moment correlation coefficient has a range of -1 to $+1$. A -1 implies that a high value on one variable is associated with low values on the other variable, and a $+1$ implies that a high value on one variable is associated with a high value on the other variable. A coefficient of 0 indicates that there is no association between the variables.[23]

Therefore, with a correlation of .967 between unemployment compensation and public welfare, we can see that the overall trend in Figure 9-1 is strong and positive. If we divide the two variables in various ways, the correlation fluctuates toward a more conservative figure. When they are dichotomized at the mean, the correlation (r) equals .719; when dichotomized at the median, the correlation (r) equals .760; when trichotomized (into thirds, roughly), the correlation (r) is .813.

When treated as nominal variables, and when divided at the mean, the lambdas are .545 with public welfare as the dependent variable and .565 (with a symmetric assumption). The chi-square (χ^2) is 21.94 (sign = .001, $df = 1$) although several cells have fewer than five cases.

When divided at the median, the lambdas are .760 with public welfare as the dependent variable and .760 (with a symmetric assumption). The chi-square (χ^2) is 25.92 (sign = .001, $df = 1$) with two cells less than five. You may also notice that the simple correlation (r) from the median split provides a compromise between the interval level correlation and the mean split correlation.

---

[23] See Hayward Alker, *Mathematics and Politics*, The Macmillan Company, New York, 1965, pp. 80–88.

X_1	X_2	X_1X_2	X_3	X_1X_3	X_4	X_1X_4	
1	6	6	5	5	5	5	
2	7	14	4	8	2	4	
3	8	24	3	9	1	3	$N = 5$
4	9	36	2	8	3	12	
5	10	50	1	5	4	20	
$\overline{15}$	$\overline{40}$	$\overline{130}$	$\overline{15}$	$\overline{35}$	$\overline{15}$	$\overline{44}$	

$\overline{X}_1 = 3$ $\overline{X}_2 = 8$ $\overline{X}_3 = 3$ $\overline{X}_4 = 3$

$X_1{}^2$	$X_1 - \overline{X}_1$	$(X_1 - \overline{X})^2$	$X_2{}^2$	$X_2 - \overline{X}_2$	$(X_2 - \overline{X}_2)^2$
1	−2	4	36	−2	4
4	−1	1	49	−1	1
9	0	0	64	0	0
16	1	1	81	1	1
25	2	4	100	2	4
$\overline{55}$		$\overline{10}$	$\overline{330}$		$\overline{10}$

$X_3{}^2$	$X_3 - \overline{X}_3$	$(X_3 - \overline{X}_3)^2$	$X_4{}^2$	$X_4 - \overline{X}^4$	$(X_4 - \overline{X}_4)^2$
25	2	4	25	2	4
16	1	1	4	−1	1
9	0	0	1	−2	4
4	−1	1	9	0	0
1	−2	4	16	1	1
$\overline{55}$		$\overline{10}$	$\overline{55}$		$\overline{10}$

Formula 1 for $r = \dfrac{\sum (x - \bar{x})(y - \bar{y})}{\sqrt{\sum (x - \bar{x})^2 \sum (y - \bar{y})^2}}$

r between x_1 and $x_2 = \dfrac{(4 + 1 + 0 + 1 + 4)}{\sqrt{10(10)}} = \dfrac{10}{10} = 1$

r between x_1 and $x_3 = \dfrac{-4 - 1 + 0 - 1 - 4}{\sqrt{10(10)}} = \dfrac{-10}{10} = -1$

r between x_1 and $x_4 = \dfrac{-4 + 1 + 0 + 0 + 2}{\sqrt{10(10)}} = \dfrac{-1}{10} = -.10$

Formula 2 for $r = \dfrac{N \sum (xy) - (\sum x)(\sum y)}{\sqrt{[N \sum x^2 - (\sum x)^2][N \sum y^2 - (\sum y)^2]}}$

r between x_1 and $x_2 = \dfrac{5(130) - (15)(40)}{\sqrt{(5(55) - 225)(5(330) - 1600)}} = \dfrac{50}{\sqrt{50(50)}} = \dfrac{50}{50} = 1$

r between x_1 and $x_3 = \dfrac{5(35) - (15)(15)}{\sqrt{(5(55) - 225)(5(55) - 225)}} = \dfrac{-50}{\sqrt{50(50)}} = \dfrac{-50}{50} = -1$

r between x_1 and $x_4 = \dfrac{5(44) - (15)(15)}{\sqrt{(5(55) - 225)(5(55) - 225)}} = \dfrac{-5}{50} = -.10$

Table 9-8 Correlation coefficient

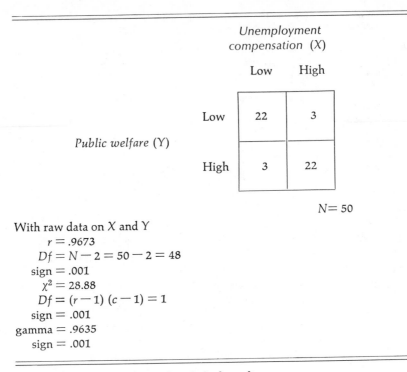

With raw data on X and Y
$$r = .9673$$
$$Df = N - 2 = 50 - 2 = 48$$
$$\text{sign} = .001$$
$$\chi^2 = 28.88$$
$$Df = (r - 1)(c - 1) = 1$$
$$\text{sign} = .001$$
$$\text{gamma} = .9635$$
$$\text{sign} = .001$$

Table 9-9   Summary of statistical results

Table 9-9 summarizes the results of using the various statistics on our initial data; the chi-square, as you can see, is larger than both of those just mentioned because there has been no Yates' correction in the results.

Controlling the third variable

To this point we have only studied two variable relationships. We have discussed the relationship between receipt of monies for public welfare and unemployment compensation. Frequently, phenomena in social science are a function of many factors, a number of which may be interrelated in various ways. "Political participation," for example, is a behavior that probably is related to a number of factors. It is often difficult to determine what the actual relationship is.

Consider, for example, the relationship between sex (A) and political participation (B). It has become almost a truism to contend that women participate in the political process less than men. In its simplest form, the contention is that political participation is a function of sex. This example is, of course, simplified. Many other factors are important in explaining differential rates of participation; it is not in fact a simple two-variable relationship. More importantly, the contention in many cases is *mistaken* because the relationship is a function of a third, *intervening* variable—socioeconomic standing (*C*), or differences in education and income.

To determine whether an additional (or alternative) variable is necessary, we *control* for the new factor. In the preceding example, we would compare males and females of similar socioeconomic standing (*ses*) to see if the relationship is truly a function of sex. This is accomplished by grouping all of the males and females of the different socioeconomic (*ses*) classes and then seeing whether males in the various ses classes still participate more when compared with females in the same ses class. Suppose, initially, that the correlation between sex and political participation was .73. We would want to compare this correlation with that obtaining when we control for ses. If the original correlation is reduced to near 0, it would indicate that the original relationship is *spurious*; the original correlation is the result of the fact that ses often varies with sex. When the effects of socioeconomic standing are controlled, the original relationship between sex and participation disappears.

When the control variable is *antecedent* to the independent variable originally postulated, it may be cited as the *explanation* for the relationship.[24] If, on the other hand, the theory said that the control factor occurred after *A* and before *B*, the control variable would offer an *interpretation* of the relationship between *A* and *B*. In this case, the interpretation need not render the relationship between *A* and *B* spurious. Instead, the control variable *intervenes* between *A* and *B* and must be built into the theory.[25] When theory is not guiding research, the problems of distinguishing dependent, independent, and control variables and of interpretation versus explanation are formidable.

Assuming that we have a theory about the order of the variables, we could get several results by controlling a variable. The three main effects of controlling that we wish to demonstrate are (1) independence (no effect), (2) the "plus-minus" effect, and (3) the "shrink-stretch" effect.[26]

[24] Claire Selltiz, Marie Jahoda, Morton Deutsch, and Stuart Cook, *Research Methods in Social Relations*, rev. 1-vol. ed., Holt, Rinehart and Winston, 1961, pp. 429–440; Oliver Benson, *Political Science Laboratory*, Charles E. Merrill, Columbus, Ohio, 1969, pp. 316–317. For an extension of this logic into the correlation coefficients, see Blalock, *Social Statistics*, pp. 337–343.

[25] Benson, *Political Science Laboratory*, p. 317. Some other excellent work on controlling the impact of the "third" variable can be found in James A. Davis, *Elementary Survey Analysis*, Prentice-Hall, Englewood Cliffs, N.J., 1971; and Frank J. Kohout, *Statistics for Social Scientists*, John Wiley & Sons, New York, 1974.

[26] Benson, *Political Science Laboratory*, pp. 302–312.

		High school and below (B—)	College (B)	Male (C—) B—	B	Female (C) B—	B
President doing good job?	No A—	150	100	75	50	75	50
	Yes A	100	150	50	75	50	75
		250	250	125	125	125	125
			$N = 500$		$N = 250$		$N = 250$
			$\gamma = .385$		$\gamma = .385$	$\gamma = .385$	

Table 9-10   Controlling variable effects: independence—"no effect"

For the first illustration we assume that the dependent variable was a question about whether or not the President is doing a good job. In Table 9-10, when sex is controlled, it makes no difference. Men and women show a positive relationship between education and the expressed belief that the President is doing a good job; the relationship shows no effect when controlled for sex.

In Table 9-11 the *plus-minus effect* is illustrated. In this case the dependent variable is the preferred size of family. The overall pattern in the first section of Table 9-11 suggests that there is no relationship between education and the preference for any family size. When we control for sex, however, highly educated males show a preference for larger families (more than two children). The more highly educated females, on the other hand, show a preference for smaller families (two children or less).

The third hypothetical example in Table 9-12 demonstrates the *shrink-stretch effect*. The dependent variable is attitude toward employment equality. The original relationship, with the full sample, shows a moderately positive relationship between higher education and a belief that there should be "strict employment equality." But when sex is controlled, the relationship for the men disappears. For the women the relationship is strengthened. Thus we can see that the positive association between attitudes on employment equality and education is substantially a product of the attitudes of women.

Another way to look at the use of control variables is to ask whether or not knowledge of the control variable provides a basis for betting on the behavior of individuals. We introduced the idea that knowing one variable can help reduce the errors made when guessing

		Male (C—) High		Female (C) High	
		High school	College	High school	College	school	College

Size of family more than 2?	No A—	125	125	75	50	50	75
	Yes A	125	125	50	75	75	50
		250	250	125	125	125	125
		$N = 500$		$N = 250$		$N = 250$	
		$\gamma = .00$		$\gamma = .385$		$\gamma = .385$	

Table 9-11   Controlling variable effects: "plus-minus" effect

the other variable earlier. Here we apply this idea to control variables. A technique designed to answer this question has been developed by James Davis; the procedures are outlined employing the data in Table 9-13.[27] The dependent variable in this example (group) is the perceived importance of interest groups to the legislative process. The dependent variable (*group*) is assumed to be related to the independent variable (*decide*), which is based on whether the legislator decided to run for public office late in life (after being in college) or early in life (when graduating from high school or before). The control variable is party (*Democrat* or *Republican*).

The odds are determined on the basis of the marginal frequencies. In our example odds ratios for A and B respectively are

$$\begin{pmatrix} \text{Late} \\ A \\ \text{Early} \end{pmatrix} \text{ and } \begin{pmatrix} \text{Approve} \\ B \\ \text{Disapprove} \end{pmatrix}$$

are $\begin{pmatrix} \text{Late} \\ A \\ \text{Early} \end{pmatrix} = \dfrac{504}{448} = 1.125$ and $\begin{pmatrix} \text{Approve} \\ B \\ \text{Disapprove} \end{pmatrix} = \dfrac{481}{471} = 1.0212$

Describing the variables singularly, we see the odds are that legislators are likely to approve of interest group activity $\left(\dfrac{481}{471} = 1.0212 \right)$, and

[27] James A. Davis, "Hierarchical Models for Significance Tests in Multivariate Contingency Tables: An exegesis of Goodman's recent papers," in *Sociological Methodology 1973–1974*, ed. Herbert L. Costner, Jossey-Bass, San Francisco, 1974, pp. 189–231.

		High school	College	High school	College	High school	College
				Male		Female	
Strict employ-ment equality?	No	150	100	62	63	88	37
	Yes	100	150	63	62	37	88

	High school	College		Male High school	College		Female High school	College
	250	250		125	125		125	125
	$N = 500$			$N = 250$			$N = 250$	
	$\gamma = .385$			$\gamma = .00$			$\gamma = .6996$	

Table 9-12   Controlling variable effects: "shrink–stretch" effect

they are more likely to have decided to enter politics later in life $\left(\dfrac{504}{448} = 1.125\right)$.

We can extend this method to derive the *conditional odds ratio*, which reflects the ratios given another variable's categories. For our example, A has the categories for deciding to enter politics rather late in life ($A = $ Late) and early in life ($A - = $ Early). Therefore the conditional odds ratio for B, given the categories for A, are

$$\left[\left(\begin{array}{c}\text{Approve} \\ B \\ \text{Disapprove}\end{array}\right)\Bigg| A = \text{Late}\right] = \left[\frac{287}{217}\Bigg| A = \text{Late}\right] = 1.323$$

The vertical line indicates a condition of A. For the condition where A is low:

$$\left[\left(\begin{array}{c}\text{Approve} \\ B \\ \text{Disapprove}\end{array}\right)\Bigg| A = \text{Early}\right] = \left[\frac{194}{254}\Bigg| A = \text{Early}\right] = .764$$

The conditional odds ratios say that these relationships are not independent; if they were independent, the conditional odds ratios would equal 1.00. What we have shown above is that those who decided to enter politics late in life are more likely to approve of interest-group activities in the legislative process (1.323), and those legislators who decided to go into public life at an early point are more likely to disapprove of interest-group activity (.764).

The situation of moving to higher-order odds is the control situation. Now we ask whether our chances are stronger if we also know

First order

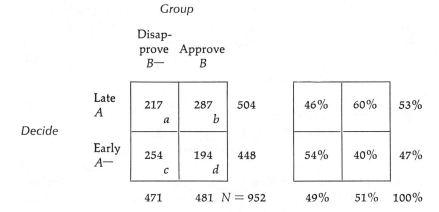

Group

	Disap-prove $B-$	Approve B					
Late A	217 a	287 b	504		46%	60%	53%
Early $A-$	254 c	194 d	448		54%	40%	47%
	471	481	$N = 952$		49%	51%	100%

Decide

Order

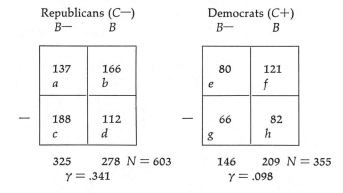

	Republicans ($C-$) $B-$	B			Democrats ($C+$) $B-$	B
$-$	137 a	166 b		$-$	80 e	121 f
	188 c	112 d			66 g	82 h
	325	278 $N = 603$			146	209 $N = 355$
		$\gamma = .341$				$\gamma = .098$

Third order

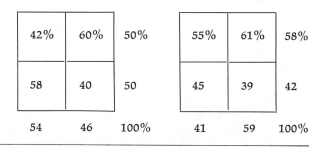

42%	60%	50%		55%	61%	58%
58	40	50		45	39	42
54	46	100%		41	59	100%

Table 9-13   Hypothetical tables for odds ratios

which party a legislator belongs to, as well as when the decision to enter politics was made. The control situation is really a third-order odds ratio; the first order was the A, and the second order was the $\overset{+}{A}\,\overset{+}{B}$ just described. So to continue the argument, if Republican legislators are designated as $C-$ and Democrats are $C+$, the third-order odds ratios are as follows:

$$\frac{\overset{+}{A}\,\overset{+}{B}\,C=+\text{ Democrats}}{\overset{+}{A}\,\overset{+}{B}\,C=-\text{ Republicans}}=\frac{fg/eh}{bc/ad}=\frac{fgad}{ehbc}=\overset{+}{A}\,\overset{+}{B}\,\overset{+}{C}$$

The third-order odds ratio is .5984 for Democrats versus Republicans. We look at these ratios somewhat differently in Table 9-14. Thus, while we earlier noted that legislators who decided to enter politics later in life were more positive toward interest-group activity in the legislature, we can now point out that the pattern is most pronounced among Republican legislators. The third-order odds ratio of .5984 says that it would be a bad bet to offer even money that Democratic legislators are more likely than Republicans to approve of interest-group activities, even if they decided to enter politics fairly late.

By glancing back at the gammas (γ) in Table 9-13, we can observe these trends in the same terms that we first set out for controlling variables. The original relationship melts into a shrink-stretch effect when controlling for *party*. The Democrats show little contribution ($\gamma = .098$), whereas the Republicans show some strength ($\gamma = .341$).

The controlling method discussed previously and the odds ratio logic both can be extended through higher orders. The odds ratio can be used with logarithms and with an extension of the correlation logic to "predict" a dependent variable. Several models for predicting can be used, and the prediction for each individual can be tested against the actual distribution; this cumulative fit is tested with the chi-square discussed earlier. Like many statistics, these techniques appear in available computer routines such as those mentioned in Chapter 10.[28]

Before moving ahead to a discussion about the significance of these relationships, let us summarize the preceding. We have seen that spuriousness occurs in one instance: where the original relationship reduces to zero and where the theory about the process says that the control variable occurs before the independent variable. Where the

[28] Lawrence S. Mayer and Phillip J. Pichotta, "A FORTRAN program for linear log odds analysis," *Behavior Research Methods and Instrumentation*, 6 (May 1974), 351. For some theory upon which these materials are based, see L. A. Goodman, "The Multivariate Analysis of Qualitative Data: Interactions among Multiple Classifications," *Journal of the American Statistical Association*, 65 (1970), 226–256; and "A Modified Multiple Regression Approach to the Analysis of Dichotomous Variables," *American Sociological Review*, 37 (1972), 28–46; and "Causal Analysis of Data from Panel Studies and Other Kinds of Surveys," *American Journal of Sociology*, 78 (1973), 1135–1191.

Variable frequencies			Odds ratios		
B	*A*	*C*	I	II	III
Group	Decide	Party			
			$+$	$+\ +$	$+\ +\ +$
—	$+$		B A C	B A C	B A C
			$-$	$-\ \ -$	$-\ \ -\ \ -$
80	121	$+$	$+$	1.5125⎫	1.2174⎫	
66	82	—	$+$	1.2424⎭		.5984
137	166	$+$	—	1.2117⎫	2.0341⎭	
188	112	—	—	.5957⎭		

Table 9-14 Party, group, and decide variables for odds ratios

relationship reduces to zero and the control variable is presumed to intervene between independent and dependent variables, we have a call for interpretation and perhaps a revision of the theory.

We have also seen that the original relationship is frequently clarified by controlling variables. Introducing controls can also cause various effects, of which we covered only three. The odds ratio was used to show how to get a better feel for the effect of the control variable, and this was explained in terms of an even bet (for full independence) to uneven bets (greater or less than 1.0).

Significance levels and statistical inference

Three major problems are associated with selecting significance levels and making statistical inferences: (1) questions about samples, sample size, and populations; (2) the appropriate levels of significance; and (3) making inferences from relationships and levels of significance.

The first problem is demonstrated amply by the example used throughout this chapter. By treating the fifty states as a sample, the various statistics and the consideration of levels of significance are justified. As we pointed out, these statistics and the logic associated with them are based on assuming a random sampling of populations.

Be aware that the controversy about whether populations can be treated as samples continues. We reject the argument (1) that if the entire population is at our disposal, there is no need to use statistics, since such measures are used as a basis for making inferences about the larger population; and (2) that if we have the population, we can draw conclusions directly from frequencies and proportions. We believe it is necessary and interesting to use appropriate statistics to talk about the relationship between two variables, even when the population is at our disposal.

Yet in what sense is our example of fifty states a sample? Many populations are treated as samples in an infinite time series or a potentially infinite population. A population of a certain student group may be considered a sample (though obviously biased by self-selection) of the potential students who join the group; and the American states, as normally studied at one point in time, provide a sample of the larger population of states over a long time series. Once again, by chance or by choice, the sample is limited to these fifty at this point in time. This latter discussion can also be framed in the terms of "hypothetical universes," "nonprobability samples," and "ex post facto hypothesis testing." [29]

What, then, constitutes an adequate sample? Proper sampling procedure and adequate size are important. As a rule of thumb, if we have less than thirty cases, we have additional problems related to statistical inference. Fortunately, fifty or more cases (appropriately selected) are common to most social science research. Three rooms in a school, or four organizations, or two political groups, or all medium-sized cities usually will produce more than fifty students, employees, citizens, or cities. Hence, with samples of this size, no special statistical considerations are needed when using significance tables[30]—other than caution.

You must be aware, though, (1) that random error in the sampling process may produce a sample in which a relationship exists in a sample but not in the population; (2) that the probability of any sample relationship's resulting solely from random error (chance) may be calculated, as we suggest shortly; and (3) that the statistical significance of a sample relationship is the probability that random error in the sampling process produced a sample having as strong a relationship as that actually observed if there were absolutely no relationships in the population from which the sample was drawn.[31]

---

[29] A brief outline of these issues is in Travis Hirshi and Hanan C. Selvin, *Delinquency Research*, The Free Press, New York, 1967, pp. 220–231. See also C. Alan Boneau, "The Effects of Violations of Assumptions Underlying the Test," *Psychological Bulletin*, 57 (1960), 49–64. The further possibility of theoretical sampling can be reviewed by reading Barney G. Glaser and Anselm L. Strauss, *The Discovery of Grounded Theory*, Aldine Publishing Company, Chicago, 1967, pp. 45–77; James S. Coleman, "Relational Analysis: The Study of Social Organizations with Survey Methods," *Human Organization*, 16 (Summer 1958), 28–36; Seymour Martin Lipset, Martin Trow, and James S. Coleman, *Union Democracy*, The Free Press, New York, 1956, pp. 470–480; and Peter Blau, "Structural Effects," *American Sociological Review*, 25 (April 1960), 178–193.

[30] For small numbers of cases where you are talking only about these smaller samples, refer to Siegel, *Nonparametric Statistics*; and Hollander and Wolf, *Nonparametric Statistical Methods*.

[31] A kind reviewer made these points in relation to our intuitive discussion of the logic of statistical decision-making.

Suppose (1) that fifty or more cases are in our sample; (2) that our null hypothesis, the straw man discussed earlier, is stated to the effect that no relationship will exist between X and Y; and (3) that we are willing to take a chance that we will reject the null hypothesis even though it is correct:[32] we now are ready to accept the statistic as being *significant*. The question remains, "At what level is the statistic to be accepted as significant?"

If our theory tells us that X and Y should be strongly related and if preliminary studies in the past have shown that X and Y are strongly related, are we going to believe that there is only a 50-50 chance that X and Y will be related? Conversely, if we know little about the relationship between X and Y and if there is little theoretical material suggesting a relationship between X and Y, are we going to be unsettled if the relationship is not strong? Under what circumstances should we demand a high association, and when are more modest correlations acceptable?

Let us look at the relationship in terms of its happening by chance so many times out of 100. An event that would happen by chance only 2 out of every 100 times is obviously a better bet than an event that might happen by chance about 25 out of 100 times. Essentially this betting is what levels of significance is about. A commonly accepted level of significance is .05, which means that a particular relationship would happen by chance only 5 out of 100 times.

Certainly, the .05 level is not sacred, though it is a good base point.[33] If we have good reason to hypothesize that the relationship exists, the .05 might be too conservative a benchmark. In these cases, it may be more realistic to expect the relationship to be so strong that it could happen only by chance about 1 every 1,000 times (sign = .001).[34]

On the other hand, the behavior of the variables may be so new that we would be happy to have the relationship occur an estimated

[32] This error is the type-I error, rejecting the null hypothesis when in fact it is true; when you accept the null hypothesis as being true, but it is false, you have committed a type-II error. For further detail, see Glass and Stanley, *Statistical Methods in Education and Psychology*, pp. 279–288.

[33] Debates over this are frequent. For a book devoted to the debate, see *The Significance Test Controversy*, eds. Denton E. Morrison and Ramon E. Henkel, Aldine Publishing Company, Chicago, 1970.

[34] The bet actually is one in which we argue that there is only 1, 5, 10, etc., chances out of 100 that there is really no relationship in the population from which the "random" sample is drawn. This bet is why the strength of the random sampling is so important. Other hedges that social scientists make against the bet are found in confidence intervals, decision or nondecision theories, and so on. For a variety of ways of looking at these problems, see Hays, *Statistics*, pp. 245–300; Blalock, *Social Statistics*, pp. 90–96; Selltiz et al., *Research Methods . . .*, pp. 414–422.

90 percent of the time (sign $= .10$). Thus, while one can use the .05 level as a benchmark, we should also consider whether or not this benchmark is relevant for our data and theory.[35]

Returning to our original example and the statistics and materials from Table 9-9, we can make the following minimum statements for unemployment compensation and public welfare: (1) the relationship between these two variables is not likely to be a product of chance; (2) the relationship between these two variables is strong, positive, and significant. Obviously, we would like to say that more payments for unemployment compensation to a state will result in more payments for public welfare. More specifically, we would like to say that unemployment compensation payments cause public welfare payments. We cannot, alas, make such a statement. Although statistical results lend some support for these statements, inferring causality also requires considering time and stabili'y and nonreversibility (recursiveness) in the presence of other variables.

To infer causality, the variables must, of course, be statistically related, yet this is not a sufficient condition. One variable must also be shown to take place before the other, and the relationship between the two variables must be shown to hold even when "the effects of other variables causally prior to both of the original variables are removed"; in other words, we need to control for these variables.[36] In this chapter we have shown that there is the statistical relationship between our variables, but we have not shown (1) that unemployment compensation payments *precede* public welfare payments or (2) that all other effects of variables related to both unemployment compensation and public welfare and preceding them are irrelevant. Nor have we presented a theory that would explain these relationships.[37] As such, we are far from meeting the standards set forth in Chapter 2 for an adequate explanation.

As a word of advice, we suggest cautious optimism when strong relationships occur and a reserved attitude about the data, theory, exceptions, and enthusiasm of fellow researchers. The work of an empirical researcher, unfortunately, is never finished. Theory is never proved, and new theory is always suspect.

---

[35] Without going into another debate, many of these conflicts are found between classic statisticians and Bayesian statisticians. An example is Ward Edwards, "Tactical Note on the Relation between Scientific and Statistical Hypothesis," *Psychological Bulletin,* 63 (1965), 400–402; and Warner Wilson, Howard L. Miller, and Jerold S. Lower, "Much Ado about the Null Hypothesis," *Psychological Bulletin,* 67 (1967), 188–196.

[36] Hirshi and Selvin, *Delinquency Research,* p. 38.

[37] Even so, we would note that arguments can be offered which allow for the simultaneous creation of theory and data analysis; Glaser and Strauss, *The Discovery of Grounded Theory,* pp. 28–32.

It should also be pointed out that we have shown how to compute only a few statistics. Many more techniques are available,[38] as is more detail about techniques we have discussed. Also, although we have shown how to compute a number of statistics (and you should do this to thoroughly understand them), the statistics discussed in this chapter are available in virtually every computer software package discussed in Chapter 10. When you thoroughly understand the procedures and assumptions underlying various statistics, you may allow the computer to do the hard computational labor.

Review questions and exercises

1 Explain the meaning and significance of the following terms:

a   Descriptive statistics
b   Mean
c   Median
d   Nonparametric statistics
e   Nominal, ordinal, and interval statistics
f   Central tendency
g   Standard deviation
h   Levels of significance
i   Chi-square
j   Strength of relationship
k   Gamma
l   Cramer's V
m   Lambda
n   Simple correlation coefficient

2 Under what conditions is one likely to require a higher level of significance?
3 Read some of the work discussed in footnote 1 on levels of statistical significance and summarize the positions discussed in your reading.
4 Discuss (a) the problems of inferring causality from the use of statistics and (b) the conditions under which this inference is more or less justified.

---

[38] An interesting book that will lead you through the maze and offer new measures is Frank M. Andrews, Laura Klem, Terrence N. Davidson, Patrick M. O'Malley, and Willard L. Rodgers, *A Guide for Selecting Statistical Techniques for Analyzying Social Science Data*, Survey Research Center, Institute for Social Research, Ann Arbor, Mich., 1974.

5 As a summary and learning exercise:

a Use the Table of Random Numbers to draw two independently random 25 percent samples from the state data in Table 9-1.

b Compute mean, median, and standard deviation.

c Use the following formula:

$$t = \frac{\overline{X} - \overline{X}'}{\sqrt{\text{Pooled variance}\left(\dfrac{1}{N} + \dfrac{1}{N'}\right)}}$$

where $\overline{X}$ = mean of the first random sample
$\overline{X}'$ = mean of the second random sample

$$\text{Pooled variance} = \frac{(N-1)\,S^2 + (N'-1)\,S'^2}{N + N' - 2}$$

where N = number of states in first sample
S^2 = variance of first sample
N' = number of states in second sample
S'^2 = variance of second sample

d Find a t-test table in a statistics text and use the degree of freedom formula ($df = N + N' - 2$) to tell whether or not the samples are significantly different. Hint: the t will have to be a bit over 2.0 if $df = 23$.

e Divide the samples at the mean and calculate the chi-square (χ^2) for the following table:

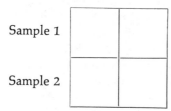

	Cases below mean	Cases above mean
Sample 1		
Sample 2		

From the χ^2, are the samples different? If so, are they systematically different; that is, is the lambda or gamma significant?

6   Below are two demonstration tables:

	Southern school districts				Northern school districts		
	Family income				Family income		
	Low	High			Low	High	
Low violence	180	270	450	Low violence	300	210	510
High violence	180	90	270	High violence	60	150	210
	360	360			360	360	
			$N = 720$				$N = 720$

a   Calculate the appropriate statistics to study the tables.
b   What are your conclusions?
c   Combine the tables into the following format:

	Family income	
	Low	High
Low violence		
High violence		

$N = 1,440$

d   Calculate the same statistics.
e   What are your conclusions?
7   Below are two set of numbers:

Case	Set 1	Case	Set 2
1	1	1	37
2	2	2	4
3	3	3	53
4	4	4	39
5	5	5	54
6	6	6	11
7	7	7	63
8	8	8	19

(Continued overleaf)

Case	Set 1	Case	Set 2
9	9	9	14
10	10	10	62
11	20	11	10
12	17	12	46
13	18	13	25
14	19	14	28
15	16	15	66
16	15	16	73
17	11	17	67
18	13	18	1
19	12	19	27
20	14	20	44

a Calculate the mean, the median, and the skewness.
b Calculate the simple correlation.
Using the mean:
c Calculate the Cramer's V.
d Calculate the lambda.
e Calculate the gamma.
f Compare the simple correlation (r), the Cramer's V, the gamma (γ). What is your conclusion? Hint: Look at the measures of skewness.

> The trouble with old-fashioned
> computers was that they never did
> what you told them to do. The
> trouble with modern computers is
> the fact that they do precisely
> what you told them to do, and not
> what you meant to tell them to do.
>
> John G. Kemeny

10

DATA PROCESSING

High-speed data processing equipment and computers are relatively new tools in the arsenal of political science, but they are being used with increasing frequency and proficiency. This chapter introduces some major considerations to be taken into account when using data processing equipment and the procedures to follow in preparing data for this type of analysis. We also provide an elementary introduction to some basic equipment you are likely to encounter. With a thorough understanding of this chapter, you should be able to take a data set and execute a large- or small-scale project using at least two pieces of data processing equipment, the key punch and the counter-sorter. Unfortunately, the background information needed to use a computer is beyond the scope of this book. However, a number of good introductions to basic computer programming are available for those who want to pursue this topic.[1] At the end of the chapter we briefly mention some "canned programs" that are available and useful for political scientists. These normally can be used with minimal assistance.

---

[1] See, for example, D. K. Carver, *Introduction to FORTRAN II and FORTRAN IV Programming,* John Wiley & Sons, New York, 1969.

The Rime of the Ancient Programmer *

It is an ancient programmer;
   He stoppeth one of three.
"By thy long printout, and error lights,
   Now wherefor stopp'st thou me?
"My problem's set, conditions met;
   It's my turn to get in.
"The 'ready' bell is tinkling loud;
   May'st hear the merry din."
The programmer, he held him fast.
   "There was a slip," quoth he,
"That made the program run awry;
   It seemed it could not be.
"My mates and I for hours did try;
   (Such torments few are given);
"Till in despair, I tore my hair,
   And shot the algorithm.
"My mates said, 'Well, he's stopped the bell;
   The error light's extinguished;
" 'And though there's insulation smell
   His method's quite distinguished.'
"But suddenly for programs weird,
   Each sinner felt an urge;
"But though once and again they cleared,
   The sums would not converge.
"So they dropped dead; at last I said,
   'I hadn't oughter done it!
" 'I'm under curse, and what is worse,
   There's no one left to run it!'
"An angel form at last appeared,
   To answer my pained queries;
"And, though it seemed to me quite weird,
   Said, 'Bless the Taylor series!'
"I blessed each term, and an angleworm,
   As 'twere my heart's dear treasure,
"And Stieltjes integrals, in turn,
   I threw in for good measure.
"Then up I rose, put on fresh clothes,
   And tried to get an answer.
"How grand the sight! It worked just right
   At each conditional transfer.

"He summeth best who loveth best
   Remainders to grow small;
"But he for whom they won't converge
   Can never sum at all!"

H. W. Kaufmann

Computers and data processing equipment appear to conjure all kinds of images in the minds of those not versed in their basic purpose and operation. We see films and hear tales of computers taking over the world, directing people's minds, and generally dehumanizing all our lives. Computers and data processing equipment should be recognized first and foremost as what they are—tools.[2] Although data processing equipment and computers generally can process data with greater speed and accuracy than a human being could in the same amount of time, they cannot substitute for a well-conceived and well-executed research project. A favorite saying among those familiar with computers is GIGO—or "garbage in, garbage out"—a reference to the fact that what comes out of a computer is only as good as what goes in. A poorly designed questionnaire, a biased sample, and inaccurately recorded data will not be corrected by electronic data processing equipment. There are numerous pitfalls in the research process. Assuming that the pitfalls preceding actual data analysis have been surmounted, we now can attempt to ensure that further errors are not created at this stage of the research.

In spite of its relatively recent debut in political science, data processing is not as new as is commonly supposed. The first punch-card was actually invented in the later part of the nineteenth century by Herman Hollerith of the United States Census Bureau. The Census Bureau had an understandable interest in the development of technology to help handle the massive information that the Census Bureau collects. The ability to process large amounts of data quickly remains a principal advantage of electronic data processing.

In addition to speed, electronic data processing offers other advantages. Electronic data processing equipment often is more accurate than its human counterpart. Computers seldom suffer from fatigue, errors of misrecording, and similar human foibles that often accompany lengthy midnight calculations. (They are, on the other hand, sometimes subject to the most annoying breakdowns at the most inopportune moments.) Kenneth Janda, author of an excellent introduction to data processing, points out additional advantages of

---

[2] For a highly readable account of the impact of computers and their potential in the decades ahead see John G. Kemeny, *Man and the Computer*, Charles Scribner's Sons, New York, 1972.

data processing: "these include . . . convenience, neatness . . . permanency, flexibility, and reproducibility." [3]

When dealing with large amounts of data, it frequently is easier to handle and store data on punchcards, tapes, and disks. Punchcards store data in a manageable and relatively permanent form, and they are easily reproduced if damaged.

Nevertheless, processing by electronic means is not always the most economical method of analyzing data. The procedure should be used with due consideration of the costs and benefits involved compared with alternatives. Normally the following considerations should weigh in this evaluation:

1   *The Number of Cases in the Study* (the size of the sample)   If the number of cases is large (Janda suggests 100 cases as a benchmark), then putting data on punchcards and analyzing it electronically may be less costly than doing it manually.

2   *The Purposes of the Study*   If complicated statistical analyses of data are intended, it might be most efficient to use a computer even if the number of cases is relatively small. If analysis may continue over a period of time, punchcards may be useful because they provide a reusable and flexible recording medium.

3   *Possible Future Uses of the Data*   Data recorded on punchcards and tapes are stored easily and shared among scholars. The Inter-University Consortium for Political Research at the University of Michigan provides a data bank containing the data base of many major studies in the discipline. These are stored on punchcards and tapes and are available at cost to participating universities. Central storage facilities make it possible to replicate earlier studies. If the data may be of interest to others, storing it on punchcards will facilitate transference of information.[4]

Preliminary steps in data processing: coding and punching the data

THE PUNCHCARD

After data are gathered—whether through content analysis, simulation, survey research, or another technique—a number of additional steps must be accomplished before data can be analyzed with electronic data processing equipment. Any errors made in these preliminary stages will be reflected in the final analysis.

[3] Kenneth Janda, *Data Processing: Applications to Political Research*, Northwestern University Press, Evanston, Ill., 1965, p. 7.
[4] Ibid., pp. 10–11.

Let us suppose that we have conducted a rather large survey and feel it can be processed most efficiently at the computing center. The first step then will be to transfer the information to a form suitable for data processing equipment. Normally the data will be transferred, at least initially, to punchcards. Sometimes data will be transferred later to tapes or disks which frequently are more efficient for handling large bodies of information. You also will need a basic guide to the information on the punchcards in order to pinpoint each piece of information. As we have pointed out previously, questionnaires sometimes are constructed with predefined formatting for punchcards. This procedure is used frequently to deal with closed or structured questions. Transferring data to punchcards will pose no great problem in this case. The questionnaire itself will provide the basic reference or codebook guidelines. More often, however, data are not completely predefined in this sense. No doubt some questions will be open-ended and potentially allow for infinite variation in response. The advantages and disadvantages of this type of format have been discussed in Chapter 6. If the questionnaire is not precoded completely, it will be necessary to develop a codebook before transferring data to computer cards. This codebook provides the necessary bridge between raw data from the original questionnaires and the transformed data on the punchcards.

The punchcard that the codebook refers to will look something like the one reproduced in Figure 10-1. Observe that the card has an eighty-column field (eighty adjacent columns). A maximum of eighty single-spaced numbers, letters, or special characters can be punched onto each card. Each column can be punched in one or more of twelve spaces. The top two punches, known as "11 and 12" or "x and y," are unmarked; they are used by themselves or in conjunction with other punches in the same column to indicate an alpha or special symbol. These punches and their printed meanings can be seen clearly in Figure 10-1. Additionally, each column is numbered from 0 to 9 on the lower edge. The bottom of the card, where the 9s appear, is commonly called the *nine-edge* of the card.

A key-punch machine is used to punch a computer card. Many key punches also will print what you have punched at the top of the card. The printing that appears at the top is essentially irrelevant as far as data processing equipment is concerned. Computers and the sorter "read" only the holes, or punches, in the card, not the printing. The printing is useful, however, in helping to visually check the accuracy of punching, and it is advised for this reason. As you can see, the pattern of punches varies, depending on the character or numeral that has been punched. This pattern is constant to each letter or numeral, although it may vary somewhat from key punch to key punch. The numerals are intuitively meaningful in that the punches correspond to the numbers printed on the surface of the card; a single

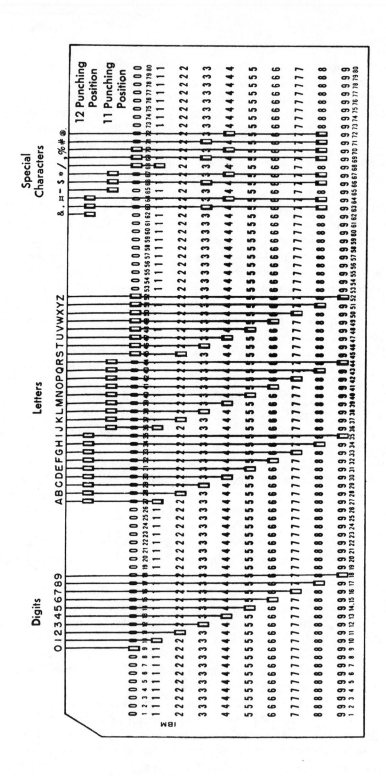

Figure 10-1

266

punch will always appear on top of the appropriate printed number of the card. If you punch a 6 and it appears slightly off the appropriate printed 6 in the specified column, you have "off-punched" that numeral. Sometimes cards slip in the key punch, producing this effect. This will be misinterpreted by data processing equipment, if not rejected outright. Punches must appear *directly* in the relevant columns! Letters and special characters also have constant punch patterns, but they are not as directly meaningful for students unfamiliar with the patterns. Letters and special characters also are characterized by multiple punching in a single column. Letters and special characters (+, /, $, %, etc.) are not used frequently to record data in political science, because they are multiple-punched and cannot be read by many computer programs. Experts in computer science predict that at some later time we will have computer programs that can read simple English. As you examine Figure 10-1, make careful note of the fact that the patterns of the numeral 0 and the letter O are not identical; they *cannot* be used interchangeably.

DEVELOPING A CODEBOOK

In setting up a codebook you should first think the project through thoroughly. Codebook construction is not difficult, but it can be done with varying degrees of flexibility and convenience. The following minimum considerations should be taken into account:

1 What is the most efficient form of referencing the data?
2 Are the punched data spaced sufficiently so that they are readable for verification?
3 Might you wish to reference a single variable on a number of dimensions?
4 Should there be some constant sequence in the patterning of response?

The number of punchcards finally used is a function of two factors: the size of the sample (the number of cases or observations) and the amount of information (the number of variables) dealing with each case. If all data for one case do not fit onto one card, the record may be continued onto subsequent cards. In this case, we normally use some means of differentiating the continuations; this is often accomplished by labelling the first card of each case or respondent as "card 1 of deck 1," with the second card being labelled "deck 2" and so on. In addition to labelling continuation cards, basic identification codes usually are repeated. By convention, identification material is usually placed in the first several columns of the card. Deck numbers are also frequently placed at the beginning of each card, although some scholars prefer to place them at the end of each card. Whatever the scheme, consistent placement must be maintained.

It also is useful to maintain constant spacing between units of information. This will facilitate checking of the punching. It is difficult to check key-punching visually if the card is solidly punched from column 1 through column 80. Of course, if space is a constraint, this is not necessary. Spacing also can be useful, however, because it leaves room for subsequent filling in of new variables or collapsed versions of variables located in their immediate vicinity.

Now let's proceed to an example of setting up a codebook. Suppose we have done a survey of the various education associations located throughout the American states. We have directed our surveys to the state affiliates of the National Education Association, the American Association of School Boards, and the American Association of School Administrators. Suppose we received responses from all three organizations in each of the fifty states. Our sample size is then the number of organizations times the number of states, or $3 \times 50 = 150$. We will need a minimum of 150 cards, one for each case, and perhaps more if our questionnaire is long. Suppose that, in fact, our survey is fairly long and we require three punchcards for each respondent. Initially we then will want to set up a format that provides at least three pieces of basic identification material: state, type of organization, and deck number. The codebook at this point might resemble Table 10-1.

Table 10-2 further exemplifies the basic form a codebook should take. Note that the exact column location of each variable is specified. A reference to the appropriate question number on the original questionnaire is cited, and the exact meaning of the transformed data is delineated. In the preceding case of question number 1, "Organization" was defined so that a punched 1 signified the respondent as an NEA affiliate, a 2 indicates the respondent to be an AASB affiliate, etc. In Table 10-2, question number 2, "State," requires two columns, since the number of possible categories exceeds the limits of one digit; in this case there are fifty states. Any data occupying more than one column must *always* be *right-justified*. The machinery presumes 01 to be equal to 1. If, on the other hand, we punched 1 in column 2 and left column 3 blank, it will read this as 10, even if we don't punch a 0 after the 1. The third item in this codebook example, "Deck Number," is not given a questionnaire reference, because it is essentially a manufactured item not in the original questionnaire. Innumerable variations of coding could be used in place of our example. For instance, we might want to be able to differentiate on the basis not only of state but also of region. This can be accomplished at the coding stage in a manner that greatly facilitates subsequent processing. For example, we might use the convention employed at the Survey Research Center and depicted in Table 10-2; which allows state-by-state and regional dif-

IBM column number	Question number	Response category
1	1	
		Organization
		1 National Education Association Affiliate
		2 American Association of School Boards Affiliate
		3 American Association of School Administrators Affiliate
2–3	2	*State*
		01 Alabama
		02 Alaska
		etc.
4		*Deck number 1*

Table 10-1 Basic identification

ferentiation without expanding the field of the variable. In the Survey Research Center's format the first digit of each response identifies the region, while the two digits together identify the state. A 0 punch in column 2 invariably would refer to a state located in the "New England" region, a 1 indicates a state in the "Middle Atlantic" region, etc. There is nothing absolute in these regional categorizations, of course; they can be varied in a number of ways that possibly are more relevant to a particular problem. Efficiency is an important consideration, however, and you should think through the possible categorizations that will be most useful for your purposes.

As you will recall from Chapter 6, some variables present no difficulty in coding. In some cases the categories are predetermined, as would be the case with the variable "sex." Other variables have explicit enough categories, but you may wonder whether to retain all possible differentiations of a category. A number of variables are naturally continuous and have an infinite number of points on the measurement scale. Others are theoretically discontinuous but nevertheless admit of numerous points. Income, for example, might admit of 150 distinctions on the survey, the same number as the total number of responses. Do we want to keep all categories; if not, where will we differentiate our categories and on what grounds? These important questions must be dealt with in the survey design or coding process. While these decisions are somewhat subjective, they should not be arbitrary. You should always bear in mind the costs and benefits of collapsing categories in the coding process. On the one hand, collapsing makes the groupings larger and more manageable, but on the other hand, a considerable amount of detailed information is lost in

IBM column number	Question number	Question and response categories
2–3	2	State and Region:

New England

01 Connecticut
02 Maine
03 Massachusetts
04 New Hampshire
05 Rhode Island
06 Vermont

Middle Atlantic

11 Delaware
12 New Jersey
13 New York
14 Pennsylvania

East North Central

21 Illinois
22 Indiana
23 Michigan
24 Ohio
25 Wisconsin

West North Central

31 Iowa
32 Kansas
33 Minnesota
34 Missouri
35 Nebraska
36 North Dakota
37 South Dakota

Solid South

41 Alabama
42 Arkansas
43 Florida
44 Georgia
45 Louisiana
46 Mississippi
47 North Carolina

Table 10-2   Coding format: state and region

Option 1	Option 2
Income	*Income*
1 $000–$3,999	1 $01–$1,000
2 $4,000–$6,999	2 $1,001–$3,500
3 $7,000–$9,999	3 $3,501–$4,999
4 $10,000–$14,000	4 $5,000–$6,999
5 $14,001–$18,999	5 $7,000–$9,999
6 $19,000–$25,999	6 $10,000 and above
7 $26,000 and above	

Table 10-3   **Alternative categorizations of income**

doing so. For example, what considerations should be made in choosing between the two schemes for categorizing income presented in Table 10-3? An obvious consideration, of course, is the sample and the subject with which we are dealing. Option 2 might be a perfectly reasonable schema if we are dealing with students and their incomes (as opposed to their parents'). Using option 1 on a sample of students might not differentiate students at all, since the vast majority probably would fall in category 1. On the other hand, option 1 might be applicable if we were sampling the entire population of the United States. Category choice should be justified; the first category, for example, might be justified on the grounds that it approximates the levels established by the federal government as the poverty level. Needless to say, if we were doing a cross-national sample, this categorization would be inadequate.

In some cases we may want to combine the benefits of the breadth of responses with more collapsed categories. We can accomplish this by establishing two separate variables. For example, one question might be the open-ended query, "What do you see as some of the most important problems facing America?" We may have come up with a variety of responses, perhaps as many as 50 different answers from our sample of 150 individuals. We may want to retain the information and therefore provide space in our codebook for the variety, in this case allocating two columns for the 50 different responses. In addition, we might want a collapsed version of this response as well. Later, some computer programs can combine response categories, but this is the exception rather than the rule. It is generally preferable to have the foresight to plan for this yourself. You may then develop broader categories that will group responses effectively. This may yield, for example, nine groupings, which necessitates only one column on the punchcard. These groupings, in this particular example, might be "pollution and ecology," "peace and war," "economic recession," "local problems," "state problems," "international affairs," etc.

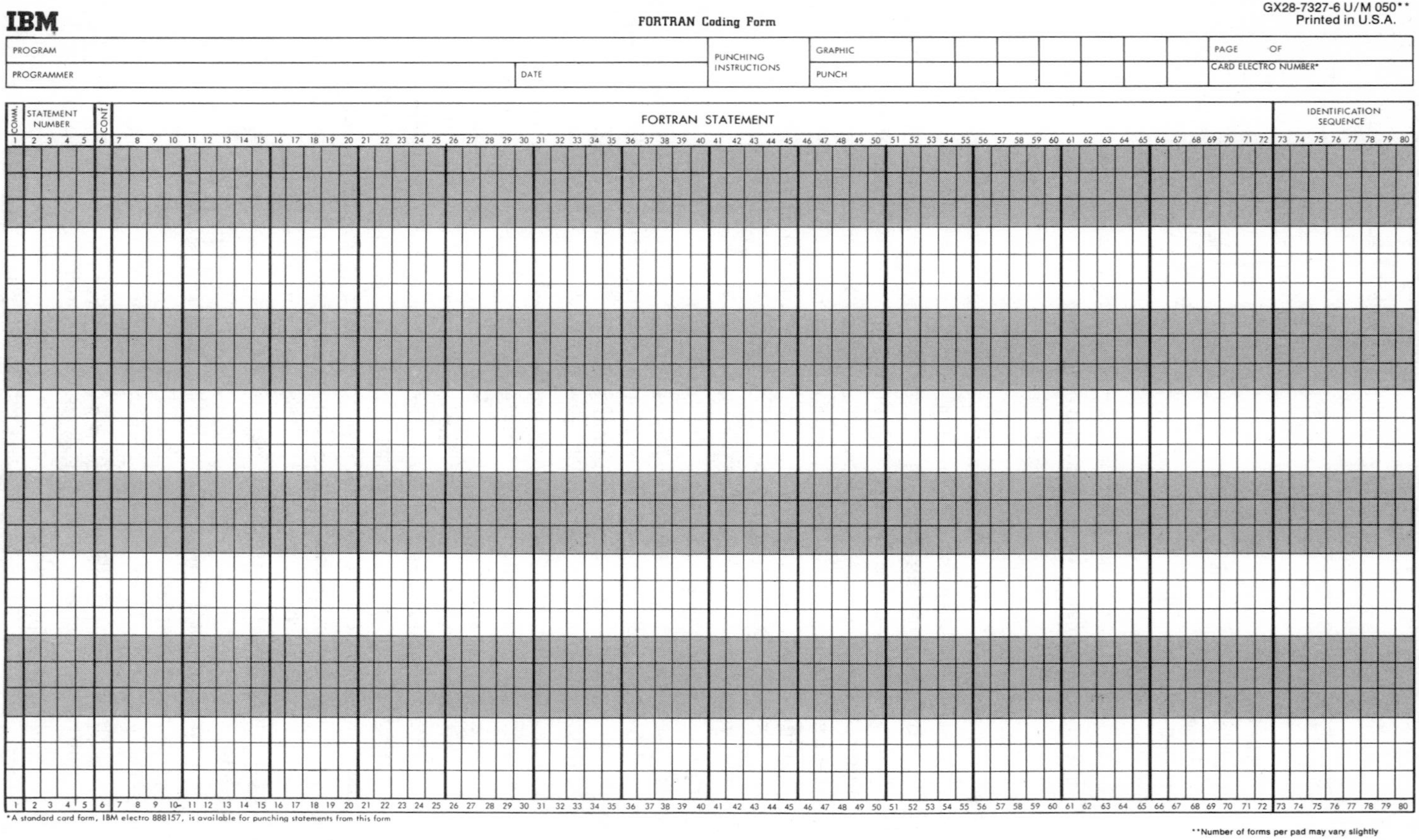
IBM
FORTRAN Coding Form
GX28-7327-6 U/M 050**
Printed in U.S.A.
PROGRAM
PROGRAMMER
DATE
PUNCHING INSTRUCTIONS
GRAPHIC
PUNCH
PAGE OF
CARD ELECTRO NUMBER*
COMM.
STATEMENT NUMBER
CONT.
FORTRAN STATEMENT
IDENTIFICATION SEQUENCE
*A standard card form, IBM electro 888157, is available for punching statements from this form
**Number of forms per pad may vary slightly

Figure 10-2

PUNCHING DATA ONTO CARDS: THE KEY PUNCH

After completing the codebook, we will know exactly where each piece of information is to go on to the punchcard. Key-punching is a simple but somewhat tedious chore, particularly if the amount of data to be punched is large. Computer companies produce paper that is basically nothing more than an enlarged card to facilitate transferring data from the original questionnaire to punchcards (see Figure 10-2). Placing a ruler under the line you are punching will help keep your place in a large set of data. It also is useful to keep these recording sheets for future reference, particularly if there is only one set of the data. This will facilitate reproducing a lost or otherwise damaged card.

Data are punched onto cards with a key punch like the model depicted in Figure 10-3. The keyboard of the key punch resembles that of a standard typewriter. A visit to a computing center and an attempt at actually operating a key punch will clarify the following discussion.

The first step in using a key punch is to place blank cards in the hopper. The machine is turned on and off by an appropriate lever, and blank cards are fed into the machine automatically if the automatic feed button at the top of the keyboard is depressed. The REG, or register, button will position the card in the first column for punching. (With the automatic feed on, positioning will be accomplished automatically.) The cards are then punched from left to right, from column 1 to column 80. The key punch uses only capital letters. To punch numerals, the NUM button must be depressed. Similarly, special characters—also presented as uppercase in the sense of standard typewriters—require use of the NUM button. If you want the key punch to print as well as punch the recorded information, the automatic PRINT button at the top of the keyboard is depressed. A spacing bar is provided at the bottom of the keyboard to leave columns blank. The machine also has a backspace key, as indicated in Figure 10-3. Above the backspacer is a position indicator. This will tell which column is ready for punching. When column 80 is punched, the card will eject automatically. If the automatic feed is on, the next card will proceed to the punching station. To eject a card before reaching column 80, depress the REL (release) button.

The key punch has other useful mechanisms. Commonly, we might make only one error in a card and not want to punch the entire card over again. On the other hand, it frequently happens that we have a large amount of data that contain identical information in, say, the first six columns. In both cases, it is preferable not to repeat the entire procedure. Because the punching section of the key punch is in phase with the reading phase, we can duplicate information from card to card. Being in phase simply means that holes electronically sensed at the reading phase can be duplicated on the card at the punching phase. This is accomplished by pressing the DUP (duplicate)

Figure 10-3

button; information on the card in the reading station is duplicated onto the card in the punching station.

The key punch also has a cylinder drum located above the back-space key. This basically puts the mechanism under automatic control for printing, skipping columns, ejecting cards, etc.

> Instructing the key punch to skip, duplicate, or release upon reaching certain column locations is known as programming. (Programming the key punch, however, is considerably different from programming computers. . . .) The operator programs the key punch by punching a control card, wrapping the card around a cylinder or drum, and inserting the drum on a spindle in the machine. The holes in the card control the operation of the machine, causing it to perform specified functions automatically.[5]

[5] *Ibid.*, p. 51.

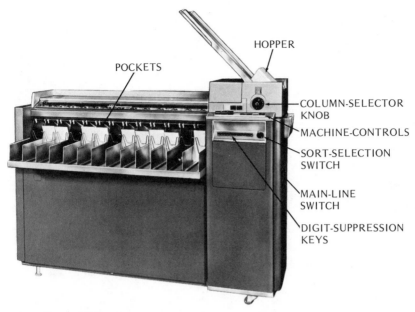

Figure 10-4

Analyzing data: the counter-sorter

One of the easiest means of categorizing large amounts of data (other than the computer itself) is by using the counter-sorter.

Figure 10-4 is a picture of a standard card sorter. Depending upon the model available, this machine can process over 600 cards per minute. Needless to say, with a large number of cards to process, the sorter can handle the task more efficiently than manual sorting. The sorter is designed to sort cards into groups on the basis of the punched holes. However, it can sort only on one column at a time. Some sorters have counters as well; these machines will sort the cards into groups and count the number of cards in each. The operation of the sorter is simple:

> A wire brush in the counter-sorter reads the punch cards. The cards run over a brass roller located underneath the brush, and when the card is between the brush and the roller, the two cannot make contact. However, when the brush passes over a hole in the card, it makes contact with the roller beneath, creating an electrical impulse that the machine uses to sort the cards into chutes.[6]

Figure 10-5 depicts this process diagrammatically.

[6] Lyman Tower Sargent and Thomas Zant, *Techniques of Political Analysis: An Introduction*, Wadsworth Publishing Company, Belmont, Calif., 1970, p. 37.

Card passing between roller and brush acts as an
insulator so that no impulse is available at the
brush.

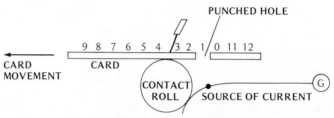

When brush makes contact with roller, a circuit
is completed and an electrical impulse is available
to instruct the machine to do a specific job.

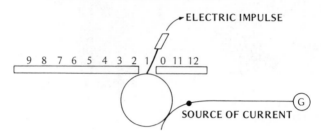

Figure 10-5

Using the sorter is not difficult. The first step is to position the movable reading brush to read the column initially selected. This is done by means of a column-selector knob. Cards then are placed in the hopper *face down* with the *nine-edge in*, toward the brush and roller. The weight must be replaced on top of the last card in the hopper to ensure that the last few cards will be processed. Check to make sure that the counter dials are set to 0 if you are using a counter-sorter. Otherwise the counter merely will add the totals processed in each grouping to those previously registered by the last user of the machine. The final step is to start the machine. The sorter then begins processing the cards, sorting them on the column designated; cards without punches in the column are sorted into the R (reject) bin.

To use the sorter to build cross-tabulations for data, additional points may prove helpful. Planning ahead can reduce the number of sortings and time involved. Obviously, you must determine which columns to "sort on" before beginning the process itself. It is helpful to go to the computing center with tables completely set up for this purpose so that you merely will have to fill in the appropriate cells. Remember always to include totals as well as individual cell frequencies. It is most efficient to sort first on the variables with the least

Identification	Boy		Girl		
of Mayor	6th grade	8th grade	6th grade	8th grade	Total
Correct name *given*	(N) %				
Incorrect name *given*					
Don't know/ *No answer*					
Totals					

Table 10–4   Identification of mayor by sex and age

number of categories when you are doing more than a one-way tabulation. This will reduce the number of sortings required.

Suppose in Table 10-4 we are setting up a table to test the hypothesis that political information (as measured by correct identification of the mayor's name) is related to grade level, with sex being posited as an intervening variable in light of the common observation that girls mature more quickly than boys. Our dependent variable in this example is clearly the level of political information. In constructing our table we should note that variables normally are totaled in the direction of the independent variable. Both the numerical (N) frequencies and the percentages should be given. Percentages are easily calculable on adding machines. It would be most efficient in this example to sort first on sex of respondent, since this variable admits of only two categories; or alternatively, on grade level, since it too has only two categories. If we sort first on sex, we then will have two groupings, boys and girls, which will tell us the total number of each in the sample. We next will take the cards that have grouped the boys and sort them on the column which contains information relating to grade level. Then we will know the number of boys in each grade surveyed. The third step involves sorting the boys in each grade grouping on the dependent variable, political information. The same procedure then is followed for the girls.

Basic computer components and operations

What is a computer? A useful definition is offered by Peter R. Senn: "A *computer* is an electronic device which is able to accept information, apply certain prescribed processes, and then supply results." Senn further notes that only the "electronic" part of the definition differentiates a computer from a slide rule or the ancient abacus. Computers are, in addition, considerably more complex and efficient than either of these.[7]

Senn's definition raises the additional question, "And how does a computer perform these tasks?" You will note that the definition implies at least three necessary components: some means of inputting information and instructions, directions for performing any manipulations, and means of producing results in readable form through output devices. Computers now use a variety of *input devices* to enter basic necessary information, both about data and about instructions. Input devices, include electromagnetic tapes, punchcards, typewritten or punched tapes, and, in some cases, vocal instructions. These are some media by which a computer is accessed, the basic communication media. Nevertheless, as Senn points out, there is an important qualification:

> Most computers do not speak English. Their input devices can do such remarkable things as read holes in cards, light beams, or typewriting, but all of these must be put into a specific computer language, the most popular being FORTRAN. This creates problems exactly analogous to translation.[8]

The term *FORTRAN* is short for "formula translation." This translation from human to mechanical terms is necessary before a computer can do anything. The process of translation is usually termed *programming*. There are a number of different machine languages available, but FORTRAN is the most generally useful problem-oriented language, and it is the basis of most programs of interest to social scientists.

Once a program is written in acceptable machine-oriented language and placed in the computer through some input device, the computer stores both the program and the data in its *memory unit*. The size of computer memory units varies, with size being somewhat, though not exclusively, dependent on the model. The "core" area tells approximately how large the memory capacity of a computer is. Generally, computers with large memory units can execute and store large amounts of data more efficiently than computers with smaller memory units.

Computers also have logical units and control or processing units. These serve the essential functions of manipulating data in the manner described by the instructions. In addition, computers have *output devices* that enable them to communicate the *results* of their

[7] Peter R. Senn, *Social Science and Its Methods*, Holbrook Press, Boston, 1971, p. 255.
[8] *Ibid.*

operations. Output devices also vary; results may be printed out on a printer, on a typewriter, on magnetic tape, on punchcards, and others. Output devices are frequently the same as input devices.[9]

COMPUTER PROGRAMS OF SPECIAL RELEVANCE TO SOCIAL SCIENCE

A number of computer programs have been written by programming experts with special relevance to social science problems. These programs make it possible for a person with a minimal knowledge of basic computer procedures to use the computer in analyzing data. *Canned* (prewritten) *programs* usually have the additional advantage of being "debugged" (although unforeseen bugs occasionally crop up, particularly when a program is adapted to a new system). For beginning programmers, debugging can be costly and time-consuming. In addition, many of the more advanced statistical operations used by social scientists involve complex, multistep procedures that can be handled best by someone with thorough and advanced knowledge of programming. Because of the complexity, the high costs of writing new programs, and the general availability of good, well-documented canned programs, most social scientists tend to work with existing programs rather than attempting to write their own. Nevertheless, a canned program can become a poor crutch if you do not thoroughly understand its procedures. Although canned programs can easily execute complex mathematical manipulations of data, you eventually will have to interpret the results, and therefore a thorough understanding of the procedures is required.

A fairly large computing center may offer a choice of several canned programs to execute the same procedure. There normally will be slight variations in the procedures involved in different programs as well as varying options for handling data. One factor to consider in evaluating different programs is the extent to which they are accompanied by well-detailed *users' manuals*. The better programs provide detailed information about the procedures involved in each program, the formulas used, the options available, the necessary information for accessing the programs, the constraints operative in different programs, and a thorough description of what the output or results will look like. These are important considerations in evaluating how a program relates to a particular problem as well as in interpreting its procedures and results. Some programs are better equipped than others with regard to *diagnostic error messages* that help locate internal errors in the program, errors made in accessing the program, and errors resulting from the violation by your data of the constraints of the

[9] *Ibid.*, pp. 255–257.

program. A well-documented program is better and easier to work with than one that does not contain thorough information.

Computer terminology distinguishes between computing "hardware" and "software." *Hardware* simply refers to the physical apparatus, the machinery, the computer itself. *Software*, on the other hand, refers to the methods of instructing the computer—called computer programming. The past fifty years have seen major developments in both these aspects of computer science. As we pointed out previously, the development of canned programs has been one significant aspect of software development. There are now a large number of statistical *library* packages available as well as thousands of small *single-purpose* programs. As Ronald E. Anderson points out in his survey of current software systems relevant to social data, the number of programs is so large that it is virtually incalculable. But help is at hand:

> Currently an organization at the University of Wisconsin, called the National Program Library and Central Program Inventory Service for the Social Sciences (NPL/CPIS), under the direction of James R. Taylor, has begun to serve as a central information clearing house. Such efforts hopefully will solve some of our information and program dissemination problems.[10]

Computer programs can be categorized in several ways, by purpose or variety of purpose, by developing source, by degree of relatedness among constituent programs, etc. Anderson distinguishes *statistical libraries* and *integrated statistical packages* or *systems* as follows:

> A collection of programs maintained as a unit is called a *library*; if the programs are closely related, e.g., all statistical, then the library is called a *package*. If a package of programs is tightly integrated such that output from one program is automatically input to another system, then it is frequently called a *system* or a software system.[11]

Similarly, software can be distinguished in terms of where it was developed. Generally speaking, most available social science programs have been developed in university environments, through noncommercial means. One statistical library, the Scientific Subroutine Package, or SSP, is an exception to this generalization, since it was manufactured, designed, and distributed through IBM.

The following pages briefly discuss some common programs

---

[10] Ronald E. Anderson, "A Survey of Application Software for Social Data Analysis Instruction," in *Proceedings of the Second Annual Conference on Computers in Undergraduate Curricula*, Dartmouth College, 1971, p. 135.
[11] *Ibid.*

available that are generally relevant to social science. In addition to the programs listed, you may find it useful to examine the IBM publication *Catalog of Programs for IBM Data Processing Systems* if your computing center has IBM equipment. Information about new computer programs is also listed in the quarterly periodical *Behavioral Science*, as well as *Behavioral Research* and *Educational and Psychological Measurement*. Similarly, Kenneth Janda's book, *Data Processing*, and *Legislative Roll-Call Analysis* by Anderson, Watts, and Wilcox reference a number of programs specifically relevant to political science.

One of the first statistical libraries developed was the BMD program originating at UCLA. Many later programs are patterned after the initial BMD program.

1   *BMD: Bio-Medical Computer Programs.* This is a statistical library containing a number of component programs relevant to political scientists. BMD is probably the most widely available general program. It includes, among others, descriptive and tabulation programs, regression analysis, factor analysis, Guttman scalogram analysis, multivariate analysis, and analysis of variance. A user's manual edited by W. J. Dixon is available from the University of California Press, which provides documentation for each program in the package and describes the basic procedures necessary to use this statistical library and its subprograms. Fairly comprehensive diagnostic error messages are built into the program.

2   *SPSS: Statistical Package for the Social Sciences,* developed by Norman H. Nie, Dale H. Bent, and C. Hadlai Hull at Stanford University. The SPSS contains many of the subprograms found in BMD and a number of additional programs. SPSS includes, among others, *one-* and *two-way cross-tabulation* with frequencies, row percentages, column percentages, and total percentages; *cross-tabulation statistics* (chi-square, Fisher's Exact Test, Phi, Cramer's *V*, Contingency Coefficient, Lambda Asymmetric, Lambda Symmetric, Kendall's Tau B and Tau C, Gamma, and Sommer's D); *descriptive statistics* (mean, standard error, median, mode, standard deviation, variance, kurtosis, skewness, range, minimum, and maximum); *Correlation Analysis* (Pearson Product Moment Correlation Coefficient, Spearman and Kendall Rank Order Correlation Coefficients); *Guttman Scalogram Analysis; Factor Analysis; Multiple Regression Analysis; and Partial Correlation Analysis.*

A manual for SPSS is available from McGraw-Hill. SPSS is probably the best-documented general program available. Each subprogram is discussed in detail in both technical and nontechnical terms. Specifications are stated clearly for accessing the subprogram and for mounting the package, and extensive error messages are provided. SPSS also has a number of valuable options built into its general control program that apply to most subprograms. Many of these options are not available under other systems. These include routines enabling users to generate variable transformations, recode variables, delete missing data, sample, select and weigh specified cases, and establish, add to, or alter existing files.

SPSS was designed for the 360 computer and generally requires 256 K available bytes of core.

3 *SSP: Scientific Subroutine Package.* Developed by and distributed through IBM, SSP is a combination of over 250 FORTRAN subroutines. The component programs are divided under two general headings: statistics and mathematics. The more relevant programs appearing under the statistics subtitle include nonparametric tests, random-number generation, regression analysis (multiple linear, stepwise, and polynomial), factor analysis, correlation analysis, analysis of variance, discriminate analysis, time series analysis, and others.

This system is commonly found at computer centers using IBM data processing equipment. Although the system was originally designed for the IBM 360, many computer centers have adapted it to the 1620 and other machines. Sample size may be a constraint in this program depending on the core area available at a particular computing center. Documentation and error messages are provided.

4 *OSIRIS: Organized Set of Integrated Routines for Investigation with Statistics.* Developed at the University of Michigan's Institute for Social Research for analysis of social science data, OSIRIS is widely available at computer facilities. Like the previously mentioned programs, OSIRIS is a general statistical package. It includes various statistical measures, correlation and regression analysis, analysis of variance, multivariate analysis, factor analysis, multidimensional scaling, and cluster analysis. OSIRIS also has good file-management capabilities. Extensive documentation is available on OSIRIS from the Institute for Social Research.

5 *DATA-TEXT.* DATA-TEXT was developed at Harvard University for data processing in the behavioral and social sciences. A good manual on DATA-TEXT is now available from the Free Press. DATA-TEXT includes basic descriptive statistics, parametric and nonparametric measures of association, significance tests, analysis of variance, factor analysis, multiple regression, and basic correlation analysis.

Like OSIRIS and SPSS, DATA-TEXT has good variable-transformation capabilities, and, in some cases, fewer limitations on the number of variables, values, or cases. Comparisons with SPSS and OSIRIS indicate that CPU time for small runs may be greater with DATA-TEXT, technical documentation is not yet complete, and only the most standard statistical techniques are offered. Nevertheless, DATA-TEXT provides a good statistical package which, like the others, is being improved continually.

In addition to these general programs numerous special-purpose programs are available that are designed generally for a single task, such as computing chi-square or executing cross-tabulations on data. We cannot list these programs since they are usually idiosyncratic. Special-purpose programs are generally indexed (named) according to the task they are designed to perform; this makes them easily identifiable. A glance through your computing center's catalog of software holdings will give some idea of the variety of special-purpose programs available.

Review questions and exercises

1 Explain the meaning of the following terms:
    a   Key punch
    b   Sorter and counter-sorter
    c   Punchcard
    d   Codebook
    e   Hollerith
    f   Right justify
    g   Nine-edge
    h   Hardware
    i   Software
    j   Program
    k   Off-punch
    l   Statistical libraries
    m   Single-purpose programs
    n   Integrated statistical packages or systems
    o   Cross-tabulation
    p   Marginals
    q   Frequency
    r   Cell
    s   FORTRAN
    t   Input devices
    u   Output devices
    v   Computer
2 What are some advantages and disadvantages of using data processing equipment? What factors should be taken into account when considering whether to use data processing equipment?

3 Develop an annotated inventory of the statistical packages of your computing center that are relevant to your field.
4 If your computing center has several programs designed to perform essentially the same task, systematically outline the constraints and advantages of each.
5 Examine the user's manual of one of the larger programs we described in this chapter and note any advantages one program has over others you are familiar with.

APPENDICES

APPENDIX A

BASIC REFERENCE SOURCES IN POLITICAL SCIENCE

This appendix provides a brief overview of available reference sources that are particularly relevant to political science. Our suggestions are necessarily incomplete. A definitive listing of all possible reference sources would constitute more than several volumes. It is hoped, however, that these suggestions do offer fairly complete coverage of the major general reference works available at most university libraries.

After choosing a researchable problem, you probably will find it necessary to use library resources for a number of purposes. A general review of relevant literature frequently is included in your research paper, together with a statement that links your approach to the problem with previous work in that area. Unless you are doing field work or employing a method that will generate original data, you also may have to rely upon library sources as the data basis of your study. A thorough acquaintance with available library facilities and reference works will greatly facilitate this research process. This appendix includes a number of sources that may be useful to this end.

General guides to the literature

A number of general guides to the literature of political science are now available. They discuss periodicals, documents, abstracts, bibliographies, and a wide range of possible reference works.

GENERAL AIDS

Brock, Clifton. *The Literature of Political Science.* Bowker, New York, 1969.

Conover, Helen. *A Guide to Bibliographic Tools for Research in Foreign Affairs.* Greenwood, Westport, Conn., 1970.

Heller, Frederick. *The Information Sources of Political Science.* ABC-CLIO, Santa Barbara, Calif., 1971.

Kalvelage, Carl, Morley Segal, and Peter J. Anderson. *Research Guide for Undergraduates in Political Science.* General Learning Press, Morristown, N.J., 1972.

Mason, John. *Research Resources: Annotated Guide to the Social Sciences*. ABC-CLIO, Santa Barbara, Calif., 1968.

White, Carl. *Sources of Information in the Social Sciences*. Bedminister, Totowa, N.J., 1964.

Wynar, Lubomyr R. *Guide to Reference Materials in Political Science: A Selective Bibliography*. 2 vols. Libraries Unlimited, Littleton, Colo., 1968.

Zawodny, J. K. *Guide to the Study of International Relations*. Chandler, San Francisco, 1966.

BIBLIOGRAPHIES AND BIBLOGRAPHIC ESSAYS

The ABS Guide to Recent Publications in the Social and Behavioral Sciences. Sage Publications, New York, 1965.
> A selective annotated bibliography of books, periodicals, articles, pamphlets, and government documents.

Beck, Carl. *Political Elites: A Select Computerized Bibliography*. M.I.T. Press, Cambridge, Mass., 1968.
> An extensive listing of books and periodical articles on the various conceptual and substantive areas touched by the study of political elites.

Bibliographic Information Center for the Study of Political Science. *Bibliographic Production in Political Science: A Directory*. 2d ed. Bibliographic Information Center for the Study of Political Science, San Jose, Calif., 1972.

Foreign Affairs Bibliography: A Selection and Annotated List of Books on International Relations. Council on Foreign Relations, since 1919.
> A list of American and foreign books on all aspects of international relations.

Frey, Frederick W., Peter Stephenson, and Katherine Archer Smith (eds.). *Survey Research on Comparative Social Change: A Bibliography*. M.I.T. Press, Cambridge, Mass., 1969.
> An annotated bibliography consisting of approximately 1,600 entries drawn from 260 English language journals. Annotated items are organized by geographic area of relevance as well as by substantive areas of concern. This work is confined to studies employing the survey research technique dealing with social change.

International Bibliography of Political Science. Aldine, Chicago; since 1962.
> Lists books, periodical articles, pamphlets, and some book re-

views. This is the broadest political science index, although it is generally somewhat behind in publication.

Library of Congress Catalog. Books: Subjects. Library of Congress, Washington, since 1950.

A subject listing of books available at the Library of Congress and other major libraries.

Lindzey, Gardner, and Elliot Aronson. *The Handbook of Social Psychology.* 2d ed. 5 vols. Addison-Wesley, Reading, Mass., 1968.

The seminal collection of summary essays on various research methods (vol. 2), the theories of modern social psychology (vol. 1), the individual in a social context—attitudes, personality, socialization and others (vol. 3), group psychology (vol. 4), and applied social psychology (vol. 5).

Press, Charles. *Main Street Politics: Policy-making at the Local Level: A Survey of the Periodical Literature Since 1950.* Michigan State University, Lansing, 1962.

As the title indicates, this work is devoted to the periodical literature relevant to community decision-making. It covers the period from 1951–1961. Annotations are quite extensive, and the author provides an initial overview of this area.

Robinson, James (ed.). *Political Science Annual.* 5 vols. Bobbs-Merrill, Indianapolis, since 1966.

Excellent, thorough bibliographic essays on a number of subjects such as Political Socialization; Legislative Institutions and Processes; and Public Opinion and Opinion Change; Education and Political Behavior; Community Power Studies; Participant Observation; Political Internships and Research; Crisis Decision-making: An Inventory and Appraisal of Concepts, Theories, Hypotheses, and Techniques of Analysis; and many others.

Wynar, Lubomyr. *American Political Parties.* Libraries Unlimited, Littleton, Colo., 1969.

A fairly comprehensive bibliography of research materials related to the organization, development, and study of American political parties.

Periodicals

Periodicals necessarily constitute one of the most important sources of recent work in political science. We have subdivided this category into three sections—indices, abstracts, and major journals— to facilitate dealing with the extensive periodical materials available. Students will probably find that abstracts provide a convenient starting point in researching any given topic. The *International Political Science*

Abstracts is a valuable source because it provides a brief overview of relevant articles. The abstracts in this source generally are written by the author of the article. Indices, on the other hand, normally provide only subject, title, and author citations, which may not always accurately direct students to all relevant material.

PERIODICAL INDICES

ABC POL SCI: Advance Bibliography of Contents: Political Science and Government. American Bibliographical Center–CLIO Press, Santa Barbara, Calif., since 1969.
>A "current contents" service which reproduces the table of contents for about 260 journals in political science and related fields. No annotation is provided.

Public Affairs Information Service Bulletin. Public Affairs Information Service, New York, since 1915.
>One of the most up-to-date indexes available, covering over 1,000 English language periodicals, as well as books, pamphlets, and some government documents.

Reader's Guide to Periodical Literature. H. W. Wilson, New York, since 1900.
>Appears semimonthly with indexing provided quarterly and annually. Indexes more than 150 general, nontechnical periodicals ranging from *The Yale Law Review* to *Mademoiselle*, as well as many current-events reports appearing in periodicals such as *Time, Newsweek*, and similar magazines.

Social Sciences and Humanities Index. H. W. Wilson, New York, since 1907.
>Indexes over 200 major scholarly journals in the social sciences and the humanities including most journals relevant to political science. Appears quarterly with annual indexing of accumulations. Prior to 1965 this periodical index was named the *International Index to Periodicals*.

ABSTRACTS OF PERIODICAL ARTICLES

Dissertation Abstracts: Abstracts of Dissertations Available on Microfilm or as Xerographic Reproductions. University Microfilm, A Xerox Company, Ann Arbor, Mich., since 1938.
>Abstracts written by the authors of doctoral dissertations from over 200 major Canadian and American universities are provided. This source is published monthly in two sections entitled "The Humanities" and "The Sciences." Annual indexing by subject and author with some cross-classification to other relevant subjects.

International Political Science Abstracts. Basil Blackwell, Oxford, since 1951.

>   Appears quarterly giving 150- to 200-word abstracts of articles appearing in more than 200 English and foreign language journals. Indexing is provided by subject and author.

Peace Research Abstracts Journal. International Peace Research Association, Clarkson, Ont., since 1964.

>   Appears monthly with indexing provided semiannually and annually. Approximately 9,000 abstracts appear each year.

Psychological Abstracts. The American Psychological Association, Washington, since 1927.

>   Appears monthly with annual indexes. Abstracts include approximately 15,000 articles annually.

Sociological Abstracts. Sociological Abstracts, New York, since 1952.

>   Appears eight times per year with a cumulative index in the eighth issue. Listings are provided according to author, subject, and periodical. Usually contains about 5,000 abstracts annually.

U.S. Government Research and Development Reports. Clearinghouse for Federal and Technical Information, Springfield, Va., since 1946.

>   A government abstracting journal that covers research done under government auspices. Many of the materials mentioned in this source will probably not be readily available at small libraries. This abstract is published semimonthly with quarterly indexes by subject, personal author, and corporate author.

MAJOR JOURNALS IN POLITICAL SCIENCE

In recent years an increasing number of journals have appeared in political science. For lack of space, we have not included all possible journals of interest. Students are reminded also to examine the journals in relevant outside fields such as sociology, economics, psychology, and others. In addition to the more specialized periodical literature available, we feel that the following general journals of political science are valuable.

American Journal of Political Science, since 1957.

>   Of rather recent vintage, formerly called the *Midwest Journal of Political Science,* the *AJPS* has quickly established a reputation for quality publications. This journal is also published quarterly and also includes book reviews and official notices of professional interest to political scientists.

The American Political Science Review, since 1906.

>   This journal is probably the most prestigious periodical in the

discipline. It usually includes a number of articles of especially high quality as well as lengthy and brief reviews of major new books in the field.

American Politics Quarterly, since 1973.

A new journal devoted exclusively to research on American politics. Articles appearing during the *APQ's* first year were largely empirical.

The Annals of the American Academy of Political and Social Science, since 1890.

Published bimonthly, the *Annals* devote each issue to a detailed discussion of a relevant topic of current concern based upon articles by a number of experts on that subject.

Daedalus. The American Academy of Arts and Sciences, since 1846.

Daedalus is published quarterly with an entire issue devoted to a single subject, again with a number of experts writing articles on that topic.

The Journal of Politics, since 1939.

This journal is the official publication of the Southern Political Science Association. It appears quarterly and generally includes a number of high-quality articles on a variety of subjects. Book reviews are also included in *The Journal of Politics.*

Political Science Quarterly, since 1886.

This journal is somewhat more traditional in orientation than the preceding journals. It includes articles by statesmen as well as academicians focusing on both domestic and international policy. Includes book reviews.

The Western Political Quarterly, since 1948.

Appearing quarterly, the *WPQ* is the official publication of the Western Political Science Association. During election years it traditionally has devoted one entire issue to the general subject of "Elections in the West" with detailed discussion of elections in each of the Western states. More frequently the *WPQ* devotes its issue to a wide variety of subjects.

In addition to these more general political science journals, a number of specialized journals are directly relevant to given subdivisions within the field.

International relations

American Journal of International Law, since 1970.

Official journal of the American Society of International Law. It is the most prestigious of American international law journals, carrying articles and other contents by the leading scholars of the field. More oriented to practicing international lawyers and law school personnel than to political scientists. Important cases and documents presented.

Foreign Affairs: An American Quarterly Review, since 1922.
A prestigious journal publishing articles by major statesmen as well as academicians with particular relevance to current situations of international importance. *Foreign Affairs* also includes annotated book lists, recent government documents, pamphlets, etc.

Foreign Policy, since 1970.
A lively journal covering American foreign policy, with some attention to broader concerns. Covers essentially the same field as *Foreign Affairs,* but tends to be less "establishment" oriented in the sense of presenting frequent critiques of foreign policy subjects by academics of all opinion. Each issue contains a series of short articles; no book reviews or other information.

International Organization, since 1947.
A quarterly publication of the World Peace Organization; this journal is useful for its general scholarly articles on issues related to the subject of international relations and especially international organizations, and also as an accounting of the activities of the various international organizations. The latter are generally summarized in the second portion of each journal.

International Studies Quarterly (formerly *Background*), since 1957.
Official publication of the International Studies Association, the *International Studies Quarterly* is one of the most prestigious journals in the field of international relations. Its bibliographic articles have been frequently recognized for their thoroughness.

The Journal of Conflict Resolution, since 1957.
Appears quarterly with special relevance to problems related to war and peace. This journal has been the outlet for some of the most pioneering empirical and theoretical work in the study of international relations.

Journal of Peace Research, since 1964.
A journal edited by the staff of the International Peace Research Institute, Oslo, Norway, it is known for its attention to pioneering methodological approaches to the study of international relations, with particular attention to factors affecting peace and stability. The scope of its articles is interdisciplinary.

Orbis, since 1957.
A journal on international relations and foreign policy, it is published by the University of Pennsylvania. Each issue has a large number of articles on a broad range of subjects. The articles are primarily concerned with policy analysis. *Orbis* also has one of

the better collections of book reviews each issue, which deal only with international and foreign policy.

World Politics: A Quarterly Journal of International Relations, since 1948.

World Politics is published by the Center of International Studies at Princeton University. This journal is known for its orientation toward high-calibre, more theoretical works dealing especially with international and comparative policies.

Comparative politics and area-study periodicals

Comparative Political Studies, since 1968.

A quarterly journal which usually carries a number of articles on a single country or, more frequently, comparative, cross-national studies. This journal appears to be particularly oriented toward contemporary empirical methods in contrast to many of the more descriptively oriented, specialized journals in comparative politics.

Comparative Politics, since 1968.

A new quarterly publication of the political science program at the City University of New York. The first issue was an overview of the general field of comparative politics; subsequent issues have been devoted to comparative analysis of a variety of political institutions and processes.

Comparative politics has only recently emerged with specialized general journals of relevance to the field. Area-study periodicals, on the other hand, have been available for a long time. In addition to the preceding general journals of comparative politics, students frequently will find articles of general relevance to the study of comparative politics in the general journals discussed previously, such as *The American Political Science Review, The Journal of Politics,* the *American Journal of Political Science, World Politics,* and others.

Area studies: Africa

Africa: A List of Current Social Science Research by Private Scholars and Academic Centers. U.S. Department of State, External Research Division, Washington, 1952-1968.

Covers social science research in progress and/or recently completed, covering all African countries. Particularly useful for alerting oneself to research which is not being widely publicized in the professional and/or commercial press.

Africa Today. Graduate School of International Studies, University of Denver, Denver, since 1973.

African Abstracts. International African Institute, London, since 1950.

Abstracts articles of particular relevance to anthropologists with occasional reference to articles of possible interest to political science.

African Studies Newsletter. African Studies Association, Columbia University, New York, since 1968.

Published six to nine times per year, the *African Studies Newsletter* provides essentially summary information on recent publications and research relevant to Africa in general.

Canadian Journal of African Studies, since 1967.

Current Bibliography on African Affairs. African Bibliographic Center, Washington, 1962–1967; and Greenwood Periodicals, Westport, Conn., since 1968.

A bimonthly list of new books and articles of relevance to Africa subdivided by disciplinary area of pertinence.

Journal of Modern African Studies, since 1963.

United States and Canadian Publications on Africa, since 1960. Stanford University: Hoover Institute, Stanford, since 1962.

An annual listing of relevant books, articles, and pamphlets generally dealing with Africa. This listing is somewhat dated normally and is not annotated.

In addition to the preceding general bibliographic sources on African politics, the following journal may prove useful:

African Quarterly, Indian Council for Africa, since 1963.

Area studies: Asia

Asia: A List of Current Social Science Research by Private Scholars and Academic Centers. U.S. Department of State, External Research Division, Washington, 1952–1968.

Now-defunct summarizing service listing current and recently completed research done under governmental auspices.

Bibliography of Asian Studies, since 1956. Appearing in *Journal of Asian Studies.*

Fairly extensive, unannotated listing of new works relevant to Asian Studies based on a perusal of books, pamphlets, articles, etc.

Cumulative Bibliography of Asian Studies, 1941–1965. G. K. Hall, Boston, 1969.

Southeast Asia: A Critical Bibliography. Kennedy G. Tregonning, University of Arizona Press, Tucson, 1969.

An annotated reference guide to the literature dealing with the countries of Southeast Asia. Contains over 2,000 entries organized geographically and topically.

Southern Asia Social Science Bibliography. UNESCO, Research Center on Social and Economic Development in Southern Asia, Delhi, 1954–1965. 12 vols.

> Annotated bibliography with rather extensive abstracts provided, organized by geographic area and subject.

The following journals are a few of the many area or country studies available on Asia:

Asia, since 1964.

Asian Studies, since 1963.

Asian Survey, since 1961.

The China Quarterly, since 1960.

Contemporary Japan, since 1955.

Japan Interpreter (formerly *Journal of Social and Political Ideas in Japan*), since 1963.

Journal of Asian Studies, since 1941.

Modern Asian Studies, since 1967.

Pacific Affairs, since 1928.

Area studies: Eastern Europe and the Soviet Union

The American Bibliography of Russian and East European Studies. Indiana University Press, Bloomington, since 1956.

> An annual unannotated bibiography of recent work on the Soviet Union and Eastern Europe. Covers only books and articles published within the recent year and appearing in the English language. This bibliography is organized by geographic area, subject field and country.

Horecky, Paul E. (ed.). *East Central Europe: A Guide to Basic Publications.* University of Chicago Press, Chicago, 1969.

> An annotated collection of prominent work on Czechoslovakia, East Germany, Hungary, Poland, and the East Central European area in general. This Guide includes books, periodicals, and general articles covering more than 500,000 titles.

Horecky, Paul E. (ed.). *Southeastern Europe: A Guide to Basic Publications.* University of Chicago Press, Chicago, 1969.

> Similar to the previous title by Horecky, this volume covers Albania, Bulgaria, Greece, Romania, and Yugoslavia.

New York, Public Library, Slavonic Division, *Dictionary Catalog of the Slavonic Collection, The New York Public Library Reference Department.* G. K. Hall, Boston, 1959.

> A basic listing of the holdings of the New York Public Library on the Baltic and Slavic countries. Many of the works cited in this

listing are in Russian and have not been translated. This is, how-ever, one of the largest collections available.

Journals of particular relevance to students interested in the *Soviet Union* and *Eastern Europe* in general include some of the following:

Analysis of Current Developments in the Soviet Union. Institute for the Study of the USSR, Munich; other publications include *Studies on the Soviet Union* (now discontinued).

The Central European Journal. University of Colorado, Boulder, since 1967.

Current Digest on the Soviet Press. American Association for the Advancement of Slavic Studies, Ohio State University, Columbus, since 1929.

Eastern European Quarterly. University of Colorado, Boulder, since 1967.

Problems of Communism, a bimonthly publication of the U.S. Information Agency, Washington, since 1952.

The Slavic Review. American Association for the Advancement of Slavic Studies, Banta, Menasha, Wis., since 1941.

The Slavonic and East European Review. University of London's School of Slavonic and East European Studies, London, since 1922.

Soviet Law and Government. International Arts & Sciences Press, New York, since 1962.

Soviet Studies from the University of Glasgow, Blackwell, Oxford, since 1949.

Studies in Comparative Communism: An Interdisciplinary Journal. School of Politics and International Relations, University of Southern California, since 1968.

Area studies: Latin America

Guide to Latin American Studies. 2 vols. Martin H. Sable, Latin American Center, University of California, Los Angeles, 1967.

An annotated bibliographic guide to the literature on Latin America arranged by discipline and subject subdivisions.

Handbook of Latin American Studies. University of Florida Press, Gainesville, since 1935.

Appears annually with classifications of significant published work on Latin America. Annotations are provided, organized by field of relevance and cross-indexed by author and subject.

Indice General de Publicaciones Periodicas Latino Americanas: Humanidades y Ciencias Sociales (Index to Latin American Periodicals:

Humanities and Social Sciences). Scarecrow Press, Metuchen, New Jersey, since 1961.

> Quarterly and annually cumulated index to periodical literature dealing with Latin America in Spanish with a listing of English equivalents provided as well.

Latin American Development: A Selected Bibliography (1950–1967). Jerry L. Weaver (ed.), ABC-CLIO Press, Santa Barbara, Calif.

Latin American Research Review. Latin American Studies Association, since 1965.

> A periodical published three times a year providing an inventory of current research dealing with Latin America, with a general description of this research as well as more general recent bibliographic materials in this area.

Specific periodicals are also available on Latin America in general and on specific Latin American countries in particular. Good journals in this area which are in English include:

Journal of Inter-American Studies. University of Miami Press, Coral Gables, Fla., since 1959.

Latin American Digest. Center for Latin American Studies, University of Arizona, Tempe, since 1966.

The Latin American Research Review. University of Texas, Austin, since 1965.

Numerous additional journals are available in Spanish and Portuguese.

Area studies: Western Europe, Great Britain, and the Commonwealth

Australian Journal of Politics and History, since 1944.

Australian Quarterly, since 1929.

Indian Political Science Review, since 1966.

The Journal of Commonwealth Political Studies, since 1961.

Parliamentary Affairs, with special relevance to Great Britain, since 1947.

The Political Quarterly (Great Britain), since 1930.

Political Science (New Zealand), since 1948.

Political Scientist (India), since 1964.

Political Studies (Great Britain), since 1953.

Politics (Australia), since 1966.

Politische Vierteljahresschrift (Germany), since 1960.

Revue Française de Science Politique (France), since 1951.

Periodicals especially relevant to public policy and public administration

Administrative Science Quarterly. Graduate School of Business and Public Administration, Cornell University, since 1965.

Polity. Political Science Association of New England, New York, and Pennsylvania, since 1968.

Public Administration Review. American Society for Public Administration, since 1940.

Public Choice (formerly *Papers on Non-market Decision-making),* since 1966.

A quarterly publication stressing work employing the application of economic models to political science.

The Public Interest. Freedom House, since 1965.

Particular attention to issues of current public interest. Frequently devotes an entire issue to a single policy issue.

Public Policy, Harvard University Kennedy School of Government, since 1970.

Periodicals of special relevance to urban politics

Public Management. International City Managers' Association, since 1919.

Public Personnel Management. International Personnel Management Association, Chicago, since 1940.

Urban Affairs Quarterly. City University of New York, since 1965.

Urban Research News. Bureau of Community Planning, University of Illinois, Urbana, since 1966.

Report on current research in this area.

General interdisciplinary journals of importance

American Behavioral Scientist. Metron, Princeton, N.J., since 1957.

Frequently devotes an entire issue to a single topic. Broadly interdisciplinary in subject matter of articles as well as methodologies used. Appears monthly.

Behavioral Scientist. Mental Health Research Institute of the University of Michigan, since 1956.

Stress on empirically based articles generally applicable to human behavior. Advanced sections on game theory and computer programming.

Psychology Today, since 1967.

A monthly publication frequently including interviews with highly respected philosophers, psychologists, and others. Frequently includes lengthy articles on current debates within psychology as well as articles more directly dealing with contemporary social problems.

The Public Opinion Quarterly. American Association for Public Opinion Research, since 1937.

Generally high-quality articles on the methodology of polling and the results of current empirical research on public opinion.

Social Problems. Society for the Study of Social Problems, since 1953.

Social Research. Graduate Faculty of Political and Social Science of the New School for Social Research, New York, since 1934.

A journal appearing quarterly which is frequently centered around one theme per issue. Articles are normally of high quality and written by academicians in a number of the social sciences.

Society, since 1963.

Formerly titled *Trans-action,* this monthly journal published at Rutgers University, emphasizes current social issues and recent research relevant to these problems. Includes book reviews.

Book reviews

Most major journals in political science carry book reviews. In addition, basic reference sources are available which are specifically devoted to book reviews.

Book Review Digest. H. W. Wilson, New York, since 1905.

An index and digest for reviews appearing in more than seventy-five periodicals. Arrangement within volumes is alphabetical by author, with a title and subject index also provided. Generally, reviews of a book will appear in the volume of the *Digest* corresponding with date of publication or in the immediate succeeding year.

Book Review Index. Gale Research, Detroit, since 1965.

An index only, for reviews appearing in more than 200 journals. This index covers more political science journals than the preceding *Digest.*

Index to Book Reviews in the Humanities. P. Thomson, Detroit, since 1960.

Although specifically directed to the humanities, this index does cover many books in the social sciences providing an index to more than 700 periodicals.

Index to the Times. Times Newspapers Ltd., London, since 1960.

Lists book reviews appearing in the *Times* by book title.

International Bibliography of Political Science. Aldine, Chicago, since 1962.

> This previously mentioned general bibliographic source also frequently cites reviews of books.

The New York Times Index. The New York Times Corporation, New York, since 1913.

> Under the general heading Book Reviews, a listing of book reviews appearing in the *New York Times* is provided by author and title.

Social Sciences and Humanities Index. H. W. Wilson, New York, since 1907.

> This source also lists reviews under the name of the author.

Newspapers

Newspapers frequently are used as sources of data and general information in political science. Many newspapers do not keep cumulative indexes. The *New York Times* and the *London Times* do keep indexes that greatly facilitate their use.

Christian Science Monitor. Index to the Christian Science Monitor. H. M. Cropsey, Corvallis, Oreg., since 1959.

> An annual index to each of the regional editions of this newspaper.

London Times Index, ceased.

> A comprehensive index to the *London Times.*

New York Times Index. New York, since 1851.

> A comprehensive index to all the material reported in the daily and Sunday *New York Times.* The *New York Times* generally is available at most libraries on microfilm. It is wise to cross-check topics under several relevant titles or subject headings to ensure complete coverage.

The Wall Street Journal. Index, 1957– . Dow Jones and Co., New York, since 1958.

> This index is divided into two parts; the first deals with corporate news indexed by company name, and the second part deals with general news by subject.

Guides to government documents

Each year the United States government publishes an extremely large number of documents. Some of these documents are not distributed widely, but a large number are available at most libraries. If given sufficient advance notice, your librarian usually can obtain documents

that the library does not presently hold. There are also a sizeable number of depositories for government documents throughout the United
States. If your library is not a depository for government documents,
probably another library in your vicinity has these resources. Locating
government documents can be an onerous task if you are not familiar
with the basic reference tools available to these sources. Some of these
directories include the following:

Congressional Quarterly Weekly Report. Congressional Quarterly,
Washington, since 1964.

> An objective summary and analysis of events in Congress and the
> federal government. Provides voting data for the House and the
> Senate on selected measures as well as portions of major speeches.

Monthly Catalog of United States Government Publications. Super-
intendent of Documents, Washington, since 1895.

> An index to the publications of all branches including congres-
> sional, departmental, and bureau publications. An annual index
> is also contained in the back of each volume.

Monthly Checklist of State Publications. Library of Congress, Washington, since 1910.

> Efficient reference to state government publications. Lists all
> items received by the Library of Congress alphabetically by state
> and issuing agency. An annual index is also provided with con-
> tent and title listings. Not exhaustive in coverage, but a good
> starting point.

Statistical sources

A large number of statistical sources are available, of which the following brief citations are only a small portion. Before undertaking a
research project, it is important to check what data sources are available at your library. The items suggested below are among the most
commonly used and most widely available sources of statistical information. They generally are considered highly reliable sources of
information, an important consideration in any research project.

R. Scammon. *America Votes: A Handbook of Contemporary American
Election Statistics.* Governmental Affairs Institute and *Congressional
Quarterly,* Washington, since 1956.

> This source provides data by state on presidential, senatorial,
> congressional, and gubernatarial elections since the 1940s.

Book of the States. Council of State Governments, Chicago, since 1935.

> Contains information on the structure and functional activities
> of the fifty state governments. Includes information on elections,
> finance, services, legislation, etc.

Congressional District Data Book, U.S. Bureau of the Census, Washington, since 1963.
> This source provides statistical data on 254 items for each congressional district. These items are drawn from the decenial United States census.

County and City Data Book. Bureau of the Census, Washington, since 1949.
> Also based upon the United States census, the *County and City Data Book* contains statistical information for each county in the United States, standard metropolitan statistical areas, and cities with populations of more than 25,000.

Demographic Yearbook. United Nations Publications, New York, since 1948.
> One of the best single sources for worldwide population data.

Europa Yearbook. Europa Publications, London, since 1959.
> Contains descriptive and statistical information on each European country and a directory of government officials.

Foreign Statistical Documents. Hoover Institute, Stanford, Calif., 1967.
> A bibliography rather than a data source, this publication provides a convenient bibliography of general statistics as well as international trade and agriculture statistics.

Historical Statistics of the United States, Colonial Times to 1957. U.S. Government Printing Office, Washington, since 1910.
> A compilation of more than 8,000 statistical time series data on American social and economic development.

Municipal Yearbook. International City Managers' Association, Washington, since 1934.
> Contains extensive descriptive and statistical information on cities of the United States, includes listing of recent data and information sources.

SS Data. Laboratory for Political Research of the University of Iowa, since 1971.
> Published quarterly, this newsletter communicates information relevant to the acquisition of social science data archives. Includes short abstracts describing variables and sample. Includes data in history, sociology, political science, and others. Also lists new bibliographic reference books and major archives throughout the world.

Statistical Abstracts of the United States. U.S. Census Bureau, Washington, since 1878.
> An annual compendium that provides the major statistical data produced by the federal government. It is divided into sections on population, education, elections, communication, and others.

Statistical Sources. 2d ed. Paul Wasserman et al., Gale Research Co., Detroit, 1966.

> A subject index to sources for statistical information on industrial, social, educational, financial, and other statistics for the United States and selected foreign countries.

Statistical Yearbook. United Nations, New York, since 1948.

> A publication of the United Nations which provides extensive data for the various countries of the world on population, income, education, etc. Information is not always complete for all countries.

Yearbook of International Trade Statistics. United Nations, New York, since 1950.

> An annual U.N. publication giving detailed annual trade statistics for 142 countries.

Yearbook of National Accounts Statistics. United Nations, New York, since 1954.

> Extensive economic data on approximately 100 countries.

Data archives

A large number of central data archives now accumulate and distribute at a moderate cost data that were the basis of some significant studies in the discipline. Although space limitations prohibit listing their holdings, the following list of archives provides addresses for those interested in seeing what existing data are available. Usually the data are distributed on computer tapes or cards.

MAJOR ARCHIVES*

Project TALENT Data Bank
AMERICAN INSTITUTE FOR RESEARCH
P.O. Box 1113
Palo Alto, California 94302

Evert Brouwer, Manager
AMSTERDAMS SOCIAALWETENSCHAPPELIJK DATA ARCHIEF
University of Amsterdam
Room 143 - Roetersstraat 15
Amsterdam, Netherlands

Source: SS Data, University of Iowa, Laboratory for Political Research.

William Kleka, Director
BEHAVIORAL SCIENCES LABORATORY
University of Cincinnati
Cincinnati, Ohio 45221

Philippe Laurent
BELGIAN ARCHIVES FOR THE SOCIAL SCIENCES
Van Evenstraat 2A, Room 04–05
3000 Louvain, Belgium

Data Archivist
BUREAU OF APPLIED SOCIAL RESEARCH
Columbia University
New York, New York 10025

Arthur S. Banks, Director
CENTER FOR COMPARATIVE POLITICAL RESEARCH
State University of New York
Binghamton, New York 13901

Alice Robbin
DATA & PROGRAM LIBRARY SERVICE
4451 Social Science Building
University of Wisconsin
Madison, Wisconsin 53706

David Amos
DATA LIBRARY
Computing Centre
University of British Columbia
Vancouver 8, British Columbia
Canada

Librarian
Information Documentation Center
DUALABS, INC.
1601 N. Kent Street, Suite 900
Arlington, Virginia 22209

Stein Rokkan, Director
EUROPEAN CONSORTIUM FOR POLITICAL RESEARCH
Data Information Service
Gamel Kalvedalsveien 12
N–5000 Bergen, Norway

Thomas Atkinson, Director
Data Bank
INSTITUTE FOR BEHAVIORAL RESEARCH
York University
4700 Keele Street
Downsview, Ontario
Canada

Data Librarian
INTERNATIONAL DATA LIBRARY & REFERENCE SERVICE
Survey Research Center
University of California
Berkeley, California 94720

Survey Research Archive
Historial Archive
International Relations Archive
INTER-UNIVERSITY CONSORTIUM FOR POLITICAL RESEARCH
P.O. Box 1248
Ann Arbor, Michigan 48106

ISR SOCIAL SCIENCE ARCHIVE
P.O. Box 1248
Ann Arbor, Michigan 48106

Manuel J. Carvajal, Director
LATIN AMERICAN DATA BANK
Room 471 International Studies Building
University of Florida
Gainseville, Florida 32601

Gerald J. Rosenkrantz, Chief
Machine-readable Archives Branch
NATIONAL ARCHIVES (NNPD)
Washington, D.C. 20408

Patrick Bova
NATIONAL OPINION RESEARCH CENTER
University of Chicago
6030 South Ellis Avenue
Chicago, Illinois 60637

Lorraine Borman
NORTHWESTERN UNIVERSITY INFORMATION CENTER
Vogelback Computing Center
Northwestern University
Evanston, Illinois 60201

Eugene J. Watts
OHIO DATA ARCHIVES
Ohio Historical Society
Ohio Historical Center
Columbus, Ohio 43211

Richard Hofstader, Director
POLIMETRICS LABORATORY
Department of Political Science
Ohio State University
Columbus, Ohio 43210

Elizabeth Powell, Associate Director
POLITICAL SCIENCE DATA ARCHIVE
Department of Political Science
Michigan State University
East Lansing, Michigan 48823

Ronald Weber, Director
POLITICAL SCIENCE LABORATORY AND DATA ARCHIVE
Department of Political Science
248 Woodburn Hall
Indiana University
Bloomington, Indiana 47401

Philip K. Hastings
ROPER PUBLIC OPINION RESEARCH CENTER
P.O. Box 624
Williams College
Williamstown, Massachusetts 02167

SOCIAL DATA EXCHANGE ASSOCIATION
333 Grotto Avenue
Providence, Rhode Island

James Grifhorst
SOCIAL SCIENCE DATA ARCHIVE
Laboratory for Political Research
321A Schaeffer Hall
University of Iowa
Iowa City, Iowa 52242

Daniel Amick
SOCIAL SCIENCE DATA ARCHIVE
Survey Research Laboratory
414 Kinley Hall
Urbana, Illinois 61810

Peter C. Tolos
SOCIAL SCIENCE DATA ARCHIVE
UCLA Survey Research Center
Los Angeles, California 90024

Tony Falsetto
SOCIAL SCIENCE DATA ARCHIVES
Department of Sociology
Carleton University
Ottawa 1, Canada

Everett C. Ladd, Jr.
SOCIAL SCIENCE DATA CENTER
University of Connecticut
Storrs, Connecticut 06268

Neal E. Cutler
SOCIAL SCIENCE DATA CENTER
University of Pennsylvania
3508 Market Street - Suite 350
Philadelphia, Pennsylvania 19104

Sue A. Dodd
SOCIAL SCIENCE DATA LIBRARY
University of North Carolina
Room 10 Manning Hall
Chapel Hill, North Carolina 27514

Judith S. Rowe
SOCIAL SCIENCE USER SERVICE
Princeton University Computer Center
87 Prospect Avenue
Princeton, New Jersey 08540

Jack Elinson
SOCIOMEDICAL RESEARCH ARCHIVES
Columbia University School of Public Health
Black Research Building
630 West 168th Street
New York, New York 10032

Director
SSRC SURVEY ARCHIVE
University of Essex
Colchester
England

William E. Bicker, Director
Neal McGowan, Senior Programmer
STATE DATA PROGRAM
Institute of Governmental Studies
109 Moses Hall
University of California
Berkeley, California 94720

Cees P. Middendorp
STEINMETZ ARCHIVES
Information and Documentation Centre for the Social Sciences
Royal Netherlands Academy of Arts and Sciences
Keizersgracht 569-571
Amsterdam, Netherlands

ZENTRALARCHIV FUR EMPIRISCHE SOZIALFORSCHUNG
Universitat zu Koln
5 Koln
Bachemer Str. 40
Germany

APPENDIX B
THE RESEARCH REPORT

A number of considerations arise when an investigator is faced with the task of writing a research report. In this appendix we briefly discuss three considerations about which questions most often arise: format, audience, and length. Many good sources are available for students desiring greater detail, yet this brief overview should answer most basic questions.

Format

The first step in any formal writing is to outline the entire paper so that the presentation is a logical series of steps that takes the reader from introductory remarks through summary and conclusion. Some presentations of the "classic" format follow:

Babbie	*Selltiz et al.*	*Tichy*
Purpose and overview	Statement of the problem	Background
Review of literature		Statement of problems
Study design and execution	Research procedures	
	The results	Discussion of procedures
Analysis and Interpretation	Implications	
		Statement of results
Summary and conclusions		Conclusions and recommendations

INTRODUCTION

The introduction generally outlines the problem under investigation, and the general rationale for the study and the report. The problem may stem from conflicting theories and/or findings, a practical problem, etc. The introduction should contain a clear and concise definition of the problem under investigation. Frequently the introduction also will outline subsequent sections of the report so that readers are given a general guide to the subsequent discussion.

REVIEW OF THE LITERATURE

A review of the literature is an integral part of the general setting of the problem under investigation. The review of the literature can be included in the introduction itself, set aside as a separate section of the paper, or interwoven in the central text.

All research builds upon the work of others. The section of the report discussing other literature on your topic is designed to fit your research into the larger research tradition. In this connection you should ask, "How does my work add to the existing literature? How have problems similar to mine been investigated in the past? How do my procedures differ? In what respects is the existing research incomplete or inconclusive?"

In terms of general format, we generally recommend that it is better to discuss the literature in terms of summary positions. This format is generally more economical and interesting than simply listing author 1, author 2, author 3, etc. For examples of good summary essays on the literature, we suggest that you look at the essays in the *Political Science Annual*, volume I, edited by James Robinson.

RESEARCH PROCEDURES

The research procedures section of the paper outlines the research techniques employed in detail. Conventionally this would include a discussion of the sampling procedure, sample size, locale, statistical analysis, computer packages, etc. The research procedures should be precise enough to allow interested readers to go to a selected source, for example, if they were interested in more detail on a specific program employed. Triangulation helps considerably at this point. If a sample is used, for example, compare your sample with the population, if possible, and demonstrate how your sample compares with others employed in previous research. Similarly, indicate means of validating your measures whenever possible. If your scales are correlated with others or have shown consistency across other samples or populations, this is helpful in evaluating your research.

PRESENTATION OF RESULTS

The body of the paper presents the results. Normally summary tables are included, with appropriate statistics given at the bottom of each table. The text provides commentary on the tables and normally goes beyond mere description of the data by offering tentative explanations for the findings. Wherever appropriate, the discussion should be integrated to consider your findings relative to other studies on the same subject.

RESULTS AND CONCLUSIONS

The concluding section of the report generally summarizes the findings. Frequently, the conclusion also will offer suggestions for future research by pointing out new questions raised by the study. In their final sections some reports make policy recommendations as well. This is common in technical reports executed within bureaucracies and government agencies.

This general format can be varied, of course. One common variation is to present the conclusions and recommendations first. Format is somewhat dependent upon the audience, the party or parties to whom the report is directed.

Audience

In addition to affecting the format somewhat, the audience frequently will also have some bearing on the style and language employed. We endorse the position that *all* reports should be readable by almost anyone. They should be precise in defining terms and avoid unnecessary jargon whenever possible. Nevertheless, differences in background influence both readers and writers of reports. Researchers addressing themselves to a highly specialized audience in technical journals can assume that the audience is familiar with certain general literature in the area and with certain concepts and terminology. These assumptions cannot be made in writing a term paper or a general report addressed to the public. As a general guideline, we suggest that researchers consider rather carefully who their audience is and their background in writing the report. Since the basic goal of a report is to *communicate* a study's results, we must always consider the mose effective means of achieving this.

Length

One of the first questions students ask an instructor is, "How long does the report need to be?" The instructor normally responds somewhat cryptically, "Long enough." While we tend to agree with the instructor that it is difficult to set absolute parameters on length, perhaps general guidelines can be offered. Students should remember that the most important thing is that the report cover all necessary information. Sometimes this can be achieved concisely, and sometimes it cannot.

Length again depends somewhat on purpose. If the report is to be a research note (commonly published in a professional journal), it is generally quite short. Research notes generally run from five to ten pages, and they usually emphasize the presentation of results rather than the other portions of the report emphasized here, such as the review of the literature, etc. Conventional research articles (and many term papers) often include lengthy theoretical introductions and discussions of the analyses and run about twenty-five pages including tables, footnotes, and figures.

In summary, we suggest that students begin the process of report writing by constructing a basic outline of the sections to be included and the major points to be discussed. It is convenient to collect citations and short commentary on the related literature on index cards. These provide ready reference in writing footnotes and the review of the literature. After the first draft of the report is written, it should be revised and polished. One basic embarrassment to avoid is poor writing. It detracts from the content of the report and makes reading tedious rather than enjoyable. Poor writing results from bad punctuation and spelling, monotonous sentence structure, bad grammar, and poor transition between ideas. The following are useful references on writing style and format:

Babbie, Earl R. *Survey Research Methods*, Wadsworth, Belmont, 1973.

Leggett, Glen. *Handbook for Writers*. Prentice-Hall, New York, 1952.

Perrin, Porter G. *Handbook for Current English*, 3d ed. Scott, Foresman and Company, Glenview, Ill., 1968.

Selltiz, Claire, Jahoda, Deutsch and Cook. *Research Methods in Social Relations*, rev. 1-vol. ed. Holt, Rinehart and Winston, New York, 1961.

Strunk, William, Jr., and E. B. White. *Elements of Style*. Macmillan Company, New York, 1959.

Tichy, H. J., *Effective Writing*. John Wiley, New York, 1966.

Turabian, Kate L. *A Manual for Writers of Term Papers, Theses, and Dissertations*. University of Chicago Press, Chicago, 1964.

Watkins, Floyd C., et al. *Practical English Handbook*, 4th ed. Houghton Mifflin, Boston, 1974.

APPENDIX C
SOME SEMANTIC DIFFERENTIAL SCALES
WHICH HAVE BEEN USED IN VARIOUS STUDIES

1. angular-rounded
2. bass-treble
3. beautiful-ugly
4. black-white
5. blatant-muted
6. boring-interesting
7. brave-cowardly
8. bright-dark
9. calm-agitated
10. calm-exciting
11. chaotic-ordered
12. clean-dirty
13. clear-hazy
14. colorful-colorless
15. concentrated-diffuse
16. controlled-accidental
17. deep-shallow
18. definite-uncertain
19. deliberate-careless
20. dull-exciting
21. dull-sharp
22. emotional-rational
23. empty-full
24. even-uneven
25. expensive-cheap
26. fair-unfair
27. familiar-strange
28. fast-slow
29. ferocious-peaceful
30. formal-informal
31. fragrant-foul
32. fresh-stale
33. gentle-violent
34. genuine-artificial
35. gliding-scraping
36. good-bad
37. happy-sad
38. hard-soft
39. healthy-sick
40. heavy-light
41. high-class–low-class
42. high-low
43. honest-dishonest
44. hot-cold
45. humorous-serious
46. important-trivial
47. intimate-remote
48. kind-cruel
49. labored-easy
50. large-small
51. long-short
52. loose-tight
53. loud-soft
54. lush-austere
55. masculine-feminine
56. meaningless-meaningful
57. mild-intense
58. modern–old-fashioned
59. near-far
60. nice-awful
61. obvious-subtle
62. pleasant-unpleasant
63. pleasing-annoying
64. powerful-weak
65. pungent-bland
66. pushing-pulling
67. red-green
68. relaxed-tense

Source: From *Tests and Measurements: Assessment and Prediction,* by Jum C. Nunnally, Jr. Copyright 1959 McGraw-Hill Book Company. Used with permission of McGraw-Hill Book Company.

69. repeated-varied
70. repetitive-varied
71. resting-busy
72. rich-poor
73. rich-thin
74. rough-smooth
75. rugged-delicate
76. rumbling-whining
77. sacred-profane
78. safe-dangerous
79. simple-complex
80. sincere-insincere
81. solid-hollow
82. static-dynamic
83. steady-fluttering
84. strong-weak

85. superficial-profound
86. sweet-bitter
87. sweet-sour
88. tasty-distasteful
89. thick-thin
90. unbelievable-believable
91. unique-commonplace
92. usual-unusual
93. vague-precise
94. valuable-worthless
95. vibrant-still
96. wet-dry
97. wide-narrow
98. yellow-blue
99. young-old

APPENDIX D

APPROXIMATE SAMPLING ERROR OF PERCENTAGES*
(In percentages)

Reported	Number of interviews							
percentages	1500	1000	700	500	400	300	200	100
50	3.1	3.6	4.2	4.9	5.4	6.2	7.5	10.5
30 or 70	2.8	3.3	3.8	4.5	4.9	5.7	6.9	9.6
20 or 80	2.5	2.9	3.4	3.9	4.3	4.9	6.0	8.4
10 or 90	1.8	2.2	2.5	2.9	3.2	3.7	4.5	6.3
5 or 95	1.3	1.6	1.8	2.1	2.4	2.7	3.3	4.6

* The figures in this table represent *two* standard errors. Hence, for most items the chances are 95 in 100 that the value being estimated lies within a range equal to the reported percentages, plus or minus the sampling error.

Source: The Survey Research Center. Formulas and detail of calculations appear in L. Kish and Hess, *The Survey Research Center's National Sample of Dwellings*, Institute for Social Research, Ann Arbor, Mich., 1965.

APPENDIX D (Continued)

APPROXIMATE SAMPLING ERROR OF DIFFERENCES
(In percentages)

Size of subgroups	For percentages from 35% to 65%						
	1500	1000	700	500	300	200	100
1500	4.4	4.8	5.2	5.8	6.9	8.1	11.0
1000		5.1	5.5	6.1	7.2	8.3	11.0
700			5.9	6.4	7.5	8.6	11.0
500				6.9	7.9	8.9	12.0
300					8.7	9.7	12.0
200						11.0	13.0
100							15.0
	For percentages around 20% and 80%						
1500	3.6	3.8	4.2	4.6	5.6	6.5	8.8
1000		4.1	4.4	4.9	5.7	6.7	8.9
700			4.8	5.2	6.0	6.9	9.0
500				5.5	6.3	7.2	9.3
300					7.0	7.8	9.7
200						8.5	10.0
100							12.0
	For percentages around 10% and 90%						
1500	2.6	2.9	3.2	3.5	4.2	4.9	6.6
1000		3.1	3.3	3.6	4.3	5.0	6.7
700			3.6	3.9	4.5	5.2	6.8
500				4.1	4.7	5.4	6.9
300					5.2	5.8	7.3
200						6.4	7.7
100							8.9
	For percentages around 5% and 95%						
1500	2.0	2.2	2.4	2.6	3.1	3.7	5.0
1000		2.3	2.5	2.7	3.2	3.8	5.0
700			2.7	2.9	3.4	3.9	5.1
500				3.1	3.6	4.0	5.2
300					3.9	4.4	5.5
200						4.8	5.8
100							6.7

* The values shown are the differences required for significance (two standard errors) in comparisons of percentages derived from two different national surveys or from two different subgroups of the same study.

APPENDIX E
STATISTICAL TABLES

Table 1. Random Numbers

10097	32533	76520	13586	34673	54876	80959	09117	39292	74945
37542	04805	64894	74296	24805	24037	20636	10402	00822	91665
08422	68953	19645	09303	23209	02560	15953	34764	35080	33606
99019	02529	09376	70715	38311	31165	88676	74397	04436	27659
12807	99970	80157	36147	64032	36653	98951	16877	12171	76833
66065	74717	34072	76850	36697	36170	65813	39885	11199	29170
31060	10805	45571	82406	35303	42614	86799	07439	23403	09732
85269	77602	02051	65692	68665	74818	73053	85247	18623	88579
63573	32135	05325	47048	90553	57548	28468	28709	83491	25624
73796	45753	03529	64778	35808	34282	60935	20344	35273	88435
98520	17767	14905	68607	22109	40558	60970	93433	50500	73998
11805	05431	39808	27732	50725	68248	29405	24201	52775	67851
83452	99634	06288	98083	13746	70078	18475	40610	68711	77817
88685	40200	86507	58401	36766	67951	90364	76493	29609	11062
99594	67348	87517	64969	91826	08928	93785	61368	23478	34113
65481	17674	17468	50950	58047	76974	73039	57186	40218	16544
80124	35635	17727	08015	45318	22374	21115	78253	14385	53763
74350	99817	77402	77214	43236	00210	45521	64237	96286	02655
69916	26803	66252	29148	36936	87203	76621	13990	94400	56418
09893	20505	14225	68514	46427	56788	96297	78822	54382	14598
91499	14523	68479	27686	46162	83554	94750	89923	37089	20048
80336	94598	26940	36858	70297	34135	53140	33340	42050	82341
44104	81949	85157	47954	32979	26575	57600	40881	22222	06413
12550	73742	11100	02040	12860	74697	96644	89439	28707	25815
63606	49329	16505	34484	40219	52563	43651	77082	07207	31790
61196	90446	26457	47774	51924	33729	65394	59593	42582	60527
15474	45266	95270	79953	59367	83848	82396	10118	33211	59466
94557	28573	67897	54387	54622	44431	91190	42592	92927	45973
42481	16213	97344	08721	16868	48767	03071	12059	25701	46670
23523	78317	73208	89837	68935	91416	26252	29663	05522	82562
04493	52494	75246	33824	45862	51025	61962	79335	65337	12472
00549	97654	64051	88159	96119	63896	54692	82391	23287	29529
35963	15307	26898	09354	33351	35462	77974	50024	90103	39333
59808	08391	45427	26842	83609	49700	13021	24892	78565	20106
46058	85236	01390	92286	77281	44077	93910	83647	70617	42941

Source: The RAND corporation. *A Million Random Digits.* The Free Press, New York, 1955. By the kind permission of the publishers.

Table 1 (continued)

32179	00597	87379	25241	05567	07007	86743	17157	85394	11838
69234	61406	20117	45204	15956	60000	18743	92423	97118	96338
19565	41430	01758	75379	40419	21585	66674	36806	84962	85207
45155	14938	19476	07246	43667	94543	59047	90033	20826	69541
94864	31994	36168	10851	34888	81553	01540	35456	05014	51176
98086	24826	45240	28404	44999	08896	39094	73407	35441	31880
33185	16232	41941	50949	89435	48581	88695	41994	37548	73043
80951	00406	96382	70774	20151	23387	25016	25298	94624	61171
79752	49140	71961	28296	69861	02591	74852	20539	00387	59579
18633	32537	98145	06571	31010	24674	05455	61427	77938	91936
74029	43902	77557	32270	97790	17119	52527	58021	80814	51748
54178	45611	80993	37143	05335	12969	56127	19255	36040	90324
11664	49883	52079	84827	59381	71539	09973	33440	88461	23356
48324	77928	31249	64710	02295	36870	32307	57546	15020	09994
69074	94138	87637	91976	35584	04401	10518	21615	01848	76938
09188	20097	32825	39527	04220	86304	83389	87374	64278	58044
90045	85497	51981	50654	94938	81997	91870	76150	68476	64659
73189	50207	47677	26269	62290	64464	27124	67018	41361	82760
75768	76490	20971	87749	90429	12272	95375	05871	93823	43178
54016	44056	66281	31003	00682	27398	20714	53295	07706	17813
08358	69910	78542	42785	13661	58873	04618	97553	31223	08420
28306	03264	81333	10591	40510	07893	32604	60475	94119	01840
53840	86233	81594	13628	51215	90290	28466	68795	77762	20791
91757	53741	61613	62269	50263	90212	55781	76514	83483	47055
89415	92694	00397	58391	12607	17646	48949	72306	94541	37408
77513	03820	86864	29901	68414	82774	51908	13980	72893	55507
19502	37174	69979	20288	55210	29773	74287	75251	65344	67415
21818	59313	93278	81757	05686	73156	07082	85046	31853	38452
51474	66499	68107	23621	94049	91345	42836	09191	08007	45449
99559	68331	62535	24170	69777	12830	74819	78142	43860	72834
33713	48007	93584	72869	51926	64721	58303	29822	93174	93972
85274	86893	11303	22970	28834	34137	73515	90400	71148	43643
84133	89640	44035	52166	73852	70091	61222	60561	62327	18423
56732	16234	17395	96131	10123	91622	85496	57560	81604	18880
65138	56806	87648	85261	34313	65861	45875	21069	85644	47277
38001	02176	81719	11711	71602	92937	74219	64049	65584	49698
37402	96397	01304	77586	56271	10086	47324	62605	40030	37438
97125	40348	87083	31417	21815	39250	75237	62047	15501	29578
21826	41134	47143	34072	64638	85902	49139	06441	03856	54552
73135	42742	95719	09035	85794	74296	08789	88156	64691	19202
07638	77929	03061	18072	96207	44156	23821	99538	04713	66994
60528	83441	07954	19814	59175	20695	05533	52139	61212	06455
83596	35655	06958	92983	05128	09719	77433	53783	92301	50498
10850	62746	99599	10507	13499	06319	53075	71839	06410	19362
39820	98952	43622	63147	64421	80814	43800	09351	31024	73167

Table 1 (continued)

59580 06478	75569 78800	88835 54486	23768 06156	04111 08408
38508 07341	23793 48763	90822 97022	17719 04207	95954 49953
30692 70668	94688 16127	56196 80091	82067 63400	05462 69200
65443 95659	18288 27437	49632 24041	08337 65676	96299 90836
27267 50264	13192 72294	07477 44606	17985 48911	97341 30358
91307 06991	19072 24210	36699 53728	28825 35793	28976 66252
68434 94688	84473 13622	62126 98408	12843 82590	09815 93146
48908 15877	54745 24591	35700 04754	83824 52692	54130 55160
06913 45197	42672 78601	11883 09528	63011 98901	14974 40344
10455 16019	14210 33712	91342 37821	88325 80851	43667 70883
12883 97343	65027 61184	04285 01392	17974 15077	90712 26769
21778 30976	38807 36961	31649 42096	63281 02023	08816 47449
19523 59515	65122 59659	86283 68258	69572 13798	16435 91529
67245 52670	35583 16563	79246 86686	76463 34222	26655 90802
60584 47377	07500 37992	45134 26529	26760 83637	41326 44344
53853 41377	36066 94850	58838 73859	49364 73331	96240 43642
24637 38736	74384 89342	52623 07992	12369 18601	03742 83873
83080 12451	38992 22815	07759 51777	97377 27585	51972 37867
16444 24334	36151 99073	27493 70939	85130 32552	54846 54759
60790 18157	57178 65762	11161 78576	45819 52979	65130 04860
03991 10461	93716 16894	66083 24653	84609 58232	88618 19161
38555 95554	32886 59780	08355 60860	29735 47762	71299 23853
17546 73704	92052 46215	55121 29281	59076 07936	27954 58909
32643 52861	95819 06831	00911 98936	76355 93779	80863 00514
69572 68777	39510 35905	14060 40619	29549 69616	33564 60780
24122 66591	27699 06494	14845 46672	61958 77100	90899 75754
61196 30231	92962 61773	41839 55382	17267 70943	78038 70267
30532 21704	10274 12202	39685 23309	10061 68829	55986 66485
03788 97599	75867 20717	74416 53166	35208 33374	87539 08823
48228 63379	85783 47619	53152 67433	35663 52972	16818 60311
60365 94653	35075 33949	42614 29297	01918 28316	98953 73231
83799 42402	56623 34442	34994 41374	70071 14736	09958 18065
32960 07405	36409 83232	99385 41600	11133 07586	15917 06253
19322 53845	57620 52606	66497 68646	78138 66559	19640 99413
11220 94747	07399 37408	48509 23929	27482 45476	85244 35159
31751 57260	68980 05339	15470 48355	88651 22596	03152 19121
88492 99382	14454 04504	20094 98977	74843 93413	22109 78508
30934 47744	07481 83828	73788 06533	28597 20405	94205 20380
22888 48893	27499 98748	60530 45128	74022 84617	82037 10268
78212 16993	35902 91386	44372 15486	65741 14014	87481 37220
41849 84547	46850 52326	34677 58300	74910 64345	19325 81549
46352 33049	69248 93460	45305 07521	61318 31855	14413 70951
11087 96294	14013 31792	59747 67277	76503 34513	39663 77544
52701 08337	56303 87315	16520 69676	11654 99893	02181 68161
57275 36898	81304 48585	68652 27376	92852 55866	88448 03584

Table 1 (continued)

20857 73156	70284 24326	79375 95220	01159 63267	10622 48391
15633 84924	90415 93614	33521 26665	55823 47641	86225 31704
92694 48297	39904 02115	59589 49067	66821 41575	49767 04037
77613 19019	88152 00080	20554 91409	96277 48257	50816 97616
38688 32486	45134 63545	59404 72059	43947 51680	43852 59693
25163 01889	70014 15021	41290 67312	71857 15957	68971 11403
65251 07629	37239 33295	05870 01119	92784 26340	18477 65622
36815 43625	18637 37509	82444 99005	04921 73701	14707 93997
64397 11692	05327 82162	20247 81759	45197 25332	83745 22567
04515 25624	95096 67946	48460 85558	15191 18782	16930 33361
83761 60873	43253 84145	60833 25983	01291 41349	20368 07126
14387 06345	80854 09279	43529 06318	38384 74761	41196 37480
51321 92246	80088 77074	88722 56736	66164 49431	66919 31678
72472 00008	80890 18002	94813 31900	54155 83436	35352 54131
05466 55306	93128 18464	74457 90561	72848 11834	79982 68416
39528 72484	82474 25593	48545 35247	18619 13674	18611 19241
81616 18711	53342 44276	75122 11724	74627 73707	58319 15997
07586 16120	82641 22820	92904 13141	32392 19763	61199 67940
90767 04235	13574 17200	69902 63742	78464 22501	18627 90872
40188 28193	29593 88627	94972 11598	62095 38787	00441 58997
34414 82157	86887 55087	19152 00023	12302 80783	32624 68691
63439 75363	44989 16822	36024 00867	76378 41605	65961 73488
67049 09070	93399 45547	94458 74284	05041 49807	20288 34060
79495 04146	52162 90286	54158 34243	46978 35482	59362 95938
91704 30552	04737 21031	75051 93029	47665 64382	99782 93478

Table 2. Significant Values of *G* for Testing H_0

N	Two-tailed Test $\alpha = .05$	Two-tailed Test $\alpha = .01$	One-tailed Test $\alpha = .05$	One-tailed Test $\alpha = .01$
4			1.000	
5	1.000		0.800	1.000
6	0.867	1.000	0.733	0.867
7	0.714	0.905	0.619	0.810
8	0.643	0.786	0.571	0.714
9	0.556	0.722	0.500	0.667
10	0.511	0.644	0.467	0.600
11	0.491	0.600	0.418	0.564
12	0.455	0.576	0.394	0.545
13	0.436	0.564	0.359	0.513
14	0.407	0.51 ,	0.363	0.473
15	0.390	0.505	0.333	0.467
16	0.383	0.483	0.317	0.433
17	0.368	0.471	0.309	0.426
18	0.346	0.451	0.294	0.412
19	0.333	0.439	0.287	0.392
20	0.326	0.421	0.274	0.379
21	0.314	0.410	0.267	0.371
22	0.307	0.394	0.264	0.359
23	0.296	0.391	0.257	0.352
24	0.290	0.377	0.246	0.341
25	0.287	0.367	0.240	0.333
26	0.280	0.360	0.237	0.329
27	0.271	0.356	0.231	0.322
28	0.265	0.344	0.228	0.312
29	0.261	0.340	0.222	0.310
30	0.255	0.333	0.218	0.301
31	0.252	0.325	0.213	0.295
32	0.246	0.323	0.210	0.290
33	0.242	0.314	0.205	0.288
34	0.237	0.312	0.201	0.280
35	0.234	0.304	0.197	0.277
36	0.232	0.302	0.194	0.273
37	0.228	0.297	0.192	0.267
38	0.223	0.292	0.189	0.263
39	0.220	0.287	0.188	0.260
40	0.218	0.285	0.185	0.256
z	1.960	2.576	1.645	2.326

Source: Linton C. Freeman, *Elementary Applied Statistics*, John Wiley & Sons, New York, 1965, p. 249. Reprinted by permission.

Table 3.   Significant Values of r for Testing H_0

df	Two-tailed Test $\alpha = .05$	$\alpha = .01$	One-tailed Test $\alpha = .05$	$\alpha = .01$
1	.997	.9999	.998	.9995
2	.950	.990	.900	.980
3	.878	.959	.805	.934
4	.811	.917	.729	.882
5	.754	.874	.669	.833
6	.707	.834	.622	.789
7	.666	.798	.582	.750
8	.632	.765	.549	.716
9	.602	.735	.521	.685
10	.576	.708	.497	.658
11	.553	.684	.476	.634
12	.532	.661	.458	.612
13	.514	.641	.441	.592
14	.497	.623	.426	.574
15	.482	.606	.412	.558
16	.468	.590	.400	.542
17	.456	.575	.389	.528
18	.444	.561	.378	.516
19	.433	.549	.369	.503
20	.423	.537	.360	.492
21	.413	.526	.352	.482
22	.404	.515	.344	.472
23	.396	.505	.337	.462
24	.388	.496	.330	.453
25	.381	.487	.323	.445
26	.374	.479	.317	.437
27	.367	.471	.311	.430
28	.361	.463	.306	.423
29	.355	.456	.301	.416
30	.349	.449	.296	.409
35	.325	.418	.275	.381
40	.304	.393	.257	.358
45	.288	.372	.243	.338
50	.273	.354	.231	.322
60	.250	.325	.211	.295
70	.232	.303	.195	.274
80	.217	.283	.183	.256
90	.205	.267	.173	.242
100	.195	.254	.164	.230

Source: Linton C. Freeman, *Elementary Applied Statistics*, John Wiley & Sons, New York, 1965 p. 250. Reprinted by permission.

Table 4. Distribution of χ^2

	Probability (two-tailed)*													
df	.99	.98	.95	.90	.80	.70	.50	.30	.20	.10	.05	.02	.01	.001
1	$.0^3157$	$.0^3628$	.00393	.0158	.0642	.148	.455	1.074	1.642	2.706	3.841	5.412	6.635	10.827
2	.0201	.0404	.103	.211	.446	.713	1.386	2.408	3.219	4.605	5.991	7.824	9.210	13.815
3	.115	.185	.352	.584	1.005	1.424	2.366	3.665	4.642	6.251	7.815	9.837	11.345	16.268
4	.297	.429	.711	1.064	1.649	2.195	3.357	4.878	5.989	7.779	9.488	11.668	13.277	18.465
5	.554	.752	1.145	1.610	2.343	3.000	4.351	6.064	7.289	9.236	11.070	13.388	15.086	20.517
6	.872	1.134	1.635	2.204	3.070	3.828	5.348	7.231	8.558	10.645	12.592	15.033	16.812	22.457
7	1.239	1.564	2.167	2.833	3.822	4.671	6.346	8.383	9.803	12.017	14.067	16.622	18.475	24.322
8	1.646	2.032	2.733	3.490	4.594	5.527	7.344	9.524	11.030	13.362	15.507	18.168	20.090	26.125
9	2.088	2.532	3.325	4.168	5.380	6.393	8.343	10.656	12.242	14.684	16.919	19.679	21.666	27.877
10	2.558	3.059	3.940	4.865	6.179	7.267	9.342	11.781	13.442	15.987	18.307	21.161	23.209	29.588
11	3.053	3.609	4.575	5.578	6.989	8.148	10.341	12.899	14.631	17.275	19.675	22.618	24.725	31.264
12	3.571	4.178	5.226	6.304	7.807	9.034	11.340	14.011	15.812	18.549	21.026	24.054	26.217	32.909
13	4.107	4.765	5.892	7.042	8.634	9.926	12.340	15.119	16.985	19.812	22.362	25.472	27.688	34.528
14	4.660	5.368	6.571	7.790	9.467	10.821	13.339	16.222	18.151	21.064	23.685	26.873	29.141	36.123
15	5.229	5.985	7.261	8.547	10.307	11.721	14.339	17.322	19.311	22.307	24.996	28.259	30.578	37.697
16	5.812	6.614	7.962	9.312	11.152	12.624	15.338	18.418	20.465	23.542	26.296	29.633	32.000	39.252
17	6.408	7.255	8.672	10.085	12.002	13.531	16.338	19.511	21.615	24.769	27.587	30.995	33.409	40.790
18	7.015	7.906	9.390	10.865	12.857	14.440	17.338	20.601	22.760	25.989	28.869	32.346	34.805	42.312
19	7.633	8.567	10.117	11.651	13.716	15.352	18.338	21.689	23.900	27.204	30.144	33.687	36.191	43.820
20	8.260	9.237	10.851	12.443	14.578	16.266	19.337	22.775	25.038	28.412	31.410	35.020	37.566	45.315

df													
21	8.897	9.915	11.591	13.240	15.445	17.182	20.337	23.858	26.171	29.615	32.671	36.343	38.932	46.797
22	9.542	10.600	12.338	14.041	16.314	18.101	21.337	24.939	27.301	30.813	33.924	37.659	40.289	48.268
23	10.196	11.293	13.091	14.848	17.187	19.021	22.337	26.018	28.429	32.007	35.172	38.968	41.638	49.728
24	10.856	11.992	13.848	15.659	18.062	19.943	23.337	27.096	29.553	33.196	36.415	40.270	42.980	51.179
25	11.524	12.697	14.611	16.473	18.940	20.867	24.337	28.172	30.675	34.382	37.652	41.566	44.314	52.620
26	12.198	13.409	15.379	17.292	19.820	21.792	25.336	29.246	31.795	35.563	38.885	42.856	45.642	54.052
27	12.879	14.125	16.151	18.114	20.703	22.719	26.336	30.319	32.912	36.741	40.113	44.140	46.963	55.476
28	13.565	14.847	16.928	18.939	21.588	23.647	27.336	31.391	34.027	37.916	41.337	45.419	48.278	56.893
29	14.256	15.574	17.708	19.768	22.475	24.577	28.336	32.461	35.139	39.087	42.557	46.693	49.588	58.302
30	14.953	16.306	18.493	20.599	23.364	25.508	29.336	33.530	36.250	40.256	43.773	47.962	50.892	59.703

* For one-tailed applications, simply *halve* the probability shown: that is, .10 (two-tailed) becomes, .10/2 or .05 for a one-tailed probability.

Source: Ronald A. Fisher and Frank Yates. *Statistical Tables for Biological, Agricultural and Medical Research.* Edinburgh: Oliver & Boyd, Ltd. By permission of Longman Group Limited. Table V. Reprinted from *Basic Statistical Methods* (2nd ed.), N. M. Downie and R. W. Heath, Harper & Row, 1965.

Table 5. Areas under the normal curve: fractions of unit area from 0 to Z

/	0.00	0.01	0.02	0.03	0.04	0.05	0.06	0.07	0.08	0.09
0.0	0.0000	0.0040	0.0080	0.0120	0.0160	0.0199	0.0239	0.0279	0.0319	0.0359
0.1	.0398	.0438	.0478	.0517	.0557	.0596	.0636	.0675	.0714	.0753
0.2	.0793	.0832	.0871	.0910	.0948	.0987	.1026	.1064	.1103	.1141
0.3	.1179	.1217	.1255	.1293	.1331	.1368	.1406	.1443	.1480	.1517
0.4	.1554	.1591	.1628	.1664	.1700	.1736	.1772	.1808	.1844	.1879
0.5	.1915	.1950	.1985	.2019	.2054	.2088	.2123	.2157	.2190	.2224
0.6	.2257	.2291	.2324	.2357	.2389	.2422	.2454	.2486	.2517	.2549
0.7	.2580	.2611	.2642	.2673	.2704	.2734	.2764	.2794	.2823	.2852
0.8	.2881	.2910	.2939	.2967	.2995	.3023	.3051	.3078	.3106	.3133
0.9	.3159	.3186	.3212	.3238	.3264	.3289	.3315	.3340	.3365	.3389
1.0	.3413	.3438	.3461	.3485	.3508	.3531	.3554	.3577	.3599	.3621
1.1	.3643	.3665	.3686	.3708	.3729	.3749	.3770	.3790	.3810	.3830
1.2	.3849	.3869	.3888	.3907	.3925	.3944	.3962	.3980	.3997	.4015
1.3	.4032	.4049	.4066	.4082	.4099	.4115	.4131	.4147	.4162	.4177
1.4	.4192	.4207	.4222	.4236	.4251	.4265	.4279	.4292	.4306	.4319
1.5	.4332	.4345	.4357	.4370	.4382	.4394	.4406	.4418	.4429	.4441
1.6	.4452	.4463	.4474	.4484	.4495	.4505	.4515	.4525	.4535	.4545
1.7	.4554	.4564	.4573	.4582	.4591	.4599	.4608	.4616	.4625	.4633
1.8	.4641	.4649	.4656	.4664	.4671	.4678	.4686	.4693	.4699	.4706
1.9	.4713	.4719	.4726	.4732	.4738	.4744	.4750	.4756	.4761	.4767
2.0	.4772	.4778	.4783	.4788	.4793	.4798	.4803	.4808	.4812	.4817
2.1	.4821	.4826	.4830	.4834	.4838	.4842	.4846	.4850	.4854	.4857
2.2	.4861	.4864	.4868	.4871	.4875	.4878	.4881	.4884	.4887	.4890
2.3	.4893	.4896	.4898	.4901	.4904	.4906	.4909	.4911	.4913	.4916
2.4	.4918	.4920	.4922	.4925	.4927	.4929	.4931	.4932	.4934	.4936
2.5	.4938	.4940	.4941	.4943	.4945	.4946	.4948	.4949	.4951	.4952
2.6	.4953	.4955	.4956	.4957	.4959	.4960	.4961	.4962	.4963	.4964
2.7	.4965	.4966	.4967	.4968	.4969	.4970	.4971	.4972	.4973	.4974
2.8	.4974	.4975	.4976	.4977	.4977	.4978	.4979	.4979	.4980	.4981
2.9	.4981	.4982	.4982	.4983	.4984	.4984	.4985	.4985	.4986	.4986
3.0	.4987	.4987	.4987	.4988	.4988	.4989	.4989	.4989	.4990	.4990
3.1	.4990	.4991	.4991	.4991	.4992	.4992	.4992	.4992	.4993	.4993
3.2	.4993	.4993	.4994	.4994	.4994	.4994	.4994	.4995	.4995	.4995
3.3	.4995	.4995	.4995	.4996	.4996	.4996	.4996	.4996	.4996	.4997
3.4	.4997	.4997	.4997	.4997	.4997	.4997	.4997	.4997	.4997	.4998
3.6	.4998	.4998	.4999	.4999	.4999	.4999	.4999	.4999	.4999	.4999
4.9	.5000									

Source: Harold O. Rugg. *Statistical Methods Applied to Education*. Boston: Houghton Mifflin Company, 1917. Table III, pp. 389–390. With the kind permission of the publishers. Reproduced by permission from *Statistical Methods*, 6th edition, by George W. Snedecor & William G. Cochran. © 1967 by the Iowa State University Press.

INDEX